D1614246

Mathematical Methods in Image Reconstruction

SIAM Monographs on Mathematical Modeling and Computation

About the Series

In 1997, SIAM began a new series on mathematical modeling and computation. Books in the series develop a focused topic from its genesis to the current state of the art; these books

- present modern mathematical developments with direct applications in science and engineering;
- describe mathematical issues arising in modern applications;
- develop mathematical models of topical physical, chemical, or biological systems;
- present new and efficient computational tools and techniques that have direct applications in science and engineering; and
- illustrate the continuing, integrated roles of mathematical, scientific, and computational investigation.

Although sophisticated ideas are presented, the writing style is popular rather than formal. Texts are intended to be read by audiences with little more than a bachelor's degree in mathematics or engineering. Thus, they are suitable for use in graduate mathematics, science, and engineering courses.

By design, the material is multidisciplinary. As such, we hope to foster cooperation and collaboration between mathematicians, computer scientists, engineers, and scientists. This is a difficult task because different terminology is used for the same concept in different disciplines. Nevertheless, we believe we have been successful and hope that you enjoy the texts in the series.

Joseph E. Flaherty

Frank Natterer and Frank Wübbeling, *Mathematical Methods in Image Reconstruction*

Per Christian Hansen, *Rank-Deficient and Discrete Ill-Posed Problems: Numerical Aspects of Linear Inversion*

Michael Griebel, Thomas Dornseifer, and Tilman Neunhoeffer, *Numerical Simulation in Fluid Dynamics: A Practical Introduction*

Khosrow Chadan, David Colton, Lassi Päivärinta, and William Rundell, *An Introduction to Inverse Scattering and Inverse Spectral Problems*

Charles K. Chui, *Wavelets: A Mathematical Tool for Signal Analysis*

Mathematical Methods in Image Reconstruction

Frank Natterer
Frank Wübbeling

Universität Münster
Münster, Germany

Society for Industrial and Applied Mathematics

Philadelphia

Library of Congress Cataloging-in-Publication Data

Mathematical methods in image reconstruction / Frank Natterer...[et al.]
     p. cm. — (SIAM monographs on mathematical modeling and computation)
   Includes bibliographical references and index.
   ISBN 0-89871-472-9
     1. Image processing—Congresses. I. Natterer, F. (Frank), 1941- II. Series.

TA1637 .M356 2001
621.36'7--dc21

                                   00-053804

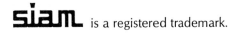

Contents

Preface   ix

List of Symbols   xi

1 Introduction   1
  1.1 The Basic Example   1
  1.2 Overview   2
  1.3 Mathematical Preliminaries   3
     1.3.1 Fourier analysis   3
     1.3.2 Some integral operators   5
     1.3.3 The Moore–Penrose generalized inverse   5
     1.3.4 The singular value decomposition   5
     1.3.5 Special functions   6
     1.3.6 The fast Fourier transform   8

2 Integral Geometry   9
  2.1 The Radon Transform   9
  2.2 The Ray Transform   17
  2.3 The Cone Beam Transform   23
  2.4 Weighted Transforms   27
     2.4.1 The attenuated ray transform   27
     2.4.2 The Feig–Greenleaf transform   30
     2.4.3 The windowed ray transform   31
  2.5 Integration over Curved Manifolds   31
     2.5.1 Computing an even function on S^2 from its integrals over equatorial circles   32
     2.5.2 Reduction of problems on the sphere to the Radon transform   33
     2.5.3 Reconstruction from spherical averages   34
     2.5.4 More general manifolds   36
  2.6 Vector Fields   36

3 Tomography   41
  3.1 Transmission Tomography   41
     3.1.1 Parallel scanning geometry   41

	3.1.2	Fan beam scanning geometry	42
	3.1.3	3D helical scanning	43
	3.1.4	3D cone beam scanning	43
3.2	Emission Tomography		44
3.3	Diffraction Tomography		46
3.4	Magnetic Resonance Imaging		51
3.5	Electron Tomography		54
3.6	Radar		55
	3.6.1	Synthetic aperture radar	55
	3.6.2	Range–Doppler radar	56
3.7	Vector Tomography		57
	3.7.1	Doppler tomography	57
	3.7.2	Schlieren tomography	58
	3.7.3	Photoelastic tomography	58
3.8	Seismic Tomography		59
	3.8.1	Travel time tomography	59
	3.8.2	Reflection tomography	60
	3.8.3	Waveform tomography	60
3.9	Historical Remarks		62

4 Stability and Resolution   **63**
4.1	Stability	63
4.2	Sampling	65
4.3	Resolution	71
4.4	The FFT on Nonequispaced Grids	78

5 Reconstruction Algorithms   **81**
5.1	The Filtered Backprojection Algorithm		81
	5.1.1	Standard parallel scanning	83
	5.1.2	Parallel interlaced scanning	87
	5.1.3	Standard fan beam scanning	90
	5.1.4	Linear fan beam scanning	93
	5.1.5	Fast backprojection	95
	5.1.6	The point spread function	96
	5.1.7	Noise in the filtered backprojection algorithm	97
	5.1.8	Filtered backprojection for the exponential Radon transform	99
	5.1.9	Filtered backprojection for the attenuated Radon transform	99
5.2	Fourier Reconstruction		100
	5.2.1	Standard Fourier reconstruction	100
	5.2.2	The gridding method	102
	5.2.3	The linogram algorithm	106
	5.2.4	Fourier reconstruction in diffraction tomography and MRI	108
5.3	Iterative Methods		110
	5.3.1	ART	110
	5.3.2	The EM algorithm	118
	5.3.3	Other iterative algorithms	124

5.4   Direct Algebraic Algorithms 125
5.5   3D Algorithms 127
     5.5.1   The FDK approximate formula 128
     5.5.2   Grangeat's method 129
     5.5.3   Filtered backprojection for the cone beam transform 131
     5.5.4   Filtered backprojection for the ray transform 133
     5.5.5   The Radon transform in 3D 133
5.6   Circular Harmonic Algorithms 134
     5.6.1   Standard parallel scanning 134
     5.6.2   Standard fan beam scanning 136
5.7   ART for Nonlinear Problems 137

6   Problems That Have Peculiarities   **139**
6.1   Unknown Orientations 139
     6.1.1   The geometric method 139
     6.1.2   The moment method 141
     6.1.3   The method of Provencher and Vogel 142
     6.1.4   The 2D case 143
6.2   Incomplete Data 144
     6.2.1   Uniqueness and stability 144
     6.2.2   Reconstruction methods 147
     6.2.3   Truncated projections in PET 148
     6.2.4   Conical tilt problem in electron tomography 150
6.3   Discrete Tomography 151
6.4   Simultaneous Reconstruction of Attenuation and Activity 152
6.5   Local Tomography 155
6.6   Few Data 159

7   Nonlinear Tomography   **161**
7.1   Tomography with Scatter 161
7.2   Optical Tomography 163
     7.2.1   The transport model 163
     7.2.2   The diffusion model 165
     7.2.3   The linearized problem 168
     7.2.4   Calderon's method 170
     7.2.5   The transport-backtransport algorithm 172
     7.2.6   The diffusion-backdiffusion algorithm 174
7.3   Impedance Tomography 176
7.4   Ultrasound Tomography 178
     7.4.1   Frequency domain ultrasound tomography 179
     7.4.2   Time domain ultrasound tomography 185

Bibliography   **189**

Index   **209**

Preface

Since the advent of computerized tomography in the seventies, many imaging techniques have emerged and have been introduced in radiology, science, and technology. Some of these techniques are now in routine use, most are still under development, and others are the subject of mainly academic research, their future usefulness in debate.

This book makes an attempt to describe these techniques in a mathematical language, to provide the adequate mathematical background and the necessary mathematical tools. In particular, it gives a detailed analysis of numerical algorithms for image reconstruction.

We concentrate on the developments of the last 10 to 15 years. Previous results are given without proof, except when new proofs are available. It is assumed that, or at least helpful if, the reader is familiar with the tomography literature of the eighties.

The backbone of the theory of imaging is still integral geometry. We survey this field as far as is necessary for imaging purposes. Imaging techniques based on or related to integral geometry are briefly described in the section on tomography. In contrast, the section on algorithms is fairly detailed, at least in the two-dimensional (2D) case. In the three-dimensional (3D) case, we derive exact and approximate inversion formulas for specific imaging devices. We describe their algorithmic implementation, which largely parallels the 2D case. The development in the field of algorithms is still quite lively, in particular in the 3D area. While some fundamental principles, such as filtered backprojection, seem to be well established, much of this section may well turn out to be just a snapshot of the present scene. General trends, such as the present revival of Fourier and iterative methods, become visible.

In the last part of the book we deal with imaging techniques that are usually referred to as tomography but that are only remotely related to the straight line paradigm of tomography. These can be formulated as bilinear inverse problems of partial differential equations. We give a common framework and describe simple numerical methods based on standard iterative techniques of tomography.

The book is aimed at mathematicians, engineers, physicists, and other scientists with the appropriate mathematical skills who want to understand the theoretical foundations of image reconstruction and to solve concrete problems.

Often the proofs are sketchy or even missing in cases in which suitable references are easily available. We hope that the readability does not suffer from these omissions, which are necessary to keep this report at a reasonable length.

A Web page for this book has been created at http://www.siam.org/books/mm05. It includes any necessary corrections, updates, and additions. Code fragments and additional papers can be found on the authors' site at http://www.inverse-problems.de/.

Thanks are due to Thomas Dierkes, Oliver Dorn, and Helmut Sielschott for their support in the preparation of the book. We particularly want to thank Mrs. Berg, who patiently LaTeXed the manuscript from the first drafts to the final version. The advice of the reviewers is gratefully acknowledged; it helped us to improve the manuscript in many ways. Last but not least, we want to thank the SIAM staff for their efficient cooperation.

F. Natterer
F. Wübbeling
April 2000

List of Symbols

Symbol		Page
Rf	Radon transform	9
Pf	ray transform	17
Df	cone beam transform	23
$R_\mu f$	attenuated Radon transform	27
$T_\mu f$	cxponential Radon transform	27
$\mathcal{P}f$	vectorial ray transform	36
$\mathcal{R}^p f$	Radon probe transform	36
$\mathcal{R}^\perp f$	Radon normal transform	36
$I^\alpha f$	Riesz potential	5
Hf	Hilbert transform	5
A^T	transpose of matrix A	
A^*	adjoint of operator A	
$x \cdot \theta$	inner product	
$\lvert x \rvert$	Euclidean norm	
$\theta^\perp$	subspace perpendicular to θ	
$\theta_\perp$	unit vector perpendicular to θ	
E_θ	orthogonal projection on $\theta^\perp$	18
$\lfloor t \rfloor$	largest integer $\leq t$	
$\mathbb{R}^n$	n-dimensional euclidean space	
$\mathbb{C}^n$	complex n-dimensional space	
$\mathbb{Z}^n$	n-dimensional vectors with integer components	
$L_p(X)$	space of p-integrable functions on X	
$\mathcal{S}(X)$	Schwartz space on X	3
$\mathcal{S}'(X)$	space of tempered distributions on X	3
H^α, H_0^α	Sobolev spaces	17

Symbol		Page
S^{n-1}	unit sphere in $\mathbb{R}^n$	
T^n	tangent bundle to S^{n-1}	17
C^n	unit cylinder in $\mathbb{R}^n$	9
$SO(n)$	special orthogonal group in $\mathbb{R}^n$	
$\hat{f}, \tilde{f}$	Fourier transform and its inverse	3
$C_\ell^\lambda(x)$	Gegenbauer polynomials	6
$J_v(x)$	Bessel function of the first kind	7
$H_v(x)$	Hankel function of the first kind	47
$T_\ell(x), U_\ell(x)$	Chebyshev polynomials	6
$Y_\ell(x)$	spherical harmonic of degree ℓ	6
$\delta(x)$	Dirac δ function	4
$\operatorname{sinc}(x)$	sinc function	65
D^k	$(\frac{\partial}{\partial x_1})^{k_1} \dots (\frac{\partial}{\partial x_n})^{k_n}$	3
$\int$	integrals without specification are over the whole space	

Chapter 1

Introduction

1.1 The Basic Example

The prime example of imaging is still computerized tomography. "Tomography" is derived from the Greek word $\tau o\mu os$, slice. It stands for a variety of different techniques for imaging two-dimensional (2D) cross sections of three-dimensional (3D) objects. In the simplest case, let us consider an object whose linear attenuation coefficient with respect to X rays at the point x is $f(x)$. The cross section to be imaged is scanned by thin X-ray beams L, providing us with

$$g(L) = \int_L f(x)dx. \qquad (1.1)$$

The problem now is to compute an approximation to f from the integrals (1.1).

In principle, this problem was solved by Radon (1917).

If L is modeled as the straight line $x \cdot \theta = s$, where $\theta \in S^1$ and $s \in \mathbb{R}^1$, then (1.1) can be written as

$$g(\theta, s) = \int_{x\cdot\theta=s} f(x)dx = (Rf)(\theta, s). \qquad (1.2)$$

R is known as the Radon transform. Radon's inversion formula

$$f(x) = \frac{1}{4\pi^2} \int_{S^1} \int_{\mathbb{R}^1} \frac{\frac{d}{ds}g(\theta, s)}{x \cdot \theta - s} ds d\theta \qquad (1.3)$$

yields f in terms of g. Radon's inversion formula can be implemented numerically to yield a reliable and fast algorithm for the reconstruction of the image f from the data g (filtered backprojection algorithm; see section 5.1). As an example, we present in Figure 1.1 an abdominal cross section that was computed from the data produced by a clinical CT scanner. Such a data set is called a sinogram in the language of tomography. It is just a visualization of the Radon transform of the cross section. So why do we write a book on imaging? We give a few answers.

1. Explicit inversion formulas such as (1.3) are just the starting point for developing numerical algorithms. The right way to convert (1.3) into an accurate and efficient algorithm is by no means obvious.

 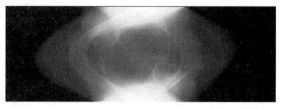

Figure 1.1. *Abdominal cross section (left) computed from the sinogram (right).*
Each row of the sinogram contains the detector output for one position of the X-ray source.

2. In many cases, the model is much more complex than (1.2), and no exact inversion formula such as (1.3) exists. Thus one has to develop numerical methods quite independent from analytical tools.

3. Often it is not possible or not desirable to measure all the data entering an inversion formula such as (1.3). Then questions of uniqueness and stability arise.

4. Suppose we want to recover f with a certain spatial resolution. How do we need to sample g in order to achieve this resolution? What is the minimal number of sampling points?

5. A thorough understanding of the model problem (1.1) may help one to deal with related imaging techniques, such as ultrasound, magnetic resonance, impedance, and laser imaging.

As an introduction to tomography we recommend Herman (1980). A survey on the many applications of tomography is given by Deans (1983). The practitioner might want to consult Kak and Slaney (1987) for the more practical aspects. For the more theoretical aspects, see Natterer (1986).

1.2 Overview

In the rest of Chapter 1, we collect some mathematics, mainly for reference purposes. In Chapter 2, we give a short account of integral geometry, which is still the backbone of the mathematical theory of imaging. We define the relevant integral transforms, and we derive inversion formulas that serve as the starting point for many of the reconstruction algorithms in Chapter 5. We also discuss uniqueness and derive inequalities that will be used to prove stability estimates in Chapter 4. In Chapter 3, we give a more detailed description of various tomographic imaging techniques. In Chapter 4, we look at the reconstruction problem from two aspects: ill-posedness and sampling. Both aspects are crucial for the design of imaging devices. Chapter 5 on reconstruction algorithms is the central part of this report. We give a detailed description of many of the basic algorithms of tomography, and we discuss the role of the various parameters of these algorithms and their proper usage. In Chapter 6, we consider problems that do not fit into the framework of Chapter 5—data are not sufficient; the objects that have to be recovered are rather special; important pieces of information, such as the projection angles, are unknown; or only special features, such as edges, are sought for. We not only give algorithms for the cases that take into account these peculiarities, but we discuss stability and uniqueness in light of the mathematical theories in previous chapters. In Chapter 7, we deal with imaging techniques that can be formulated as inverse problems of partial differential equations. It turns out that some of the techniques used in tomography extend to these nonlinear problems, yielding reconstruction algorithms quite similar to, although more complex than, the algorithms of tomography.

1.3 Mathematical Preliminaries

1.3.1 Fourier analysis

The Fourier transform plays an important role in imaging for two reasons. First, it is closely related to integral geometric transforms such as the Radon and ray transforms. Second, it is an indispensable tool in the study of sampling and discretization processes. For $f \in L_1(\mathbb{R}^n)$, the Fourier transform $\hat{f}$ and the inverse Fourier transform $\tilde{f}$ are defined by

$$\hat{f}(\xi) = (2\pi)^{-n/2} \int_{\mathbb{R}^n} e^{-ix \cdot \xi} f(x) dx,$$

$$\tilde{f}(\xi) = (2\pi)^{-n/2} \int_{\mathbb{R}^n} e^{ix \cdot \xi} f(x) dx.$$

We use both transforms for other functions f, such as for functions in $L_2(\mathbb{R}^n)$ and even for the tempered distributions $\mathcal{S}'(\mathbb{R}^n)$, the dual space of the Schwartz space $\mathcal{S}(\mathbb{R}^n)$. We recommend Yosida (1968), Schwartz (1973), and Stein and Weiss (1971) as general references.

We list a few properties of the Fourier transform. Let $f \in \mathcal{S}'(\mathbb{R}^n)$. Then we have the inversion formula

$$f = \tilde{\hat{f}}.$$

If $f_r(x) = f(rx), r > 0$, we have

$$\hat{f}_r(\xi) = r^{-n} \hat{f}(r^{-1}\xi). \tag{1.4}$$

Likewise, if $f_y(x) = f(x + y)$ for $y \in \mathbb{R}^n$, then

$$\hat{f}_y(\xi) = e^{i\xi \cdot y} \hat{f}(\xi). \tag{1.5}$$

For $k = (k_1, \ldots, k_n)$, $k_i \geq 0$ integer, we have

$$(D^k f)^\wedge(\xi) = i^{|k|} \xi^k \hat{f}(\xi), \quad (x^k f)^\wedge = i^{|k|} D^k \hat{f}. \tag{1.6}$$

Here $D^k = (\frac{\partial}{\partial x_1})^{k_1} \ldots (\frac{\partial}{\partial x_n})^{k_n}$, $x^k = x_1^{k_1} \cdots x_n^{k_n}$, and $|k| = k_1 + \cdots + k_n$. For $f \in \mathcal{S}'(\mathbb{R}^n)$, $g \in \mathcal{S}(\mathbb{R}^n)$, the convolution

$$(f * g)(x) = \int_{\mathbb{R}^n} f(x - y) g(y) dy$$

is defined, and we have

$$(f * g)^\wedge = (2\pi)^{n/2} \hat{f} \hat{g}, \quad (fg)^\wedge = (2\pi)^{-n/2} \hat{f} * \hat{g}. \tag{1.7}$$

If $f \in L_2(\mathbb{R}^n)$, then $\hat{f} \in L_2(\mathbb{R}^n)$, too. If $f, g \in L_2(\mathbb{R}^n)$, then we have Parseval's relation

$$\int_{\mathbb{R}^n} \hat{f} g \, dx = \int_{\mathbb{R}^n} f \hat{g} \, dx. \tag{1.8}$$

Since $\tilde{\bar{f}}(\xi) = \overline{\hat{f}}(\xi)$, these relations have their counterpart for $\tilde{f}$.

We need a few special Fourier transforms. For δ the Dirac δ function, i.e., $\delta \in \mathcal{S}'(\mathbb{R}^n)$ and $\delta f = f(0)$ for $f \in \mathcal{S}(\mathbb{R}^n)$, we have

$$\hat{\delta} = (2\pi)^{-n/2}. \tag{1.9}$$

An approximation δ_Ω to δ can be defined by

$$\hat{\delta}_\Omega(\xi) = \begin{cases} (2\pi)^{-n/2}, & |\xi| < \Omega, \\ 0, & |\xi| \geq \Omega. \end{cases}$$

One obtains

$$\delta_\Omega(x) = (2\pi)^{-n/2} \Omega^n \frac{J_{n/2}(\Omega|x|)}{(\Omega|x|)^{n/2}}; \tag{1.10}$$

see section 1.3.5. The shah distribution

$$\mathrm{shah}_h = \sum_{k \in \mathbb{Z}^n} \delta_{hk},$$

where $\delta_y f = f(y)$, has the Fourier transform

$$(\mathrm{shah}_{2\pi/h})^\wedge = (2\pi)^{-n/2} h^n \mathrm{shah}_h.$$

This is Poisson's formula. More generally, we have for $f \in \mathcal{S}(\mathbb{R}^n)$

$$\sum_{\ell \in \mathbb{Z}^n} \hat{f}\left(\xi - \frac{2\pi}{h}\ell\right) = (2\pi)^{-n/2} h^n \sum_{\ell \in \mathbb{Z}^n} f(h\ell) e^{-ih\xi \cdot \ell}. \tag{1.11}$$

We use the Fourier transform to define the Hilbert spaces $H^\alpha(G)$, $H_0^\alpha(G)$ for sufficiently regular domains $G \subseteq \mathbb{R}^n$ and $\alpha \in \mathbb{R}$. For $G = \mathbb{R}^n$, we put

$$\|f\|_{H^\alpha(\mathbb{R}^n)}^2 = \int_{\mathbb{R}^n} (1 + |\xi|^2)^\alpha |\hat{f}(\xi)|^2 \, d\xi.$$

$H_0^\alpha(G)$ is the closure of $C_0^\infty(G)$ with respect to the norm in $H^\alpha(\mathbb{R}^n)$. For $\alpha \geq 0$, $H^\alpha(G)$ consists of those functions f on G that can be extended to functions f^* in $H^\alpha(\mathbb{R}^n)$, and $\|f\|_{H^\alpha(G)}$ is the lower bound of $\|f^*\|_{H^\alpha(\mathbb{R}^n)}$ for all such extensions. For $\alpha \leq 0$, $H^\alpha(G)$ is the dual of $H^{-\alpha}(G)$, i.e.,

$$\|f\|_{H^\alpha(G)} = \sup_{g \in H_0^{-\alpha}(G)} \frac{\int_\Omega f g \, dx}{\|g\|_{H_0^{-\alpha}(G)}}.$$

See Adams (1975) as a general reference.

1.3.2   Some integral operators

The Hilbert transform in $\mathbb{R}^1$ is defined by the principal value integral

$$(Hf)(x) = \frac{1}{\pi} \int_{\mathbb{R}^1} \frac{f(y)}{x-y} dy, \quad f \in L_2(\mathbb{R}^1). \tag{1.12}$$

One can show that

$$(Hf)^\wedge(\xi) = -i \, \text{sgn}(\xi) \hat{f}(\xi). \tag{1.13}$$

The Abel integral equation

$$\int_0^x \frac{f(t)}{\sqrt{x^2 - t^2}} = g(x) \tag{1.14}$$

has the solution

$$\begin{aligned}
f(x) &= \frac{2}{\pi} \frac{d}{dx} \int_0^x \frac{t g(t)}{\sqrt{x^2 - t^2}} dt \\
&= \frac{2}{\pi} \left\{ g(0) + x \int_0^x \frac{g'(t)}{\sqrt{x^2 - t^2}} dt \right\};
\end{aligned}$$

see Gorenflo and Vessella (1991).

The Riesz potential I^α in $\mathbb{R}^n$ is defined by

$$(I^\alpha f)^\wedge(\xi) = |\xi|^{-\alpha} \hat{f}(\xi), \quad \alpha < n. \tag{1.15}$$

1.3.3   The Moore–Penrose generalized inverse

Let H, K be Hilbert spaces and let $A : H \to K$ be a linear bounded operator. The Moore–Penrose generalized solution f^+ to $Af = g$ is defined as follows: f^+ is the element with smallest norm in the set of the minimizers of $\|Af - g\|$ (if this set is nonempty, i.e., if $g \in \text{range}(A) + \text{range}(A)^\perp$). It can be shown that f^+ is the unique solution to the normal equation

$$A^*Af = A^*g \tag{1.16}$$

in $\overline{\text{range}(A^*)}$. The linear operator A^+ defined by $f^+ = A^+g$ for $g \in \text{range}(A) + \text{range}(A)^\perp$ is called the Moore–Penrose generalized inverse. For a comprehensive treatment see Groetsch (1977).

1.3.4   The singular value decomposition

Let A be a bounded linear operator of a Hilbert space H into the Hilbert space K. By the singular value decomposition (SVD) we mean a representation of A in the form

$$Af = \sum_k \sigma_k (f, f_k) g_k, \tag{1.17}$$

where (f_k), (g_k) are orthonormal systems in H, K, respectively, and σ_k are positive numbers, the singular values of A. The sum may be finite or infinite. The adjoint of A is given by

$$A^*g = \sum_k \sigma_k (g, g_k) f_k, \tag{1.18}$$

and the operators

$$A^*Af = \sum_k \sigma_k^2(f, f_k)f_k, \qquad (1.19)$$

$$AA^*g = \sum_k \sigma_k^2(g, g_k)g_k \qquad (1.20)$$

are self-adjoint operators in H, K, respectively. The spectrum of A^*A, AA^* consists of the eigenvalues σ_k^2 and possibly the eigenvalue 0, whose multiplicity may be infinite. The generalized inverse of A is

$$A^+g = \sum_k \sigma_k^{-1}(g, g_k)f_k. \qquad (1.21)$$

See Bertero and Boccacci (1998) for the use of the singular value decomposition in imaging.

1.3.5   Special functions

Special functions are used extensively in imaging. A standard reference is Abramowitz and Stegun (1970). We collect some frequently used formulas for the convenience of the reader.

The Gegenbauer polynomials C_ℓ^λ of degree ℓ are orthogonal polynomials on $[-1, +1]$ with weight function $(1-x^2)^{\lambda-1/2}, \lambda > -1/2$. Special cases are the Chebyshev polynomials of the first kind ($\lambda = 0$),

$$T_\ell(x) = \cos(\ell \arccos x), \quad |x| \le 1,$$

the Chebyshev polynomials of the second kind ($\lambda = 1$),

$$U_\ell(x) = \frac{\sin((\ell + 1) \arccos x)}{\sin(\arccos x)}, \quad |x| \le 1,$$

and the Legendre polynomials P_ℓ for $\lambda = \frac{1}{2}$.

We have the inequalities

$$|T_\ell(x)| \le 1, \qquad |P_\ell(x)| \le 1$$

for $|x| \le 1$ and

$$|T_\ell(x)| \ge \frac{1}{2}(x + \sqrt{x^2 - 1})^\ell$$

for $|x| \ge 1$. This estimate indicates exponential growth of T_ℓ with x outside $[-1, +1]$.

A spherical harmonic Y_ℓ of degree ℓ is the restriction to S^{n-1} of a harmonic polynomial homogeneous of degree ℓ on $\mathbb{R}^n$; see Seeley (1966). There exist exactly

$$N(n, \ell) = \frac{(2\ell + n - 2)(n + \ell - 3)!}{\ell!(n - 2)!}$$

linearly independent spherical harmonics of degree ℓ, and spherical harmonics of different degree are orthogonal in $L_2(S^{n-1})$. For $n = 3$, the $N(3, \ell) = 2\ell + 1$ linear independent spherical harmonics of degree ℓ are

$$Y_{\ell,m}(\theta) = P_\ell^m(\cos\psi)\sin m\varphi,$$
$$Y_{\ell,-m}(\theta) = P_\ell^m(\cos\psi)\cos m\varphi,$$
$$Y_{\ell,0}(\theta) = P_\ell(\cos\psi),$$

where $\theta = (\cos\varphi\sin\psi, \sin\varphi\sin\psi, \cos\psi)^T$, $m = 1, \ldots, \ell$, and

$$P_\ell^m(t) = (-1)^m(1-t^2)^{m/2}\frac{d^m P_\ell(t)}{dt^m}.$$

For $n = 2$, the spherical harmonics of degree ℓ are $\cos\ell\varphi$, $\sin\ell\varphi$ for $\ell \neq 0$, and 1 for $\ell = 0$, where $\theta = (\cos\varphi, \sin\varphi)^T$.

An important result on spherical harmonics is the Funk–Hecke theorem: For a function h on $[-1, +1]$, we have

$$\int_{S^{n-1}} h(\theta \cdot \omega)Y_\ell(\omega)d\omega = C_{n,\ell}(h)Y_\ell(\theta),$$

$$C_{n,\ell}(h) = c_{n,\ell}\int_{-1}^{+1} h(t)C_\ell^{(n-2)/2}(t)(1-t^2)^{(n-3)/2}dt$$

with some positive constant $c_{n,\ell}$. For $n = 2$, this reads

$$\int_0^{2\pi} h(\cos(\varphi - \psi))e^{i\ell\varphi}d\varphi = 2\int_{-1}^{+1} h(t)T_{|\ell|}(t)(1-t^2)^{-1/2}dt\, e^{i\ell\psi}.$$

The Bessel function of the first kind of real order ν is defined by

$$J_\nu(x) = \left(\frac{z}{2}\right)^\nu\sum_{k=0}^\infty\frac{(-z^2/4)^k}{k!\Gamma(\nu+k+1)}.$$

For ν an integer, we have the integral representation

$$J_\nu(x) = \frac{1}{2\pi}\int_0^{2\pi} e^{ix\sin\varphi - i\nu\varphi}d\varphi.$$

The asymptotic behavior of $J_\nu(x)$ as both ν and x tend to infinity is crucial in the investigation of resolution in section 4.3. Debye's asymptotic relation states that $J_\nu(x)$ is negligible if, in a sense, $\nu > x$. More precisely, we have for $0 < \vartheta < 1$

$$0 \leq J_\nu(\vartheta\nu) \leq (2\pi\nu)^{-1/2}(1-\vartheta^2)^{-1/4}e^{-(\nu/3)(1-\vartheta^2)^{3/2}}.$$

We also need the modified Bessel functions

$$I_\nu(z) = \left(\frac{z}{2}\right)^\nu\sum_{k=0}^\infty\frac{(z^2/4)^k}{k!\Gamma(\nu+k+1)}$$

of order ν. For z real, $z \to \infty$, we have

$$I_\nu(z) = \frac{e^z}{\sqrt{2\pi z}}\left(1 + O\left(\frac{1}{z}\right)\right);$$

see Abramowitz and Stegun (1970), formula 9.7.1.

1.3.6 The fast Fourier transform

The discrete counterpart of the Fourier integral is the discrete Fourier transform of length $2q$:

$$\hat{y}_k = \sum_{j=-q}^{q-1} e^{-\pi ijk/q} y_j, \quad k = -q, \ldots, q-1. \tag{1.22}$$

A straightforward evaluation of (1.22) requires $O(q^2)$ operations. Any algorithm of lower complexity, usually $q \log q$, is called a fast Fourier transform (FFT). Standard references are Nussbaumer (1982) and Briggs and Henson (1995).

In tomography the FFT is mostly used for the evaluation of the Fourier transform

$$\hat{f}(\xi) = (2\pi)^{-1/2} \int e^{-ix\cdot\xi} f(x) dx \tag{1.23}$$

and multidimensional extensions. Assume that f is sampled with stepsize $h > 0$ and that f vanishes outside $[-\rho, \rho]$. Applying the trapezoidal rule to (1.23) leads to the approximation

$$\hat{f}(\xi) = (2\pi)^{-1/2} h \sum_{j=-q}^{q-1} e^{-i\xi hj} f(hj),$$

where $q = \rho/h$. Since $\hat{f}$ is band-limited with bandwidth ρ, $\hat{f}$ needs to be sampled with a stepsize $\leq \pi/\rho$; see section 4.2. If we choose the coarsest possible stepsize π/ρ, we have to evaluate

$$\hat{f}(k\pi/\rho) = (2\pi)^{-1/2} h \sum_{j=-q}^{q-1} e^{-i\pi kj/q} f(jh). \tag{1.24}$$

This approximation makes sense only for $k = -q, \ldots, q-1$ since the right-hand side has period $2q$ in k, while the left-hand side tends to zero as $k \to \infty$. Evaluating (1.24) is a discrete Fourier transform of length $2q$.

Sometimes one has to evaluate $\hat{f}$ for a different stepsize u in the frequency domain, i.e.,

$$\hat{f}(ku) = (2\pi)^{-1/2} h \sum_{j=-q}^{q-1} e^{-iku\rho j/q} f(hj).$$

This can be done by the chirp-z algorithm; see Nussbaumer (1982). We write

$$-kj = -\frac{1}{2}k^2 + \frac{1}{2}(k-j)^2 - \frac{1}{2}j^2,$$

obtaining

$$\hat{f}(ku) = (2\pi)^{-1/2} h e^{-\frac{1}{2}uk^2\rho/q} \sum_{j=-q}^{q-1} e^{\frac{i}{2}u(k-j)^2\rho/q} e^{-\frac{i}{2}uj^2\rho/q} f(hj).$$

Apart from multiplications with exponential factors of unit modulus, this is a convolution of length $2q$, which can be done by FFT in $O(q \log q)$ time.

Chapter 2

Integral Geometry

In this section, we give an outline of the theory of some integral transforms that are relevant to tomography. In order to avoid technical difficulties, we restrict the discussion to smooth functions. For an in-depth treatment, see Helgason (1999), Gel'fand, Graev, and Vilenkin (1965), and Smith, Solmon, and Wagner (1977). We give only a few proofs; for the missing ones, see Natterer (1986).

2.1 The Radon Transform

The Radon transform R integrates a function f on $\mathbb{R}^n$ over hyperplanes. Let $H(\theta, s) = \{x \in \mathbb{R}^n : x \cdot \theta = s\}$ be the hyperplane perpendicular to $\theta \in S^{n-1}$ with (signed) distance $s \in \mathbb{R}^1$ from the origin. Each hyperplane can be represented in this way, and $H(-\theta, -s) = H(\theta, s)$. We define $(Rf)(\theta, s)$ as the integral of f over $H(\theta, s)$, i.e.,

$$(Rf)(\theta, s) = \int_{H(\theta,s)} f(x)dx. \tag{2.1}$$

We consider Rf as a function on the unit cylinder

$$C^n = \{(\theta, s) : \theta \in S^{n-1}, \ s \in \mathbb{R}^1\}$$

in $\mathbb{R}^n$. Obviously, Rf is an even function on C^n, i.e., $(Rf)(-\theta, -s) = (Rf)(\theta, s)$. Alternative notations are

$$(Rf)(\theta, s) = \int_{\mathbb{R}^n} \delta(s - x \cdot \theta) f(x) dx \tag{2.2}$$

with the one-dimensional (1D) Dirac δ function, and

$$(Rf)(\theta, s) = \int_{\theta^\perp} f(s\theta + y) dy, \tag{2.3}$$

where $\theta^\perp = \{x \in \mathbb{R}^n : x \cdot \theta = 0\}$ is the subspace orthogonal to θ.

9

We consider—with few exceptions—Rf only for functions $f \in \mathcal{S}(\mathbb{R}^n)$. Then Rf is a function on $\mathcal{S}(C^n)$, where

$$\mathcal{S}(C^n) = \left\{ g \in C^\infty(C^n) : s^\ell \frac{\partial^k}{\partial s^k} g(\theta, s) \text{ bounded}, \quad \ell, k = 0, 1, \ldots \right\}. \qquad (2.4)$$

Much of the theory of the Radon transform follows from its behavior under Fourier transform and convolution. On C^n we understand Fourier transform and convolution as acting on the second variable, i.e.,

$$(g * h)(\theta, s) = \int_{\mathbb{R}^1} g(\theta, s - t) h(\theta, t) dt, \qquad (2.5)$$

$$\hat{g}(\theta, \sigma) = (2\pi)^{-1/2} \int_{\mathbb{R}^1} g(\theta, s) e^{-is\sigma} ds \qquad (2.6)$$

for $g, h \in \mathcal{S}(C^n)$.

The following theorem is known as the "projection theorem" or "central slice theorem" in the tomography literature.

THEOREM 2.1. *Let $f \in \mathcal{S}(\mathbb{R}^n)$. Then for $\theta \in S^{n-1}$, $\sigma \in \mathbb{R}^1$,*

$$(Rf)^\wedge(\theta, \sigma) = (2\pi)^{(n-1)/2} \hat{f}(\sigma\theta).$$

Note that the symbol "$\wedge$" has two different meanings here. On the left-hand side, it stands for the 1D Fourier transform on C^n, while on the right-hand side, it stands for the usual Fourier transform in $\mathbb{R}^n$.

THEOREM 2.2. *Let $f, g \in \mathcal{S}(\mathbb{R}^n)$. Then*

$$Rf * Rg = R(f * g).$$

Here the convolution on the left-hand side is in C^n, but it is in $\mathbb{R}^n$ on the right-hand side.

Now we introduce the backprojection operator R^* by

$$(R^*g)(x) = \int_{S^{n-1}} g(\theta, x \cdot \theta) d\theta, \quad g \in \mathcal{S}(C^n). \qquad (2.7)$$

Thus for $g = Rf$, $(R^*g)(x)$ is the average of all hyperplane integrals of f through x.

Mathematically speaking, R^* is just the adjoint to R. For $g \in \mathcal{S}(\mathbb{R}^1)$, $f \in \mathcal{S}(\mathbb{R}^n)$, we have

$$\int_{\mathbb{R}^1} g(s)(Rf)(\theta, s) ds = \int_{\mathbb{R}^n} g(\theta \cdot x) f(x) dx. \qquad (2.8)$$

It follows that for $g \in \mathcal{S}(C^n)$, $f \in \mathcal{S}(\mathbb{R}^n)$,

$$\int_{S^{n-1}} \int_{\mathbb{R}^1} g \, Rf \, d\theta ds = \int_{\mathbb{R}^n} (R^*g) f \, dx.$$

The following theorem is the starting point for the filtered backprojection algorithm (see section 5.1), which is the standard reconstruction algorithm in two dimensions.

THEOREM 2.3. *Let* $f \in \mathcal{S}(\mathbb{R}^n)$ *and* $g \in \mathcal{S}(C^n)$. *Then*

$$(R^*g) * f = R^*(g * Rf).$$

Again note the different meanings of the symbol "*" here.

THEOREM 2.4. *For* $g \in \mathcal{S}(C^n)$ *even (i.e.,* $g(\theta, s) = g(-\theta, -s)$*), we have*

$$(R^*g)^\wedge(\xi) = 2(2\pi)^{(n-1)/2}|\xi|^{1-n}\hat{g}\left(\frac{\xi}{|\xi|}, |\xi|\right).$$

Although the actual numerical implementation of inversion procedures will be based on Theorem 2.3, it is of interest to have exact inversion formulas. A whole family of inversion formulas is given in the following theorem. It uses Riesz potentials on C^n. In (1.15), we introduced the Riesz potential I^α in $\mathbb{R}^n$. In the same way, we may introduce the Riesz potential on C^n by

$$(I^\alpha g)^\wedge(\theta, \sigma) = |\sigma|^{-\alpha}\hat{g}(\theta, \sigma), \quad \alpha < 1, \tag{2.9}$$

where the Fourier transform is in the sense of C^n.

THEOREM 2.5. *Let* $f \in \mathcal{S}(\mathbb{R}^n)$ *and* $g = Rf$. *Then for* $\alpha < n$,

$$f = \frac{1}{2}(2\pi)^{1-n}I^{-\alpha}R^*I^{\alpha-n+1}g.$$

Note that $I^{-\alpha}$, $I^{\alpha-n+1}$ are the Riesz potentials in $\mathbb{R}^n$ and C^n, respectively. We consider some special cases. First, let $\alpha = 0$. Then

$$f = \frac{1}{2}(2\pi)^{1-n}R^*I^{1-n}g. \tag{2.10}$$

We want to find a more explicit version for the Riesz potential. From (2.9),

$$\begin{aligned}(I^{1-n}g)^\wedge(\theta, \sigma) &= |\sigma|^{n-1}\hat{g}(\theta, \sigma) \\ &= (\mathrm{sgn}(\sigma))^{n-1}\sigma^{n-1}\hat{g}(\theta, \sigma).\end{aligned} \tag{2.11}$$

Now we make use of the Hilbert transform H (see (1.12)), which we apply to functions on C^n with respect to the second variable. According to (1.13) applying H $n-1$ times yields

$$(H^{n-1}g)^\wedge(\theta, \sigma) = \left(\frac{1}{i}\right)^{n-1}(\mathrm{sgn}(\sigma))^{n-1}\hat{g}(\theta, \sigma). \tag{2.12}$$

From (1.6),

$$(g^{(n-1)})^\wedge(\theta, \sigma) = i^{n-1}\sigma^{n-1}\hat{g}(\theta, \sigma), \tag{2.13}$$

where $g^{(n-1)}$ is the derivative of g with respect to the second variable. Combining (2.10)–(2.13), we obtain

$$f = \frac{1}{2}(2\pi)^{1-n}R^*H^{n-1}g^{(n-1)}.$$

We remark that

$$H^{n-1} = \begin{cases} (-1)^{(n-2)/2}H, & n \text{ even,} \\ (-1)^{(n-1)/2}, & n \text{ odd.} \end{cases}$$

Thus we eventually arrive at the following theorem.

THEOREM 2.6. *Let $f \in \mathcal{S}(\mathbb{R}^n)$ and $g = Rf$. Then*

$$f = c_n \begin{cases} R^* H g^{(n-1)}, & n \text{ even,} \\ R^* g^{(n-1)}, & n \text{ odd,} \end{cases}$$

$$c_n = \frac{1}{2}(2\pi)^{1-n} \begin{cases} (-1)^{(n-2)/2}, & n \text{ even.} \\ (-1)^{(n-1)/2}, & n \text{ odd.} \end{cases}$$

There is a marked difference between even and odd dimensions. For n odd, the inversion formula reads

$$f(x) = c_n \int_{S^{n-1}} g^{(n-1)}(\theta, x \cdot \theta)d\theta. \tag{2.14}$$

Thus $f(x)$ is simply an average of $g^{(n-1)}$ over all hyperplanes through x. This means that the inversion formula is local in the following sense: In order to reconstruct f at some point x, one only needs the integrals of f over hyperplanes passing through a neighborhood of x. This is not true for n even. In that case, the Hilbert transform comes in, and we have

$$f(x) = c_n \int_{S^{n-1}} (Hg^{(n-1)})(\theta, x \cdot \theta)d\theta. \tag{2.15}$$

We express the Hilbert transform by the integral (1.12), i.e.,

$$(Hg^{(n-1)})(\theta, s) = \frac{1}{2} \int_{\mathbb{R}^1} \frac{g^{(n-1)}(\theta, s+t) - g^{(n-1)}(\theta, s-t)}{t} dt.$$

Inserting this into (2.15) and interchanging the order of integration we obtain

$$f(x) = \frac{c_n}{2} \int_{\mathbb{R}^1} \frac{1}{t} \int_{S^{n-1}} \left(g^{(n-1)}(\theta, x \cdot \theta + t) - g^{(n-1)}(\theta, x \cdot \theta - t) \right) d\theta dt. \tag{2.16}$$

Since n is even, $g^{(n-1)}$ is odd, i.e., $g^{(n-1)}(-\theta, -s) = -g^{(n-1)}(\theta, s)$. Thus (2.16) simplifies into

$$f(x) = c_n \int_{\mathbb{R}^1} \frac{1}{t} \int_{S^{n-1}} g^{(n-1)}(\theta, x \cdot \theta + t)d\theta dt. \tag{2.17}$$

From this expression it is clear that the inversion for n even is not local: In order to compute f at some point x, one needs integrals of f over hyperplanes far away from x.

The formula (2.17) for $n = 2$, i.e.,

$$f(x) = \frac{1}{4\pi^2} \int_{\mathbb{R}^1} \frac{1}{t} \int_{S^1} g'(\theta, x \cdot \theta + t)d\theta dt, \tag{2.18}$$

was obtained by Radon (1917). It is called Radon's inversion formula. For $n = 3$, Radon obtained

$$f(x) = -\frac{1}{8\pi^2} \Delta \int_{S^2} g(\theta, x \cdot \theta)d\theta, \tag{2.19}$$

where Δ is the Laplacian with respect to x. Since

$$\Delta g(\theta, x \cdot \theta) = g''(\theta, x \cdot \theta),$$

this may be written as

$$f(x) = -\frac{1}{8\pi^2} \int_{S^2} g''(\theta, x \cdot \theta) d\theta,$$

and this is (2.14) for $n = 3$.

So far we have considered the case $\alpha = 0$ of Theorem 2.5. Another interesting choice of α is $\alpha = n - 1$, in which case

$$f = \frac{1}{2}(2\pi)^{1-n} I^{1-n} R^* g. \tag{2.20}$$

For n odd,

$$I^{1-n} = (-\Delta)^{(n-1)/2}$$

is a differential operator. In particular, for $n = 3$, we regain (2.19). For n even, we can restore locality of the inversion formula, at least to a certain extent, by choosing $\alpha = n - 3$. Then

$$I^{\alpha-n+1} g = I^{-2} g = -g'',$$

and Theorem 2.5 reads

$$I^{n-3} f = -\frac{1}{2}(2\pi)^{1-n} R^* g''. \tag{2.21}$$

The right-hand side can be evaluated locally in the same sense as (2.14). (2.21) is the basis of local tomography in section 6.5.

A completely different inversion formula for the Radon transform is derived by expanding f and $g = Rf$ in spherical harmonics $Y_{\ell k}$ (see section 1.3.5), i.e.,

$$f(x) = \sum_{\ell=0}^{\infty} \sum_{k=0}^{N(n,\ell)} f_{\ell k}(|x|) Y_{\ell k}(x/|x|),$$

$$g(\theta, s) = \sum_{\ell=0}^{\infty} \sum_{k=0}^{N(n,\ell)} g_{\ell k}(s) Y_{\ell k}(\theta).$$

The following theorem gives a relation between $f_{\ell k}$ and $g_{\ell k}$.

THEOREM 2.7. *Let* $f \in \mathcal{S}(\mathbb{R}^n)$ *and* $g = Rf$. *Then*

$$g_{\ell k}(s) = \frac{|S^{n-2}|}{C_\ell^{(n-2)/2}(1)} \int_s^{\infty} C_\ell^{(n-2)/2}\left(\frac{s}{r}\right) \left(1 - \frac{s^2}{r^2}\right)^{(n-3)/2} f_{\ell k}(r) r^{n-2} dr,$$

$$f_{\ell k}(r) = \frac{c_n r^{2-n}}{C_\ell^{(n-2)/2}(1)} \int_r^{\infty} (s^2 - r^2)^{(n-3)/2} C_\ell^{(n-2)/2}\left(\frac{s}{r}\right) g_{\ell k}^{(n-1)}(s) ds,$$

$$c_n = \begin{cases} \frac{(-1)^{n-1}}{2\pi^{n/2}} \frac{\Gamma((n-2)/2)}{\Gamma(n-2)}, & n > 2, \\ -\frac{1}{\pi}, & n = 2. \end{cases}$$

Here $C_\ell^{(n-2)/2}$ are the Gegenbauer polynomials; see section 1.3.5. Due to a different normalization, the formulas are different from Natterer (1986).

There is an alternative way to relate $f_{\ell k}$ to $g_{\ell k}$ by the Hankel transform. Using the expansion of f in spherical harmonics we get

$$\hat{f}(\rho\omega) = (2\pi)^{-n/2} \sum_{\ell=0}^{\infty} \sum_{k=0}^{N(n,\ell)} \int_0^\infty r^{n-1} f_{\ell k}(r) \int_{S^{n-1}} e^{-ir\rho\theta\cdot\omega} Y_{\ell k}(\theta) d\theta dr.$$

We can express the integral on S^{n-1} by the Funk–Hecke theorem (see section 1.3.5), obtaining

$$\hat{f}(\rho\omega) = \sum_{\ell=0}^{\infty} i^{-\ell} \sum_{k=0}^{N(n,\ell)} \int_0^\infty r^{n-1} (r\rho)^{(2-n)/2} f_{\ell k}(r) J_{\ell+(n-2)/2}(\rho r) dr\, Y_{\ell k}(\omega).$$

On the other hand, by Theorem 2.1,

$$\hat{f}(\rho\omega) = (2\pi)^{(1-n)/2} \hat{g}(\omega,\rho) = (2\pi)^{(1-n)/2} \sum_{\ell=0}^{\infty} \sum_{k=0}^{N(n,\ell)} \hat{g}_{\ell k}(\rho) Y_{\ell k}(\omega),$$

hence

$$\hat{g}_{\ell k}(\rho) = (2\pi)^{(n-1)/2} i^{-\ell} \rho^{(2-n)/2} \int_0^\infty r^{\frac{n}{2}} f_{\ell k}(r) J_{\ell+(n-2)/2}(\rho r) dr$$

$$= (2\pi)^{(n-1)/2} i^{-\ell} \rho^{(2-n)/2} \mathcal{H}_{\ell+(n-2)/2}(r^{\frac{n-2}{2}} f_{\ell k}),$$

where

$$\mathcal{H}_\nu f(\rho) = \int_0^\infty r f(r) J_\nu(\rho r) dr$$

is the Hankel transform of order ν. By the Hankel inversion formula, $\mathcal{H}_\nu^{-1} = \mathcal{H}_\nu$ (see, e.g., Sneddon (1972), Chapter 5); hence

$$f_{\ell k}(r) = (2\pi)^{(1-n)/2} i^{\ell} r^{\frac{2-n}{2}} \int_0^\infty \rho^{\frac{n}{2}} \hat{g}_{\ell k}(\rho) J_{\ell+(n-2)/2}(\rho r) d\rho. \qquad (2.22)$$

Of course, this is equivalent to the second formula of Theorem 2.7. It is the starting point of the Hankel inversion suggested by Higgins and Munson (1988).

For $n = 2$, the spherical harmonics are simply the exponentials and the Gegenbauer polynomials C_ℓ^0 are the Chebyshev polynomials (see section 1.3.5) of the first kind. Thus Theorem 2.7 simplifies considerably in this case. Putting

$$f(x) = \sum_\ell f_\ell(r) e^{i\ell\psi}, \qquad x = r \begin{pmatrix} \cos\psi \\ \sin\psi \end{pmatrix},$$

$$g(\theta,s) = \sum_\ell g_\ell(s) e^{i\ell\varphi}, \qquad \theta = \begin{pmatrix} \cos\varphi \\ \sin\varphi \end{pmatrix},$$

we simply have (see section 1.3.5)

$$g_\ell(s) = 2 \int_s^\infty T_{|\ell|}\left(\frac{s}{r}\right)\left(1 - \frac{s^2}{r^2}\right)^{-1/2} f_\ell(r)dr, \tag{2.23}$$

$$f_\ell(r) = -\frac{1}{\pi} \int_r^\infty (s^2 - r^2)^{-1/2} T_{|\ell|}\left(\frac{s}{r}\right) g_\ell'(s)ds. \tag{2.24}$$

This formula was obtained by Cormack (1963) and Kershaw (1962), (1970). Equation (2.24) is called Cormack's first inversion formula. Cormack's second inversion formula, with improved stability properties, is derived in Cormack (1964) and Natterer (1986).

Still another inversion formula was given by Vvedenskaya and Gindikin (1984). It starts out from Poisson's formula (1.11) in the form

$$\sum_{\ell \in \mathbb{Z}^n} f(x + \ell) = (2\pi)^{n/2} \sum_{\ell \in \mathbb{Z}^n} \hat{f}(2\pi\ell)e^{2\pi i x \cdot \ell}$$

$$= (2\pi)^{1/2} \sum_{\ell \in \mathbb{Z}^n} (Rf)^\wedge\left(\frac{\ell}{|\ell|}, 2\pi|\ell|\right)e^{2\pi i x \cdot \ell},$$

where we have used Theorem 2.1. Each $\ell \in \mathbb{Z}^n$ can be written uniquely as $\ell = mk$ with $m \in \mathbb{Z}$ and $k = (k_1, k_2, \ldots, k_n)^T \in \mathbb{Z}^n$ such that $gcd(k_1, k_2, \ldots, k_n) = 1$ and $k_1 \geq 0$. (Here we make the convention that 0 admits every natural number as divisor and gcd of a set containing only 0's is ∞.) Then

$$\sum_{\ell \in \mathbb{Z}} h(\ell) = {\sum_k}' \sum_m h(mk),$$

where the prime means that the sum extends over those $k \in \mathbb{Z}^n$ for which $gcd(k_1, \ldots, k_n) = 1$ and $k_1 \geq 0$. Applying this summation formula to the above sum, we get

$$\sum_{\ell \in \mathbb{Z}^n} f(x + \ell) = (2\pi)^{1/2} {\sum_k}' \sum_m (Rf)^\wedge\left(\frac{k}{|k|}, 2\pi|k|m\right)e^{2\pi i x \cdot km}.$$

The m sum can be evaluated by Poisson's formula (1.11) again, this time with $n = 1$ and $h = 2\pi|k|$. We obtain

$$\sum_{\ell \in \mathbb{Z}^n} f(x + \ell) = (2\pi)^{n-1/2} {\sum_k}' \frac{1}{|k|} \sum_\ell (Rf)\left(\frac{k}{|k|}, \frac{x \cdot k + \ell}{|k|}\right).$$

Now assume that supp$(f) \subseteq [0, 1]^n$. Then the sum on the left-hand side reduces to $f(x)$, and

$$f(x) = (2\pi)^{n-1/2} {\sum_k}' \frac{\ell}{|k|} \sum_\ell (Rf)\left(\frac{k}{|k|}, \frac{x \cdot k + \ell}{|k|}\right)$$

for $x \in [0, 1]^n$. This is the inversion formula of Vvedenskaya and Gindikin. It is tempting to use it as the starting point of an inversion algorithm since the right-hand side is already discretized. However, the computer implementation of this formula has not been very successful.

The ranges of integral geometric transforms are usually highly structured. The structure of the range of R is described by the following theorem.

THEOREM 2.8. *Let $g \in S(C^n)$ and*

$$p_m(\theta) = \int_{\mathbb{R}^1} s^m g(\theta, s) ds, \quad m = 0, 1, \ldots.$$

Then $g = Rf$ for some $f \in S(\mathbb{R}^n)$ if and only if $p_m(\theta)$ is a homogeneous polynomial of degree m.

For $n = 2$, a homogeneous polynomial of degree m in $\theta = \binom{\cos \varphi}{\sin \varphi}$ has the form

$$p_m(\theta) = \sum_{\substack{|\ell| \leq m \\ \ell + m \text{ even}}} c_{m\ell} e^{i\ell\varphi}.$$

We shall make use of Theorem 2.8 in Chapter 6.

Now we give the singular value decomposition of the Radon transform. Let $P_{k,\ell}$ be the polynomials of degree k orthogonal with respect to the weight function t^ℓ in $[0, 1]$, i.e.,

$$\int_0^1 t^\ell P_{k,\ell}(t) P_{m,\ell}(t) dt = \begin{cases} 1, & k = m, \\ 0 & \text{otherwise.} \end{cases}$$

The $P_{k,\ell}(t)$ are up to normalization the Jacobi polynomials $G_k(\ell + (n-2)/2, \ell + (n-2)/2, t)$; see Abramowitz and Stegun (1970), formula 22.2.2. Let $Y_{\ell k}$, $k = 0, \ldots, N(n, \ell)$, be an orthonormal basis for the spherical harmonics of degree ℓ. We define for $m \geq 0, 0 \leq \ell \leq m$, $1 \leq k \leq N(n, \ell)$

$$f_{m\ell k}(x) = 2^{1/2} P_{(m-\ell)/2, \ell + (n-2)/2}(|x|^2) |x|^\ell Y_{\ell k}(x/|x|) \tag{2.25}$$

and

$$g_{m\ell k}(\theta, s) = c(m) w(s)^{n-1} C_m^{n/2}(s) Y_{\ell k}(\theta), \tag{2.26}$$

where $C_m^{n/2}(s)$ is the Gegenbauer polynomial of degree m (see Abramowitz and Stegun (1970), formula 22.2.3) and

$$w(s) = (1 - s^2)^{1/2}.$$

$c(m)$ is a normalization factor chosen to make the norm of $g_{m\ell k}$ in $L_2(C^n, w^{1-n})$ equal to 1. From Abramowitz and Stegun (1970), formula 22.2.3,

$$c(m) = \frac{\pi 2^{1-n/2} \Gamma(m+n)}{m!(m + \frac{n}{2})(\Gamma(\frac{n}{2}))^2}.$$

We also introduce the numbers

$$\sigma_m^2 = \frac{2^n \pi^{n-1}}{(m+1) \cdots (m+n-1)}. \tag{2.27}$$

THEOREM 2.9. *The functions $f_{m\ell k}$, $m \geq 0$, $0 \leq \ell \leq m$, $1 \leq k \leq N(n, \ell)$ are complete orthonormal families in the spaces $L_2(|x| < 1)$, $L_2(C^n, w^{1-n})$, respectively. The singular value decomposition of R as an operator between these spaces is given by*

$$Rf = \sum_{m=0}^{\infty} \sigma_m \sum_{\substack{0 \leq \ell \leq m \\ \ell + m \text{ even}}} \sum_{k=1}^{N(n,\ell)} (f, f_{m\ell k})_{L_2(|x|<1)} g_{m\ell k}.$$

Thus the singular values of R are σ_m, each being of multiplicity $N(n, \ell)\lfloor \frac{m+2}{2} \rfloor$.

Theorem 2.9 was obtained by Davison (1983) and Louis (1984). The expression (2.27) is obtained by making explicit the constants in the latter paper. In both papers more general weight functions were considered.

For questions of stability, estimates of Rf in Sobolev spaces are important. Besides the Sobolev spaces $H_0^\alpha(G)$, G a sufficiently regular domain in $\mathbb{R}^n$ (see section 1.3.1), we need the Sobolev spaces $H^\alpha(C^n)$ defined by

$$\|g\|_{H^\alpha(C^n)}^2 = \int_{S^{n-1}} \int_{\mathbb{R}^1} (1 + \sigma^2)^{\alpha/2} |\hat{g}(\theta, \sigma)|^2 d\sigma d\theta.$$

With these norms we have the following theorem.

THEOREM 2.10. *Let G be bounded, and let α be a real number. Then there are positive constants $c(\alpha, G)$, $C(\alpha, G)$ such that for all $f \in H_0^\alpha(G)$*

$$c(\alpha, G)\|f\|_{H_0^\alpha(G)} \leq \|Rf\|_{H^{\alpha+(n-1)/2}(C^n)} \leq C(\alpha, G)\|f\|_{H_0^\alpha(G)}.$$

Theorem 2.10 tells that, roughly speaking, Rf is smoother than f by an order of $(n-1)/2$.

2.2 The Ray Transform

While the Radon transform R integrates over hyperplanes in $\mathbb{R}^n$, the ray transform P integrates over straight lines. Thus for $n = 2$, R and P differ only in the notation. The treatment of P parallels the one of R, so the same references can be used.

We represent straight lines in $\mathbb{R}^n$ by a direction $\theta \in S^{n-1}$ and a point $x \in \theta^\perp$ as $\{x + t\theta : t \in \mathbb{R}^1\}$. Then P may be defined by

$$(Pf)(\theta, x) = \int_{\mathbb{R}^1} f(x + t\theta)dt. \tag{2.28}$$

Thus Pf is a function on $T^n = \{(\theta, x) : \theta \in S^{n-1}, x \in \theta^\perp\}$. If $f \in \mathcal{S}(\mathbb{R}^n)$, then $Pf \in \mathcal{S}(T^n)$, where

$$\mathcal{S}(T^n) = \{g \in C^\infty(T^n) : x^\alpha D^\beta g(\theta, x) \text{ bounded}, \ \alpha, \beta \geq 0\}.$$

Fourier transform and convolution on T^n are defined by

$$\hat{g}(\theta, \xi) = (2\pi)^{(1-n)/2} \int_{\theta^\perp} e^{-ix\cdot\xi} g(\theta, x)dx, \quad \xi \in \theta^\perp, \tag{2.29}$$

$$(g * h)(\theta, x) = \int_{\theta^\perp} g(x - y)h(y)dy, \quad x \in \theta^\perp. \tag{2.30}$$

THEOREM 2.11. *Let* $f \in \mathcal{S}(\mathbb{R}^n)$. *Then for* $\theta \in S^{n-1}$, $\xi \perp \theta$,

$$(Pf)^\wedge(\theta, \xi) = (2\pi)^{1/2} \hat{f}(\xi).$$

From this theorem, we have the following uniqueness results in $\mathbb{R}^3$. Let $S_0^2 \subseteq S^2$ meet every equatorial circle of S^2 (condition of Orlov (1976)). Then $(Pf)(\theta, \cdot)$, $\theta \in S_0^2$, determines f uniquely. Indeed, let $\xi \in \mathbb{R}^3$ be arbitrary. Then if S_0^2 satisfies Orlov's condition, we can find $\theta \in S_0^2$ such that $\theta \perp \xi$. Hence $\hat{f}(\xi)$ is determined by $(Pf)^\wedge(\theta, \xi)$. That the condition of Orlov implies uniqueness can also be seen via the Radon transform. Let H be a plane. The unit vectors parallel to H form an equatorial circle that, according to Orlov's condition, contains a direction vector θ in S_0^2 for which $(Pf)(\theta, \cdot)$ is known in all of $\theta^\perp$. Hence

$$\int_H f(x)dx = \int_{x \in \theta^\perp \cap H} (Pf)(\theta, x)dx$$

is known. Thus the Radon transform of f is known, hence f by Theorem 2.6.

THEOREM 2.12. *Let* $f, g \in \mathcal{S}(\mathbb{R}^n)$. *Then*

$$Pf * Pg = P(f * g).$$

In both theorems, one has to keep in mind that different Fourier transforms and convolutions are denoted by the same symbol.

The backprojection operator P^* now is

$$(P^*g)(x) = \int_{S^{n-1}} g(\theta, E_\theta x)d\theta, \tag{2.31}$$

where E_θ is the orthogonal projection on $\theta^\perp$, i.e., $E_\theta x = x - (x \cdot \theta)\theta$. Again, P^* is just the adjoint of P, i.e.,

$$\int_{S^{n-1}} \int_{\theta^\perp} gPf d\theta dx = \int_{\mathbb{R}^n} P^*g \cdot f dx. \tag{2.32}$$

THEOREM 2.13. *Let* $f \in \mathcal{S}(\mathbb{R}^n)$ *and* $g \in \mathcal{S}(T^n)$. *Then*

$$(P^*g) * f = P^*(g * Pf).$$

THEOREM 2.14. *Let* $f \in \mathcal{S}(\mathbb{R}^n)$ *and* $g = Pf$. *Then for* $\alpha < n$, *we have*

$$f = \frac{1}{2\pi |S^{n-1}|} I^{-\alpha} P^* I^{\alpha-1} g.$$

Here $I^{-\alpha}$ *is the Riesz potential on* $\mathbb{R}^n$ *(see (1.15)), while* $I^{\alpha-1}$ *is the Riesz potential on* T^n, *which is defined by*

$$(I^{\alpha-1}g)^\wedge(\theta, \xi) = |\xi|^{1-\alpha} \hat{g}(\theta, \xi), \quad \xi \in \theta^\perp.$$

THEOREM 2.15. *Let* $f \in \mathcal{S}(\mathbb{R}^n)$. *Then for* $m = 0, 1, \ldots,$

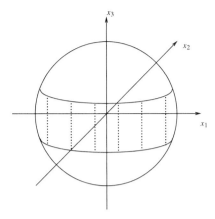

Figure 2.1. *Spherical zone for Orlov's inversion formula.*

$$\int_{\theta^{\perp}} (x \cdot y)^m (Pf)(\theta, x) dx = q_m(y), \quad y \in \theta^{\perp},$$

where q_m is a homogeneous polynomial of degree m that is independent of θ.

The inversion formula for P of Theorem 2.14 is not as useful as the inversion formula for R of Theorem 2.5. To fix ideas, consider the case $n = 3$ and put $\alpha = 0$. Then

$$f(x) = \frac{1}{(4\pi)^2} \int_{S^2} (I^{-1}g)(\theta, E_\theta x) d\theta. \tag{2.33}$$

Thus one needs $g(\theta, y)$ for all $\theta \in S^2$ and $y \in \theta^{\perp}$ in order to find the function f. In practice, it is rarely the case that g is known on all of S^2.

A formula using only a subset $S_0^2 \subset S^2$ was given by Orlov (1976). In spherical coordinates,

$$x = \begin{pmatrix} \cos\varphi \, \cos\vartheta \\ \sin\varphi \, \cos\vartheta \\ \sin\vartheta \end{pmatrix}, \qquad 0 \le \varphi < 2\pi, \qquad |\vartheta| \le \frac{\pi}{2},$$

S_0^2 is given by $\vartheta_-(\varphi) \le \vartheta \le \vartheta_+(\varphi)$, $0 \le \varphi < 2\pi$, where $\vartheta_\pm$ are functions such that $-\frac{\pi}{2} < \vartheta_-(\varphi) < 0 < \vartheta_+(\varphi) < \frac{\pi}{2}$, $0 \le \varphi < 2\pi$. For example, if $\vartheta_\pm = \pm\vartheta_0$ are constant, then S_0 is the spherical zone between the horizontal planes $x_3 = \pm \sin\vartheta_0$; see Figure 2.1.

Let $\ell(x, y)$ be the length of the intersection of S_0^2 with the subspace spanned by x, $y \in \mathbb{R}^3$. According to our assumption on $\vartheta_\pm$, $\ell(x, y) > 0$ if x, y are linearly independent.

THEOREM 2.16. *Let $f \in \mathcal{S}(\mathbb{R}^3)$ and $g(\theta, x) = (Pf)(\theta, x)$ for $\theta \in S_0^2$ and $x \in \theta^{\perp}$. Then*

$$f(x) = \Delta \int_{S_0^2} h(\theta, E_\theta x) d\theta,$$

where h is obtained from g by

$$h(\theta, x) = -\frac{1}{4\pi^2} \int_{\theta^\perp} \frac{g(\theta, x - y)}{|y|\ell(\theta, y)} dy.$$

We derive Orlov's inversion formula in a more general setting.

Inversion formulas for subsets $S_0^{n-1} \subset S^{n-1}$ can be obtained as follows. With the adjoint P^* defined as

$$(P^*g)(x) = \int_{S_0^{n-1}} g(\theta, E_\theta x) d\theta,$$

we verify immediately that Theorem 2.13 still holds. Hence for $H = P^*h$, we have

$$H * f = P^*(h * Pf). \tag{2.34}$$

For $H = \delta$, this is an inversion formula requiring only directions $\theta \in S_0^{n-1}$.

THEOREM 2.17. *For $h \in \mathcal{S}(T_0^{n-1})$, $T_0^{n-1} = \{(\theta, x) : \theta \in S_0^{n-1}, \; x \in \theta^\perp\}$,*

$$\hat{H}(\xi) = (2\pi)^{1/2} \frac{1}{|\xi|} \int_{S_0^{n-1} \cap \xi^\perp} \hat{h}(\theta, \xi) d\theta.$$

Proof. We have

$$(P^*h)^\wedge(\xi) = (2\pi)^{-n/2} \int_{\mathbb{R}^n} e^{-ix\cdot\xi}(P^*h)(x)dx$$

$$= (2\pi)^{-n/2} \int_{S_0^{n-1}} \int_{\mathbb{R}^n} e^{-ix\cdot\xi} h(\theta, E_\theta x) dx d\theta.$$

Putting $x = y + s\theta$, $y \in \theta^\perp$, we obtain

$$(P^*h)^\wedge(\xi) = (2\pi)^{-n/2} \int_{S_0^{n-1}} \int_{\theta^\perp} \int_{\mathbb{R}} e^{-iy\cdot\xi - is\theta\cdot\xi} h(\theta, y) dy ds d\theta$$

$$= (2\pi)^{(2-n)/2} \int_{S_0^{n-1}} \int_{\theta^\perp} e^{-iy\cdot\xi} h(\theta, y)\delta(\theta \cdot \xi) dy d\theta$$

$$= (2\pi)^{1/2} \int_{S_0^{n-1}} \hat{h}(\theta, E_\theta\xi)\delta(\theta \cdot \xi) d\theta$$

$$= (2\pi)^{1/2}|\xi|^{-1} \int_{S_0^{n-1} \cap \xi^\perp} \hat{h}(\theta, \xi) d\theta. \qquad \square$$

In order to get an inversion formula from (2.34), we have to determine h such that $H = \delta$ or $(P^*h)^\wedge = (2\pi)^{-n/2}$, i.e.,

$$\int_{S_0^{n-1} \cap \xi^\perp} \hat{h}(\theta, \xi) d\theta = (2\pi)^{-(n+1)/2}|\xi|. \tag{2.35}$$

A solution independent of θ is

$$\hat{h}(\theta, \xi) = \frac{|\xi|}{(2\pi)^{(n+1)/2} |S_0^{n-1} \cap \xi^\perp|} \tag{2.36}$$

with $|S_0^{n-1} \cap \xi^\perp|$ the $(n-2)$-dimensional Lebesgue measure of $S_0^{n-1} \cap \xi^\perp$. For $n = 3$ and S_0^2, the spherical zone from Figure 2.1, Colsher (1980) gave the explicit form of $\hat{h}$. With $\xi_3 = |\xi| \cos \psi$, $0 \le \psi \le \pi$, he obtained

$$\hat{h}(\theta, \xi) = \frac{|\xi|}{(2\pi)^2} \begin{cases} \frac{1}{2\pi}, & \sin \psi \le \sin \vartheta_0, \\ \frac{1}{4 \arcsin(\sin \vartheta_0 / \sin \psi)}, & \sin \psi \ge \sin \vartheta_0. \end{cases} \tag{2.37}$$

For the derivation of (2.37) we represent $\omega \in S^2 \cap \xi^\perp$ by spherical coordinates with $\xi/|\xi|$ as North Pole, i.e.,

$$\omega = \begin{pmatrix} -\sin \beta \, \cos \psi \\ \cos \beta \\ \sin \beta \, \sin \psi \end{pmatrix} \quad \text{for} \quad \xi = |\xi| \begin{pmatrix} \sin \psi \\ 0 \\ \cos \psi \end{pmatrix}.$$

$S^2 \cap \xi^\perp$ is the equatorial circle $\{\omega : 0 \le \beta < 2\pi\}$. It intersects the planes $\xi_3 = \pm \sin \vartheta_0$ for

$$\beta = \pm \arcsin \left(\frac{\sin \vartheta_0}{\sin \psi} \right)$$

provided that $\sin \psi \ge \sin \vartheta_0$. Since β is the arc length on $S^2 \cap \xi^\perp$, we have

$$|S_0^2 \cap \xi^\perp| = 4 \arcsin \left(\frac{\sin \vartheta_0}{\sin \psi} \right).$$

For $\sin \psi \le \sin \vartheta_0$, $S_0^2 \cap \xi^\perp$ is an equatorial circle; hence $|S_0^2 \cap \xi^\perp| = 2\pi$. This shows (2.37).

If Orlov's condition is not satisfied, then (2.36) does not make sense for $S_0^{n-1} \cap \xi^\perp = \phi$. In this case, we may put

$$\hat{h}(\theta, \xi) = \begin{cases} \frac{|\xi|}{(2\pi)^{(n+1)/2} |S_0^{n-1} \cap \xi^\perp|}, & |S_0^{n-1} \cap \xi^\perp| \ne 0, \\ 0 & \text{otherwise.} \end{cases}$$

This leads to the solution of minimal norm; see section 1.3.3.

Putting $n = 3$ and $H(x) = \frac{1}{|x|}$ in Theorem 2.17, i.e., $\hat{H}(\xi) = \left(\frac{2}{\pi} \right)^{1/2} |\xi|^{-2}$, we obtain for h

$$\int_{S_0^2 \cap \xi^\perp} \hat{h}(\theta, \xi) d\theta = \frac{1}{\pi} \frac{1}{|\xi|}.$$

A solution independent of θ is

$$\hat{h}(\theta, \xi) = \frac{1}{\pi |\xi| |S_0^2 \cap \xi^\perp|}.$$

We compute the inverse Fourier transform of $\hat{h}$, i.e.,

$$h(\theta, x) = \frac{1}{2\pi^2} \int_{\theta^\perp} \frac{e^{ix \cdot \xi} d\xi}{|\xi||S_0^2 \cap \xi^\perp|}, \quad x \in \theta^\perp.$$

With T a (3,2) matrix the columns of which are an orthonormal basis of $\theta^\perp$, we can write $x = Ty, \xi = T\eta$ with $y, \eta \in \mathbb{R}^2$; hence

$$h(\theta, x) = \frac{1}{2\pi^2} \int_{\mathbb{R}^2} \frac{e^{iy \cdot \eta} d\eta}{|\eta||S_0^2 \cap (T\eta)^\perp|}.$$

Introducing polar coordinates $y = ra, \eta = \rho\alpha, a, \alpha \in S^1$, we obtain

$$h(\theta, x) = \frac{1}{2\pi^2} \int_0^\infty \int_{S^1} \frac{e^{ir\rho a \cdot \alpha} d\rho d\alpha}{|S_0^2 \cap (T\alpha)^\perp|}$$

$$= \frac{1}{2\pi^2} \int_{-\infty}^{+\infty} \int_{S_+^1} \frac{e^{ir\rho a \cdot \alpha} d\rho d\alpha}{|S_0^2 \cap (T\alpha)^\perp|},$$

where S_+^1 is the half-circle in $\mathbb{R}^2$. With the help of (1.9), the ρ integral can now be carried out, yielding

$$h(\theta, x) = \frac{1}{\pi} \int_{S_+^1} \frac{\delta(ra \cdot \alpha) d\alpha}{|S_0^2 \cap (T\alpha)^\perp|}$$

$$= \frac{1}{\pi r} \frac{1}{|S_0^2 \cap (Ta_\perp)^\perp|},$$

where $a_\perp$ is a vector perpendicular to a. Since $(Ta_\perp)^\perp$ is spanned by x, θ, we have

$$h(\theta, x) = \frac{1}{\pi|x|} \frac{1}{\ell(x, \theta)}.$$

Thus we arrive at Orlov's inversion formula from Theorem 2.16.

The singular value decomposition of P was obtained by Maass (1987). With the functions $f_{m\ell k}$ from (2.25) and a certain complete orthonormal system $g_{m\ell k}$ on $L_2(T^n, w)$, where $w(y) = (1 - |y|^2)^{1/2}$, there are positive numbers $\sigma_{m\ell}$ such that

$$(Pf)(\theta, x) = \sum_{m=0}^{\infty} \sum_{\substack{0 \leq \ell \leq m \\ \ell + m \text{ even}}} \sigma_{m\ell} \sum_{k=1}^{N(n,\ell)} (f, f_{m\ell k}) g_{m\ell k}. \tag{2.38}$$

The singular values $\sigma_{m\ell}$, each having multiplicity $N(n, \ell)$, satisfy

$$\sigma_{m\ell} = O(m^{-1/2}), \quad m \to \infty, \tag{2.39}$$

uniformly in ℓ.

The Sobolev space estimate of P makes use of the norm

$$\|g\|_{H^\alpha(T^n)} = \int_{S^{n-1}} \int_{\theta^\perp} (1 + |\eta|^2)^{\alpha/2} |\hat{g}(\theta, \eta)|^2 d\eta d\theta.$$

Corresponding to Theorem 2.10, we have the following theorem.

THEOREM 2.18. *Let G be bounded and α real. Then there are positive constants $c(\alpha, G)$, $C(\alpha, G)$ such that for all $f \in H_0^\alpha(G)$*

$$c(\alpha, G)\|f\|_{H_0^\alpha(G)} \le \|Pf\|_{H^{\alpha+1/2}(T^n)} \le C(\alpha, G)\|f\|_{H_0^\alpha(G)}.$$

Thus Pf is smoother than f by the order $1/2$, independent of the dimension.

2.3 The Cone Beam Transform

Let $\theta \in S^{n-1}$ and $a \in \mathbb{R}^n$. The cone beam transform D of $f \in \mathcal{S}(\mathbb{R}^n)$ is defined by

$$(Df)(a, \theta) = \int_0^\infty f(a + t\theta)dt. \qquad (2.40)$$

Thus the difference between D and the ray transform P is mainly notational. We extend Df to a function on $\mathbb{R}^3 \times \mathbb{R}^3$ by putting

$$\begin{aligned}
(Df)(a, y) &= \int_0^\infty f(a + ty)dt \\
&= |y| \int_0^\infty f\left(a + t\frac{y}{|y|}\right) dt.
\end{aligned}$$

In other words, we extend Df in the second argument as a function homogeneous of degree -1. Such a function has a well-defined Fourier transform:

$$(Df)^\wedge(a, \eta) = (2\pi)^{-3/2} \int_{\mathbb{R}^3} (Df)(a, y)e^{-iy\cdot\eta}dy.$$

We think of a as the source of a ray with direction θ. In a typical 3D tomographic setup, the object f of compact support would be surrounded by a source curve A, and $(Df)(a, \theta)$ would be measured for $a \in A$ and $\theta \in S^2$. It is for this situation that we try to invert D. For this purpose, we give some relations between D and the Radon transform R, which in turn permit the inversion of D, provided the source curve A satisfies certain conditions. We restrict the discussion to the 3D case.

All these relations are an outflow of a formula essentially obtained by Hamaker et al. (1980): Let h be a function on $\mathbb{R}^1$, homogeneous of degree $1 - n$. Then

$$\int_{S^{n-1}} (Df)(a, \omega)h(\theta \cdot \omega)d\omega = \int_{\mathbb{R}^1} (Rf)(\theta, s)h(s - a \cdot \theta)ds.$$

We use this for $n = 3$. Then we can put $h = \delta'$, obtaining

$$\frac{\partial}{\partial s}(Rf)(\theta, s)|_{s=a\cdot\theta} = -\int_{S^2} (Df)(a, \omega)\delta'(\theta \cdot \omega)d\omega.$$

Evaluating this integral, we obtain Grangeat's formula, as follows (see Grangeat (1987), (1991)).

THEOREM 2.19. *Let $f \in \mathcal{S}(\mathbb{R}^3)$. Then for $\theta \in S^2$, $a \in \mathbb{R}^3$,*

$$\frac{\partial}{\partial s}(Rf)(\theta, a \cdot \theta) = \int_{\omega \in \theta^\perp \cap S^2} \frac{\partial}{\partial \theta}(Df)(a, \omega) d\omega,$$

where $\frac{\partial}{\partial \theta}$ is the directional derivative in the direction θ, acting on the second argument of Df.

An alternative, entirely elementary proof of Theorem 2.19 is as follows. It suffices to prove the theorem for $\theta = e_3$. In that case, it reads

$$\frac{\partial}{\partial s}(Rf)(e_3, a_3) = \int_{\omega \in S^1} \left[\frac{\partial}{\partial z}(Df)\left(a, \begin{pmatrix} \omega \\ z \end{pmatrix}\right)\right]\Bigg|_{z=0} d\omega.$$

It is easily seen that the right- and left-hand sides both coincide with

$$\int_{\mathbb{R}^2} \frac{\partial f}{\partial x_3}\left(a + \begin{pmatrix} x' \\ 0 \end{pmatrix}\right) dx',$$

hence the theorem.

Grangeat's formula can be viewed as the limiting case of a much more general result due to Palamodov (1991). Suppose we want to compute $(Rf)(\theta, s)$ from the values of $(Df)(a, \omega)$ for a on some curve C on the plane $x \cdot \theta = s$ and for ω tangent to C at a. Obviously, this is not possible. However, if C is part of a smooth surface S transverse to $x \cdot \theta = s$, and if $(Df)(a, \omega)$ is known for all $a \in S$ and ω tangent to S at a, then $\frac{\partial}{\partial s}(Rf)(\theta, s)$ can be computed. For C, a circle, and S, the cylinder perpendicular to $x \cdot \theta = s$ whose intersection with $x \cdot \theta = s$ is C, this can be shown as in the elementary proof of Grangeat's formula above. If S is a narrow tube shrinking to a point a, we regain Grangeat's result.

Other formulas relating Rf to Df can be obtained by different choices of h. Putting

$$h(s) = \int_{-\infty}^{+\infty} e^{-is\sigma} |\sigma| d\sigma,$$

i.e., $Rf * h = H\frac{\partial}{\partial s}Rf$, leads to a formula given by B. D. Smith (1985). It can be written in various ways. We may write

$$(Df)^\wedge(a, \xi) = (2\pi)^{-3/2} \int_{\mathbb{R}^3} e^{-i\xi \cdot x}(Df)(a, x) dx$$

$$= (2\pi)^{-3/2} \int_0^\infty r^2 \int_{S^2} e^{-ir\xi \cdot \omega}(Df)(a, r\omega) dr d\omega$$

$$= (2\pi)^{-3/2} \int_{S^2} \int_0^\infty r e^{-ir\xi \cdot \omega} dr (Df)(a, \omega) d\omega$$

$$= (2\pi)^{-3/2} \int_{S^2} \int_0^\infty r e^{-ir\xi \cdot \omega} dr ((Df)(a, \omega) + (Df)(a, -\omega)) d\omega$$

$$= \frac{1}{2}(2\pi)^{-3/2} \int_{S^2} \int_{-\infty}^{+\infty} |r| e^{-ir\xi \cdot \omega} dr ((Df)(a, \omega) + (Df)(a, -\omega)) d\omega$$

$$= \frac{1}{2}(2\pi)^{-3/2} \int_{S^2} (Df)(a, \omega) h(\xi \cdot \omega) d\omega.$$

Thus

$$H\frac{\partial}{\partial s}(Rf)(\theta, s)|_{s=\theta\cdot a} = 2(2\pi)^{3/2}(Df)^{\wedge}(a, \theta).$$

This is the formula of B. D. Smith (1985).

Finally, we put $h(s) = 1/s^2$, obtaining

$$\int \frac{(Rf)(\theta, s)}{(a\cdot\theta - s)^2}ds = \int_{S^2} \frac{(Df)(a, \omega)}{(\theta\cdot\omega)^2}d\omega.$$

These integrals have to be understood in the distributional sense, i.e., as the finite part of a divergent integral; see Schwartz (1973). An integration by parts on the left-hand side yields

$$\int \frac{\frac{\partial}{\partial s}(Rf)(\theta, s)}{a\cdot\theta - s}ds = \int_{S^2} \frac{(Df)(a, \omega)}{(\theta\cdot\omega)^2}d\omega$$

or, equivalently,

$$H\frac{\partial}{\partial s}(Rf)(\theta, a\cdot\theta) = \frac{1}{\pi}\int_{S^2} \frac{(Df)(a, \omega)}{(\theta\cdot\omega)^2}d\omega.$$

This formula is due to Gel'fand and Goncharov (1987).

An explicit inversion formula was given by Tuy (1983). It applies to a situation in which the source curve A satisfies Tuy's condition: A intersects each plane hitting supp(f) transversally. Analytically this means that if $a = a(\lambda), \lambda \in I$, is a parametric representation of A, then there exists for each $x \in$ supp(f) and each $\theta \in S^2$ a $\lambda = \lambda(x, \theta) \in I$ such that

$$a(\lambda(x, \theta))\cdot x = \theta\cdot x, \qquad a'(\lambda(x, \theta))\cdot\theta \neq 0.$$

THEOREM 2.20. *Suppose that the source curve A satisfies Tuy's condition. Then*

$$f(x) = (2\pi)^{-3/2}i^{-1}\int_{S^2}(a'(\lambda)\cdot\theta)^{-1}\frac{d}{d\lambda}(Df)^{\wedge}(a(\lambda), \theta)d\theta,$$

where $\lambda = \lambda(x, \theta)$.

The function $g(x, y) = (Df)(x, y)$ in its extended form satisfies John's differential equations (John (1955))

$$\frac{\partial^2 g}{\partial x_i\partial y_j} - \frac{\partial^2 g}{\partial x_j\partial y_i} = 0, \quad i, j = 1, 2, 3.$$

Let $\hat{g}$ be the Fourier transform of g with respect to the second variable. Then

$$\eta_j\frac{\partial\hat{g}}{\partial x_i}(x, \eta) - \eta_i\frac{\partial\hat{g}}{\partial x_j}(x, \eta) = 0, \quad i, j = 1, 2, 3.$$

This can be written as

$$\eta\times\nabla\hat{g}(x, \eta) = 0.$$

It follows that $\hat{g}(\cdot, \eta)$ is constant on planes orthogonal to η. Thus $\hat{g}(x, \eta)$ is known for each x such that each plane through x meets A. This can be used to compute a complete set of data in cases in which Tuy's condition is not satisfied; see Finch (1985).

In some cases one can reduce the dimensionality of the inversion problem for D by exploiting invariances. For instance, consider the case of a circle as source curve. Then the problem is invariant with respect to rotation in the source plane and with respect to scaling in the axial direction. Thus a Fourier expansion in the source plane, combined with a Mellin transform in the axial variable, reduces the problem to 1D.

To be more specific, we assume that the source curve is the unit circle in the $x_1 - x_2$ plane. Then a conveniently parametrized and scaled version of D is

$$g(\varphi, y_2, y_3) = \int_0^\infty f((1-t)\theta + t(y_2\theta_\perp + y_3 e_3))dt,$$

$$\theta = \begin{pmatrix} \cos\varphi \\ \sin\varphi \\ 0 \end{pmatrix}, \quad \theta_\perp = \begin{pmatrix} -\sin\varphi \\ \cos\varphi \\ 0 \end{pmatrix}, \quad e_3 = \begin{pmatrix} 0 \\ 0 \\ 1 \end{pmatrix},$$

where f is assumed to vanish outside the unit ball of $\mathbb{R}^3$. The Mellin transform of a function h in $\mathbb{R}^1$ is defined to be

$$(Mh)(s) = \int_0^\infty t^{s-1}h(t)dt;$$

see Sneddon (1972). We denote the Mellin transform of g, f with respect to y_3, x_3 by Mg, Mf, respectively. Obviously

$$(Mg)(\varphi, y_2, s) = \int_0^\infty (Mf)((1-t)\theta' + ty_2\theta_\perp', s)t^{-s}dt,$$

where θ', $\theta_\perp'$ are the orthogonal projections of θ, $\theta_\perp$ onto the $x_1 - x_2$ plane. Note that this is for each s a weighted Radon integral equation for $(Mf)(\cdot, s)$ in the plane. We expand Mf, Mg in Fourier series

$$(Mf)(x, s) = \sum_\ell f_\ell(r, s)e^{-i\ell\varphi}, \quad x = r\begin{pmatrix} \cos\varphi \\ \sin\varphi \end{pmatrix},$$

$$(Mg)(\varphi, y_2, s) = \sum_\ell g_\ell(y_2, s)e^{-i\ell\varphi}$$

with certain functions f_ℓ, g_ℓ. Substituting into the integral equation for Mf, we obtain after some algebra

$$g_\ell(y_2, s) = \int_0^\infty f_\ell\left(\sqrt{(1-t)^2 + t^2 y_2^2}, s\right)e^{-i\ell\alpha(t, y_2)}dt,$$

where $\alpha(t, y_2)$ is the argument of the point $\binom{1-t}{ty_2}$ in the $x_1 - x_2$ plane. Thus for each ℓ, s, we get a 1D integral equation for f_ℓ. This is clearly reminiscent of the derivation of Cormack's inversion formula (2.24). Unfortunately, it seems that there does not exist an explicit solution such as (2.24) to this integral equation, as we already have exploited all the invariances. See Natterer (1994) for details.

2.4   Weighted Transforms

In this section, we consider transforms that integrate over lines with respect to a weight function. Fairly general transforms of this type have been considered by Quinto (1983). We consider only a few examples that occur in practice.

2.4.1   The attenuated ray transform

Let $\mu \in \mathcal{S}(\mathbb{R}^n)$. The attenuated ray transform P_μ is defined by

$$(P_\mu f)(\theta, x) = \int f(x + t\theta) e^{-\int_t^\infty \mu(x+\tau\theta)d\tau} dt, \quad x \in \theta^\perp,$$

for $f \in \mathcal{S}(\mathbb{R}^n)$. If $n = 2$, it is more customary to use the attenuated Radon transform

$$(R_\mu f)(\theta, s) = \int_{x \cdot \theta = s} f(x) e^{-(D\mu)(x, \theta_\perp)} dx,$$

where $\theta = (\cos\varphi, \sin\varphi)^T$ and $\theta_\perp = (-\sin\varphi, \cos\varphi)^T$. The adjoint of R_μ is given by

$$(R_\mu^* g)(x) = \int_{S^1} e^{-(D\mu)(x, \theta_\perp)} g(\theta, x \cdot \theta) d\theta.$$

If f vanishes outside a convex set and if μ is constant within this set, then R_μ can be reduced to the exponential Radon transform

$$(T_\mu f)(\theta, s) = \int f(s\theta + t\theta_\perp) e^{\mu t} dt,$$

and the same applies to P_μ. T_μ admits a projection theorem analogous to Theorem 2.1 (see Natterer (1979)): If f has compact support, then

$$(T_\mu f)^\wedge(\theta, \sigma) = (2\pi)^{1/2} \hat{f}(\sigma\theta + i\mu\theta_\perp).$$

It follows that for $g = T_\mu f$, we have

$$\hat{g}(\theta_1, i\sigma_1) = \hat{g}(\theta_2, i\sigma_2)$$

whenever $\sigma_1\theta_1 + \mu\theta_{1,\perp} = \sigma_2\theta_2 + \mu\theta_{2,\perp}$. It is shown in Aguilar and Kuchment (1995) that this condition characterizes the range of T_μ.

We also have an inversion formula analogous to Theorem 2.5.

THEOREM 2.21. *Let $g = T_\mu f$ and $f \in \mathcal{S}(\mathbb{R}^2)$. Then*

$$f = \frac{1}{4\pi} T_{-\mu}^* I_\mu^{-1} g,$$

where I_μ^{-1} is the generalized Riesz potential

$$(I_\mu^{-1} g)^\wedge(\sigma) = \begin{cases} |\sigma| \hat{g}(\sigma), & |\sigma| > |\mu|, \\ 0 & otherwise, \end{cases}$$

and T_μ^* is the generalized backprojection

$$(T_\mu^* g)(x) = \int_{S^1} e^{\mu x \cdot \theta_\perp} g(\theta, x \cdot \theta) d\theta.$$

This theorem generalizes the Radon inversion formula to the exponential case. It is due to Tretiak and Metz (1980). It is the starting point of the filtered backprojection algorithm for the solution of $T_\mu f = g$; see section 5.1.8. For $n > 2$, the exponential ray transform was inverted in Palamodov (1996), but this formula is not easily implemented.

The attenuated Radon transform admits consistency conditions in its range similar to Theorem 2.8, as follows.

THEOREM 2.22. *Let $f, \mu \in S(\mathbb{R}^2)$ and let $g = R_\mu f$. Then for $k > m \geq 0$ integer, we have*

$$\int_{\mathbb{R}^1} \int_{S^1} s^m e^{\pm i k \varphi + \frac{1}{2}(I \pm i H) R\mu(\theta, s)} g(\theta, s) d\theta ds = 0,$$

where $\theta = (\cos\varphi, \sin\varphi)^T$ and H is the Hilbert transform (1.12), acting on the variable s.

Proof. Let

$$u(x, \theta) = h(\theta, x \cdot \theta) - (D\mu)(x, \theta_\perp),$$
$$h = \frac{1}{2}(I + i H) R\mu.$$

One can show (see Natterer (1986), Theorem 6.2) that the Fourier expansion of u contains only terms of odd and positive order, i.e.,

$$u(x, \theta) = \sum_{\ell > 0 \text{ odd}} u_\ell(x) e^{i\ell\varphi},$$

with certain functions u_ℓ. It follows that for $k > m \geq 0$

$$(x \cdot \theta)^m e^{i k \varphi + u(x, \theta)}$$

has only Fourier coefficients of positive order. Hence

$$(R_\mu^*(s^m e^{i k \varphi + h}))(x) = \int_{S^1} (x \cdot \theta)^m e^{i k \varphi + u(x, \theta)} d\theta = 0, \quad k > m \geq 0.$$

Recalling that R_μ^* is the adjoint of R_μ, we have

$$\int_{\mathbb{R}^1} \int_{S^1} s^m e^{i k \varphi + h(\theta, s)} (R_\mu f)(\theta, s) d\theta ds$$
$$= \int_{\mathbb{R}^2} (R_\mu^*(s^m e^{i k \varphi + h}))(x) f(x) dx$$
$$= 0$$

for $k > m \geq 0$. Together with the complex conjugate equation, this is the theorem. $\square$

We will make use of these consistency conditions in section 6.4.

An inversion formula for R_μ was recently obtained by Novikov (2000). We give a short derivation of Novikov's formula based on the techniques used in the proof of Theorem 2.22.

THEOREM 2.23. *Let $f, \mu \in \mathcal{S}(\mathbb{R}^2)$ and $g = R_\mu f$. Let $h = \frac{1}{2}(I + iH)R\mu$. Then*

$$f(x) = \frac{1}{4\pi} \operatorname{Re} \operatorname{div} R^*_{-\mu}(\theta e^{-h} H e^h g).$$

Proof. It suffices to prove the theorem for $f(x) = \delta(x - y)$. With this choice of f,

$$
\begin{aligned}
(He^h g)(\theta, s) &= \frac{1}{\pi} \int_{\mathbb{R}^1} \frac{1}{s - t} e^{h(\theta, t)} \int_{x \cdot \theta = t} e^{-(D\mu)(x, \theta_\perp)} \delta(x - y) dx dt \\
&= \frac{1}{\pi} \frac{1}{s - \theta \cdot y} e^{h(\theta, \theta \cdot y) - (D\mu)(y, \theta_\perp)} \\
&= \frac{1}{\pi} \frac{1}{s - \theta \cdot y} u(y, \theta),
\end{aligned}
$$

where u is as in the proof of Theorem 2.22. Using this, it remains to show that

$$\delta(x - y) = \operatorname{Re} \frac{1}{4\pi^2} \operatorname{div} \int_{S^1} \frac{\theta}{(x - y) \cdot \theta} e^{u(y, \theta) - u(x, \theta)} d\theta. \tag{2.41}$$

From the proof of Theorem 2.22, we know that

$$u(y, \theta) - u(x, \theta) = \sum_{\ell > 0 \text{ odd}} (u_\ell(y) - u_\ell(x)) e^{i\ell\varphi}.$$

It follows that with certain functions $u_\ell(x, y)$,

$$\cosh(u(y, \theta) - u(x, \theta)) = 1 + \sum_{\ell > 0 \text{ even}} u_\ell(x, y) e^{i\ell\varphi},$$

$$\sinh(u(y, \theta) - u(x, \theta)) = \sum_{\ell > 0 \text{ odd}} u_\ell(x, y) e^{i\ell\varphi}.$$

From the formula

$$\int_0^{2\pi} \frac{\sin(\ell\varphi)}{\sin \varphi} d\varphi = 2\pi, \quad \ell > 0 \text{ odd}$$

(see Gradshteyn and Ryzhik (1965), formula 3.612), we can derive

$$\int_0^{2\pi} \frac{\theta}{x \cdot \theta} e^{i\ell\varphi} d\varphi = \begin{cases} 0, & \ell \text{ odd}, \\ 2\pi x/|x|^2, & \ell = 0, \\ -2\pi i e^{i\ell\psi} x_\perp/|x|^2, & \ell > 0, \end{cases}$$

where $x_\perp/|x| = (\cos \psi, \sin \psi)^T$. Using this with x replaced by $x - y$, we obtain

$$\int_0^{2\pi} \frac{\theta}{(x-y)\cdot\theta} \cosh(u(y,\theta) - u(x,\theta))d\varphi$$

$$= 2\pi \frac{x-y}{|x-y|^2} - 2\pi i \sum_{\ell>0 \text{ even}} u_\ell(x,y)e^{i\ell\psi}\frac{(x-y)_\perp}{|x-y|^2}$$

$$= 2\pi \frac{x-y}{|x-y|^2} - 2\pi i(\cosh(u(y,\omega) - u(x,\omega)) - 1)\frac{(x-y)_\perp}{|x-y|^2},$$

where $(x-y)_\perp/|x-y| = (\cos\psi, \sin\psi)^T = \omega$, and

$$\int_0^{2\pi} \frac{\theta}{(x-y)\cdot\theta} \sinh(u(y,\theta) - u(x,\theta))d\varphi = 0.$$

Since $x\cdot\omega = y\cdot\omega$, we have

$$u(y,\omega) - u(x,\omega) = -(D\mu)(y,\omega_\perp) + (D\mu)(x,\omega_\perp)$$
$$= -\int_y^x \mu ds$$

with integration along the straight line joining x, y. This is real-valued. Hence

$$\text{Re}\int_0^{2\pi} \frac{\theta}{(x-y)\cdot\theta} e^{u(y,\theta)-u(x,\theta)}d\varphi = 2\pi \frac{x-y}{|x-y|^2}.$$

Now (2.41) follows from

$$\text{div}\frac{x}{|x|^2} = 2\pi\delta(x). \qquad \square$$

Actually, Novikov's formula is a little different from the one of Theorem 2.23. In our notation, Novikov's original formula reads

$$f(x) = \frac{1}{4\pi}\text{Re div } R_\mu^*(\theta e^h H e^{\bar{h}}\check{g})$$

with $\check{g}(\theta, s) = g(-\theta, -s)$. Using the Fourier expansion of the function u in the proof of Theorem 2.22, one can show that this formula is equivalent to Theorem 2.23.

Theorem 2.23 is the basis for the filtered backprojection algorithm for inverting R_μ in section 5.1.9.

2.4.2 The Feig–Greenleaf transform

This transform comes up in Range–Doppler radar; see section 3.6. For $f \in \mathcal{S}(\mathbb{R}^2)$, it is defined by

$$(Ff)(u,v) = \int f(tu, t+v)e^{iut^2}dt.$$

We show that F can be inverted for f real. More precisely, we show that if $f \in \mathcal{S}(\mathbb{R}^2)$ is real and $f(x,y) = 0$ for $x < 0$, then f is uniquely determined by $g = Ff$.

Proof. For the proof, we follow Feig and Greenleaf (1986). We denote by $\hat{g}$, $\hat{f}$ the 1D Fourier transforms of g, f with respect to the second argument. With this notation, we have

$$\hat{g}(u, v) = (2\pi)^{-1/2} \int \int f(tu, t + v)e^{-ivv+iut^2}dtdv$$

$$= \int \hat{f}(tu, v)e^{ivt+iut^2}dt$$

$$= e^{-i\frac{v^2}{4u}} \int \hat{f}(tu, v)e^{iu(t+\frac{v}{2u})^2}dt$$

$$= e^{-i\frac{v^2}{4u}} \frac{1}{u} \int \hat{f}(t - v/2, v)e^{it^2/u}dt,$$

where we have replaced $t + \frac{v}{2u}$ by $\frac{t}{u}$. For $v > 0$, the lower limit of the integral can be chosen to be 0 since f hence $\hat{f}$ vanishes in the left half-plane. Thus for $v > 0$,

$$\hat{g}(u, v) = e^{-i\frac{v^2}{4u}} \frac{1}{u} \int_0^{\infty} \hat{f}(t - v/2, v)e^{it^2/u}dt$$

$$= e^{-i\frac{v^2}{4u}} \frac{1}{2u} \int_0^{\infty} \frac{1}{\sqrt{t}}\hat{f}(\sqrt{t} - v/2, v)e^{it/u}dt.$$

The right-hand side is essentially an inverse Fourier transform. By a direct Fourier transform, we therefore get for $v, t > 0$

$$\frac{1}{\sqrt{t}}\hat{f}(\sqrt{t} - v/2, v) = (2\pi)^{-1} \int e^{-iu(t-v^2/4)}\hat{g}\left(\frac{1}{u}, v\right)\frac{2du}{u}.$$

Putting $x = \sqrt{t} - v/2$, we get for $x, v > 0$

$$\hat{f}(x, v) = (2\pi)^{-1}(2x + v) \int e^{-iu(x^2+vx)}\hat{g}\left(\frac{1}{u}, v\right)\frac{du}{u}.$$

Since f is real, this determines $\hat{f}(x, v)$ for $x > 0$ and all real v.   □

2.4.3   The windowed ray transform

This transform was introduced in Kaiser and Streater (1992). It is defined by

$$(P_h f)(x, \theta) = \int_{\mathbb{R}^1} f(x + t\theta)h(t)dt,$$

where h is referred to as a window. For $h = 1$ we get the usual ray transform (2.28). $P_h f$ is a function of $2n - 1$ variables. Thus inversion of P_h is an overdetermined problem.

2.5   Integration over Curved Manifolds

Many cases of reconstructing functions from integrals over curved manifolds are treated in the literature. A standard reference is Helgason (1984). We deal only with some elementary cases.

2.5.1 Computing an even function on S^2 from its integrals over equatorial circles

Let f be an even function on S^2, i.e., $f(-x) = f(x)$. For $\theta \in S^2$ put

$$(Qf)(\theta) = (Qf)(\psi, \varphi) = \int_{S^2 \cap \theta^\perp} f(x)dx, \quad \theta = \begin{pmatrix} \cos\varphi \ \sin\psi \\ \sin\varphi \ \sin\psi \\ \cos\psi \end{pmatrix}, \qquad (2.42)$$

i.e., $Qf(\theta)$ is the integral of f over the great circle with North Pole θ. Since f is even, we may restrict ψ to $0 \le \psi \le \frac{\pi}{2}$. We consider first the case in which f depends only on the distance from the North Pole of S^2, which we locate at e_3, i.e.,

$$f(x) = F(\cos u), \quad x = \begin{pmatrix} \cos v \ \sin u \\ \sin v \ \sin u \\ \cos u \end{pmatrix}.$$

Then $(Qf)(\psi, \varphi) = g(\sin\psi)$ depends only on ψ, and we may assume $\varphi = 0$. The great circle $S^2 \cap \theta^\perp$ is given by $x \cdot \theta = 0$ or, in the spherical coordinates u, v, by

$$\cos v \sin u \sin\psi + \cos u \cos\psi = 0. \qquad (2.43)$$

We consider only the quarter of the great circle for which $0 \le u \le \frac{\pi}{2} - \psi$ and $\frac{\pi}{2} \le v \le \pi$. Putting $s = \cos u$, we obtain for this quarter the parametric representation

$$x = x(s) = \begin{pmatrix} -s/\tan\psi \\ \frac{1}{\sin\psi}\sqrt{\sin^2\psi - s^2} \\ s \end{pmatrix}, \quad 0 \le s \le \sin\psi,$$

as is easily seen from (2.43). Hence, combining the four quarters,

$$g(\sin\psi) = 4 \int_0^{\sin\psi} F(s) \left| \frac{dx}{ds} \right| ds$$

$$= 4 \int_0^{\sin\psi} F(s) \frac{ds}{\sqrt{\sin^2\psi - s^2}}.$$

This is an Abel integral equation for F. Using the inversion formula from section 1.3.2, we obtain

$$F(s) = \frac{1}{2\pi} \left\{ g(0) + s \int_0^s \frac{g'(t)dt}{\sqrt{s^2 - t^2}} \right\}.$$

We use this only at the North Pole, i.e., for $s = 1$:

$$F(1) = \frac{1}{2\pi} \left\{ g(0) + \int_0^1 \frac{g'(t)dt}{\sqrt{1 - t^2}} \right\}$$

$$= \frac{1}{2\pi} \left\{ g(0) + \int_0^{\pi/2} \frac{\frac{d}{d\psi} g(\sin\psi)}{\cos\psi} \right\}.$$

Returning to the original quantities f, Qf, this means

$$f(e_3) = \frac{1}{2\pi}\left\{(Qf)(0,0) + \int_0^{\pi/2} \frac{\frac{d}{d\psi}(Qf)(\psi,0)}{\cos\psi}d\psi\right\}. \qquad (2.44)$$

Now we consider the general case of a function f depending on both u and v. Putting

$$\overline{f}(u) = \frac{1}{2\pi}\int_0^{2\pi} f(u,v)dv, \qquad \overline{Qf}(\psi) = \frac{1}{2\pi}\int_0^{2\pi}(Qf)(\psi,\varphi)d\varphi,$$

we have

$$\overline{f}(0) = f(e_3), \qquad (Q\overline{f})(\psi,0) = \overline{Qf}(\psi), \qquad (Q\overline{f})(0,0) = (Qf)(e_3).$$

Applying (2.44) to $\overline{f}$, we thus obtain

$$f(e_3) = \overline{f}(0) = \frac{1}{2\pi}\left\{(Q\overline{f})(0,0) + \int_0^{\pi/2} \frac{d(Q\overline{f})(\psi,0)}{\cos\psi}\right\}$$

$$= \frac{1}{2\pi}\left\{(Qf)(e_3) + \int_0^{\pi/2} \frac{d(\overline{Qf})(\psi)}{\cos\psi}\right\}.$$

This is the inversion formula at e_3. For general $\theta \in S^2$ it reads

$$f(\theta) = \frac{1}{2\pi}\left\{(Qf)(\theta) + \int_0^{\pi/2} \frac{d\,\overline{Qf}(\omega)}{\theta\cdot\omega}\right\},$$

$$\overline{Qf}(\omega) = \frac{1}{2\pi}\int_{\theta\perp\omega}(Qf)(\theta)d\theta. \qquad (2.45)$$

Here d stands for differentiation with respect to the azimuth. This formula was obtained by Funk (1914).

2.5.2 Reduction of problems on the sphere to the Radon transform

More generally, we may consider the operator

$$(Qf)(\xi,s) = \int_{\theta\in S^2, \xi\cdot\theta=s} f(\theta)d\theta,$$

where $\xi \in \mathbb{R}^3$, $\xi \neq 0$. We purposefully do not restrict ξ to the unit sphere. We consider the following cases.

1. $(Qf)(\xi,s)$ is known for $s = 0$ only. This is the problem solved by Funk. We give a different solution in terms of the 2D Radon transform. Of course, we have to assume that f is even. We then have

$$(Qf)(\xi,0) = 2\int_{\xi'\cdot x'=-x_3\xi_3} f(x',x_3)\frac{dx'}{x_3},$$

where $x' = (x_1, x_2)^T$, $\xi' = (\xi_1, \xi_2)^T$, and $x_3 = \sqrt{1 - |x'|^2}$. Introducing the new variable

$$y = x'/x_3, \qquad dx' = x_3^4 dy,$$

we obtain

$$\begin{aligned}(Qf)(\xi, 0) &= 2 \int_{\xi' \cdot y = -\xi_3} f(x', x_3) x_3^3 dy \\ &= (R\phi)(\xi', -\xi_3),\end{aligned}$$

where

$$\phi(y) = 2f(x', x_3) x_3^3$$

and R is the 2D Radon transform, the argument of $R\phi$ being not normalized. Thus we can recover ϕ hence f from $(Qf)(\cdot, 0)$ by means of one of the inversion formulas of the Radon transform, yielding an alternative to (2.45). We remark that this is an example for reducing integral geometric problems in spaces of constant curvature to Radon problems in Euclidean spaces; see Palamodov (1998).

2. $(Qf)(\xi, s)$ is known only for $\xi_3 = 0$, i.e., f has to be reconstructed from circles on S^2 lying in planes parallel to the x_3 axis. For this to make sense we have to assume that f is even in x_3, i.e., $f(x', -x_3) = f(x', x_3)$. In that case, we have

$$\begin{aligned}(Qf)(\xi', 0, s) &= 2 \int_{\xi' \cdot x' = s} f(x', x_3) \frac{dx'}{x_3} \\ &= (R\phi)(\xi', s),\end{aligned}$$

where

$$\phi(x') = 2f(x', x_3)/x_3.$$

Again the inversion problem is reduced to the one for the 2D Radon transform.

The inversion formulas of this section can also be obtained by the technique based on the κ-operator; see Gindikin, Reeds, and Shepp (1993).

2.5.3 Reconstruction from spherical averages

Here we want to recover a function f in $\mathbb{R}^n$ from its integrals over spheres whose midpoints are restricted to a hyperplane. The relevant integral transform is

$$(Mf)(x', r) = \int_{|y| = r} f(x' + y', y_n) d\sigma(y), \tag{2.46}$$

where $y = \binom{y'}{y_n}$, $y', x' \in \mathbb{R}^{n-1}$, $r \geq 0$, and σ is the surface measure on $|y| = r$. Obviously, $Mf = 0$ if f is odd in x_n. Therefore, we assume f to be even in x_n. Equivalently, we have

$$(Mf)(x', r) = 2 \int_{|y'| < 1} f(x' + ry', r\sqrt{1 - |y'|^2}) \frac{dy'}{\sqrt{1 - |y'|^2}},$$

where the integral is over $\mathbb{R}^{n-1}$. In order to invert M, we exploit translation invariance: With $f_a(x) = f(x' + a, x_n), a \in \mathbb{R}^{n-1}$, we obviously have

$$(Mf_a)(x', r) = (Mf)(x' + a, r).$$

We exploit this invariance by a Fourier transform with respect to x', obtaining

$$(Mf)^\wedge(\xi', r) = 2 \int_0^1 \frac{s^{n-2}}{\sqrt{1-s^2}} \hat{f}(\xi', r\sqrt{1-s^2}) \int_{S^{n-2}} e^{irs\theta \cdot \xi'} d\theta ds,$$

where $(Mf)^\wedge$, $\hat{f}$ denote Fourier transforms with respect to the first $n - 1$ variables. This is for each $\xi' \in \mathbb{R}^{n-1}$ a 1D integral equation for $\hat{f}(\xi', \cdot)$, which can be solved by using the transform

$$(H_n f)(\rho) = \rho^{1-n/2} \int_0^\infty r^{n/2} J_{(n-2)/2}(r\rho) f(r) dr.$$

H_n is simply the Fourier transform in $\mathbb{R}^n$ for radial functions and is essentially the Hankel transform already used in section 2.1. We have for $\xi \in \mathbb{R}^n$

$$(H_n(Mf)^\wedge)(\xi', |\xi|) = 2(2\pi)^{(n-1)/2} \frac{|\xi|^{2-n}}{|\xi_n|} \hat{f}(\xi). \tag{2.47}$$

Here H_n acts on $(Mf)^\wedge$ as a function of the last variable and $\hat{f}$ is now the nD Fourier transform of f. For the proof, see Fawcett (1985) and Andersson (1988).

An explicit inversion formula analogous to Radon's inversion formula (Theorem 2.6) can be obtained as follows. We define the backprojection operator M^* by

$$(M^*g)(x) = \int_{\mathbb{R}^{n-1}} g\left(y', \sqrt{|x' - y'|^2 + x_n^2}\right) dy',$$

i.e., M^* averages over all spheres containing x. Taking the nD Fourier transform yields

$$
\begin{aligned}
(M^*g)^\wedge(\xi) &= (2\pi)^{-n/2} \int_{\mathbb{R}^n} e^{-ix\cdot\xi}(M^*g)(x)dx \\
&= (2\pi)^{-n/2} \int_{\mathbb{R}^n} e^{-ix\cdot\xi} \int_{\mathbb{R}^{n-1}} g\left(y', \sqrt{|x' - y'|^2 + x_n^2}\right) dy' dx \\
&= (2\pi)^{-n/2} \int_{\mathbb{R}^{n-1}} e^{-iy'\cdot\xi'} \int_{\mathbb{R}^n} e^{-i((x'-y')\cdot\xi' + x_n\xi_n)} g\left(y', \sqrt{|x' - y'|^2 + x_n^2}\right) dx dy' \\
&= (2\pi)^{-n/2} \int_{\mathbb{R}^{n-1}} e^{-iy'\cdot\xi'} \int_{\mathbb{R}^n} e^{-ix\cdot\xi} g(y', |x|) dx dy' \\
&= \int_{\mathbb{R}^{n-1}} e^{-iy'\cdot\xi'} (H_n g(y', \cdot))(|\xi|) dy' \\
&= \sqrt{2\pi}(H_n \hat{g})(\xi', |\xi|).
\end{aligned}
$$

Combining this with (2.47), we obtain

$$\hat{f}(\xi) = \frac{1}{2}(2\pi)^{-n/2}|\xi_n||\xi|^{n-2}(M^*g)^\wedge(\xi), \quad g = Mf. \tag{2.48}$$

This formula was obtained for $n = 2$ by Nilsson (1997). For the null space and range of M, see Quinto (1982).

2.5.4   More general manifolds

Inversion formulas have been obtained for many families of manifolds. Most of them
require invariances, such as rotational or translation invariance; see Cormack (1981, 1982),
Cormack and Quinto (1980), and Quinto (1983). The standard reference for the group
theoretical approach is Helgason (1984). For approximate inversion formulas, see Beylkin
(1984).

2.6   Vector Fields

The transforms R, P are easily extended to vector fields $f \in (\mathcal{S}(\mathbb{R}^n))^n$ by applying them
componentwise. We denote the extended transforms with the same letters R, P. The
vector valued transforms give rise to some transforms that have interesting applications:
the vectorial ray transform

$$(\mathcal{P}f)(\theta, x) = \theta \cdot (Pf)(\theta, x), \quad x \in \theta^\perp,$$

the Radon probe transform

$$(\mathfrak{R}^p f)(\theta, s) = p(\theta, s) \cdot (Rf)(\theta, s),$$

where $p = p(\theta, s)$ is called the probe, and the special case $p(\theta, s) = \theta$ hereof, the Radon
normal transform

$$(\mathfrak{R}^\perp f)(\theta, s) = (\mathfrak{R}^\theta f)(\theta, s) = \theta \cdot (Rf)(\theta, s);$$

see Braun and Hauck (1991), Prince (1995), and Sharafutdinov (1994). We have $\mathcal{P}$:
$(\mathcal{S}(\mathbb{R}^n))^n \to \mathcal{S}(T^n)$, $\mathfrak{R}^p$, $\mathfrak{R}^\perp : (\mathcal{S}(\mathbb{R}^n))^n \to \mathcal{S}(C^n)$. For a recent overview, see Sparr
et al. (1995).

Since $\mathcal{P}$, $\mathfrak{R}^p$, $\mathfrak{R}^\perp$ map vector fields to scalar functions, one cannot expect these
transforms to be invertible. In fact, we have the following theorem.

THEOREM 2.24. $\mathcal{P}f = 0$ *if and only if* $f = \operatorname{grad} \psi$ *for some* ψ.

Proof. By Theorem 2.11,

$$(\mathcal{P}f)^\wedge(\theta, \xi) = \theta \cdot (Pf)^\wedge(\theta, \xi) = (2\pi)^{1/2}\theta \cdot \hat{f}(\xi), \quad \xi \in \theta^\perp.$$

Thus if $\mathcal{P}f = 0$, then $\hat{f}(\xi) \in \theta^\perp$ for each $\xi \in \theta^\perp$. Hence $\hat{f}$ maps every hyperplane of $\mathbb{R}^n$
into itself. This is possible only if $\hat{f}(\xi) = i\hat{\psi}(\xi)\xi$ with some complex valued function $\hat{\psi}$.
Hence $f = \operatorname{grad} \psi$. Conversely, $f = \operatorname{grad} \psi$ obviously implies $\mathcal{P}f = 0$. $\Box$

THEOREM 2.25. *Let* $n = 2$ *or* $n = 3$. *We have* $\mathfrak{R}^\perp f = 0$ *if and only if* $f = \operatorname{curl} \phi$ *for some*
ϕ. *(For* $n = 2$, *we put* $\operatorname{curl} \phi = (\partial\phi/\partial x_2, -\partial\phi/\partial x_1)^T$.)

Proof. By Theorem 2.1,

$$(\mathfrak{R}^\perp f)^\wedge(\theta, \sigma) = \theta \cdot (Rf)^\wedge(\theta, \sigma) = (2\pi)^{(n-1)/2}\theta \cdot \hat{f}(\sigma\theta).$$

Thus if $\mathfrak{R}^\perp f = 0$, then $\hat{f}(\xi) \in \xi^\perp$ for each ξ. Hence, for $n = 2$,

$$\hat{f}(\xi) = i\hat{\phi}(\xi) \begin{pmatrix} \xi_2 \\ -\xi_1 \end{pmatrix}$$

with some complex valued function $\hat{\phi}$, and

$$\hat{f}(\xi) = i\xi \times \hat{\phi}(\xi)$$

with some vector field $\hat{\phi}$ for $n = 3$. In any case, $f = \operatorname{curl}\phi$. Conversely, $f = \operatorname{curl}\phi$ obviously implies $\mathfrak{R}^\perp f = 0$.   □

According to the Helmholtz decomposition, every vector field in $(\mathcal{S}(\mathbb{R}^n))^n$ can be written as $f = f^s + f^i$, where the solenoidal part f^s satisfies div $f^s = 0$ and the irrotational part $f^i = \operatorname{grad}\psi$ with some function ψ on $\mathbb{R}^n$; see Morse and Feshbach (1953), p. 53. If $n = 2, 3$, $f^s = \operatorname{curl}\phi$ for some ϕ. According to Theorem 2.24 a solenoidal vector field f is uniquely determined by $\mathcal{P}f$. There exist two ways to actually determine f from $\mathcal{P}f$. The first one starts out from the following theorem.

THEOREM 2.26. *Let $n = 2$ and $f \in (\mathcal{S}(\mathbb{R}^2))^2$. Then*

$$\frac{\partial}{\partial s}(\mathcal{P}f)(\theta, s\theta_\perp) = \left(P\left(\frac{\partial f_2}{\partial x_1} - \frac{\partial f_1}{\partial x_2}\right)\right)(\theta, s\theta_\perp), \quad \theta_\perp = \begin{pmatrix} \theta_2 \\ -\theta_1 \end{pmatrix}.$$

Proof. By Theorem 2.11,

$$i\sigma(\mathcal{P}f)^\wedge(\theta, \sigma\theta) = (2\pi)^{1/2}i\sigma\theta \cdot \hat{f}(\sigma\theta)$$
$$= (2\pi)^{1/2}\left(\frac{\partial f_2}{\partial x_1} - \frac{\partial f_1}{\partial x_2}\right)^\wedge(\sigma\theta_\perp)$$
$$= \left(P\left(\frac{\partial f_2}{\partial x_1} - \frac{\partial f_1}{\partial x_2}\right)\right)^\wedge(\theta, \sigma\theta_\perp).$$

The result follows by an inverse Fourier transform.   □

The inversion procedure based on the theorem is as follows. If $n = 2$ and $f \in (\mathcal{S}(\mathbb{R}^2))^2$ is solenoidal, then $f = \operatorname{curl}\phi$, i.e., $f_1 = \partial\phi/\partial x_2$, $f_2 = -\partial\phi/\partial x_1$. Hence $\Delta\phi = \partial f_1/\partial x_2 - \partial f_2/\partial x_1$, Δ the Laplacian, can be computed from $\mathcal{P}f$ via Theorem 2.26 and from an inversion formula for P or (since $n = 2$) R; see sections 2.1 and 2.2. Since $\phi \in \mathcal{S}(\mathbb{R}^n)$, ϕ can be computed from $\Delta\phi$. Hence f can be computed from $\mathcal{P}f$.

If $n = 3$ and $f \in (\mathcal{S}(\mathbb{R}^3))^3$ is solenoidal, we may restrict $\mathcal{P}f$ to a plane, e.g., $x_3 = 0$; that is, we consider $(\mathcal{P}f)(\theta, x)$ only for $\theta = \binom{\theta'}{0}$, $x = \binom{x'}{0}$. Then with $f' = (f_1, f_2, 0)^T$, we have

$$(\mathcal{P}f)(\theta, x) = (\mathcal{P}f')(\theta', x'),$$

and the 3D problem is reduced to a 2D problem for f'. Hence $(\operatorname{curl} f)_3 = \partial f_2/\partial x_1 - \partial f_1/\partial x_2$ can be computed exactly as in the 2D case above. Proceeding in the same way with the planes $x_2 = 0$, $x_1 = 0$, we find the other components of curl f and hence f.

The second method for computing f from $\mathcal{P}f$ makes use of the following inversion formula, which is analogous to Theorem 2.14.

THEOREM 2.27. *Let $g = \mathcal{P}f$ and $f \in (\mathcal{S}(\mathbb{R}^n))^n$ be solenoidal. Then for $\alpha < n$,*

$$f = \frac{n-1}{2\pi|S^{n-2}|} I^{-\alpha} \mathcal{P}^* I^{\alpha-1} g,$$

where

$$(\mathcal{P}^* g)(x) = \int_{S^{n-1}} g(\theta, E_\theta x)\theta d\theta.$$

Proof. By Theorem 2.11,

$$\hat{g}(\theta, \xi) = \theta \cdot (Pf)^\wedge(\theta, \xi) = (2\pi)^{1/2} \theta \cdot \hat{f}(\xi), \quad \xi \in \theta^\perp.$$

Since div $f = 0$, we have $\hat{f}(\xi) \cdot \xi = 0$. Let $\theta_1, \ldots, \theta_{n-1}$ be an orthonormal basis of $\xi^\perp$. Then

$$\hat{f}(\xi) = \sum_{j=1}^{n-1} (\theta_j \cdot \hat{f}(\xi))\theta_j$$

$$= (2\pi)^{-1/2} \sum_{j=1}^{n-1} \hat{g}(\theta_j, \xi)\theta_j.$$

If $u \in SO(n)$ leaves ξ fixed, $u\theta_1, \ldots, u\theta_{n-1}$ is also an orthonormal basis of $\xi^\perp$; hence

$$\hat{f}(\xi) = (2\pi)^{-1/2} \sum_{j=1}^{n-1} \hat{g}(u\theta_j, \xi)u\theta_j.$$

We may think of u as an element of $SO(n-1)$. Averaging over $SO(n-1)$ with respect to the normalized Haar measure on $SO(n-1)$ yields

$$\hat{f}(\xi) = (2\pi)^{-1/2} \sum_{j=1}^{n-1} \int_{SO(n-1)} \hat{g}(u\theta_j, \xi)u\theta_j du$$

$$= (2\pi)^{-1/2} \frac{1}{|S^{n-2}|} \sum_{j=1}^{n-1} \int_{\xi^\perp \cap S^{n-1}} \hat{g}(\theta, \xi)\theta d\theta,$$

where we have used the formula

$$\int_{SO(n-1)} h(u\theta_j) du = \frac{1}{|S^{n-2}|} \int_{S^{n-2}} h(\theta) d\theta,$$

which is valid for continuous functions on S^{n-1}. Since the integral is the same for each j, we have

$$\hat{f}(\xi) = (2\pi)^{-1/2} \frac{n-1}{|S^{n-2}|} \int_{\xi^\perp \cap S^{n-1}} \hat{g}(\theta, \xi)\theta d\theta$$

$$= (2\pi)^{-1/2} \frac{n-1}{|S^{n-2}|} |\xi| \int_{S^{n-1}} \hat{g}(\theta, \xi)\theta\delta(\xi \cdot \theta) d\theta.$$

By Fourier inversion we obtain for the Riesz potential

$$
\begin{aligned}
I^{\alpha} f(x) &= (2\pi)^{-n/2} \int_{\mathbb{R}^n} e^{ix\cdot\xi} |\xi|^{-\alpha} \hat{f}(\xi) d\xi \\
&= (2\pi)^{-(n+1)/2} \frac{n-1}{|S^{n-2}|} \int_{\mathbb{R}^n} e^{ix\cdot\xi} |\xi|^{1-\alpha} \int_{S^{n-1}} \hat{g}(\theta,\xi)\theta\delta(\xi\cdot\theta) d\theta d\xi \\
&= (2\pi)^{-(n+1)/2} \frac{n-1}{|S^{n-2}|} \int_{S^{n-1}} \theta \int_{\mathbb{R}^n} e^{ix\cdot\xi} |\xi|^{1-\alpha} \hat{g}(\theta,\xi)\delta(\xi\cdot\theta) d\xi d\theta \\
&= (2\pi)^{-(n+1)/2} \frac{n-1}{|S^{n-2}|} \int_{S^{n-1}} \theta \int_{\theta^{\perp}} e^{ix\cdot\xi} |\xi|^{1-\alpha} \hat{g}(\theta,\xi) d\xi d\theta \\
&= (2\pi)^{-1} \frac{n-1}{|S^{n-2}|} \int_{S^{n-1}} \theta(I^{\alpha-1}g)(\theta, E_\theta x) d\theta \\
&= (2\pi)^{-1} \frac{n-1}{|S^{n-2}|} (\mathcal{P}^*(I^{\alpha-1}g))(x).
\end{aligned}
$$

The result follows by applying $I^{-\alpha}$.   □

For $\alpha = 1$, Theorem 2.27 was obtained by Sharafutdinov (1994), Theorem 2.12.2, in a more general context by different means.

So much for the inversion of $\mathcal{P}$. As for the inversion of $\mathfrak{R}^{\perp}$, we know from Theorem 2.25 that only the irrotational part of f can be recovered from $\mathfrak{R}^{\perp}f$. More generally, we have the following inversion results.

THEOREM 2.28. *Let $n = 2$ or 3 and $g = \mathfrak{R}^p f$. If f is irrotational, then*

$$
f = \operatorname{grad} \psi, \quad \frac{\partial}{\partial s}(R\psi)(\theta,s) = \frac{g(\theta,s)}{p(\theta,s)\cdot\theta}.
$$

Proof. Since f is irrotational, we have $f = \operatorname{grad} \psi$ for some ψ. Hence $\hat{f}(\xi) = i\hat{\psi}(\xi)\xi$. Applying Theorem 2.1 twice, we obtain

$$
\begin{aligned}
(Rf)^{\wedge}(\theta,\sigma) &= (2\pi)^{(n-1)/2} \hat{f}(\sigma\theta) \\
&= (2\pi)^{(n-1)/2} i\sigma\theta\hat{\psi}(\sigma\theta) \\
&= i\sigma\theta(R\psi)^{\wedge}(\theta,\sigma) \\
&= \theta\left(\frac{\partial}{\partial s}R\psi\right)^{\wedge}(\theta,\sigma);
\end{aligned}
$$

hence

$$
(Rf)(\theta,s) = \theta\left(\frac{\partial}{\partial s}R\psi\right)(\theta,s).
$$

Since

$$
g(\theta,s) = p(\theta,s)\cdot(Rf)(\theta,s),
$$

the result follows.   □

THEOREM 2.29. *Let $n = 3$ and $g_j = \Re^{p_j} f$, $j = 1, 2$, with $f \in \mathcal{S}(\mathbb{R}^3))^3$, where p_1, p_2 are such that*

$$U^T = (p_1 \times \theta, p_2 \times \theta, \theta)$$

is invertible. If f is solenoidal, then

$$f = \operatorname{curl} \phi, \quad \frac{\partial}{\partial s} R\phi = U^{-1} \begin{pmatrix} g_1 \\ g_2 \\ 0 \end{pmatrix}.$$

Proof. Since f is solenoidal, $f = \operatorname{curl} \phi$ for some ϕ with $\operatorname{div} \phi = 0$. Hence $\hat{f} = i\xi \times \hat{\phi}(\xi)$, $\xi \cdot \hat{\phi}(\xi) = 0$. Applying Theorem 2.1 twice yields

$$\begin{aligned}
(Rf)^\wedge(\theta, \sigma) &= 2\pi \hat{f}(\sigma\theta) \\
&= 2\pi i\sigma\theta \times \hat{\phi}(\sigma\theta) \\
&= i\sigma\theta \times (R\phi)^\wedge(\theta, \sigma) \\
&= \theta \times \left(\frac{\partial}{\partial s} R\phi \right)^\wedge (\theta, \sigma).
\end{aligned}$$

By taking the inverse Fourier transform, we obtain

$$(Rf)(\theta, s) = \theta \times \left(\frac{\partial}{\partial s} R\phi \right) (\theta, s);$$

hence

$$g_j = p_j \cdot Rf = p_j \cdot \left(\theta \times \frac{\partial}{\partial s} R\phi \right) = (p_j \times \theta) \frac{\partial}{\partial s} R\phi. \tag{2.49}$$

From Theorem 2.1, we immediately obtain

$$\theta \cdot \frac{\partial}{\partial s} R\phi = R(\operatorname{div} \phi) = 0.$$

Combining this with (2.49) yields the result.   □

Chapter 3

Tomography

Methods of tomography are used in almost every branch of science, not only in radiology, and an exhaustive review of the applications of tomography is impossible. In this section, we describe only a few examples, which demonstrate the wide variety of tomographic techniques. The state of the art in the medical field can be seen in the NRC report edited by Budinger (1996) and in Morneburg (1995). The lively development in other fields is reflected in Lavrent'ev (1995) and Beck et al. (1995).

3.1 Transmission Tomography

In transmission tomography one probes an object with nondiffractive radiation, e.g., X rays for the human body. If I_0 is the intensity of the sources, $f(x)$ the linear attenuation coefficient of the object at the point x, L the ray along which the radiation propagates, and I the intensity of the radiation past the object, then

$$I = I_0 e^{-\int_L f(x)dx} \tag{3.1}$$

or

$$\int_L f(x)dx = \log \frac{I_0}{I}. \tag{3.2}$$

In the simplest case, the ray L is thought of as a straight line, but modeling L as strip or cone, possibly with a weight function to account for detector inhomogeneities, may be more appropriate.

The rays are usually arranged in a regular pattern, which we refer to as scanning geometry. We give a few examples of scanning geometries that are used in practice.

3.1.1 Parallel scanning geometry

Parallel scanning is a 2D geometry, that is, only one slice of the object is scanned at a time. The rays are arranged in parallel bunches, giving rise to a two-parameter family of straight

41

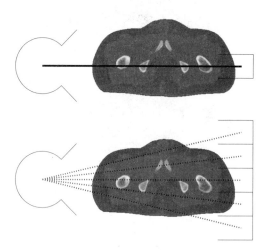

Figure 3.1. *Dual motion scanners. Top: First generation (one source, one detector). Bottom: Second generation (one source, several detectors).*

lines $L_{j\ell}$, $j = 0, \ldots, p - 1$, $\ell = -q, \ldots, q$, where $L_{j\ell}$ is the straight line making an angle $\varphi_j = j\Delta\varphi$ with the x_2-axes and having (signed) distance $s_\ell = \ell\Delta s$ from the origin, i.e., $x \cdot \theta_j = s_\ell$, $\theta_j = (\cos\varphi_j, \sin\varphi_j)^T$.

Parallel scanning is conveniently modeled by the 2D Radon transform; see section 2.1. The measured values $g_{j\ell}$ are simply

$$g_{j\ell} = (Rf)(\theta_j, s_\ell), \qquad j = 0, \ldots, p - 1, \quad \ell = -q, \ldots, q. \tag{3.3}$$

This geometry requires a dual motion scanner; see Figure 3.1.

The X-ray tube moves along a straight line. It is fired at each position s_ℓ, and I is measured by a detector behind the object, which is moved, too. After the whole slice is scanned, the process is repeated with a new angular orientation. This technique was used in the early days of CT (first-generation scanners). It is still used in applications in which the scanning time is not crucial, but in the medical field it has been replaced by faster techniques. An obvious improvement is the use of more than one detector, permitting the measurement of several rays at a time (second-generation scanner). The third generation uses the fan beam scanning geometry.

3.1.2 Fan beam scanning geometry

Many detectors are used in fan beam scanning. In a third-generation scanner, the X-ray source and the detectors are mounted on a common rotating frame; see Figure 3.2. During the rotation, the detectors are read out in small time intervals. Equivalently, we may assume that the X-ray tube is fired at a number of discrete source positions. Denoting the jth source position by $r\theta(\beta_j)$, $\theta(\beta) = (\cos\beta, \sin\beta)^T$, and the angle the ℓth ray in the fan emanating from the source at $r\theta(\beta_j)$ makes with the central ray (which may or may not be measured) by α_ℓ, the measured values correspond to the 2D cone beam transform (see section 2.3):

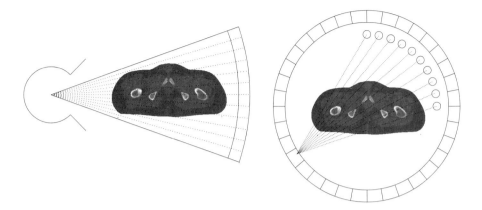

Figure 3.2. *Fan beam scanning. Left: Third-generation scanner (rotating detector-or-source system). Right: Fourth-generation scanner (stationary detector ring, rotating source).*

$$g_{j\ell} = (Df)(r\theta(\beta_j),\ \theta(\alpha_\ell + \beta_j + \pi)), \tag{3.4}$$
$$j = 0, \ldots, p - 1, \quad \ell = -q, \ldots, q.$$

Note that $\alpha_\ell > 0$ for rays lying to the left of the rotation center viewed from the source. In the simplest case, if the detectors are on a circle around the source, $\alpha_\ell = (\ell + \delta)\Delta\alpha$, where δ is the detector setoff. δ is chosen either 0 or $\pm 1/4$. For a linear detector array with distance d from the source, $\alpha_\ell = \arctan(\ell\Delta\alpha/d)$, possibly with a detector setoff of $\pm 1/4$. Other choices of α_ℓ occur in practice, too. For instance, in a fourth-generation scanner (see Figure 3.2), the detectors are at $r\theta(\beta_j)$ and the source is rotating continuously on a circle of radius d around the origin. The detectors are read out at discrete time intervals. This gives rise to fan beam projections with vertices at the detectors.

Of course, one can pass from one of these (and those of section 5.1) 2D scanning geometries to another one by interpolation ("rebinning"; see Herman (1980)), at least approximately. However, rebinning usually introduces artifacts. It is preferable to develop a specially adapted reconstruction algorithm for each scanning geometry.

3.1.3 3D helical scanning

Instead of doing the fan beam scan slice by slice, one can move the 3D object continuously in the direction of the axis of symmetry of a fan beam scanner; this is 3D helical scanning. Equivalently, one may think of a fan beam scanner in which the source runs on a helix around the object.

3.1.4 3D cone beam scanning

In 3D cone beam scanning, a source runs around the object on a curve, together with a 2D detector array; see Figure 3.3. In the simplest case, the curve is a circle. This situation can be

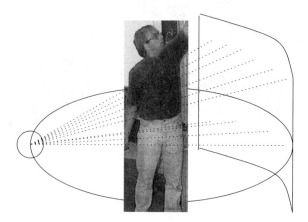

Figure 3.3. *Cone beam scanner with source on a circle.*

modeled by the 3D cone beam transform in very much the same way as for third-generation fan beam scanners.

The number of rays actually measured varies between 100 (say) in industrial tomography to 10^6–10^8 in radiological applications.

3.2   Emission Tomography

In emission tomography one determines the distribution f of a radiopharmaceutical in the interior of an object by measuring the radiation outside the object in a tomographic fashion. If μ is the attenuation distribution of the object—the quantity one determines in transmission tomography—then the intensity measured by a detector collimated to pick up only radiation along the straight line L is given by

$$I = \int_L f(x) e^{-\int_{L(x)} \mu(y) dy} dx, \tag{3.5}$$

where $L(x)$ is the section of L between x and the detector. This is the mathematical model for single particle emission computed tomography (SPECT). Thus SPECT gives rise to the attenuated ray transform

$$(P_\mu f)(\theta, x) = \int_{\mathbb{R}^1} f(x + t\theta) e^{-\int_t^\infty \mu(x+\tau\theta) d\tau} dt, \quad x \in \theta^\perp, \quad \theta \in S^2. \tag{3.6}$$

In positron emission tomography (PET), the sources eject the particles pairwise in opposite directions, and they are detected in coincidence mode, i.e., only events with two particles arriving at opposite detectors at the same time are counted. In that case, (3.5) has to be replaced by

$$I = \int_L f(x) e^{-\int_{L_+(x)} \mu(y) dy - \int_{L_-(x)} \mu(y) dy} dx,$$

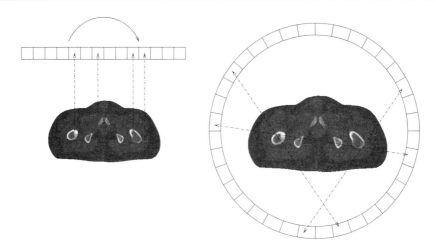

Figure 3.4. *Emission tomography. Left: SPECT. Right: PET.*

where $L_+(x)$, $L_-(x)$ are the two half-lines of L with endpoint x. Since the exponent adds up to the integral over L, we can write

$$I = e^{-\int_L \mu(y)dy} \int_L f(x)dx. \qquad (3.7)$$

Thus PET can be modeled with the ray transform of f and μ, the relevant transform being

$$e^{-P\mu(\theta,x)}(Pf)(\theta,x), \quad x \in \theta^\perp. \qquad (3.8)$$

In emission tomography one is interested in f, not μ. Usually one determines f from the measurements, assuming μ to be known or simply ignoring it. The interesting question of determining f and μ simultaneously is addressed in section 6.4.

Typical 2D devices for emission tomography are shown in Figure 3.4. In principle, a 3D object can be treated as a stack of 2D problems, as in transmission tomography. This means that oblique rays are not measured, resulting in poor statistics. Therefore, fully 3D devices are to be preferred. In PET one puts the object to be imaged into a cylinder that is completely covered by detectors; see Figure 3.5.

Emission tomography is essentially stochastic in nature. Due to the small number of events the stochastic aspect is much more pronounced than in transmission tomography. Thus besides the models using integral transforms, stochastic models have been set up for emission tomography. These models are completely discrete. We describe the widely used model of Shepp and Vardi (1982).

We subdivide the reconstruction region into pixels or voxels. The number of events in pixel (or voxel) j is a *Poisson* random variable φ_j whose expectation $f_j = E\varphi_j$ is a measure for the activity in pixel/voxel j. The vector $f = (f_1, \ldots, f_m)^T$ is the sought-for quantity. The measurement vector $g = (g_1, \ldots, g_n)$ is considered as a realization of the random variable $\gamma = (\gamma_1, \ldots, \gamma_n)$, where γ_i is the number of events detected in detector i. The model is described by the (n, m) matrix $A = (a_{ij})$, whose elements are

$$a_{ij} = \text{Prob}(\text{event in pixel/voxel } j \text{ is detected in detector } i),$$

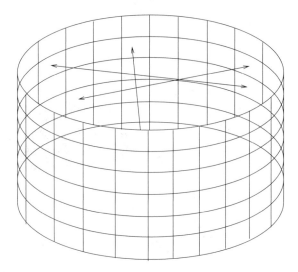

Figure 3.5. *3D PET.*

where Prob denotes probability. These probabilities are determined either theoretically or by measurements. We have

$$E(\gamma) = Af.$$

f is determined by the maximum likelihood method, which consists in maximizing the likelihood function

$$L(f) = \prod_{i=1}^{n} \frac{(Af)_i^{g_i}}{g_i!} e^{-(Af)_i}. \tag{3.9}$$

Variants of the expectation maximization (EM) algorithm were suggested for doing this; see section 5.3.2.

3.3   Diffraction Tomography

X rays travel along straight lines. This is why X-ray tomography can be modeled by the ray transform. For other sources of radiation, such as ultrasound and microwaves, the situation is more complex. These waves do not travel along straight rays. Their exact paths depend on the internal structure of the object under investigation and are unknown. We can no longer think in terms of simple projections and linear integral equations. More sophisticated nonlinear models have to be used.

In diffraction tomography, one models the process by the inverse scattering problem for the wave equations and solves it either in the Born or Rytov approximation. Thus the straight line assumption has been given up in diffraction tomography, but the use of the said approximations restricts diffraction tomography to weakly scattering objects. The fully nonlinear problem is treated in section 7.4.

The object to be imaged is given by a function f, which vanishes outside the object. f is related to the refraction index n of the object by $f = n^2 - 1$. The object is irradiated

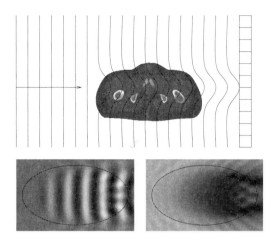

Figure 3.6. *Diffraction tomography. Top: Incident plane wave (left) generates a scattered wave, which is measured by a detector array (right). The process is repeated for many incidence directions. Bottom: Wave scattered by an elliptical homogeneous object; scattered wave (left), Scattered wave scaled by the incoming wave (right).*

by a plane wave

$$e^{-ikt}u_I(x), \quad u_I(x) = e^{ikx \cdot \theta} \tag{3.10}$$

with wave number $k = \frac{2\pi}{\lambda}$, λ the wave length, traveling in the direction of the unit vector θ. The resulting wave $e^{-ikt}u(x)$ satisfies the reduced wave equation

$$\Delta u + k^2(1 + f)u = 0 \tag{3.11}$$

plus suitable boundary condition at infinity. Now $u(x)$ is measured outside the object for many directions θ; see Figure 3.6. From all these measurements, f has to be determined.

In order to derive the Born approximation, we put $u = u_I + v$ in (3.11), where v satisfies the Sommerfeld radiation condition and the differential equation

$$\Delta v + k^2 v = -k^2(u_I + v)f. \tag{3.12}$$

Now we assume that the scattered field v is small in comparison with the incident field u_I. Then we can neglect v on the right-hand side of (3.12), obtaining

$$\Delta v + k^2 v = -k^2 u_I f. \tag{3.13}$$

This equation can readily be solved for v with the help of Green's function G for the differential operator $-\Delta - k^2$ with Sommerfeld's radiation condition as boundary condition. For $n = 2$, we have

$$G_2(x) = \frac{i}{4}H_0(k|x|) \tag{3.14}$$

with H_0 the zero order Hankel function of the first kind, and

$$G_3(x) = \frac{e^{ik|x|}}{4\pi|x|} \tag{3.15}$$

for $n = 3$. Using G_n, $n = 2, 3$, we can rewrite (3.13) as

$$v(x) = k^2 \int G_n(x - x')e^{ikx' \cdot \theta} f(x')dx'. \qquad (3.16)$$

Assume that f is supported in $|x| < \rho$ and that u, hence v, is measured on the plane $r\theta + \theta^\perp$ for each θ for some r with $|r| > \rho$. Then the function

$$(U_r f)(\theta, y) = \frac{1}{k} v(r\theta + y)/u_I(r\theta + y)$$

$$= ke^{-ikr} \int G_n(r\theta + y - x')e^{ikx' \cdot \theta} f(x')dx' \qquad (3.17)$$

is available for $y \in \theta^\perp$. We call $U_r : L_2(|x| < \rho) \to L_2(T^n)$ the propagation operator; see Devaney (1982). For $r > \rho$, it yields the transmitted wave, and for $r < -\rho$, the reflected wave.

The Rytov approximation is obtained by putting $u = u_I e^{v/u_I}$. The resulting differential equation for v is

$$(\Delta + k^2)v = -k^2 u_I \left(f + k^{-2} \left| \nabla \left(\frac{v}{u_I} \right) \right|^2 \right).$$

Neglecting the second term on the right-hand side leads to the Rytov approximation. The differential equation for v is the same as (3.13). So the Rytov approximation leads to the same propagation operator U_r as the Born approximation. The mathematical treatment is the same; only the physical interpretation is different. For the validity of the Born approximation, we must have

$$|Rf| \ll \frac{\pi}{k}, \qquad (3.18)$$

where R is the Radon transform (2.1). This is a slight extension of the condition given in Kak and Slaney (1987), p. 214. The Rytov approximation requires

$$\left| \frac{1}{f} \nabla \left(\frac{v}{u_I} \right) \right| \ll k^2; \qquad (3.19)$$

see Kak and Slaney (1987), p. 216. Thus while (3.18) puts a restriction on the size and the strength of the scattering object, (3.19) restricts the variation of the scaled scattered field.

In the following, we extend the "central slice theorem" (Theorem 2.1) to the propagation operator U_r of (3.17).

THEOREM 3.1. *Let $f \in L_2(|x| < \rho)$, and let*

$$a(\eta) = \begin{cases} \sqrt{k^2 - |\eta|^2}, & |\eta| < k, \\ i\sqrt{|\eta|^2 - k^2}, & |\eta| \geq k. \end{cases}$$

Then for $|r| > \rho$ and $\eta \in \theta^\perp$,

$$(U_r f)^\wedge(\theta, \eta) = ik\sqrt{\frac{\pi}{2}} e^{ir(\varepsilon a(\eta) - k)} \frac{1}{a(\eta)} \hat{f}((\varepsilon a(\eta) - k)\theta + \eta),$$

where $\varepsilon = 1$ for $r > \rho$ and $\varepsilon = -1$ for $r < -\rho$. The Fourier transform on the left-hand side is the $(n-1)$-dimensional Fourier transform in $\theta^{\perp}$.

Proof. For $n = 2$ see Devaney (1982). Since the proof for $n = 3$ is somehow inaccessible in the open literature, we give a common proof for $n = 2, 3$. All we need is the plane wave decomposition of G_n, to wit

$$G_n(x) = ic_n \int_{\mathbb{R}^{n-1}} e^{i(|x_n|a(z) - \tilde{x} \cdot z)} \frac{dz}{a(z)}, \quad x = \begin{pmatrix} \tilde{x} \\ x_n \end{pmatrix},$$

$$c_2 = \frac{1}{4\pi}, \quad c_3 = \frac{1}{8\pi^2};$$

(3.20)

see Morse and Feshbach (1953), p. 823, for $n = 2$. For $n = 3$, the formula can be obtained from Courant and Hilbert (1962), p. 196, or by direct calculation from the integral representation of J_ν in section 1.3.5 and formula 6.646 of Gradshteyn and Ryzhik (1965).

Let $r > \rho$ and $x = r\theta + y$, $x' = r'\theta + y'$ with $y, y' \in \theta^{\perp}$. Using (3.20) with θ as North Pole, we obtain

$$G_n(x - x') = ic_n \int_{\theta^{\perp}} e^{i((r-r')a(z) - (y-y') \cdot z)} \frac{dz}{a(z)}.$$

Using this in (3.17), we obtain

$$(U_r f)(\theta, y) = ike^{-ikr} c_n \int_{\mathbb{R}^1} \int_{\theta^{\perp}} \int_{\theta^{\perp}} e^{i((r-r')a(z) - (y-y') \cdot z)} \frac{dz}{a(z)} f(r'\theta + y')e^{ikr'} dy' dr'.$$

The integration with respect to $x' = r'\theta + y'$ is a Fourier transform in $\mathbb{R}^n = \mathbb{R}\theta + \theta^{\perp}$; hence

$$(U_r f)(\theta, y) = ike^{-ikr} c_n (2\pi)^{n/2} \int_{\theta^{\perp}} e^{i(ra(z) - y \cdot z)} \hat{f}((a(z) - k)\theta - z) \frac{dz}{a(z)}.$$

The integration with respect to z is a $(n-1)$D Fourier transform in $\theta^{\perp}$. From the Fourier inversion formula, we obtain

$$(U_r f)^{\wedge}(\theta, \eta) = ike^{-ikr} c_n (2\pi)^{n-1/2} e^{ira(\eta)} \hat{f}((a(\eta) - k)\theta + \eta) \frac{1}{a(\eta)}.$$

This is the theorem for $r > \rho$. A quick perusal of the proof yields the result for $r < -\rho$. □

The theorem shows that $\hat{f}$ is determined by $(U_r f)^{\wedge}$ on semispheres around $-k\theta$ with vertex at 0 for $r > \rho$ and vertex at $-2k\theta$ for $r < -\rho$; see Figure 3.7.

As θ varies over S^{n-1} and η over $|\eta| < k$, these semispheres fill out the region

$$\begin{aligned}|\xi| < \sqrt{2}k \quad &\text{for} \quad r > \rho, \quad &&\text{i.e., transmission,} \\ \sqrt{2}k < |\xi| < 2k \quad &\text{for} \quad r < -\rho, \quad &&\text{i.e., reflection.}\end{aligned}$$

Thus from the transmitted wave a low pass filtered version of f with cutoff $\sqrt{2}k$ can be obtained, while from the reflected wave only a band pass filtered version of f with the

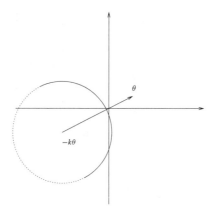

Figure 3.7. *Semispheres on which $\hat{f}$ is determined by Theorem* 3.1. *Solid line:* $r > \rho$ *(transmitted wave). Dashed line:* $r < -\rho$ *(reflected wave).*

low frequencies missing can be obtained. For $|\eta| > k$, $a(\eta)$ becomes imaginary, making Theorem 3.1 less useful.

Using Theorem 3.1 reduces the reconstruction problem to computing f from its irregularly sampled Fourier transform. This is taken up in section 5.2.

For k large, Theorem 3.1 reduces to Theorem 2.11: Putting $w = ve^{-ikx\cdot\theta}$ in (3.13) yields

$$\Delta w + 2ik\theta \cdot \nabla w = -k^2 f.$$

Neglecting Δw, we obtain the differential equation

$$\theta \cdot \nabla w = \frac{ik}{2} f,$$

whose solution is

$$w(r\theta + y) = \frac{ik}{2} \int_{-\infty}^{r} f(s\theta + y)ds, \quad y \in \theta^{\perp}.$$

It follows that for $r > \rho$,

$$(U_r f)(\theta, y) = \frac{1}{k} w(r\theta + y)$$
$$= \frac{i}{2}(Pf)(\theta, y)$$

with P the ray transform (2.28). Thus from Theorem 2.11, we expect to have approximately

$$(U_r f)^{\wedge}(\theta, \eta) = i\sqrt{\frac{\pi}{2}} \hat{f}(\eta), \quad \eta \in \theta^{\perp},$$

for k large. Letting $k \to \infty$ for η fixed in the formula of Theorem 3.1 shows that this is in fact the case.

3.4 Magnetic Resonance Imaging

The physical phenomenon exploited in magnetic resonance imaging (MRI) is the precession of the spin of a proton in a magnetic field of strength H about the direction of that field with Larmor frequency γH, where γ is the gyromagnetic ratio. By making the magnetic field vary in space in a controlled way the local magnetization $M_0(x)$ (together with the relaxation times $T_1(x)$, $T_2(x)$) can be imaged; see Lauterbur (1973). Since MRI is a rather complex technique, we start with a simplified model, which shows that the basic idea of tomography is behind MRI.

Suppose we only want to image the proton density f of a specimen. We expose the specimen to the magnetic field $H(x) = H_0 + G \cdot x$, where H_0 is a very strong spatially constant magnetic field and $G \cdot x$ is the gradient field. The Larmor frequency within the specimen is now

$$\omega(x) = \gamma(H_0 + G \cdot x).$$

Thus all the spins in the plane $G \cdot x = s$ have the same Larmor frequency. Upon probing the specimen with an electromagnetic field of frequency $\gamma(H_0 + s)$, we get a resonance phenomenon whose strength is proportional to

$$g(G, s) = \int_{x \cdot G = s} f(x) dx.$$

Thus MRI amounts to sampling the 3D Radon transform of f.

A more detailed description of MRI is based on the Bloch equation. We follow the presentation of Hinshaw and Lent (1983).

The magnetization $M(x, t)$ satisfies the Bloch equation

$$\frac{\partial M}{\partial t} = \gamma M \times H - \frac{1}{T_2}(M_1 e_1 + M_2 e_2) - \frac{1}{T_1}(M_3 - M_0)e_3. \qquad (3.21)$$

The significance of T_1, T_2, M_0 becomes apparent if we solve (3.21) for the static field $H = H_0 e_3$ with initial values $M(x, 0) = M^0(x)$. We obtain with $\omega_0 = \gamma H_0$

$$
\begin{aligned}
M_1(x, t) &= e^{-t/T_2}(M_1^0 \cos \omega_0 t + M_2^0 \sin \omega_0 t), \\
M_2(x, t) &= e^{-t/T_2}(-M_1^0 \sin \omega_0 t + M_2^0 \cos \omega_0 t), \\
M_3(x, t) &= e^{-t/T_1} M_3^0 + (1 - e^{-t/T_1}) M_0.
\end{aligned}
\qquad (3.22)
$$

Thus the magnetization rotates in the $x_1 - x_2$ plane with Larmor frequency ω_0 and returns to the equilibrium position $(0, 0, M_0)$ with speed controlled by T_2 in the x_1, x_2 plane and T_1 in the x_3-direction.

In an MRI scanner, one generates the field

$$H(x, t) = (H_0 + G(t) \cdot x)e_3 + H_1(t)(\cos(\omega_0 t)e_1 + \sin(\omega_0 t)e_2),$$

where G and H_1 are under the control of the experimentor. In the jargon of MRI, $H_0 e_3$ is the static field, $G(t) \cdot x e_3$ is the gradient field, and the term containing H_1 is the radio frequency field. The solution M of the Bloch equation for the input G, H_1 produces in the detecting system the output signal

$$S(t) = -\frac{d}{dt} \int_{\mathbb{R}^3} M(x, t) \cdot B(x) dx,$$

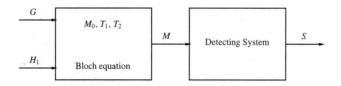

Figure 3.8. *MRI system.*

where B characterizes the detection system. Depending on the choice of H_1, various approximations to S can be made.

In one approximation, H_1 is constant in the small interval $[0, \tau]$ and $\gamma \int_0^\tau H_1 dt = \frac{\pi}{2}$. In the jargon of MRI, H_1 is a short $\frac{\pi}{2}$ pulse. In that case,

$$S(t) = \int_{\mathbb{R}^3} M_0(x) e^{-i\gamma \int_0^t G(s)ds \cdot x - t/T_2(x)} dx. \tag{3.23}$$

Choosing

$$G(t) = \begin{cases} g\theta, & \tau \le t, \\ 0 & \text{otherwise,} \end{cases} \tag{3.24}$$

with $g > 0$ and $\theta \in S^2$, we get for $\tau \le t \ll T_2$ approximately

$$
\begin{aligned}
S(t) &= \int_{\mathbb{R}^3} M_0(x) e^{-i\gamma g(t-\tau)\theta \cdot x} dx \\
&= (2\pi)^{3/2} \hat{M}_0(\gamma g(t-\tau)\theta),
\end{aligned} \tag{3.25}
$$

where $\hat{M}_0$ is the 3D Fourier transform of M_0. Thus observing $S(t)$ for $\theta \in S^2$ and $\tau \le t \ll T_2$ provides the values of $\hat{M}_0$. From Theorem 2.1 we obtain

$$(RM_0)^\wedge(\theta, t) = 2\pi \hat{M}_0(t\theta), \tag{3.26}$$

where R is the 3D Radon transform. Thus RM_0 can be obtained from S.

Assume that $S(t)$ is measured for the discrete directions

$$\theta_{jk} = \begin{pmatrix} \cos \varphi_k \sin \psi_j \\ \sin \varphi_k \sin \psi_j \\ \cos \psi_j \end{pmatrix},$$

$$\varphi_k = 2\pi k/m, \quad k = 0, \dots, m-1,$$
$$\psi_j = (j - 1/2)\pi/m, \quad j = 1, \dots, m, \tag{3.27}$$

and for discrete times $t_\ell = \ell \Delta t, \ell = 0, \dots, q$. From (3.26), $(RM_0)(\theta_{jk}, s)$ can be computed by an inverse 1D Fourier transform. This is just the data needed for the inversion algorithm in section 5.5.5.

One can also try to determine M_0 directly from (3.25) by a 3D inverse Fourier transform. In order to avoid the trouble with interpolation in Fourier space (see section 5.2), it is advantageous to choose G such that the Fourier transform of M_0 is obtained on a Cartesian grid in $\mathbb{R}^3$. This can be achieved by the choice

$$G_1(t) = \begin{cases} g_1, & \tau \leq t, \\ 0 & \text{otherwise,} \end{cases}$$

$$G_i(t) = \begin{cases} g_i, & 0 \leq t \leq \tau, \\ 0 & \text{otherwise} \end{cases} \tag{3.28}$$

for $i = 2, 3$. Then for $t \geq \tau$,

$$S(t) = \int_{\mathbb{R}^3} M_0(x) e^{-i\gamma((t-\tau)g_1 x_1 + \tau g_2 x_2 + \tau g_3 x_3)} dx$$

$$= (2\pi)^{3/2} \hat{M}_0(\gamma(t-\tau)g_1, \tau\gamma g_2, \tau\gamma g_3).$$

If this is done for g_1 fixed,

$$g_{2k} = k\Delta g, \qquad g_{3\ell} = \ell\Delta g, \qquad k, \ell = -m, \ldots, m,$$

and

$$t_j = j\Delta t + \tau, \qquad j = 1, \ldots, n,$$

we obtain $\hat{M}_0$ on a Cartesian grid with stepsizes $\gamma g_1 \Delta t$, $\tau\gamma\Delta g$, $\tau\gamma\Delta g$ in the x_1, x_2, x_3 direction, respectively.

In a second approximation, H_1 is the shaped pulse

$$H_1(t) = \phi(ta\gamma g)e^{i\gamma g x_3 t},$$

where ϕ is a smooth positive function such that its Fourier transform $\hat{\phi}$ is essentially supported in $[-1, 1]$, e.g.,

$$\phi(t) = e^{-(t-\tau/2)^2/8}.$$

Then with $x' = \begin{pmatrix} x_1 \\ x_2 \end{pmatrix}$ and $G' = \begin{pmatrix} G_1 \\ G_2 \end{pmatrix}$,

$$S(t) = \int_{\mathbb{R}^2} M_0'(x', x_3) e^{-i\gamma \int_0^t G'(s)ds \cdot x' - t/T_2(x', x_3)} dx', \tag{3.29}$$

where

$$M_0'(x', x_3) = \int_{\mathbb{R}} M_0(x', x_3') \hat{\phi}\left(\frac{x_3' - x_3}{a}\right) dx_3'.$$

Thus the shaped pulse selects a slice of thickness $2a$. (3.29) is the analogue of (3.23). If we choose, correspondingly to (3.24),

$$G'(t) = \begin{cases} g\theta', & \tau \leq t, \\ 0 & \text{otherwise} \end{cases}$$

with $g > 0$, $\theta' \in S^1$, (3.29) becomes approximately

$$S(t) = \int_{\mathbb{R}^2} M_0'(x', x_3) e^{-i\gamma g(t-\tau)\theta' \cdot x'} dx'.$$

With

$$t_\ell = \ell \Delta t + \tau, \quad \ell = 0, \ldots, q,$$

$$\theta_j' = \begin{pmatrix} \cos \varphi_j \\ \sin \varphi_j \end{pmatrix}, \quad \varphi_j = 2\pi j/p, \quad j = 0, \ldots, p - 1,$$

this gives rise to the values of $RM_0'(\cdot, x_3)$, R the 2D Radon transform needed in the standard parallel geometry as used in transmission tomography; see section 3.1. On the other hand, if we choose G' analogously to (3.28), i.e.,

$$G_1'(t) = \begin{cases} g_1, & \tau \leq t, \\ 0 & \text{otherwise,} \end{cases}$$

$$G_2'(t) = \begin{cases} g_2, & 0 \leq t \leq \tau, \\ 0 & \text{otherwise,} \end{cases}$$

we get the 2D Fourier transform of $M_0'(\cdot, x_3)$ on a Cartesian grid. This yields $M_0'(\cdot, x_3)$ immediately by a 2D inverse FFT.

From technical reasons (see Ahn, Kim, and Cho (1986)) it is more convenient to use

$$G'(t) = \eta \begin{pmatrix} \cos \xi t \\ \sin \xi t \end{pmatrix} + \eta \xi t \begin{pmatrix} -\sin \xi t \\ \cos \xi t \end{pmatrix},$$

i.e.,

$$\int_0^t G'(t) dt = \eta t \begin{pmatrix} \cos \xi t \\ \sin \xi t \end{pmatrix}.$$

Now (3.29) becomes for $t \ll T_2$

$$S(t) = \int_{\mathbb{R}^2} M_0'(x', x^3) e^{-i\gamma \eta t (x_1 \cos \xi t + x_2 \sin \xi t)} dx'$$

$$= 2\pi M_0'(\gamma \eta t \cos \xi t, \gamma \eta t \sin \xi t, x_3)^\wedge.$$

Thus we get $M_0'(\cdot, x_3)^\wedge$ on a spiral. This gives rise to a Fourier reconstruction problem; see section 5.2.

3.5   Electron Tomography

In electron tomography, the object to be imaged (a very small particle; typically a few hundred Å) is placed onto the specimen stage of a transmission electron microscope. The electron beam of the microscope generates a 2D projection of the 3D object. This is done for many orientations of the object, providing the ray transform $(Pf)(\theta, \cdot)$ of the electron density f of the object for many directions θ. Thus the mathematical problem is to invert

P. See Frank (1992) for a state-of-the-art review. A Nobel prize (Klug in 1982) is related to this kind of electron microscopy.

Due to experimental limitations, the inversion formulas for P of section 2.2 do not apply. In the simplest case (single-axis tilting), the object is fixed on the stage, which is tilted around a fixed axis perpendicular to the electron beam through an angular range $-\vartheta$ to ϑ, where ϑ is the maximal tilt angle, typically $60°$. Since each plane perpendicular to the axis of rotation can be dealt with separately, this amounts to a stack of 2D reconstruction problems for the 2D Radon transform with limited angular range; see section 6.2. In conical tilting the stage has a fixed tilting angle ϑ but is rotated around its center through $180°$. This amounts to sampling $(Pf)(\theta, \cdot)$ for θ on the cone centered at the origin and making an angle ψ_0 with the direction of the electron beam. This cone does not satisfy the completeness condition in section 2.2, meaning that this reconstruction problem is not uniquely solvable. In section 6.2.4 we give a formula for the generalized inverse. One of the main problems in electron microscopy is that the object is damaged by the exposure. A way out of this problem is to put many identical objects onto the stage; this results in many projections of the same object, but at unknown (in fact, random) orientations. Thus a single projection provides many projections of the object at different but (alas!) unknown orientations. The problem then is to find these orientations. This subject will be taken up in section 6.1.

3.6   Radar

Tomographic methods are used in various ways in radar. We give two typical examples.

3.6.1   Synthetic aperture radar

In synthetic aperture radar (SAR), a plain terrain is surveyed by a radar antenna carried by a plane flying with constant speed along a straight trajectory; see Hellsten and Andersson (1987). The quantity to be imaged is the ground reflectivity function $f : \mathbb{R}^2 \to \mathbb{R}^1$. The strength of the radar signal reflected by a surface element dS at point x in the plane with distance r from the antenna is

$$\frac{1}{r^2} f(x) dS.$$

The reflected signal received at time t originates from those points x in the plane whose distance to the antenna is $tc/2$ with c the speed of light. Thus with (y, h), $y \in \mathbb{R}^2$, the position of the plane at time t, the total reflected signal at time t is

$$\frac{1}{r^2} \int_{|y-x|=\sqrt{r^2-h^2}} f(x) dx, \quad r = tc/2.$$

This gives rise to the integral transform

$$g(y, r) = \int_{S^1} f(y + r\theta) d\theta$$

of f, which is called the average reflectivity function. The problem is to recover f in $\mathbb{R}^2$ from the values of g on $\mathbb{R}^1 \times \mathbb{R}^1_+$. Obviously, $g = 0$ if f is odd with respect to the x_1 axis.

In order to eliminate this source of nonuniqueness, one builds the antenna to illuminate only the half-plane $x_1 > 0$. Equivalently, we may assume that f is even with respect to x_1. With this restriction, f is uniquely determined by g. An inversion formula is given in section 2.5, leading to the filtered backprojection algorithm of section 5.1. Highly efficient backprojection algorithms have been suggested in this context; see Nilsson (1997).

3.6.2   Range–Doppler radar

The problem in range–Doppler radar is to find the range and the velocity of an object from the radar echo ψ_e of the radar signal ψ reflected by the object. The object is described by a reflectivity function $D(x, y)$ in the normalized variables $x = 2r/c$, $y = 2f_0 v/c$ in the range–velocity plane. Here r is the range, v the velocity, c the speed of light, and f_0 the carrier frequency.

In wideband radar, the radar echo of an object at x, y in the range–velocity plane with unit reflectivity is

$$\psi_{x,y}(t) = \sqrt{y}\psi(y(t - x));$$

see Maass (1989). The reflected signal for an object with reflectivity function D is obtained by linear superposition, i.e.,

$$\psi_e(t) = \int\int D(x, y)\psi_{x,y}(t)dxdy.$$

The problem is to recover D from $\psi_e(t)$ for $t \in \mathbb{R}$ and many choices of ψ. A standard way to do this is to compute the function

$$g(x_0, y_0) = \int \psi_e(t)\overline{\psi}_{x_0,y_0}(t)dt.$$

In the wideband case, we choose $\psi(t) = \delta(t - t_0)$ with some $t_0 \in \mathbb{R}$, obtaining

$$\psi_e(t) = \int\int D(x, y)\sqrt{y}\delta(y(t - x) - t_0)dxdy$$
$$= \int \frac{1}{\sqrt{y}}D(t - t_0/y, y)dy,$$

hence

$$g(x_0, y_0) = \int \psi_e(t)\sqrt{y_0}\delta(y_0(t - x_0) - t_0)dt$$
$$= \frac{1}{\sqrt{y_0}}\psi_e(x_0 + t_0/y_0)$$
$$= \int \frac{1}{\sqrt{yy_0}}D(x_0 + t_0/y_0 - t_0/y, y)dy.$$

Thus we arrive at integrals of D along the hyperbolas $x = x_0 + t_0/y_0 - t_0/y$. Putting

$$f(x, y) = \frac{1}{\sqrt{y}}D(-x/y, y),$$

we convert the hyperbolas into straight lines, and we obtain

$$g(x_0, y_0) = \frac{1}{\sqrt{y_0}} \int f(t_0 - y(x_0 + t_0/y_0), y) dy,$$

which is just a repararametrization of the Radon transform of f.

In narrowband radar, we assume

$$\psi(t) = u(t) e^{2\pi i f_0 t}.$$

Here $u(t)$ is slowly varying and f_0 large. The echo of a single object at range r moving with constant velocity v and unit reflectivity is

$$\psi_{x,y}(t) = \psi(t - x) e^{-2\pi i y t}.$$

We have

$$g(x_0, y_0) = \int \int D(x, y) e^{\pi i (y_0 - y)(x_0 + x)} A_\psi(x - x_0, y - y_0) dx dy,$$

where

$$A_\psi(x, y) = \int \psi(t + x/2) \overline{\psi}(t - x/2) e^{-2\pi i y t} dt.$$

One can show (see Feig and Grünbaum (1986)) that it is possible to choose ψ in such a way that

$$A_\psi(x, y) \sim \delta(x - \mu y),$$

where $\mu \in \mathbb{R}^1$ is arbitrary. Then

$$g(x_0, y_0) \sim \int \int D(x, y) e^{\pi i (y_0 - y)(x_0 + x)} \delta((x - x_0) - \mu(y - y_0)) dx dy$$

$$= e^{\pi i x_0^2/\mu} \int D(\mu y, y_0 - x_0(\mu + y)) e^{-\pi i \mu y^2} dy.$$

In section 2.4, we give an inversion formula for D real.

3.7 Vector Tomography

So far the quantity to be imaged has been a scalar function. In many cases, vector valued functions or vector fields have to be imaged. We give some examples.

3.7.1 Doppler tomography

Consider a fluid in a finite volume with local sound speed $c(x) > 0$ and velocity $v(x) \in \mathbb{R}^n$. Let x_0, x_1 be sources and receivers, respectively, for ultrasound signals propagating along the straight line L between x_0, x_1. The effective speed of sound along L is $c(x) + \theta \cdot v(x)$, where $\theta = (x_1 - x_0)/|x_1 - x_0|$, is the direction vector of L. Thus the travel time of a signal traveling from x_0 to x_1 is

$$T_{01} = \int_{x_0}^{x_1} \frac{ds}{c(x) + \theta \cdot v(x)},$$

where $x = x_0 + s\theta$. If sources and receivers are interchanged, the travel time is

$$T_{10} = \int_{x_0}^{x_1} \frac{ds}{c(x) - \theta \cdot v(x)}.$$

If $|v| \ll c$, then we have approximately

$$T_{01} + T_{10} = 2 \int_{x_0}^{x_1} \frac{ds}{c(x)}, \tag{3.30}$$

$$T_{10} - T_{01} = 2 \int_{x_0}^{x_1} \frac{\theta \cdot v(x)}{c^2(x)} ds. \tag{3.31}$$

The measurements (3.30) can be modeled by the ray transform; see section 2.2. If T_{01}, T_{10} are measured for sufficiently many source and receiver pairs, c can be computed from (3.30). (3.31) gives rise to the vectorial ray transform. We show in section 2.6 that the solenoidal part of the vector field $c^{-2}(x)v(x)$ is uniquely determined by (3.31), and an explicit inversion formula is available.

3.7.2   Schlieren tomography

Let $m = n(x)$ be the refractive index of a medium in a finite volume of $\mathbb{R}^3$. By a Schlieren arrangement (see Braun and Hauck (1991)), one measures the line integrals

$$I(x_0, x_1) = \int_{x_0}^{x_1} (b \times \theta) \cdot \operatorname{grad} n(x) ds, \tag{3.32}$$

where $\theta = (x_1 - x_0)/|x_1 - x_0|$. If x_1, x_2 are restricted to some plane, and b is chosen perpendicular to that plane, then I is essentially the normal Radon transform $\mathfrak{R}^\perp$ of the vector field $\operatorname{grad} n$; see section 2.6. One can show that $\operatorname{grad} n$ is uniquely determined by (3.32), and an inversion formula is given.

3.7.3   Photoelastic tomography

Photoelastic tomography is sometimes called integrated photoelasticity; see Aben and Puro (1997). It can be used to determine the flow in a medium by measuring the change of polarization of light as it passes through the medium. The propagation of light is modeled by

$$\frac{d}{dx_2} E = -i P E, \tag{3.33}$$

where $E = (E_1, E_3)^T$ is the electrical vector in the plane orthogonal to the direction of propagation (the x_2-axis), and

$$P = \frac{1}{n_0} \begin{pmatrix} (\varepsilon_{11} - \varepsilon_{33})/2 & \varepsilon_{13} \\ \varepsilon_{13} & -(\varepsilon_{11} - \varepsilon_{33})/2 \end{pmatrix}, \tag{3.34}$$

where ε is the dielectric tensor and n_0 is the refractive index of the medium at rest. It is assumed that $E(x_2^1)$ can be measured for each choice of $E(x_2^0)$. This means that the solution operator of (3.33) is known. For P small this means that the line integrals of P in the direction x_2 can be determined. If ε is generated by a flow with velocity vector v, then

$$\frac{1}{n_0}\varepsilon_{ij} = \alpha_0\delta_{ij} + \alpha_1\left(\frac{\partial v_i}{\partial x_j} + \frac{\partial v_j}{\partial x_i}\right),$$

where α_0, α_1 are material constants and δ is the unit matrix. Thus we arrive at the problem of determining the vector field v from line integrals.

3.8   Seismic Tomography

Geophysics is one of the fields in which tomographic methods were used much earlier than in radiology. We describe some models of increasing complexity.

3.8.1   Travel time tomography

Let $c = c(x)$ be the speed of sound in a domain $B \subseteq \mathbb{R}^3$, and let q (the source) and r (the receiver) be points on the boundary ∂B of B. The travel time of a signal traveling from r to q is

$$\int_{\Gamma_c(r,q)} \frac{ds}{c}, \tag{3.35}$$

where $\Gamma_c(r, q)$ is the geodesic with respect to the metric $ds = \frac{1}{c}|dx|$, i.e., the solution of

$$\frac{d}{dt}\frac{\dot{x}}{c(x)} = \nabla\frac{1}{c(x)}$$

connecting r and q. The problem is to recover c from (3.35) for many source–receiver pairs q, r.

Since c appears in Γ_c, (3.35) is a nonlinear problem. Assuming that we know a reference sound speed $c_0 \sim c$ and putting $f = \frac{1}{c} - \frac{1}{c_0}$, we obtain the linearized version

$$g(r, q) = \int_{\Gamma_{c_0}(r,q)} f(x)ds. \tag{3.36}$$

If c_0 is constant, then $\Gamma_{c_0}(r, q)$ is just the straight line connecting r, q. Hence (3.36) is, except for notation, the ray transform. (3.36) was used for the determination of the inner structure of the earth early in this century by Herglotz and Wiechert; see Romanov (1969) and Goldin (1986). It is also the model used in cross-borehole tomography, where transducers and receivers are located in two boreholes and the domain in between is being imaged; see Dines and Lytle (1979). Since vertical lines cannot be measured, this is an example of limited angle tomography; see section 6.2.

3.8.2   Reflection tomography

Travel time tomography makes use only of the first arrival times of a seismogram. However, seismic data is much richer and contains the whole time history of the signal. Suppose the travel time between two points x, y of the medium is $\tau(x, y)$, and let

$$I(r, q, t) = \{x : \tau(r, x) + \tau(x, q) = t\} \tag{3.37}$$

be the set of points x for which a signal starting at q, being reflected at x, and arriving at r needs time t for its journey. If we model the medium by a reflectivity function f and if we ignore multiple reflections, then the signal from source q observed at receiver r at time t is something like

$$g(r, q, t) = \int_{I(r,q,t)} f(x)dx. \tag{3.38}$$

If the signals are traveling along straight lines, then $I(r, q, t)$ is an ellipsoid with foci at r, q. If, in addition, r, q are far away from the support of f, then $I(r, q, t)$ is close to a plane at points x, where $f(x) \neq 0$, and (3.38) is essentially the Radon transform. An obvious approximate inversion procedure is as follows. Consider the set

$$\begin{aligned} J(x) &= \{(r, q, t) : \tau(r, x) + \tau(x, q) = t\} \\ &= \{(r, q, t) : x \in I(r, q, t)\}. \end{aligned}$$

It consists of all triples (r, q, t) for which—ignoring multiple reflections—receiver r receives at time t an echo from the point x of the medium due to a signal issued from source q. Summing up over all these echos from x, we get

$$f(x) \sim \int_{J(x)} g(r, q, t)drdsdt. \tag{3.39}$$

Note that (3.39) corresponds to the backprojection operator R^*; see Miller, Oristaglio, and Beylkin (1987).

3.8.3   Waveform tomography

While reflection tomography as described above is purely heuristic, waveform tomography is a more accurate model based on the wave equation. The signal $u(x, t)$ generated at source q is a solution of

$$\frac{\partial^2 u}{\partial t^2} = c^2(\Delta u + \delta(x - q)\delta(t)), \quad t > 0, \tag{3.40}$$

$$u = 0 \quad \text{for} \quad t < 0.$$

The signal received at receiver r is

$$g(r, q, t) = u(r, t).$$

The problem is to recover c from g. This is again a nonlinear problem, which we will deal with in Chapter 7.

The problem is greatly simplified by linearizing (3.40). Assuming

$$\frac{1}{c^2} = \frac{1}{c_0^2}(1 + f)$$

with some known reference speed c_0 and f small, we put $u = u^0 + v$, where u^0 is the solution of (3.40) with $c = c_0$. We obtain

$$\frac{\partial^2 v}{\partial t^2} = c_0^2 \Delta v - f \frac{\partial^2 u}{\partial t^2},$$
$$v = 0 \quad \text{for} \quad t < 0.$$

Linearization means to replace u by u^0. In this context we speak of Born approximation. The result is

$$\frac{\partial^2 v}{\partial t^2} = c_0^2 \Delta v - f \frac{\partial^2 u^0}{\partial t^2},$$
$$v = 0 \quad \text{for} \quad t < 0.$$

This equation is easily solved for v by the use of Kirchhoff's formula; see Courant and Hilbert (1962). The result is

$$v(x, t) = -\frac{1}{4\pi c_0^2} \frac{\partial^2}{\partial t^2} \int f(y) \frac{u^0(y, t - |x - y|/c_0)}{|x - y|} dy.$$

Making use of

$$u^0(x, t) = -\frac{1}{4\pi} \frac{\delta(t - |x - q|/c_0)}{|x - q|}$$

yields

$$v(x, t) = \frac{1}{16\pi^2 c_0^2} \frac{\partial^2}{\partial t^2} \int f(y) \frac{\delta(t - (|x - y| + |y - q|)/c_0)}{|x - y||y - q|} dy.$$

The integral can be evaluated by the formula

$$\int f(y)\delta(\phi(y))dy = \int_\Gamma f(y) \frac{d\sigma(y)}{|\nabla\phi(y)|},$$

where $\Gamma = \{y : \phi(y) = 0\}$ and σ is the surface measure on Γ. We obtain

$$v(x, t) = \frac{1}{16\pi^2 c_0^2} \frac{\partial^2}{\partial t^2} \int_{I_{(r,q,t)}} f(y) \frac{d\sigma(y)}{||x - y|(q - y) - |q - y|(x - y)|},$$

where $I_{r,q,t} = \{y : c_0 t = |r - y| + |y - q|\}$. $u = u^0 + v$ is the solution of (3.40) within the Born approximation. With g our data function, the solution of the inverse problem now calls for computing f from

$$g(r, q, t) = \frac{1}{16\pi^2 c_0^2} \frac{\partial^2}{\partial t^2} \int_{I(r,q,t)} f(y) \frac{d\sigma(y)}{||r - y|(q - y) - |q - y|(r - y)|}. \tag{3.41}$$

Thus we arrive at a relation very similar to the equation (3.38) of reflection tomography. Such a relation is also obtained if the background speed c_0 is not constant; see Miller, Oristaglio, and Beylkin (1987).

3.9   Historical Remarks

The history of tomography is thoroughly covered in the monograph of Webb (1990). We make only a few additions concerning inversion methods.

It seems that the first description of a tomographic scanner with an exact inversion method (based on Radon's inversion Theorem 2.6) was given by Wloka (1953). The patent of Frank (1938) precedes this work by many years; however, it uses as an inversion method straight backprojection without the necessary filtering. Cormack (1963) derived an inversion formula (2.24) and did reconstructions from data of an experimental scanner. The first commercially available scanner of Hounsfield (1973) used the Kaczmarz method (see section 5.3.1) as a reconstruction technique, although techniques based on Radon's inversion formula were already used by Bracewell (1956) in radio astronomy. The reconstruction algorithms in the medical field were developed independently of Radon's work by using Fourier analysis. Shepp and Logan (1974) recognized that the filtered backprojection algorithm can be viewed as an implementation of Radon's inversion formula. Fourier methods were also used in electron tomography (see Crowther, DeRosier, and Klug (1970)), while Vainstein (1970) used Radon's inversion formula in this context.

Chapter 4

Stability and Resolution

4.1 Stability

Problems in image reconstruction are usually not well-posed in the sense of Hadamard. This means that they suffer from one of the following deficiencies:

(i)   They are not solvable (in the strict sense) at all.

(ii) They are not uniquely solvable.

(iii) The solution does not depend continuously on the data.

For a thorough treatment of such problems see Tikhonov and Arsenin (1977). We give only a short account of the theory.

Let H, K be Hilbert spaces, and let $A : H \to K$ be a bounded linear operator. We consider the problem of solving

$$Af = g \qquad (4.1)$$

for f. (i) means that g is not in the range of A, (ii) means that A is not injective, and (iii) means that A^{-1} is not continuous.

One could do away with (i) and (ii) by using the generalized inverse A^+; see 1.3.3. But A^+ does not have to be continuous. To restore continuity, we introduce the notion of a regularization of A^+. This is a family $(T_\gamma)_{\gamma > 0}$ of linear continuous operators $T_\gamma : K \to H$, which are defined on all of K and for which

$$\lim_{\gamma \to 0} T_\gamma g = A^+ g$$

on the domain of A^+. Obviously, $\|T_\gamma\| \to \infty$ as $\gamma \to 0$ if A^+ is unbounded. With the help of regularization, we can solve (4.1) approximately in the following way. Let $g^\varepsilon \in K$ be an approximation to g such that $\|g - g^\varepsilon\| \le \varepsilon$. Let $\gamma(\varepsilon)$ be such that, as $\varepsilon \to 0$,

$$\gamma(\varepsilon) \to 0, \qquad \|T_{\gamma(\varepsilon)}\| \varepsilon \to 0.$$

Then, as $\varepsilon \to 0$,

$$\begin{aligned}
\|T_{\gamma(\varepsilon)}g^\varepsilon - A^+g\| &\le \|T_{\gamma(\varepsilon)}(g^\varepsilon - g)\| + \|T_{\gamma(\varepsilon)}g - A^+g\| \\
&\le \|T_{\gamma(\varepsilon)}\|\varepsilon + \|T_{\gamma(\varepsilon)}g - A^+g\| \\
&\to 0.
\end{aligned}$$

Hence $T_{\gamma(\varepsilon)}g^\varepsilon$ is close to A^+g if g^ε is close to g.

The number γ is called a regularization parameter. Determining a good regularization parameter is a major issue in the theory of ill-posed problems.

We discuss three examples of regularization.

1. *The truncated SVD.*

   Let

   $$Af = \sum_{k=1}^\infty \sigma_k(f, f_k)g_k$$

   be the SVD of A; see section 1.3.4. Then

   $$T_\gamma g = \sum_{\sigma_k \ge \gamma} \sigma_k^{-1}(g, g_k)f_k \tag{4.2}$$

   is a regularization with $\|T_\gamma\| \le \frac{1}{\gamma}$.

2. *Tikhonov–Phillips regularization.*

   Here we put

   $$T_\gamma = (A^*A + \gamma I)^{-1}A^*. \tag{4.3}$$

   Equivalently, $f_\gamma = T_\gamma g$ can be defined by minimizing

   $$\|Af - g\|^2 + \gamma\|f\|^2.$$

   In terms of the SVD of A, we have

   $$T_\gamma g = \sum_{k=1}^\infty F_\gamma(\sigma_k)\sigma_k^{-1}(g, g_k)f_k, \tag{4.4}$$

   $$F_\gamma(\sigma) = \frac{1}{1 + \gamma/\sigma^2}.$$

3. *Early stopping of iterative methods.*

   Suppose

   $$f^{k+1} = B_k f^k + C_k g$$

   is an iterative method for solving $Af = g$ with bounded linear operators B_k, C_k. Assume that $f^k \to A^+g$. For each $\gamma > 0$ let $k(\gamma)$ be an index such that $k(\gamma) \to \infty$ for $\gamma \to 0$. Then

   $$T_\gamma f = f^{k(\gamma)}$$

   is a regularization.

A good measure for the degree of ill-posedness of (4.1) is the rate of decay of the singular value σ_k. It is clear from (4.2) that the ill-posedness is more pronounced the faster the decay. A polynomial decay is usually considered manageable, while an exponential decay indicates that only very poor approximations to f in (4.1) can be computed.

The SVD gives us all the information we need about an ill-posed problem. In many cases, the SVD is hard to obtain. A less demanding tool for studying ill-posed problems is a Sobolev space estimate. Assume that $H = L_2(G)$ with some bounded domain G in $\mathbb{R}^n$. Assume further that for some $\alpha > 0, m > 0$,

$$\|Af\| \geq m\|f\|_{H^{-\alpha}(G)}. \tag{4.5}$$

Then one can show (see, e.g., Natterer (1986), Chapter IV) that

$$\|Af\| \leq \varepsilon, \qquad \|f\|_{H^\beta(G)} \leq \rho \tag{4.6}$$

for some $\beta, \rho > 0$ implies

$$\|f\|_{L_2(G)} \leq c\varepsilon^{\frac{\beta}{\alpha+\beta}} \rho^{\frac{\alpha}{\alpha+\beta}} \tag{4.7}$$

with a constant c depending only on m, α, β. This can be interpreted in the following way. Assume as above that g in (4.1) is known with accuracy ε, and that f is known to satisfy $\|f\|_{H^\beta}(G) \leq \rho$. Then it is possible to compute an approximation to f with accuracy $c\varepsilon^{\beta/(\alpha+\beta)}\rho^{\alpha/(\alpha+\beta)}$. Thus $\beta/(\alpha+\beta)$ is a measure of ill-posedness of (4.1). If this number is close to 1 (i.e., $\alpha \ll \beta$), then the ill-posedness is not much of a problem. However, if this number is close to 0, the loss in accuracy is dramatic. For values between these two extremes the ill-posedness is noticeable but manageable.

We discuss the ill-posedness of the Radon problem in light of these findings. The singular values of R are given in Theorem 2.9. Since they decay polynomially the ill-posedness is not very pronounced. The stability estimate of Theorem 2.10 shows that we have $\alpha = (n - 1)/2$ for $A = R$, the Radon transform in (4.1). If f is very smooth, i.e., $f \in H^\beta(G)$ for $\beta \gg 1$, then $\alpha/(\alpha + \beta) \sim 1$, and the problem $Rf = g$ is only slightly ill-posed. In most applications f will be piecewise smooth. Such functions are in $H^\beta(G)$ for $\beta < 1/2$. Thus $\alpha/(\alpha + \beta)$ is close to $1 - 1/n$, which is between the extreme cases 0 and 1. Hence both the singular value decomposition and the stability estimate indicate that the ill-posedness of $Rf = g$ is not serious. The same holds for $Pf = g$, where P is the ray transform, as can be seen from (2.38), (2.39), and Theorem 2.18.

We remark that this holds only if Rf, Pf are known in all of C^n, T^n, respectively. In section 6.2, we shall see that problems with incomplete data tend to be seriously ill-posed.

4.2 Sampling

In this section we collect some basic facts of the Fourier theory of sampling as used in communication theory and image processing; see Jerry (1977) and Pratt (1978), Part 2.4. The Fourier theory deals with functions (or distributions) whose Fourier transforms have compact support. The simplest example is the function

$$f(x) = \text{sinc}(\Omega x), \quad \text{sinc}(x) = \begin{cases} \frac{\sin x}{x}, & x \neq 0, \\ 1, & x = 0. \end{cases} \tag{4.8}$$

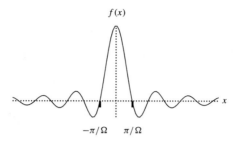

$$f(x)$$

$$-\pi/\Omega \qquad \pi/\Omega$$

Figure 4.1. *Graph of $f(x) = \mathrm{sinc}(\Omega x)$.*

It is readily seen that $\hat{f}(\xi) = 0$ for $|\xi| > \Omega > 0$. From Figure 4.1 we see that f is positive in $|x| < \pi/\Omega$ and decays in an oscillating way outside of this interval. Thus f represents an object of size $2\pi/\Omega$. More generally a function (or distribution) in $\mathbb{R}^n$ whose Fourier transform vanishes outside $|\xi| \le \Omega$ is called band-limited with bandwidth Ω, or Ω-band-limited. The smallest detail represented by such a function is of size $2\pi/\Omega$. We call a function f essentially Ω-band-limited if $\hat{f}(\xi)$ is negligible for $|\xi| \ge \Omega$.

The basic question in sampling theory is under what conditions can a function be recovered from its values on a discrete lattice. In $\mathbb{R}^n$ such a lattice can be described by a real nonsingular (n, n) matrix $W = (w_1, \ldots, w_n)$, $w_i \in \mathbb{R}^n$, $i = 1, \ldots, n$, in the form

$$L_W = \left\{ x \in \mathbb{R}^n : x = \sum_{i=1}^{n} k_i w_i, \quad k_i \in \mathbb{Z} \right\}$$
$$= \left\{ x \in \mathbb{R}^n : x = Wk, \quad k \in \mathbb{Z}^n \right\}$$
$$= W\mathbb{Z}^n.$$

Thus L_W is the lattice generated by the columns $w_1, \ldots, w_n$ of W. The reciprocal lattice $L_W^\perp$ is defined to be $L_{2\pi(W^{-1})^T}$. We remark that W is not determined uniquely by L_W, but $L_W^\perp$ and $|\det(W)|$ are.

In view of the applications we have in mind we formulate the sampling theorems for L_2-functions, although they also hold for distributions. The first one, which is due to Petersen and Middleton (1962), concerns sampling in $\mathbb{R}^n$.

THEOREM 4.1. *Let $f \in L^2(\mathbb{R}^n)$, and let $\hat{f} = 0$ outside some compact set $K \subseteq \mathbb{R}^n$. Assume that $\overset{\circ}{K} + \xi \cap \overset{\circ}{K} + \xi' = \emptyset$ for ξ, $\xi' \in L_W^\perp$, and $\xi \ne \xi'$, where $\overset{\circ}{K}$ is the interior of K. Then f is uniquely determined by its values on L_W. If f_1, f_2 both satisfy the assumptions on f, then*

$$\int_{\mathbb{R}^n} f_1 \overline{f}_2 \, dx = |\det(W)| \sum_{x \in L_W} f_1(x) \overline{f}_2(x).$$

The theorem follows immediately from Poisson's formula (1.11), which, after a change of variables, assumes the form

$$\sum_{\eta \in L_W^\perp} \hat{f}(\xi - \eta) = (2\pi)^{-n/2} |\det(W)| \sum_{x \in L_W} f(x) e^{-i\xi \cdot x}.$$

If f satisfies the hypothesis of the theorem, then the left-hand side reduces to $\hat{f}(\xi)$ for $\xi \in \overset{\circ}{K}$, demonstrating that $\hat{f}$ is uniquely determined by the values of f on L_W. To derive the integral formula we write Poisson's formula for $\xi = 0$ in the form

$$\int_{\mathbb{R}^n} f(x)dx = |\det(W)| \sum_{x \in L_W} f(x) - (2\pi)^{n/2} \sum_{0 \neq \eta \in L_W^\perp} \hat{f}(\eta).$$

The second sum on the right-hand side vanishes if $\hat{f}$ vanishes outside $K - K$, provided that L_W satisfies the hypothesis of the theorem. Putting $f = f_1 \overline{f}_2$ yields the integral formula. □

As a by-product of this derivation we note that

$$\int_{\mathbb{R}^n} f(x)dx = |\det(W)| \sum_{x \in L_W} f(x)$$

if supp$(f) \subseteq K - K$, i.e., the trapezoidal rule for the evaluation of integrals is exact in this case.

We remark that Theorem 4.1 also contains a statement on the stability of the reconstruction process. Namely, for $f_1 = f$, $f_2 = \overline{f}$ we have

$$\|f\|_{L_2(\mathbb{R}^n)}^2 = |\det(W)| \sum_{x \in L_W} |f|^2(x).$$

This means that recovering f from its samples on L_W is stable in the L_2 sense.

Let us consider the 1D case with $K = [-\Omega, \Omega]$. W reduces now to a (positive) real number $W = \Delta x$, and the reciprocal lattice is generated by $2\pi/\Delta x$. Thus the condition of the theorem means $\Delta x \leq \pi/\Omega$. This is known as the Nyquist condition in communication theory. We arrive at the Shannon sampling theorem.

THEOREM 4.2. *Let $f \in L^2(\mathbb{R}^1)$ be Ω-band-limited, and let $0 < \Delta x \leq \pi/\Omega$. Then f is uniquely determined by the values $f(\ell\Delta x)$, $\ell \in \mathbb{Z}$. If f_1, f_2 satisfy the assumptions on f, then*

$$\int_{\mathbb{R}^1} f_1 \overline{f}_2 dx = \Delta x \sum_{\ell \in \mathbb{Z}} f_1(\ell\Delta x) \overline{f}_2(\ell\Delta x).$$

We also have

$$\int_{\mathbb{R}^1} f(x)dx = \Delta x \sum_{\ell \in \mathbb{Z}} f(\ell\Delta x)$$

if f has bandwidth 2Ω and, as in the theorem, $\Delta x \leq \pi/\Omega$.

So far we have considered the general theory of sampling in $\mathbb{R}^n$. When we deal with integral geometric transforms we also have to sample periodic functions. We give a version of the Petersen–Middleton theorem that suits our purposes.

Let f be a function in $\mathbb{R}^n$ with n linear independent periods $p_1, \ldots, p_n \in \mathbb{R}^n$, i.e.,

$$f(x + p_i) = f(x), \quad i = 1, \ldots, n.$$

Let $P = (p_1, \ldots, p_n)$ and define the lattices L_P, $L_P^\perp$ as above. Then f can be viewed as a function on $\mathbb{R}^n/L_P$ which may be identified with

$$P[0,1)^n = \left\{ x \in \mathbb{R}^n : x = \sum_{i=1}^{n} \lambda_i p_i, \quad 0 \le \lambda_i < 1 \right\}.$$

The Fourier transform of a periodic function is defined by

$$\hat{f}(\xi) = \frac{1}{|\det(P)|} \int_{\mathbb{R}^n/L_P} e^{-ix\cdot\xi} f(x) dx, \quad \xi \in L_P^\perp. \tag{4.9}$$

Note that $\hat{f}$ is now a function on the discrete set $L_P^\perp$. For such functions the inverse Fourier transform is defined by

$$\tilde{f}(x) = \sum_{\xi \in L_P^\perp} e^{ix\cdot\xi} f(\xi). \tag{4.10}$$

Of course, we have $\tilde{\hat{f}} = f$ and $\hat{\tilde{f}} = f$.

For instance, if $n = 1$ and $p_1 = 2\pi$ is the (only) period of f, then $\mathbb{R}^n/L_P = [0, 2\pi)$, $L_P^\perp = \mathbb{Z}$, and

$$\hat{f}(k) = \frac{1}{2\pi} \int_0^{2\pi} e^{-ixk} f(x) dx, \quad k \in \mathbb{Z}.$$

Thus $\hat{f}(k)$ is just the kth Fourier coefficient of the 2π periodic function f, and the inverse transform is just the usual Fourier series

$$\tilde{f}(x) = \sum_{k \in \mathbb{Z}} e^{-ixk} f(k).$$

A lattice L_W suitable for sampling a periodic function must have the same periods as f, i.e., $L_P \subseteq L_W$. Then the sampling can be done on L_W/L_P. We have $L_P \subseteq L_W$ if and only if $P = WM$ with an integer matrix M, and in that case, $L_W^\perp \subseteq L_P^\perp$. For instance, if $n = 1$ and $p_1 = 2\pi$, a suitable sampling lattice is L_W with $W = 2\pi/M$, M an integer > 0. We have $L_W/L_P = \{0, \frac{2\pi}{M}, \ldots, \frac{2\pi}{M}(M-1)\}$ and $L_W^\perp = M\mathbb{Z}$.

Now we can formulate the sampling theorem for periodic functions; see Natterer (1993a).

THEOREM 4.3. *Let $f \in L_2(\mathbb{R}^n/L_P)$, and let $\hat{f} = 0$ outside a finite set $K \subseteq L_P^\perp$. Assume that $K + \xi \cap K + \xi' = \emptyset$ for $\xi, \xi' \in L_W^\perp$ and $\xi \ne \xi'$. Then f is uniquely determined by its values on L_W/L_P. If f_1, f_2 both satisfy the assumptions on f, then*

$$\int_{\mathbb{R}^n/L_P} f_1 \overline{f_2} dx = |\det(W)| \sum_{x \in L_W/L_P} f_1(x) \overline{f_2}(x).$$

The proof is again based on Poisson's formula (1.11), which now reads

$$\sum_{\eta \in L_W^\perp} \hat{f}(\xi - \eta) = \left| \frac{\det(W)}{\det(P)} \right| \sum_{x \in L_W/L_P} f(x) e^{ix\cdot\xi}.$$

for $\xi \in L_P^\perp$ and f a P-periodic function.

Again, let us consider the 1D case. With f a 2π periodic function sampled on $L_W/L_P = \{0, \frac{\pi}{M}, \ldots, \frac{\pi}{M}(2M-1)\}$, with K the set $\{-\Omega, -\Omega+1, \ldots, \Omega-1\}$, Ω an integer, the condition of the theorem means $M \geq \Omega$. Hence we have proved the following.

THEOREM 4.4. *Let* $f \in L^2(0, 2\pi)$, *and assume that the Fourier coefficients* $\hat{f}(k)$ *(see (4.9)) vanish for* $k < -\Omega$ *and* $k \geq \Omega$, Ω *an integer. Then* f *is uniquely determined by its values on* $\{0, \frac{\pi}{M}, \ldots, \frac{\pi}{M}(2M-1)\}$ *provided that* $M \geq \Omega$. *If* f_1, f_2 *satisfy the assumption on* f, *then*

$$\int_0^{2\pi} f_1 \overline{f}_2 dx = \frac{\pi}{M} \sum_{\ell=0}^{2M-1} f_1\left(\frac{\pi}{M}\ell\right) \overline{f}_2\left(\frac{\pi}{M}\ell\right).$$

Of course, this theorem is just an elementary statement about trigonometric polynomials.

In tomography we have to deal with functions of several variables which are periodic in only some of them. We obtain sampling theorems for such functions by combining the above results.

Let $f(x, y)$, $x \in \mathbb{R}^m$, $y \in \mathbb{R}^{n-m}$, be a function in $\mathbb{R}^n$ which has periods $p_1, \ldots, p_m \in \mathbb{R}^m$ in x, i.e., $f(x + p_i, y) = f(x, y)$, $i = 1, \ldots, m$. Let $P = (p_1, \ldots, p_m)$ and assume that P is nonsingular. The lattices L_P, $L_P^\perp$ in $\mathbb{R}^m$ are defined as above. We view f as a function on $\mathbb{R}^m/L_P \times \mathbb{R}^{n-m}$. The Fourier transform of f is defined by

$$\hat{f}(\xi, \eta) = \frac{1}{|\det(P)|}(2\pi)^{(m-n)/2} \int_{\mathbb{R}^m/L_P} \int_{\mathbb{R}^{n-m}} e^{-i(x\cdot\xi + y\cdot\eta)} f(x, y) dx dy,$$

$$\xi \in L_P^\perp, \quad \eta \in \mathbb{R}^{n-m}.$$

Sampling f on a lattice $L_W \subseteq \mathbb{R}^n$ makes sense only if L_W has the periods p_i, meaning that $\overline{p}_i = \binom{p_i}{0} \in L_W$, $i = 1, \ldots, m$. This is the case if and only if $\overline{P} = (\overline{p}_1, \ldots, \overline{p}_m) = WM$ with an integer matrix M. In that case, the sampling can be restricted to $L_W/L_{\overline{P}}$. The sampling theorem reads as follows.

THEOREM 4.5. *Let* $f \in L_2(\mathbb{R}^m/L_P \times \mathbb{R}^{n-m})$ *and let* $\hat{f} = 0$ *outside a bounded set* $K \subset L_P^\perp \times \mathbb{R}^{n-m}$. *Assume that the translates of* K *with respect to the lattice* $L_W^\perp$ *are mutually disjoint. Then* f *is uniquely determined by its values on* $L_W/L_{\overline{P}}$. *If* f_1, f_2 *both satisfy the assumptions on* f, *then*

$$\int_{\mathbb{R}^m/L_P} \int_{\mathbb{R}^{n-m}} f_1 \overline{f}_2 dx dy = |\det(W)| \sum_{L_W/L_{\overline{P}}} f_1(x) \overline{f}_2(x).$$

For a function in $\mathbb{R}^2$ that is 2π-periodic in the first argument, a suitable sampling lattice L_W has to satisfy $\binom{2\pi}{0} \in L_W$. The Fourier transform $\hat{f}(k, \eta)$ is just the kth Fourier coefficient of the Fourier transform with respect to the second variable, i.e.,

$$\hat{f}(k, \eta) = (2\pi)^{-3/2} \int_0^{2\pi} \int_{\mathbb{R}^1} e^{-i(kx + \eta y)} f(x, y) dx dy.$$

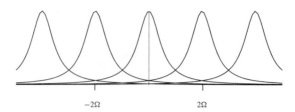

-2Ω 2Ω

Figure 4.2. *The Fourier transform of $S_W f$ for $K = [-\Omega, \Omega]$ and the lattice $L_W = \frac{\pi}{\Omega}\mathbb{Z}$, $L_W^{\perp} = 2\Omega\mathbb{Z}$. $(S_W f)^{\wedge}$ is the superposition of the graphs.*

The actual reconstruction of a function from its samples can be done by means of simple and explicit formulas. We restrict the discussion to sampling in $\mathbb{R}^n$. Let χ be the characteristic function of the set K, and let

$$(S_W f)(x) = \det(W)(2\pi)^{-n/2} \sum_{y \in L_W} f(y)\check{\chi}_K(x - y). \tag{4.11}$$

Then under the assumptions of Theorem 4.1, we have $f = S_W f$. In the 1D case described in Theorem 4.2, this is just the familiar sinc series

$$f(x) = \sum_{\ell} f(\ell\Delta x) \operatorname{sinc}\left(\pi \frac{x - \ell\Delta x}{\Delta x}\right).$$

In order to see what happens if f is not band-limited, we compute the Fourier transform of (4.11). By means of Poisson's formula (1.11), one obtains

$$(S_W f)^{\wedge}(\xi) = \chi_K(\xi) \sum_{\eta \in L_W^{\perp}} \hat{f}(\xi - \eta). \tag{4.12}$$

Thus within K, $(S_W f)^{\wedge}$ is a superposition of $\hat{f}$ and of shifted replicas of $\hat{f}$ with shifts in $L_W^{\perp}$.

Now assume that K, L_W satisfy the hypothesis of Theorem 4.1, and $\hat{f} = 0$ outside K. Then the sum in (4.12) reduces to the single term $\hat{f}(\xi)$ inside K, and it follows that $(S_W f)^{\wedge} = \hat{f}$ in K, i.e., f is uniquely determined by $S_W f$, hence by its values on L_W, and we have $S_W f = f$. However, if the support of $\hat{f}$ is not contained in K, then the shifted replicas of $\hat{f}$ affect the values of $(Sf)^{\wedge}$ in K, and $(Sf)^{\wedge}$ and $\hat{f}$ are no longer identical. This situation is sketched in Figure 4.2.

The error $a = Sf - f$ is called the aliasing error. It is clear from Figure 4.2 that aliasing is not only a high-frequency phenomenon; it also affects the low-frequency parts of f.

The only way to prevent aliasing when sampling a function that is not band-limited is to band-limit the function by a low pass filter prior to sampling. This means that f is replaced by the function

$$f_{\phi} = (\hat{f}\hat{\phi})^{\sim} = (2\pi)^{-n/2} f * \phi, \tag{4.13}$$

where $\hat{\phi}$ is a low pass filter, i.e., $\hat{\phi}(\xi) = 0$ for $|\xi| > \Omega$. Then ϕ is Ω-band-limited. The simplest case is the ideal low pass

$$\hat{\phi}(\xi) = \begin{cases} 1, & |\xi| \le \Omega, \\ 0, & |\xi| > \Omega. \end{cases} \tag{4.14}$$

Filtering with the ideal low pass is not always satisfactory since it leads to a high-frequency ringing artifact. This stems from the discontinuity of $\hat{\phi}$ at $|\xi| = \Omega$. One can avoid this artifact—at the expense of a slight loss in resolution—by using a filter with a continuous transition, such as the cosine filter

$$\hat{\phi}(\xi) = \begin{cases} \cos \frac{|\xi|\pi}{2\Omega}, & |\xi| \le \Omega, \\ 0, & |\xi| > \Omega. \end{cases} \tag{4.15}$$

Many other choices are possible and have been studied in the literature. Although much is known about how to select an "optimal" filter, making a good choice seems still to be more an art than a science.

4.3 Resolution

In the applications described in Chapter 3, all the integral transforms of section 2 are sampled on discrete sets. In this section, we study the influence of discrete sampling on the possible resolution in the sought-for function f.

We start with the Radon transform R. Let f be supported in $|x| < 1$, and assume that $(Rf)(\theta, s) = 0$ for $\theta \in A$, where A is a discrete set, $|A| = p$. From Theorem 2.9 and (2.26), we have

$$(Rf)(\theta, s) = w(s)^{n-1} \sum_{m=0}^{\infty} C_m^{n/2}(s) h_m(\theta),$$

where $h_m \in H'_m$, the harmonic polynomials of degree m with parity m. Assume that A is such that $h_m = 0$ if h_m vanishes on A. This is the case if and only if $p \ge \dim H'_m$ unless A lies on an algebraic variety of degree m. An instructive example was given by Louis (1982) for $n = 3$, in which case $\dim H'_m = (m + 2)(m + 1)$. Consider the choice (3.27) of A, where $|A| = m^2$. This is about twice as many as for the set (m odd)

$$A': \begin{array}{ll} \varphi_k = 2\pi k/m, & k = 0, \dots, m - 1, \\ \psi_j = (j - 1/2)/(m + 1), & j = 1, \dots, (m + 1)/2, \end{array}$$

where $|A'| = m(m + 1)/2$. However, A does not lead to a better resolution than A' since the function

$$Y_{m,-m}(\theta) = P_m^m(\cos \psi) \sin m\varphi,$$

which is in H'_m, vanishes on A; see section 1.3.5.

Thus, generically, $h_m = 0$ for $p \ge \dim H'_m$. Let $m(p)$ be the largest m for which this is the case. Then $h_m = 0$ for $m \le m(p)$. Taking the Fourier transform of Rf and using Theorem 2.1, we obtain

$$\hat{f}(\sigma\theta) = (2\pi)^{(2-n)/2}(2\sigma)^{-n/2} \sum_{m > m(p)} \frac{i^{-m}\Gamma(m + n)}{m!\Gamma(\frac{n}{2})} J_{m+n/2}(\sigma) h_m(\theta),$$

where the Fourier transform of $w C_m^{n/2}$ is taken from Gradshteyn and Ryzhik (1965), formula 7.321.

$J_{m+n/2}(\sigma)$ is negligible for $|\sigma| < m + n/2$; see section 1.3.5. Hence $\hat{f}(\sigma\theta)$ is negligible for $|\sigma| < m(p) + n/2$, or, asymptotically, for $|\sigma| \leq m(p)$. Thus if f has essential bandwidth Ω and $(Rf)(\theta, s) = 0$ for p directions θ and $s \subseteq \mathbb{R}^1$, then f is small provided that $\Omega \leq m(p)$. From

$$\dim H_m' = \binom{m+n-1}{m-1} = \frac{m^{n-1}}{(n-1)!}\left(1 + O\left(\frac{1}{m}\right)\right),$$

we find that this is asymptotically the case if and only if

$$p \geq \frac{\Omega^{n-1}}{(n-1)!}.$$

This is the condition that p has to satisfy if f is to be recovered from p complete views. Thus to see details of size $2\pi/\Omega$ in an object of radius 1, one has to use at least $\Omega^{n-1}/(n-1)!$ views.

The resolution for the ray transform can be reduced to the Radon case. Assume that $(Pf)(\theta, s) = 0$ for p directions θ_j. Then for every $\omega \perp \theta_j$,

$$(Rf)(\omega, s) = \int_{\substack{y \perp \theta_j \\ y \cdot \omega = s}} (Pf)(\theta_j, y) dy = 0.$$

This implies $h_m(\omega) = 0$ whenever $\omega \perp \theta_j$ for some j. It follows that the polynomial h_m must have degree $\geq p$, since the lowest degree polynomial with this property is $\prod_{j=1}^p \omega \cdot \theta_j$. Thus the expansion of Rf starts with $m = p$. Now we can argue as in the Radon case. The result is that f can be recovered reliably from $(Pf)(\theta_j, \cdot)$, $j = 1, \ldots, p$, if and only if $p \geq \Omega$.

So much for the case of continuously measured projections at arbitrary directions. We now turn to the practically more important case of fully but regularly discretized data.

Theorems 4.1–4.5 are the basis of our treatment of the fully discrete case. We start with the simplest case, namely, standard parallel scanning in 2D tomography; see (3.3). Assume that $f \in \mathcal{S}(\mathbb{R}^2)$ vanishes for $|x| \geq \rho$, and assume f to be essentially Ω-band-limited, i.e., $\hat{f}(\xi)$ is negligible in an appropriate sense for $|\xi| > \Omega$. Let $g(\varphi, s) = (Rf)(\theta, s)$, where $\theta = (\cos\varphi, \sin\varphi)^T$. g is 2π-periodic in its first argument. The Fourier transform of g in the sense of Theorem 4.5 is

$$\hat{g}(k, \sigma) = (2\pi)^{-3/2} \int_0^{2\pi} \int_{-\rho}^{\rho} e^{-i(k\varphi + \sigma s)} g(\varphi, s) ds d\varphi.$$

For the s-integral we obtain from Theorem 2.1

$$\int_{-\rho}^{\rho} e^{-i\sigma s} g(\varphi, s) ds = 2\pi \hat{f}(\sigma\theta);$$

hence

$$\hat{g}(k, \sigma) = (2\pi)^{-1/2} \int_0^{2\pi} e^{-ik\varphi} \hat{f}(\sigma\theta) d\varphi. \qquad (4.16)$$

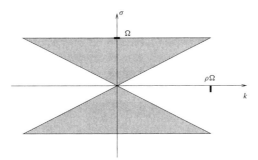

Figure 4.3. *The set K of* (4.18) *for* $\rho = 2$.

From (4.16) it is clear that $\hat{g}(k, \sigma)$ is negligibly small for $|\sigma| \geq \Omega$. Inserting for $\hat{f}$ in (4.16) the Fourier integral yields

$$\hat{g}(k, \sigma) = (2\pi)^{1/2} \int_0^{2\pi} e^{-ik\varphi} \int_{|x|<\rho} e^{-i\sigma\theta \cdot x} f(x) dx d\varphi$$

$$= (2\pi)^{1/2} \int_{|x|<\rho} f(x) \int_0^{2\pi} e^{-ik\varphi - i\sigma\theta \cdot x} d\varphi dx.$$

With $x = |x|\left(\begin{smallmatrix} \cos \psi \\ \sin \psi \end{smallmatrix}\right)$, we have $\theta \cdot x = |x| \cos(\varphi - \psi)$, hence

$$\int_0^{2\pi} e^{-ik\varphi - i\sigma\theta \cdot x} d\varphi = \int_0^{2\pi} e^{-ik\varphi - i\sigma|x|\cos(\varphi - \psi)} d\varphi$$

$$= e^{-ik\psi} \int_0^{2\pi} e^{-ik\varphi - i\sigma|x|\cos \varphi} d\varphi$$

$$= 2\pi i^k e^{-ik\psi} J_k(-\sigma|x|),$$

where J_k is the first kind Bessel function of order k; see section 1.3.5. Thus

$$\hat{g}(k, \sigma) = (2\pi)^{3/2} i^k \int_{|x|<\rho} e^{-ik\psi} f(x) J_k(-\sigma|x|) dx. \tag{4.17}$$

Now we make use of Debye's asymptotic relation for the Bessel function; see section 1.3.5. It states that $|J_k(t)|$ decays exponentially as $|k|, |t| \rightarrow \infty$ provided that $|t| \leq \vartheta |k|$ with an arbitrary constant $\vartheta < 1$. Loosely speaking, $|J_k(t)|$ is small for $|t| < |k|$ and $|t|, |k|$ is large. We conclude from (4.17) that $\hat{g}(k, \sigma)$ is small for $|\sigma\rho| < |k|$. Combining this with our conclusion from (4.16), we find that $\hat{g}$ is small outside the set

$$K = \{(k, \sigma) : |\sigma| < \Omega, \ |\sigma\rho| < |k|\}; \tag{4.18}$$

see Figure 4.3.

With the help of Theorem 4.5, we now can find the correct sampling conditions for the function g. Assume $g(\varphi, s)$ is sampled at

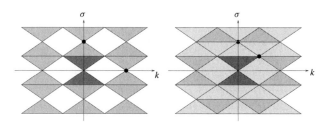

Figure 4.4. *Translates of K with respect to the reciprocal lattice for standard parallel scanning (left) and interlaced scanning (right). Dots indicate the generators of the reciprocal lattice, i.e., the columns of $2\pi(W^{-1})^T$.*

$$\varphi = \varphi_j = j\Delta\varphi, \quad \Delta\varphi = \frac{\pi}{p}, \quad j = 0, \ldots, p-1, \tag{4.19}$$

$$s = s_\ell = \ell\Delta s, \quad \Delta s = \frac{\rho}{q}, \quad \ell = -q, \ldots, q.$$

Since $g(\varphi + \pi, -s) = g(\varphi, s)$, this means that g is known on the lattice L_W generated by

$$W = \begin{pmatrix} \Delta\varphi & 0 \\ 0 & \Delta s \end{pmatrix}.$$

The reciprocal lattice $L_W^\perp$ is generated by

$$2\pi(W^{-1})^T = \begin{pmatrix} 2\pi/\Delta\varphi & 0 \\ 0 & 2\pi/\Delta s \end{pmatrix}.$$

From Figure 4.3 we see that the translates of K with respect to $L_W^\perp$ are mutually disjoint—except possibly for boundary points—if and only if

$$2\pi/\Delta\varphi \geq 2\rho\Omega, \quad 2\pi/\Delta s \geq 2\Omega$$

or

$$\Delta\varphi \leq \frac{\pi}{\rho\Omega}, \quad \Delta s \leq \frac{\pi}{\Omega}. \tag{4.20}$$

These are the correct sampling conditions for the standard parallel scanning scheme (4.19). In practice one wants to use as few data as possible for obtaining a certain resolution Ω. This means that one stipulates equality in (4.20). In that case, the relation between p, q is $p = \pi q$. Since p, q are integers, this equality is to be understood in an approximate sense. Some of the translates of K with respect to $L_W^\perp$ in the case of equality in (4.20) are drawn in Figure 4.4. It is clear that they do not cover the plane completely. Diamond-shaped regions between the translates remain uncovered. This indicates that the sampling is not optimal as far as the number of data is concerned. If (4.20) is satisfied with equality, then the number of data is

$$\frac{\pi}{\Delta\varphi}\frac{2\rho}{\Delta s} = \frac{2}{\pi}\rho^2\Omega^2. \tag{4.21}$$

In order to get a nonoverlapping covering of the plane, hence a more efficient sampling scheme, we choose as reciprocal lattice

$$2\pi (W^{-1})^T = \begin{pmatrix} \rho\Omega & 0 \\ \Omega & 2\Omega \end{pmatrix};$$

see Figure 4.4. This leads to the lattice L_W with

$$W = \frac{\pi}{\Omega\rho} \begin{pmatrix} 2 & -1 \\ 0 & \rho \end{pmatrix}.$$

This lattice is 2π-periodic in φ if $\Omega\rho$ is an integer. This can always be achieved by slight changes in Ω and ρ. In that case, L_W is given by the parallel interlaced scheme

$$\varphi = \varphi_j = j\Delta\varphi, \quad \Delta\varphi = \frac{\pi}{\Omega\rho},$$

$$s = s_{j\ell} = \ell\Delta s, \quad \Delta s = \frac{\pi}{\Omega}, \quad \ell + j \text{ even.} \tag{4.22}$$

If $\Omega\rho$ is even, then j in (4.22) can be restricted to $j = 0, \ldots, \Omega\rho - 1$ since $g(\varphi_{j+\Omega\rho}, s) = g(\varphi_j, -s)$ in that case. This means that the number of data in (4.22) is

$$\frac{\pi}{\Delta\varphi} \frac{1}{2} \frac{2\rho}{\Delta s} = \frac{1}{\pi}\rho^2\Omega^2, \tag{4.23}$$

which is only one-half the number (4.21) required by the standard parallel scheme (4.19). Hence for $\Omega\rho$ even, the interlaced scheme (4.22) yields the same resolution as the standard scheme (4.19) with only one-half the data. Interlaced scanning was suggested by Rattey and Lindgren (1981) based on the previous analysis and by Cormack (1978) in a purely geometric fashion.

So far we have considered the parallel scanning geometry. For the fan beam geometry, the treatment is the same, although technically more complicated. In this case, the 2π-periodic function

$$g(\beta, \alpha) = (Rf)(\theta, r\sin\alpha), \quad \theta = \begin{pmatrix} \cos(\beta + \alpha - \pi/2) \\ \sin(\beta + \alpha - \pi/2) \end{pmatrix}, \tag{4.24}$$

is sampled at the points β_j, α_ℓ in (3.4). We have $P = 2\pi\begin{pmatrix} 1 & 0 \\ 0 & 1 \end{pmatrix}$ and $L_P^\perp = \mathbb{Z}^2$. The Fourier transform of g is now

$$\hat{g}(k, m) = \frac{1}{4\pi^2} \int_0^{2\pi} \int_0^{2\pi} g(\beta, \alpha)e^{-ik\beta - im\alpha}, \quad k, m \in \mathbb{Z}.$$

A lengthy analysis (see Palamodov (1995)) shows that $\hat{g}$ is small outside the set

$$K = \{(k, m) \in \mathbb{Z}^2 : |k - m| < \Omega r, \ |k|r < |k - m|\rho\}; \tag{4.25}$$

see Figure 4.5. The standard fan beam sampling scheme is

$$\beta_j = j\Delta\beta, \quad \Delta\beta = \frac{2\pi}{p}, \quad j = 0, \ldots, p - 1,$$

$$\alpha_\ell = \ell\Delta\alpha, \quad \Delta\alpha = \frac{\overline{\alpha}}{q}, \quad \ell = -q, \ldots, q, \tag{4.26}$$

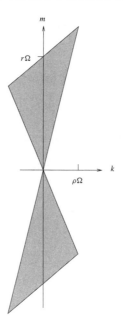

Figure 4.5. *The set K of* (4.25) *for* $\rho/r = 1/3$.

with the fan angle $2\bar{\alpha}$, $\bar{\alpha} = \arcsin(\rho/r)$. Thus the sampling lattice L_W and its reciprocal $L_W^{\perp}$ are generated by

$$W = \begin{pmatrix} \Delta\beta & 0 \\ 0 & \Delta\alpha \end{pmatrix}, \quad 2\pi(W^{-1})^T = \begin{pmatrix} 2\pi/\Delta\beta & 0 \\ 0 & 2\pi/\Delta\alpha \end{pmatrix}.$$

From Figure 4.5 we see that the translates of K from (4.25) with respect to $L_W^{\perp}$ are mutually disjoint—except possibly for boundary points—if and only if

$$2\pi/\Delta\beta \geq 2\Omega r \frac{\rho}{r+\rho}, \qquad 2\pi/\Delta\alpha \geq 2\Omega r$$

or

$$\Delta\beta \leq \frac{r+\rho}{r}\frac{\pi}{\Omega\rho}, \qquad \Delta\alpha \leq \frac{\pi}{\Omega r}. \tag{4.27}$$

These are the sampling conditions for the standard fan beam scanning geometry (4.26).

The minimal number of data is

$$\frac{2\bar{\alpha}}{\Delta\alpha}\frac{2\pi}{\Delta\beta} = \frac{1}{\pi}\frac{4r}{r+\rho}\frac{\arcsin\rho/r}{\rho/r}\rho^2\Omega^2. \tag{4.28}$$

The sampling conditions (4.27) are the best possible. Violating them leads to severe artifacts in the reconstruction. Various differing conditions have been given in the literature: the suboptimal results

$$\Delta\beta \leq \frac{\pi}{\Omega\rho}, \qquad \Delta\beta \leq \left(1 - \frac{\rho}{r}\right)\frac{\pi}{\Omega\rho}$$

of Natterer (1986) and Joseph and Schulz (1980), respectively, and the overly optimistic one

$$\Delta\beta \leq 2\min\left(1, \frac{1+3\rho/r}{2}\right)\frac{\pi}{\Omega\omega}$$

of Rattey and Lindgren (1981). For large r all these results coincide, but for $r \sim \rho$ the difference is substantial.

Some of the $L_W^{\perp}$-translates of K are sketched in Figure 4.6. As in the parallel case we see that the translates do not cover the plane completely. However, if we put

$$2\pi(W^{-1})^T = \Omega\left(\begin{array}{cc} \rho & 0 \\ \rho-r & 2r \end{array}\right),$$

then the coverage is complete. The lattice L_W with

$$W = \frac{\pi}{\Omega\rho}\left(\begin{array}{cc} 2 & 1-\rho/r \\ 0 & \rho/r \end{array}\right)$$

is 2π-periodic if Ωr, $\Omega\rho$ are integer. In that case, L_W can be written as

$$\alpha = \alpha_{\ell} = \ell\Delta\alpha, \quad \Delta\alpha = \frac{\pi}{\Omega r},$$

$$\beta = \beta_{\ell j} = j\Delta\beta + \ell(r/\rho - 1)\Delta\alpha, \quad \Delta\beta = \frac{2\pi}{\Omega\rho}. \tag{4.29}$$

The number of data in (4.29) is

$$\frac{2\bar{\alpha}}{\Delta\alpha}\frac{2\pi}{\Delta\beta} = \frac{2}{\pi}\frac{\arcsin\rho/r}{\rho/r}\rho^2\Omega^2.$$

If $\Omega\rho$ is even, then each line occurs exactly twice in (4.29). More precisely, the pairs (ℓ, j) and $(-\ell, j+\ell-\Omega\rho/2)$ parametrize the same line. Thus the actual number in that case is only one-half this number, leaving us with

$$\frac{1}{\pi}\frac{\arcsin\rho/r}{\rho/r}\rho^2\Omega^2 \tag{4.30}$$

data. For $r \gg \rho$ (e.g., $r \geq 2\rho$), this is essentially the number (4.23) of the parallel interlaced scheme. Note that (4.30) is by a factor of $4r/(r+\rho)$—a number between 2 and 4—smaller than the number (4.28) for the standard fan beam geometry.

In Figure 4.7, the rays of efficient and standard fan beam geometries with the same resolution are displayed. It can be seen with the naked eye that the efficient geometry is much less dense and, incidentally, more regular than the standard scheme.

Unfortunately, it is difficult to implement the efficient scanning geometry (4.29) for a commercial scanner. For details, see Natterer (1993a, 1995).

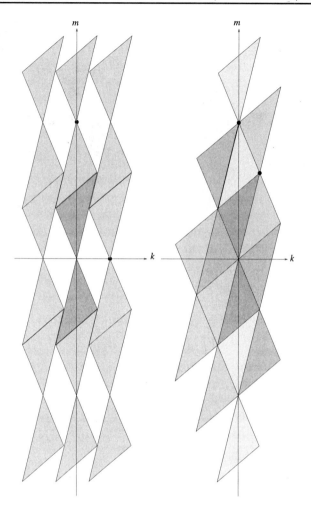

Figure 4.6. *Translates of K with respect to the reciprocal lattice for standard fan beam scanning (left) and for efficient fan beam scanning (right). Dots indicate the generators of the reciprocal lattice, i.e., the columns of the matrix $2\pi(W^{-1})^T$.*

More flexible efficient sampling schemes were suggested by Faridani (1990). For applications to diffraction tomography see Faridani (1998). The 3D case is largely unexplored; see, however, Desbat (1996) and Palamodov (1995).

4.4   The FFT on Nonequispaced Grids

In some applications, we have to evaluate

$$\hat{y}_k = \sum_{\ell=-q}^{q-1} e^{-\pi i x_\ell k/q} y_\ell, \quad k = -q, \ldots, q-1, \tag{4.31}$$

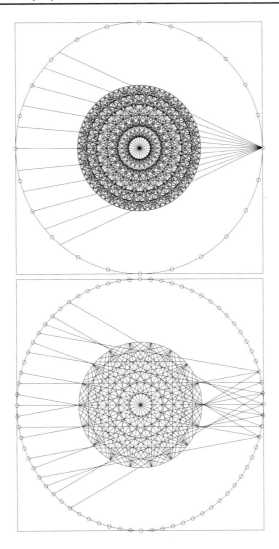

Figure 4.7. *Fan beam geometries with the same resolution. Radius of the circular reconstruction region is ρ, radius of the circle of sources $r = 2\rho$, $\Omega\rho = 15$. Top: Standard geometry (4.27) with 264 lines. Bottom: Efficient geometry (4.29) with 99 lines.*

or

$$\hat{y}_\ell = \sum_{k=-q}^{q-1} e^{-\pi i x_\ell k/q} y_k, \quad \ell = -q, \ldots, q-1, \tag{4.32}$$

where x_k is arbitrary. For $x_k = k$ we are back at (1.22). We refer to (4.31) as ned (nonequispaced data) and to (4.32) as ner (nonequispaced results); see the survey article of Ware (1998).

We follow the treatment of Fourmont (1999). It is based on the following lemma.

Let $0 < \beta < \alpha$ and $\alpha + \beta < 2\pi$. Let ϕ be a function continuous in $[-\alpha, \alpha]$, vanishing outside $[-\alpha, \alpha]$ and nonzero in $[-\beta, \beta]$. Then for $x \in \mathbb{R}^1$ and $|\xi| \le \beta$,

$$e^{-ix\xi} = \frac{(2\pi)^{-1/2}}{\phi(\xi)} \sum_m \hat{\phi}(x - m) e^{-im\xi}. \tag{4.33}$$

Putting $\xi = \beta k/q$, $x = \frac{\pi}{\beta} x_\ell$, in (4.33) yields for $|k| \le q$

$$e^{-i\pi x_\ell k/q} = \frac{(2\pi)^{-1/2}}{\phi(\beta k/q)} \sum_m \hat{\phi}\left(\frac{\pi}{\beta} x_\ell - m\right) e^{-i\beta mk/q}. \tag{4.34}$$

Inserting (4.34) into (4.31) and rearranging, we obtain

$$\hat{y}_k = \frac{(2\pi)^{-1/2}}{\phi(\beta k/q)} \sum_m e^{-i\beta mk/q} \sum_{\ell=-q}^{q-1} \hat{\phi}\left(\frac{\pi}{\beta} x_\ell - m\right) y_\ell, \quad k = -q, \ldots, q-1. \tag{4.35}$$

Likewise, inserting (4.34) into (4.32), we obtain

$$\hat{y}_\ell = (2\pi)^{-1/2} \sum_m \hat{\phi}\left(\frac{\pi}{\beta} x_\ell - m\right) \sum_{k=-q}^{q-1} e^{-i\beta mk/q} \frac{y_k}{\phi(\beta k/q)}, \quad \ell = -q, \ldots, q-1. \tag{4.36}$$

Now we choose ϕ such that $\hat{\phi}$ is decaying rapidly away from 0. A good choice for ϕ is

$$\phi(\xi) = \begin{cases} I_0(K\sqrt{\alpha^2 - \xi^2}), & |\xi| \le \alpha, \\ 0, & |\xi| > \alpha, \end{cases} \tag{4.37}$$

with I_0 the modified Bessel function of order 0; see section 1.3.5. In that case,

$$\hat{\phi}(x) = \sqrt{\frac{2}{\pi}} \frac{\sinh(\alpha\sqrt{K^2 - x^2})}{\sqrt{K^2 - x^2}}; \tag{4.38}$$

see Oberhettinger (1993). For alternative choices of ϕ see Dutt and Rohklin (1993), Beylkin (1995), and Steidl (1998). The treatment in these works is very similar, except that (4.33) holds only approximately.

(4.35) is the nonequispaced FFT in the ned case. The ℓ-sum in (4.35) can be evaluated quickly since $\hat{\phi}$ is decaying fast; only the terms with $|\frac{\pi}{\beta} x_\ell - m| \le K$ need to be taken into account. The m-sum is an equispaced FFT of length $2Q$, where $Q = \frac{\pi}{\beta} q$. Typically $\beta = \frac{\pi}{2}$, i.e., $Q = 2q$. The process is finished by scaling with $\phi(\beta k/q)$.

Likewise, (4.36) is the nonequispaced FFT in the ner case. It starts with the scaling operation, followed by an equispaced FFT of length $2Q$, and ends with doing the m-sum, which again can be computed quickly since only the terms with $|\frac{\pi}{\beta} x_\ell - m| \le K$ contribute significantly.

A good choice for α, β is α slightly smaller than $\frac{3}{2}\pi$, $\beta = \frac{1}{2}\pi$. In that case, it suffices to choose $K = 3, 6$ for single and double precision, respectively. See Fourmont (1999) for details.

Chapter 5

Reconstruction Algorithms

In this section, we give a detailed description of reconstruction algorithms for standard situations. Some nonstandard cases are dealt with in Chapter 6. We make use of the inversion formulas of Chapter 2 and of the material on sampling of Chapter 4.

5.1 The Filtered Backprojection Algorithm

The filtered backprojection algorithm is the most important reconstruction algorithm in tomography. It can be viewed as a numerical implementation of the inversion formula of Theorem 2.6 for the Radon transform. However, it is easier to start out from Theorem 2.3, as follows. Let $g = Rf$ and $V = R^*v$. Then

$$V * f = R^*(v * g). \tag{5.1}$$

The idea is to choose V as an approximation to the Dirac δ function and to determine v from $V = R^*v$. Then $V * f$ is an approximation to f which can be computed by convolving ("filtering") the data g by v, followed by a backprojection of the convolved data. This explains the name of the algorithm.

We consider only radially symmetric functions V, i.e., $V(\xi)$ depends on $|\xi|$ only. Then v can be assumed to be an even function of s only. Theorem 2.4 yields

$$\hat{V}(\xi) = 2(2\pi)^{(n-1)/2}|\xi|^{1-n}\hat{v}(|\xi|), \tag{5.2}$$

where $\hat{V}$, $\hat{v}$ are the n and 1D Fourier transforms, respectively.

Now we choose V. We want to design the algorithm in such a way that it reconstructs faithfully functions f of (essential) bandwidth Ω. This is the case if $\hat{V}(\xi) = (2\pi)^{-n/2}$ for $|\xi| \leq \Omega$, and we assume that $\hat{V}(\xi) = 0$ for $|\xi| > \Omega$.

More generally, we allow for a filter factor $\hat{\phi}(\sigma)$ which is close to 1 for $|\sigma| \leq 1$ and which vanishes for $|\sigma| > 1$. We put

$$\hat{V}_\Omega(\xi) = (2\pi)^{-n/2}\hat{\phi}(|\xi|/\Omega). \tag{5.3}$$

81

For the corresponding function v_Ω with $R^* v_\Omega = V_\Omega$, we obtain from (5.2)

$$\hat{v}_\Omega(\sigma) = \frac{1}{2}(2\pi)^{1/2-n}|\sigma|^{n-1}\hat{\phi}(\sigma/\Omega). \tag{5.4}$$

In light of Theorem 2.6, (5.4) is easy to understand: multiplication in Fourier space with $|\sigma|^{n-1}$ corresponds—up to a constant factor—to the operation $H(\frac{\partial}{\partial s})^{n-1}$ for n even and to $(\frac{\partial}{\partial s})^{n-1}$ for n odd. Many choices of $\hat{\phi}$ have been suggested in the literature; see Chang and Herman (1980) and Smith and Keinert (1985). We restrict ourselves to a few widely used filters. For $\hat{\phi}$ the ideal low pass, i.e., $\hat{\phi}(\sigma) = 1$ for $0 \le \sigma \le 1$ and $\hat{\phi} = 0$ elsewhere, we obtain for $n = 2$ the Ram–Lak filter

$$v_\Omega(s) = \frac{\Omega^2}{4\pi^2}u(\Omega s), \quad u(s) = \operatorname{sinc}(s) - \frac{1}{2}\left(\operatorname{sinc}\left(\frac{s}{2}\right)\right)^2 \tag{5.5}$$

with the sinc function (4.8). It is named after Ramachandran and Lakshminarayanan (1971) but was suggested, in a slightly different form, by Bracewell and Riddle (1967). For $s = \frac{\pi}{\Omega}\ell$, $\ell \in \mathbb{Z}$, (5.5) simplifies into

$$v_\Omega\left(\frac{\pi}{\Omega}\ell\right) = \frac{\Omega^2}{2\pi^2}\begin{cases} 1/4, & \ell = 0, \\ 0, & \ell \neq 0 \text{ even}, \\ -1/(\pi^2\ell^2), & \ell \text{ odd}. \end{cases} \tag{5.6}$$

Another possibility is the cosine filter factor

$$\hat{\phi}(\sigma) = \begin{cases} \cos\frac{\sigma\pi}{2}, & 0 \le \sigma \le 1, \\ 0, & \sigma > 1. \end{cases}$$

In contrast to the filter factors discussed above, it vanishes at the cutoff point $\sigma = 1$. Thus there is a continuous transition between the regions where $\hat{\phi}(\sigma) > 0$ and where $\hat{\phi}(\sigma) = 0$. The corresponding filter for $n = 2$ is

$$v_\Omega(s) = \frac{\Omega^2}{8\pi^2}\left(u\left(s\Omega + \frac{\pi}{2}\right) + u\left(s\Omega - \frac{\pi}{2}\right)\right) \tag{5.7}$$

with the function u from (5.5).

Shepp and Logan (1974) suggested the filter factor

$$\hat{\phi}(\sigma) = \begin{cases} \operatorname{sinc}(\sigma\pi/2), & 0 \le \sigma \le 1, \\ 0, & \sigma > 1, \end{cases}$$

yielding for $n = 2$

$$v_\Omega(s) = \frac{\Omega^2}{2\pi^3}u(\Omega s), \quad u(s) = \begin{cases} \frac{\frac{\pi}{2}-s\sin s}{(\frac{\pi}{2})^2-s^2}, & s \neq \pm\frac{\pi}{2}, \\ \frac{1}{\pi}, & s = \pm\frac{\pi}{2}. \end{cases} \tag{5.8}$$

Again considerable simplification occurs for $s = \frac{\pi}{\Omega}\ell$, $\ell \in \mathbb{Z}$, in which case

$$v_\Omega\left(\frac{\pi}{\Omega}\ell\right) = \frac{\Omega^2}{\pi^4}\frac{1}{1-4\ell^2}. \tag{5.9}$$

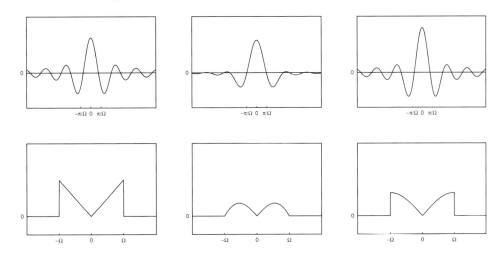

Figure 5.1. *Filters v_Ω (top row) and their Fourier transforms $\hat{v}_\Omega$ (bottom row). Left: Ram–Lak (5.5). Middle:* cos *(5.7). Right: Shepp–Logan (5.8).*

The filters v_Ω from (5.5), (5.7), and (5.8) are graphed in Figure 5.1.

For $n = 3$, Marr, Chen, and Lauterbur (1981) suggested the filter factor

$$\hat{\phi}(\sigma) = \begin{cases} (\mathrm{sinc}(\sigma\pi/2))^2, & 0 \leq \sigma \leq 1, \\ 0, & \sigma > 1, \end{cases}$$

leading to the filter

$$v_\Omega(s) = \frac{\Omega^3}{4\pi^6} \frac{\sin(\pi u)(2u^2 - 1)}{u(u-1)(u+1)}, \quad u = \frac{\Omega s}{\pi}, \tag{5.10}$$

which, for $s = \frac{\pi}{\Omega}\ell,\ \ell \in \mathbb{Z}$, reduces to

$$v_\Omega\left(\frac{\pi}{\Omega}\ell\right) = \frac{\Omega^3}{8\pi^5} \begin{cases} 2, & \ell = 0, \\ -1, & |\ell| = 1, \\ 0, & |\ell| > 1. \end{cases} \tag{5.11}$$

We see that this filter amounts to taking second order differences. In view of the inversion formula (2.14) for $n = 3$, this is not surprising.

Once v has been chosen, (5.1) has to be evaluated to obtain the approximation $V * f$ to f. This has to be done in a discrete setting. The necessary discretization of (5.1) depends of course on the way the function $g = Rf$ is sampled. Therefore, we consider the different scanning modes separately.

5.1.1 Standard parallel scanning

Here $g(\theta, s)$ is available for

$$\theta = \theta_j = \begin{pmatrix} \cos\varphi_j \\ \sin\varphi_j \end{pmatrix}, \quad \varphi_j = j\Delta\varphi, \quad \Delta\varphi = \frac{\pi}{p}, \quad j = 0,\dots,p-1,$$

$$s = s_\ell = \ell\Delta s, \quad \Delta s = \frac{\rho}{q}, \quad \ell = -q,\dots,q. \tag{5.12}$$

f is assumed to be zero outside the reconstruction region $|x| < \rho$, and we assume f to be essentially Ω-band-limited.

In a first step, we discretize the convolution integral

$$(v_\Omega * g)(\theta,s) = \int_{-\rho}^{\rho} v_\Omega(s-t)g(\theta,t)dt.$$

v_Ω is band-limited with bandwidth Ω, and g, as a function of the second argument, is essentially Ω-band-limited since f is, as follows immediately from Theorem 2.1. Hence we may apply Theorem 4.2 to the functions $f_1(t) = v_\Omega(s-t)$, $f_2(t) = g(\theta,t)$ and the lattice $L_W = \Delta s \mathbb{Z}$ provided that

$$\Delta s \le \frac{\pi}{\Omega}, \tag{5.13}$$

obtaining

$$(v_\Omega * g)(\theta,s) = \Delta s \sum_{\ell=-q}^{q} v_\Omega(s-s_\ell)g(\theta,s_\ell). \tag{5.14}$$

Strictly speaking, this is not quite correct since g is not strictly Ω-band-limited, but the error in (5.14) is negligible if, as we have assumed, f hence g is essentially Ω-band-limited.

In a second step, we discretize the backprojection

$$R^*(v_\Omega * g)(x) = \int_0^{2\pi} (v_\Omega * g)(\theta, x\cdot\theta)d\varphi, \quad \theta = \begin{pmatrix} \cos\varphi \\ \sin\varphi \end{pmatrix}. \tag{5.15}$$

The function $h(\varphi) = (v_\Omega * g)(\theta, x\cdot\theta)$ has period 2π (in fact even π). We want to show that h is essentially $2\Omega\rho$-band-limited, i.e., that

$$\hat{h}(k) = \frac{1}{2\pi}\int_0^{2\pi} e^{-ik\varphi}(v_\Omega * g)(\theta, x\cdot\theta)d\varphi, \quad k \in \mathbb{Z},$$

is negligible for $|k| > 2\Omega\rho$. We have by (1.7) and Theorem 2.1

$$(v_\Omega * g)(\theta, x\cdot\theta) = ((v_\Omega * g)^\wedge)^\sim(\theta, x\cdot\theta)$$

$$= (2\pi)^{1/2}(\hat{v}_\Omega\hat{g})^\sim(\theta, x\cdot\theta)$$

$$= \int_{-\Omega}^{\Omega} \hat{v}_\Omega(\sigma)\hat{g}(\theta,\sigma)e^{i\sigma x\cdot\theta}d\sigma$$

$$= (2\pi)^{1/2}\int_{-\Omega}^{\Omega} \hat{v}_\Omega(\sigma)\hat{f}(\sigma\theta)e^{i\sigma x\cdot\theta}d\sigma$$

$$= (2\pi)^{-1/2}\int_{|y|<\rho} f(y)\int_{-\Omega}^{\Omega} \hat{v}_\Omega(\sigma)e^{i\sigma\theta\cdot(x-y)}d\sigma dy,$$

and hence

$$\hat{h}(k) = (2\pi)^{-3/2} \int_{|y|<\rho} f(y) \int_{-\Omega}^{\Omega} \hat{v}_\Omega(\sigma) \int_0^{2\pi} e^{i\sigma\theta\cdot(x-y)-ik\varphi} d\varphi d\sigma dy.$$

The φ integral has already been encountered in the derivation of (4.17). We have found there that it equals

$$2\pi i^k e^{-ik\psi} J_k(-\sigma|x-y|),$$

where ψ is such that $y - x = |x - y|\binom{\cos\psi}{\sin\psi}$. Hence finally we obtain

$$\hat{h}(k) = (2\pi)^{-1/2} i^k \int_{|y|<\rho} f(y) e^{-ik\psi} \int_{-\Omega}^{\Omega} \hat{v}_\Omega(\sigma) J_k(-\sigma|x-y|) d\sigma dy. \tag{5.16}$$

Thus again by Debye's asymptotic relation as in (4.17), $\hat{h}(k)$ is small for $2\Omega\rho < |k|$, i.e., h has essential bandwidth $2\Omega\rho$.

The trapezoidal rule with stepsize $\Delta\varphi$ is exact for functions of bandwidth $2\Omega\rho$ provided that $\Delta\varphi \leq \frac{2\pi}{2\Omega\rho}$; see section 4.2. Thus we have approximately

$$\int_0^{2\pi} (v_\Omega * g)(\theta, x\cdot\theta) d\varphi = \frac{\pi}{p} \sum_{j=0}^{2p-1} (v_\Omega * g)(\theta_j, x\cdot\theta_j)$$

$$= \frac{2\pi}{p} \sum_{j=0}^{p-1} (v_\Omega * g)(\theta_j, x\cdot\theta_j) \tag{5.17}$$

provided that

$$\Delta\varphi \leq \frac{\pi}{\Omega\rho}. \tag{5.18}$$

Note that (5.13) and (5.18) are equivalent to (4.20), which is the necessary and sufficient condition for (5.12) to have resolution Ω.

Combining (5.14) with (5.17) leads to

$$(V_\Omega * f)(x) = \frac{2\pi}{p} \Delta s \sum_{j=0}^{p-1} \sum_{\ell=-q}^{q} v_\Omega(x\cdot\theta_j - s_\ell) g(\theta_j, s_\ell). \tag{5.19}$$

This defines an algorithm for the computation of $(V_\Omega * f)(x)$ from the discrete data (5.12).

Let us study the complexity of (5.19). For each x, it requires $O(pq)$ operations. Since f has essential bandwidth Ω, (5.19) has to be evaluated on a lattice with stepsize $\frac{\pi}{\Omega}$, i.e., for $O(\Omega^2)$ values of x. Thus we end up with $O(\Omega^2 pq)$ operations. In view of (4.20) this is a complexity of $O(\Omega^4)$ at least.

A substantial reduction of this complexity is possible by an interpolation step. Since the function $v_\Omega * g$ is Ω-band-limited—as is v_Ω—it suffices to compute the values $(v_\Omega * g)(\theta_j, s_\ell)$. This requires $O(pq^2)$ operations or $O(pq \log q)$ operations if FFT is used. The values $(v_\Omega * g)(\theta_j, x\cdot\theta_j)$, which are needed in (5.19), are then computed by linear interpolation. The evaluation of (5.19) can now be done in only $O(p)$ operations for each

x. Thus the algorithm requires only $O(\Omega^2 p) + O(pq^2) = O(\Omega^3)$ operations. This is the final form of the filtered backprojection algorithm for standard parallel data.

ALGORITHM 5.1 (filtered backprojection algorithm for standard parallel geometry)

Data: The values $g_{j,\ell} = g(\theta_j, s_\ell)$, $j = 0, \ldots, p-1$, $\ell = -q, \ldots, q$, from (5.12).

Step 1: For $j = 0, \ldots, p-1$, carry out the discrete convolution

$$h_{j,k} = \Delta s \sum_{\ell=-q}^{q} v_\Omega(s_k - s_\ell)g_{j,\ell}, \quad k = -q, \ldots, q.$$

Step 2: For each reconstruction point x, compute the discrete backprojection

$$f_{FB}(x) = \frac{2\pi}{p} \sum_{j=0}^{p-1} ((1 - \vartheta)h_{j,k} + \vartheta h_{j,k+1}),$$

where $k = k(j, x)$ and $\vartheta = \vartheta(j, x)$ are determined by

$$t = \frac{x \cdot \theta_j}{\Delta s}, \quad k = \lfloor t \rfloor, \quad \vartheta = t - k.$$

Here $\lfloor t \rfloor$ is the largest integer $\leq t$.

Result: $f_{FB}(x)$ is an approximation to $f(x)$.

The algorithm depends on the parameters Ω, p, q and on the choice of v_Ω. It is designed to reconstruct a function f with support in the circle $|x| < \rho$ and with essential bandwidth Ω. The conditions (4.20) (or (5.14) and (5.18)) should be satisfied. In the following, we study the effect of violating these conditions and of unsuitable choices of v_Ω.

1. The condition $\Delta s \leq \frac{\pi}{\Omega}$ has to be strictly satisfied. Otherwise, (5.14) does not hold even approximately, and the convolution step yields results that are completely unacceptable.

2. If the condition $\Delta\varphi \leq \frac{\pi}{\Omega\rho}$ is not satisfied, then the number p of directions permits artifact free reconstructions only within a circle of radius $\rho' < \rho$, where $\Delta\varphi = \frac{\pi}{\Omega\rho'}$. This means that large artifacts occur in a distance of $2\rho'$ from high-density objects. This can be avoided if we sacrifice resolution by choosing instead of Ω a bandwidth $\Omega' < \Omega$ such that $\Delta\varphi = \frac{\pi}{\Omega'\rho}$ in the convolution step.

3. Filter functions v_Ω whose "kernel sum"

$$\sum_\ell v_\Omega(s_\ell)$$

does not vanish should not be used. In order to see what is wrong with a nonvanishing kernel sum, we compute for $\Delta s \leq \frac{\pi}{\Omega}$

$$\hat{v}_\Omega(0) = (2\pi)^{-1/2} \int_{\mathbb{R}^1} v_\Omega(s)ds = (2\pi)^{-1/2} \sum_\ell v_\Omega(s_\ell).$$

The evaluation of the integral by the trapezoidal is correct since v_Ω has bandwidth Ω. From (5.2) we see that

$$\hat{V}_\Omega(\xi) = 2\sqrt{2\pi}\,\frac{1}{|\xi|}\hat{v}_\Omega(0) + \mathrm{O}(1)$$

for $|\xi| \to 0$. Thus $\hat{V}_\Omega$ has a singularity at the origin if the kernel sum is $\neq 0$. In that case, V_Ω cannot be a good approximation to the δ function whose Fourier transform is constant.

4. Sometimes one wants to work with filters $v_{\Omega,h}$ that are linear interpolates of a band-limited filter v_Ω, i.e.,

$$v_{\Omega,h}(s) = \frac{s - \ell h}{h}v_\Omega((\ell + 1)h) + \frac{(\ell + 1)h - s}{h}v_\Omega(\ell h), \quad \ell h \le s < (\ell + 1)h.$$

In that case, one has to make sure that each interpolation point $h\ell$ coincides with a sampling point $k\Delta s$, i.e., $h = M\Delta s$ with an integer M. This was noticed by K. T. Smith (1985) and was analyzed in Natterer and Faridani (1990).

   We remark that the interpolation step in the backprojection algorithm is equivalent to using the interpolated filter $v_{\Omega,h}$ with $h = \Delta s$ in the convolution step. For v_Ω, the Shepp–Logan filter (5.8), one can show that for $h = \pi/\Omega$

$$\hat{v}_{\Omega,h}(\sigma) = \frac{1}{2}(2\pi)^{-3/2}|\sigma|\phi(\sigma/\Omega),$$

$$\phi(\sigma) = \left|\mathrm{sinc}\,\frac{\sigma\pi}{2}\right|^3; \tag{5.20}$$

see Shepp and Logan (1974) or Natterer and Faridani (1990). Thus we can interpret the filtered backprojection algorithm implemented in Algorithm 5.1 as a filtered backprojection algorithm without interpolation as given in (5.19) using the (non–band-limited) filter (5.20).

5. Usually linear interpolation in Step 2 is sufficient. However, for difficult functions f—typically if f contains high-density objects at the boundary of the reconstruction region—linear interpolation generates visible artifacts. In that case, an oversampling procedure similar to the one of Algorithm 5.2 below is advisable.

5.1.2   Parallel interlaced scanning

Here $g(\theta, s)$ is available for

$$\theta = \theta_j, \quad s = s_\ell \quad \text{as in (5.12), but only for } \ell + j \text{ even.} \tag{5.21}$$

Again we assume f to be zero outside $|x| < \rho$ and essentially Ω-band-limited. p has to be even.

We write (5.1) for $v = v_\Omega$ in the form

$$(V_\Omega * f)(x) = \int_0^{2\pi} \int_{\mathbb{R}^1} v_\Omega(x \cdot \theta - s)g(\theta, s)\,ds\,d\varphi, \quad \theta = \begin{pmatrix} \cos\varphi \\ \sin\varphi \end{pmatrix}.$$

For the discretization of this integral, we use Theorem 4.5 for the lattice L_W from (4.22) or (5.21) and the set K from (4.18) or Figure 4.3. We put $f_1(\varphi, s) = v_\Omega(x \cdot \theta - s)$ and compute the Fourier transform of f_1 in the sense of Theorem 4.5, i.e.,

$$\hat{f}_1(k, \sigma) = (2\pi)^{-3/2} \int_0^{2\pi} \int_{\mathbb{R}^1} f_1(\varphi, s) e^{-i(k\varphi + s\sigma)} d\varphi ds$$

$$= (2\pi)^{-3/2} \int_0^{2\pi} \int_{\mathbb{R}^1} v_\Omega(x \cdot \theta - s) e^{-i(k\varphi + s\sigma)} d\varphi ds$$

$$= (2\pi)^{-1} \hat{v}_\Omega(\sigma) \int_0^{2\pi} e^{-ik\varphi - ix \cdot \theta\sigma} d\varphi.$$

The last integral has been evaluated in the derivation of (4.17). We obtain

$$\hat{f}_1(k, \sigma) = i^k e^{-ik\psi} \hat{v}_\Omega(\sigma) J_k(-\sigma|x|).$$

Again by Debye's asymptotic relation, we find that $\hat{f}_1(k, \sigma)$ is small for $|\sigma|\rho < |k|$, and of course $\hat{f}_1(k, \sigma) = 0$ for $|\sigma| > \Omega$. Hence $\hat{f}_1$ is small outside the set K of (4.18). The same is true for $f_2(\varphi, s) = g(\theta, s)$, as we have found in (4.17). Hence we can apply Theorem 4.5 to f_1, f_2. With $W = \frac{\pi}{\rho\Omega}\left(\begin{smallmatrix} 2 & -1 \\ 0 & \rho \end{smallmatrix}\right)$, $p = \rho\Omega$, $\Delta s = \pi/\Omega$, the hypothesis of the theorem is met, and we have $\det(W) = (2\pi/p)\Delta s$. Hence

$$(V_\Omega * f)(x) = \int_0^{2\pi} \int_{\mathbb{R}^1} v_\Omega(x \cdot \theta - s) g(\theta, s) ds d\varphi = \int_0^{2\pi} \int_{\mathbb{R}^1} f_1(\varphi, s) f_2(\varphi, s) ds d\varphi$$

$$= \frac{2\pi}{p} \Delta s \sum_{j=0}^{2p-1} \sum_{\ell=-q}^{q} {}' v_\Omega(x \cdot \theta_j - s_\ell) g(\theta_j, s_\ell) \qquad (5.22)$$

$$= 2 \frac{2\pi}{p} \Delta s \sum_{j=0}^{p-1} \sum_{\ell=-q}^{q} {}' v_\Omega(x \cdot \theta_j - s_\ell) g(\theta_j, s_\ell),$$

where the prime indicates that the ℓ-sum extends only over those ℓ for which $\ell + j$ is even. Thus we arrive at an expression analogous to (5.19), except that only the data with $j + \ell$ even are used, which is compensated for by a factor of 2.

The complexity of (5.22) is the same as the one of (5.19), namely, $O(\Omega^4)$. In (5.19) we reduced the complexity to $O(\Omega^3)$ by linear interpolation. Unfortunately, simple linear interpolation in (5.22) causes disastrous artifacts. In light of the 1D sampling theorem, this is easy to understand. The ℓ-sum in (5.22) is a discrete approximation to $v_\Omega * g$. But this approximation is very poor since the stepsize, due to the lack of the terms with $\ell + j$ odd, is $2\Delta s$, while the sampling theorem requires a stepsize of Δs. Nevertheless, (5.22) is a good approximation to $(V_\Omega * f)(x)$. This is possible only if the errors in the ℓ-sums cancel out when the j-sum is formed. Thus the success of (5.22) depends on a subtle interplay of the errors caused in the convolution step by insufficient sampling. The interpolation step as done in (5.19) hinders this subtle interplay.

Nevertheless, we can find an implementation with complexity $O(\Omega^3)$ of (5.22). We simply do the interpolation with a stepsize $\Delta s' \ll \Delta s$, e.g., $\Delta s' = \Delta s/M$. For M sufficiently large ($M = 16$ will do), the influence of the interpolation error is negligible.

ALGORITHM 5.2 (filtered backprojection for parallel interlaced geometry)

Data: The values $g_{j,\ell} = g(\theta_j, s_\ell)$, $j = 0, \ldots, p-1$, $\ell = -q, \ldots, q$, $\ell + j$ even from (5.12). p has to be even.

Step 1: Choose an integer $M > 0$ sufficiently large ($M = 16$ will do) and compute for $j = 0, \ldots, p-1$

$$h_{j,k} = 2\Delta s \sum_{\substack{\ell=-q \\ \ell+j \text{ even}}}^{q} v_\Omega \left(k\frac{\Delta s}{M} - s_\ell \right) g(\theta_j, s_\ell), \quad k = -Mq, \ldots, Mq.$$

Step 2: For each reconstruction point x, compute

$$f_{FB}(x) = \frac{2\pi}{p} \sum_{j=0}^{p-1} ((1 - \vartheta)h_{j,k} + \vartheta h_{j,k+1}),$$

where $k = k(j, x)$ and $\vartheta = \vartheta(j, x)$ are determined by

$$t = M\frac{x \cdot \theta_j}{\Delta s}, \quad k = \lfloor t \rfloor, \quad \vartheta = t - k.$$

Result: $f_{FB}(x)$ is an approximation to $f(x)$.

We study the various assumptions underlying this algorithm.

1. The algorithm is designed to reconstruct a function f supported in $|x| < \rho$ with essential bandwidth Ω. The sampling conditions (4.22), i.e.,

$$\Delta\varphi = \frac{\pi}{\Omega\rho}, \qquad \Delta s = \frac{\pi}{\Omega},$$

have to be satisfied. In contrast to the standard parallel geometry, oversatisfying these conditions (i.e., choosing $\Delta\varphi < \pi/\Omega\rho$ or $\Delta\varphi < \pi/\Omega$) may cause the translates of K (see Figure 4.4) to overlap, resulting in large artifacts. Thus p, q have to be tied to each other by $p = \pi q$. While this condition only prevents redundancy of the data in the standard case, it is mandatory for the interlaced geometry.

2. Only filters v_Ω with a continuous transition from nonzero to zero values, such as the cosine filter (5.7), should be used. This is because the additional filtering of the interpolation step in the standard case is not present here. Thus the only filtering done here stems from v_Ω. If v_Ω does not have a continuous transition, the ringing artifacts mentioned at the end of section 4.2 show up.

3. The artifacts produced by Algorithm 5.2 are quite different from those of Algorithm 5.1. This difference becomes clear from Figure 4.4. In the standard case, the translates of K meet only at high frequencies, while in the interlaced case they meet also at the edges $\rho|\sigma| = |k|$ in the low-frequency part. Thus the low-frequency component of aliasing is more pronounced in the interlaced geometry. One remedy is to restrict the support of f to a region slightly smaller than $|x| < \rho$ ($|x| < 0.95\rho$ will do). This reduces the overlap of the supports of $\hat{f}$ and its replicas along the edges $\rho|\sigma| = |k|$.

5.1.3   Standard fan beam scanning

Here the function Df is sampled at the points (3.4). This means that the function

$$g(\beta, \alpha) = (Rf)(\theta, r \sin \alpha), \quad \theta = \theta(\beta + \alpha - \pi/2),$$

is sampled at $\beta = \beta_j$, $\alpha = \alpha_\ell$. As usual, $\theta(\varphi) = (\cos \varphi, \sin \varphi)^T$. In standard fan beam scanning, we assume

$$\beta_j = j \Delta \beta, \quad \Delta \beta = \frac{2\pi}{p}, \quad j = 0, \ldots, p - 1,$$

$$\alpha_\ell = (\ell + \delta) \Delta \alpha, \quad \ell = -q, \ldots, q.$$

$$(5.23)$$

Here q is chosen such that the whole reconstruction region $|x| < \rho$ is covered by the rays. δ is the detector setoff, which is either 0 or $\pm 1/4$.

First, we derive the fan beam analogue of (5.1). In parallel coordinates φ, s, it reads, with $v = v_\Omega$,

$$(V_\Omega * f)(x) = \int_0^{2\pi} \int_{\mathbb{R}^1} v_\Omega(x \cdot \theta - s) Rf(\theta, s) d\varphi ds. \qquad (5.24)$$

The relation between φ, s and the fan beam coordinates β, α is

$$\varphi = \alpha + \beta - \pi/2, \qquad s = r \sin \alpha.$$

The region $[0, 2\pi) \times (-\frac{\pi}{2}, \frac{\pi}{2})$ of the $\beta - \alpha$ plane is mapped in a one-to-one fashion onto the domain $[0, 2\pi) \times (-r, r)$ in the $\varphi - s$ plane, and we have

$$\frac{\partial(\varphi, s)}{\partial(\beta, \alpha)} = \begin{vmatrix} 1 & 1 \\ 0 & r \cos \alpha \end{vmatrix} = r \cos \alpha.$$

Thus (5.24) in the new coordinates reads

$$(V_\Omega * f)(x) = r \int_0^{2\pi} \int_{-\pi/2}^{\pi/2} v_\Omega(x \cdot \theta - r \sin \alpha) g(\beta, \alpha) \cos \alpha d\alpha d\beta,$$

$$\theta = \theta(\beta + \alpha - \pi/2).$$

$$(5.25)$$

For the discretization of this integral we assume f to be essentially Ω-band-limited and zero outside $|x| < \rho$. Then, according to section 4.2, the lattice L_W with

$$W = \begin{pmatrix} \Delta \beta & 0 \\ 0 & \Delta \alpha \end{pmatrix}$$

is a good sampling lattice for g provided that (4.27) holds. We use (5.25) with v_Ω being an Ω-band-limited filter such as (5.5), (5.7), or (5.8). Then the function

$$f_1(\beta, \alpha) = v_\Omega(x \cdot \theta - r \sin \alpha)$$

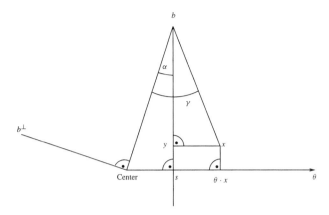

Figure 5.2. *Proof of* (5.28).

has the same properties as $f_2 = g$, i.e., its Fourier transform is small outside the set K from Figure 4.5. Thus we can apply Theorem 4.5 to L_W, f_1, f_2 to obtain, with good accuracy,

$$(V_\Omega * f)(x) = r \Delta\alpha \Delta\beta \sum_{j=0}^{p-1} \sum_{\ell=-q}^{q} v_\Omega(x \cdot \theta(\beta_j + \alpha_\ell - \pi/2) - r \sin \alpha_\ell) g(\beta_j, \alpha_\ell) \cos \alpha_\ell. \quad (5.26)$$

This is the fan beam analogue of (5.19) and defines an algorithm for the computation of $V_\Omega * f$ from the fan beam data (5.23). Again the complexity of this algorithm is $O(\Omega^4)$.

In order to obtain an $O(\Omega^3)$ algorithm, we have a closer look at the terms $|x \cdot \theta - s|$ in (5.24); see Figure 5.2.

Let γ be the angle between $x - b$ and $-b$, where $b = r\theta(\beta)$ is the source position, and let $b_\perp = r\theta(\beta + \frac{\pi}{2})$. Corresponding to our convention on the sign of α, we take γ positive if x, viewed from the source b, lies to the left of the central ray; i.e., we have

$$\cos \gamma = \frac{(b - x) \cdot b}{|b - x||b|}, \qquad \gamma \geq 0 \quad \text{for} \quad x \cdot b_\perp \leq 0, \qquad \gamma \leq 0 \quad \text{for} \quad x \cdot b_\perp \geq 0. \quad (5.27)$$

Let y be the orthogonal projection of x onto the line with parallel coordinates θ, s. Then $|x \cdot \theta - s| = |x - y|$. Considering the rectangular triangle xyb, we see that $|x - y| = |b - x| \sin |\gamma - \alpha|$, and hence

$$|x \cdot \theta - s| = |b - x| \sin |\gamma - \alpha|. \quad (5.28)$$

From (5.4) we see that v_Ω has the homogeneity property

$$v_\Omega(t\sigma) = t^{-n} v_{t\Omega}(\sigma).$$

For $n = 2$, we thus get from (5.28)

$$v_\Omega(x \cdot \theta - s) = |b - x|^{-2} v_{\Omega|b-x|}(\sin(\gamma - \alpha)).$$

Using this in (5.25), we obtain

$$(V_\Omega * f)(x) = r \int_0^{2\pi} |b - x|^{-2} \int_{-\pi/2}^{\pi/2} v_{\Omega|b-x|}(\sin(\gamma - \alpha))g(\beta, \alpha) \cos \alpha d\alpha d\beta. \quad (5.29)$$

Here $b = r\theta(\beta)$. $\gamma = \gamma(x, \beta)$ is determined in (5.27) and is independent of α. Thus the α-integral in (5.29) is a convolution. Unfortunately, the convolution kernel depends on x via the bandwidth parameter $\Omega|b - x|$. This means that the convolution has to be done for each x, leading again to the complexity $O(\Omega^4)$. In order to get a complexity of $O(\Omega^3)$, we make an approximation: We replace $\Omega|b - x|$ by Ωr, i.e., we assume $|x| \ll r$. Then (5.29) becomes approximately

$$(V_\Omega * f)(x) = r \int_0^{2\pi} |b - x|^{-2} \int_{-\pi/2}^{\pi/2} v_{\Omega r}(\sin(\gamma - \alpha))g(\beta, \alpha) \cos \alpha d\alpha d\beta. \quad (5.30)$$

This formula can now be treated exactly as in the parallel case.

ALGORITHM 5.3 (filtered backprojection algorithm for standard fan beam geometry)

Data: The values $g_{j,\ell} = g(\beta_j, \alpha_\ell)$, $j = 0, \ldots, p - 1$, $\ell = -q, \ldots, q$, from (5.23).

Step 1: For $j = 0, \ldots, p - 1$, carry out the discrete convolutions

$$h_{j,k} = \Delta\alpha \sum_{\ell=-q}^{q} v_{\Omega r}(\sin(\alpha_k - \alpha_\ell))g_{j\ell} \cos \alpha_\ell, \quad k = -q, \ldots, q.$$

Step 2: Let $b_j = r\theta(\beta_j)$, $b_{j,\perp} = r\theta(\beta_j + \frac{\pi}{2})$. For each reconstruction point x, compute the discrete weighted backprojections

$$f_{FB}(x) = r\Delta\beta \sum_{j=0}^{p-1} |b_j - x|^{-2}((1 - \vartheta)h_{j,k} + \vartheta h_{j,k+1}),$$

where $k = k(j, x)$ and $\vartheta = \vartheta(j, x)$ are determined by

$$\gamma = \pm \arccos \frac{(b_j - x) \cdot b_j}{|b_j - x||b_j|}, \quad \text{``+'' for } x \cdot b_{j,\perp} \leq 0, \quad \text{``−'' for } x \cdot b_{j,\perp} \geq 0,$$

$$t = \frac{\gamma}{\Delta\alpha}, \quad k = \lfloor t \rfloor, \quad \vartheta = t - k.$$

Result: $f_{FB}(x)$ is an approximation to $f(x)$.

Again we make a few remarks concerning the role of the various parameters in this algorithm.

1. The algorithm is designed to reconstruct a function f that is supported in $|x| < \rho$ and that is essentially Ω-band-limited. The conditions

$$\Delta\alpha \leq \frac{\pi}{\Omega r}, \quad \Delta\beta \leq \frac{r + \rho}{r} \frac{\pi}{\Omega\rho}$$

have to be satisfied to prevent aliasing.

2. Due to the approximation $\Omega|b - x| \sim \Omega r$, which we made in (5.30), the algorithm, as it stands, is accurate only if $\rho \ll r$, e.g., $\rho \le r/3$. For $\rho \sim r$, i.e., if sources are close to reconstruction points, this approximation leads to intolerable inaccuracies. In that case, we recommend reconstruction algorithms of the circular harmonic type (see section 5.6) or the rebinning approach below.

An alternative way to implement filtered backprojection for the fan beam geometry is based on exact rebinning. We assume that $\Delta\alpha$, $\Delta\beta$ are related by a relation of the form

$$m\Delta\alpha = n\Delta\beta, \tag{5.31}$$

where m, n are relatively prime. Then

$$\beta_j + \alpha_\ell = j\Delta\beta + (\ell + \delta)\Delta\alpha$$
$$= (jm + \ell n)\Delta\varphi + \delta\Delta\alpha,$$

where $\Delta\varphi = \Delta\alpha/n$. Since m, n are relatively prime, $k = jm + \ell n$ runs through all the integers as j, ℓ run through the integers. Thus (5.26) assumes the form

$$(V_\Omega * f)(x) = r\Delta\alpha\Delta\beta \sum_{k=-qn}^{qn+m(p-1)} {\sum_{\ell}}' v_\Omega(x \cdot \theta(\varphi_k) - r\sin\alpha_\ell)g_{j\ell}\cos\alpha_\ell, \tag{5.32}$$

where $j = (k - \ell n)/m$ and $\varphi_k = k\Delta\varphi + \delta\Delta\alpha - \pi/2$. The prime indicates that the sum extends only over those ℓ for which j is an integer between 0 and $p - 1$ and $|\ell| \le q$. (5.32) can be implemented very much in the same way as (5.29), but without the—questionable—approximation $v_{|\Omega||b-x|} \sim v_{\Omega r}$. Putting

$$h_k(s) = {\sum_{\ell}}' v_\Omega(s - r\sin\alpha_\ell)g_{j\ell}\cos\alpha_\ell,$$

we have

$$(V_\Omega * f)(x) = r\Delta\alpha\Delta\beta \sum_{k=-qn}^{qn+(p-1)m} h_k(x \cdot \theta(\varphi_k)).$$

In the algorithm, $h_k(s)$ is computed for a discrete set of values $s_\ell = \ell\Delta s'$, where, as in Algorithm 5.2, $\Delta s' \ll r\sin\Delta\alpha$. In between these values, h_k is computed by linear interpolation.

The implementation of the filtered backprojection algorithm for the efficient fan beam geometry (4.29) parallels the one of the parallel interlaced geometry (Algorithm 5.2). Filtered backprojection algorithms for general fan beam schemes are given in Besson (1996).

5.1.4   Linear fan beam scanning

Here the detector positions within a fan are uniformly distributed on the line perpendicular to the central ray of the fan; see Figure 5.3. We need the explicit form of the algorithm in this case mainly for the derivation of the FDK algorithm in 3D cone beam tomography in section 5.5.1.

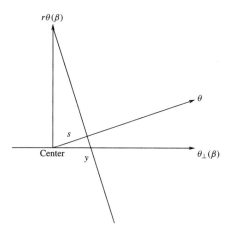

Figure 5.3. *Linear fan beam geometry.*

The sampled function is

$$g(\beta, y) = (Rf)(\theta(\varphi), s),$$

where the coordinates β, y are related to the parallel coordinates φ, s by

$$\varphi = \beta + \arctan \frac{y}{r} - \frac{\pi}{2}, \quad s = \frac{ry}{(r^2 + y^2)^{1/2}}. \tag{5.33}$$

We assume g to be sampled at β_j from (5.23) and

$$y_\ell = (\ell + \delta)\Delta y, \quad \ell = -q, \dots, q.$$

From (5.33),

$$\left| \frac{\partial(\varphi, s)}{\partial(\beta, y)} \right| = \frac{r^3}{(r^2 + y^2)^{3/2}}.$$

Introducing the coordinates β, y in (5.24), we obtain

$$(V_\Omega * f)(x) = \int_0^{2\pi} \int_{-\rho}^{\rho} v_\Omega(x \cdot \theta(\varphi) - s) g(\beta, y) \frac{r^3 \, dy \, d\beta}{(r^2 + y^2)^{3/2}}, \tag{5.34}$$

where (5.33) has to be inserted for φ, s. We compute $|x \cdot \theta(\varphi) - s|$ in the orthogonal system $\theta(\beta), \theta_\perp(\beta) = \theta(\beta - \pi/2)$. We have with $\alpha = \arctan \frac{y}{r}$

$$\begin{aligned}
\theta(\varphi) &= (\theta(\varphi) \cdot \theta(\beta))\theta(\beta) + (\theta(\varphi) \cdot \theta_\perp(\beta))\theta_\perp(\beta) \\
&= \sin\alpha\,\theta(\beta) + \cos\alpha\,\theta_\perp(\beta) \\
&= \frac{1}{(r^2 + y^2)^{1/2}}(y\theta(\beta) + r\theta_\perp(\beta)), \\
x &= (x \cdot \theta(\beta))\theta(\beta) + (x \cdot \theta_\perp(\beta))\theta_\perp(\beta),
\end{aligned}$$

and hence

$$x \cdot \theta(\varphi) - s = \frac{1}{(y^2 + r^2)^{1/2}} (yx \cdot \theta(\beta) + rx \cdot \theta_\perp(\beta) - ry)$$

$$= \frac{r - x \cdot \theta(\beta)}{(y^2 + r^2)^{1/2}} \left(\frac{rx \cdot \theta_\perp(\beta)}{r - x \cdot \theta(\beta)} - y \right)$$

$$= c(z - y).$$

Using the homogeneity relation

$$v_\Omega(c(z - y)) = c^{-2} v_{c\Omega}(z - y),$$

where

$$c = \frac{r - x \cdot \theta(\beta)}{(y^2 + r^2)^{1/2}}, \quad z = \frac{rx \cdot \theta_\perp(\beta)}{r - x \cdot \theta(\beta)},$$

we obtain from (5.34)

$$(V_\Omega * f)(x) = \int_0^{2\pi} \int_{-\rho}^{\rho} c^{-2} v_{c\Omega}(z - y) g(\beta, y) \frac{r^3 dy d\beta}{(r^2 + y^2)^{3/2}}$$

$$= r^3 \int_0^{2\pi} \frac{1}{(r - x \cdot \theta(\beta))^2} \int_{-\rho}^{\rho} v_{\Omega c}(z - y) g(\beta, y) \frac{dy}{(r^2 + y^2)^{1/2}} d\beta.$$

Here we make the approximation $c \sim 1$. As in the case of the standard fan beam geometry this is justified if the support of f is well inside the interior of $|x| \leq r$. Then we obtain approximately

$$(V_\Omega * f)(x) = \int_{S^1} \frac{r^2}{(r - x \cdot \theta)^2} \int_{-\rho}^{\rho} v_\Omega \left(\frac{rx \cdot \theta_\perp}{r - x \cdot \theta} - y \right) g(\theta, y) \frac{r dy}{(r^2 + y^2)^{1/2}} d\theta. \quad (5.35)$$

This can be implemented exactly as (5.30). With the stepsizes

$$\Delta y \leq \frac{\pi}{\Omega}, \quad \Delta \beta \leq \frac{r + \rho}{r} \frac{\pi}{\Omega \rho},$$

we obtain resolution Ω.

5.1.5 Fast backprojection

The most time-consuming part in the filtered backprojection algorithm is the backprojection. To fix ideas, let us consider the standard parallel scanning geometry from 5.1.1. For p directions on a $p \times p$ grid, it needs $O(p^3)$ operations. Nilsson (1997), Brandt et al. (1998), and Götz and Druckmüller (1996) independently found an algorithm of complexity $O(p^2 \log p)$. The ideas are essentially the same and are related to the divide and conquer strategy of computer science and to the multigrid idea of numerical analysis. We follow Nilsson (1997). We consider only the 2D case and assume that $g = Rf$ is sampled for the directions $\theta_j = (\cos \varphi_j, \sin \varphi_j)^T$ with $\varphi_j = \pi j / p$, $j = 0, \ldots, p - 1$. We compute the backprojection at the points of a $p \times p$ grid which lie inside a circle around the origin.

Suppose $p = 2^m$ with some integer $m > 0$. We compute an approximation to the discrete backprojection

$$f(x) = \sum_{j=0}^{p-1} g(\theta_j, x \cdot \theta_j)$$

on a $p \times p$ grid approximately in the following way.

Step 1. For $j = 0, 1, 2, \ldots, p - 1$, compute

$$f_j^1(x) = g(\theta_j, x \cdot \theta_j).$$

Since f_j^1 is constant along the lines $x \cdot \theta_j = s$, it suffices to compute $f_j^1(x)$ at $2p$ points x. We need $p \cdot 2p$ operations.

Step 2. For $j = 0, 2, 4, \ldots, p - 2$, compute

$$f_j^2(x) = f_j^1(x) + f_{j+1}^1(x).$$

Since f_j^1, f_{j+1}^1 are constant along the lines $x \cdot \theta_j = s$, $x \cdot \theta_{j+1} = s$, respectively, f_j^2 is almost constant along the lines $x \cdot \tilde{\theta}_j = s$, where $\tilde{\theta}_j = (\theta_j + \theta_{j+1})/\sqrt{2}$. Hence it suffices to compute f_j^2 only for a few, say, two, points on each of those lines. This means we have to evaluate f_j^2 at $4p$ points, requiring $\frac{p}{2} \cdot 4p$ operations.

Step 3. For $j = 0, 4, 8, \ldots, p - 4$, compute

$$f_j^3(x) = f_j^2(x) + f_{j+2}^2(x).$$

With exactly the same reasoning as in Step 2, we find that it suffices to compute $f_j^3(x)$ for $8p$ points, requiring $\frac{p}{4} \cdot 8p$ operations.

Proceeding in this fashion, we arrive in step m at an approximation f_j^m to f, which has to be evaluated at $2^m p$ points. Hence the number of operations for steps 1 to m is

$$p \cdot 2p + \frac{p}{2} \cdot 4p + \frac{p}{4} \cdot 8p + \cdots + \frac{p}{2^{m-1}} 2^m p = mp^2,$$

and this is $p^2 \log p$. Of course, this derivation is heuristic, but practical experience in the papers mentioned above suggests that methods along these lines can be made to work. In particular, the application to SAR in Nilsson (1997) looks promising.

5.1.6   The point spread function

The function V in (5.1) is the point spread function, i.e., the system response for $f = \delta$, the Dirac δ function. Suppose that complete projections $(Rf)(\theta_j, \cdot)$, $j = 1, \ldots, p$, are sampled. Then with the backprojection evaluated by a quadrature rule with nodes θ_j and weights α_j on S^{n-1}, the filtered backprojection algorithm yields the reconstruction

$$\sum_{j=1}^{p} \alpha_j (v * (Rf))(\theta_j, x \cdot \theta_j) = (V_p * f)(x),$$

$$V_p(x) = \sum_{j=1}^{p} \alpha_j v(x \cdot \theta_j).$$

Figure 5.4. *Point spread function of the filtered backprojection algorithm with Ram–Lak filter for $\Omega = 64$, $p = 16$ in a square of sidelength 2.*

Thus V_p is the point spread function of the filtered backprojection algorithm.

Looking at the point spread function (see Figure 5.4), we see that the condition (4.20), i.e., $\Omega\rho \leq p$ for reliable reconstruction of an object with (essential) bandwidth Ω from p complete views, is correct. The point spread function is an approximate δ function for $|x| \leq \frac{2p}{\Omega}$, permitting accurate reconstruction in $|x| \leq \frac{p}{\Omega}$. Outside $|x| \leq \frac{2p}{\Omega}$ streak-like artifacts occur (their number being $2p$).

5.1.7 Noise in the filtered backprojection algorithm

It is easy to derive formulas for the noise in reconstructed images provided the noise in the data is known; see Morneburg (1995) and Kak and Slaney (1987). We assume that the input g of a reconstruction procedure is

$$g = Rf + n,$$

where n is a random variable with

$$En = 0,$$
$$En(\theta, s)n(\theta', s') = \sigma^2(\theta, s)\delta(\theta - \theta')\delta(s - s'),$$

E being the mathematical expectation. Then the reconstructed density

$$f_V(x) = (V * f)(x) = \int_{S^{n-1}} \int_{\mathbb{R}^1} g(\theta, s)v(x \cdot \theta - s)ds d\theta$$

from (5.1) is a random variable, too, and

$$Ef_V(x) = 0,$$
$$E|f_V^2(x)| = \int_{S^{n-1}} \int_{\mathbb{R}^1} v^2(x \cdot \theta - s)\sigma^2(\theta, s)ds d\theta;$$

see, e.g., Papoulis (1965).

We consider two noise models.

1. $g = -\ell n(I/I_0)$, where I is a Poisson distributed random variable with mean value

$$\overline{I} = I_0 e^{-Rf},$$

hence with variance $E(I - \overline{I})^2 = \overline{I}$, and I_0 is some constant. Unfortunately, the logarithm of a Poisson distributed random variable has infinite expectation and variance. However, since $\overline{I}$ is large, we may model I as a random variable with mean value $\overline{I}$ and variance $\overline{I}$ which assumes values only in $(\overline{I} - \Delta I, \overline{I} + \Delta I)$, where ΔI has the order of magnitude $\sqrt{\overline{I}}$. Then $(I - \overline{I})/\overline{I}$ is small, and we have approximately

$$
\begin{aligned}
g &= \ell n I_0 - \ell n I = \ell n I_0 - \ell n(\overline{I} + (I - \overline{I})) \\
  &= \ell n I_0 - \ell n \overline{I} - \frac{I - \overline{I}}{\overline{I}},
\end{aligned}
$$

and hence

$$\sigma^2(\theta, s) = \frac{E(I - \overline{I})^2}{\overline{I}^2} = \frac{1}{\overline{I}}.$$

2. Again $g = -\ell n(I/I_0)$, but now I is normally distributed with mean value $\overline{I}$ and variance $E(I - \overline{I})^2 = \sigma^2$. By the same arguments as above, we get approximately

$$\sigma^2(\theta, s) = \frac{\sigma^2}{\overline{I}^2}.$$

Assuming that $\overline{I}$ is not varying too much over the domain of integration, we see that for both noise models the crucial quantity for noise amplification is

$$
\begin{aligned}
\kappa^2 &= \int_{S^{n-1}} \int_{\mathbb{R}^1} v^2(x \cdot \theta - s)\, ds\, d\theta \\
         &= |S^{n-1}| \int_{\mathbb{R}^1} v^2(s)\, ds \\
         &= |S^{n-1}| \int_{\mathbb{R}^1} |\hat{v}(\sigma)|^2 d\sigma \\
         &= |S^{n-1}| \frac{1}{2} (2\pi)^{1-2n} \int_0^\Omega \sigma^{2n-2} |\hat{\phi}(\sigma/\Omega)|^2 d\sigma;
\end{aligned}
$$

see (5.4). κ depends only on the dimension and the filter. For $n = 2$, we have

$$\kappa^2 = \frac{1}{24\pi^2} \Omega^3 \qquad \text{for the Ram–Lak filter (5.5),}$$

$$\kappa^2 = \frac{1}{4\pi^4} \Omega^3 \qquad \text{for the Shepp–Logan filter (5.8),}$$

$$\kappa^2 = \frac{1}{2}\left(\frac{1}{6} - \frac{1}{\pi^2}\right)(2\pi)^{-2}\Omega^3 \quad \text{for the cos filter (5.7).}$$

For $n = 3$, we get for the Marr filter (5.10)

$$\kappa^2 = \frac{12}{\pi^5}(2\pi)^{-1/2}\Omega^5.$$

The difference between $n = 2, 3$ in the power of Ω indicates the difference in sensitivity already alluded to in section 4.1: The reconstruction from plane integrals is much more sensitive to noise than the reconstruction from line integrals.

5.1.8 Filtered backprojection for the exponential Radon transform

The inversion formula for T_μ in Theorem 2.21 can be implemented in very much the same way as in section 5.1.1. We only have to replace the filter v_Ω by the filter

$$v_{\Omega,\mu} = v_\Omega - v_{|\mu|},$$

where $v_{|\mu|}$ is the Ram–Lak filter (5.5) with cutoff $|\mu|$. In the formula for the backprojection (Step 2 of Algorithm 5.1), the weight $\exp(-\mu x \cdot \theta_j)$ has to be added.

5.1.9 Filtered backprojection for the attenuated Radon transform

As in the exponential case, the implementation of the inversion formula for the attenuated Radon transform R_μ (see Theorem 2.23) is an obvious extension of the filtered backprojection algorithm. First, we have to compute the function

$$g_\mu = \operatorname{Re} e^{-h} H e^h g, \quad g = R_\mu f.$$

Putting $h = h_1 + ih_2$, $h_1 = \frac{1}{2}R\mu$, $h_2 = \frac{1}{2}HR\mu$, we have

$$g_\mu = e^{-h_1}(\cos h_2 H e^{h_1} \cos h_2 + \sin h_2 H e^{h_1} \sin h_2)g.$$

The Hilbert transform can be computed by convolution: With ϕ a low pass filter as in (5.3), we can define an approximation H_Ω to H by

$$(H_\Omega g)^\wedge(\sigma) = \hat{\phi}(\sigma/\Omega)(Hg)^\wedge(\sigma)$$
$$= \frac{\operatorname{sgn}(\sigma)}{i} \hat{\phi}(\sigma/\Omega)\hat{g}(\sigma);$$

see (1.13). It follows that

$$H_\Omega g = v_\Omega * g,$$
$$v_\Omega(s) = \frac{1}{2\pi} \int_{-\Omega}^{\Omega} \hat{\phi}(\sigma/\Omega)\frac{\operatorname{sgn}(\sigma)}{i} e^{is\sigma} d\sigma.$$

For ϕ the ideal low pass, we obtain

$$v_\Omega(s) = \frac{\Omega}{\pi} u(\Omega s), \quad u(s) = (1 - \cos s)/s.$$

This corresponds to the Ram–Lak filter (5.5). Thus g_μ can be computed for each direction θ by premultiplying the emission data g, 1D convolution with v_Ω, and postmultiplying. Once g_μ is computed, we have to carry out the weighted backprojection

$$R^*_{-\mu}(\theta g_\mu)(x) = \int_{S^1} \theta e^{(D\mu)(x,\theta_\perp)} g_\mu(\theta, x \cdot \theta) d\theta,$$

which can be done as in section 5.1.1 by the trapezoidal rule. The reconstruction is finished by computing

$$f = \frac{1}{4\pi} \operatorname{div} R^*_{-\mu}(\theta g_\mu),$$

which can easily be done by finite differences.

Alternatively, one may carry out the div operator under the integral sign, leading to the inversion formula

$$f(x) = \frac{1}{4\pi} \int_{S^1} e^{(D\mu)(x,\theta_\perp)} g'_\mu(\theta, x \cdot \theta) d\theta$$

$$+ \frac{1}{4\pi} \int_{S^1} \frac{\partial}{\partial \theta} (D\mu)(x, \theta_\perp) e^{(D\mu)(x,\theta_\perp)} g_\mu(\theta, x \cdot \theta) d\theta,$$

where $\frac{\partial}{\partial \theta}$ denotes the directional derivative in direction θ with respect to the first argument of $D\mu$ and the prime denotes differentiation with respect to the second argument of g_μ. Again the derivatives can easily be carried out by finite differences.

It seems that the filtered backprojection algorithm for R_μ behaves, by and large, as the one for R. For actual reconstructions see Kunyansky (2000).

5.2   Fourier Reconstruction

By Fourier reconstruction we mean the direct numerical implementation of the relation between $\hat{f}$ and the Fourier transform of the data as expressed by Theorems 2.1 and 2.11. To fix ideas, we restrict ourselves to the 2D Radon transform. Here Theorem 2.1 reads

$$\hat{f}(\sigma\theta) = (2\pi)^{-1/2} \hat{g}(\theta, \sigma), \qquad g = Rf. \tag{5.36}$$

Thus f can be recovered from g by doing a 1D Fourier transform on g for each θ, followed by a 2D inverse Fourier transform to yield f. The algorithms differ in the way interpolation in Fourier space is done.

5.2.1   Standard Fourier reconstruction

Here we do the interpolation simply by taking nearest neighbors. For the standard parallel scanning geometry this leads to the following algorithm.

ALGORITHM 5.4 (standard Fourier reconstruction; this algorithm is not recommended)

Data: The numbers $g_{j,\ell} = g(\theta_j, s_\ell)$, $j = 0, \ldots, p-1$, $\ell = -q, \ldots, q$, from (5.12).

Step 1: For $j = 0, \ldots, p-1$, carry out the discrete Fourier transform

$$\hat{g}_{j,r} = (2\pi)^{-1/2} \frac{\rho}{q} \sum_{\ell=-q}^{q} e^{-i\pi r\ell/q} g_{j,\ell}, \qquad r = -q, \ldots, q. \tag{5.37}$$

$\hat{g}_{j,r}$ is an approximation to $\hat{g}(\theta_j, \frac{\pi}{\rho}r) = (2\pi)^{1/2}\hat{f}(\frac{\pi}{\rho}r\theta_j)$. Thus the first step yields—up to aliasing errors—the value of $\hat{f}$ on a polar coordinate grid with radial sampling distance $\frac{\pi}{\rho}$. In the next step, we perform an interpolation from this polar coordinate grid to a Cartesian grid with the same sampling distance.

Step 2: For each $k \in \mathbb{Z}^2$, $|k| \leq q$, find integers j, r such that $r\theta_j$ is as close as possible to k and put

$$\hat{f}_k = (2\pi)^{-1/2}\hat{g}_{j,r}. \tag{5.38}$$

$\hat{f}_k$ is an approximation to $\hat{f}(\frac{\pi}{\rho}k)$ obtained by nearest neighbor interpolation in the polar coordinate grid $\{\frac{\pi}{\rho}r\theta_j, \ j = 0, \ldots, p-1, r = -q, \ldots, q\}$. Nearest neighbor interpolation can be replaced by any other interpolation method, e.g., bilinear interpolation.

Step 3: Compute an approximation f_m to $f(\frac{\rho}{q}m)$, $m \in \mathbb{Z}^2$, by the discrete 2D inverse Fourier transform

$$f_m = \frac{1}{2\pi}\left(\frac{\pi}{\rho}\right)^2 \sum_{|k|<q} e^{i\pi m \cdot k/q}\hat{f}_k, \quad |m| < q. \tag{5.39}$$

The algorithm is designed to reconstruct a function f supported in $|x| < \rho$ with essential bandwidth Ω, provided (4.20) is satisfied, i.e., $p = \rho\Omega$, $q = \frac{\rho}{\pi}\Omega$. Then the stepsize of $\frac{\rho}{q}$ in (5.37) and $\frac{\pi}{\rho}$ in (5.38) are correct in the sense of the sampling theorem. The Fourier transforms in Steps 1 and 3 require $pq \log q$, $q^2 \log q$ operations, respectively, if done by FFT. Assuming that the interpolation in Step 2 can be done in O(1) operation per point, we arrive at a complexity of the order $\Omega^2 \log \Omega$. This is much less than the Ω^3 operation the filtered backprojection algorithm needs; see section 5.1. The interest in direct Fourier reconstruction is due to this favorable operation count.

Unfortunately, the algorithm in its present form produces serious artifacts. Since the discretizations in Step 1 and Step 3 are correct in the sense of the sampling theorem, these artifacts must come from the interpolation in Step 2. In fact, the error analysis given in Natterer (1986) shows that this is the case. This error analysis also shows that local interpolation in angular direction is justified, but it is not sufficient in radial direction. On a heuristic level, this is easy to understand: The radial stepsize in the polar coordinate grid $\{\frac{\pi}{\rho}r\theta_j : j = 0, \ldots, p-1, r = -q, \ldots, q\}$ is $\frac{\pi}{\rho}$, independent of the numbers p, q. However, local interpolation formulas require the stepsize to tend to zero in order to keep the interpolation error small.

There are several methods to improve the standard Fourier algorithm.

Since angular interpolation is justified, we can move each point $\frac{\pi}{\rho}k$, $k \in \mathbb{R}^2$, on the Cartesian grid to $\frac{\pi}{\rho}|k|\theta_j$ with θ_j suitably chosen, leaving us with the problem of computing

$$\hat{f}\left(\frac{\pi}{\rho}|k|\theta_j\right) = (2\pi)^{-1}\frac{\rho}{q}\sum_{\ell=-q}^{q} e^{-i\pi|k|\ell/q}g_{j,\ell}, \quad k \in \mathbb{Z}^2, \quad |k| \leq q.$$

This is an instance of a nonequispaced FFT of type ner from (4.32). Applying (4.36), we obtain

$$\hat{f}\left(\frac{\pi}{\rho}|k|\theta_j\right) = (2\pi)^{-1/2}\sum_m \hat{\phi}\left(\frac{\pi}{\beta}|k| - m\right)z_{m,j},$$

$$z_{m,j} = (2\pi)^{-1}\frac{\rho}{q}\sum_{\ell=-q}^{q}e^{-i\beta m\ell/q}\frac{g_{j,\ell}}{\phi(\beta\ell/q)}.$$

Thus Step 1 of Algorithm 5.4 is replaced by an FFT of length $2Q$, $Q = \frac{\pi}{\beta}q$, on the weighted data $g_{j,\ell}/\phi(\beta\ell/q)$, yielding the intermediate results $z_{m,j}$. Instead of the simple interpolation in Step 2, we use the more sophisticated interpolation involving $\hat{\phi}$, with an additional local interpolation (linear will do) in the angular direction. Step 3 of Algorithm 5.4 remains the same. For details, see Fourmont (1999).

Following a suggestion of Pasciak (1981), one can avoid radial interpolation largely by moving the points $\frac{\pi}{\rho}k$—at which we need $\hat{f}$—horizontally for $|k_2| > |k_1|$ and vertically otherwise onto the closest ray $\{t\theta_j : t > 0\}$ in the polar coordinate grid to the point ξ_k on that ray. We have

$$\xi_k = \frac{\pi}{\rho}\frac{k_2}{\sin\varphi_j}\theta_j, \quad |k_2| > |k_1|,$$

$$\xi_k = \frac{\pi}{\rho}\frac{|k_1|}{\cos\varphi_j}\theta_j \quad \text{otherwise},$$

(5.40)

and hence

$$\hat{f}(\xi_k) = (2\pi)^{-1/2} = \begin{cases} \hat{g}\left(\theta_j, \frac{\pi}{\rho}\frac{k_2}{\sin\varphi_j}\right), & |k_2| > |k_1|, \\ \hat{g}\left(\theta_j, \frac{\pi}{\rho}\left|\frac{k_1}{\cos\varphi_j}\right|\right) & \text{otherwise}. \end{cases}$$

Note that j depends on k. (5.40) requires the knowledge of $\hat{g}(\theta_j, \sigma_r)$ for $\sigma_r = rh$ with

$$h = \frac{\pi}{\rho}\max\left\{\frac{1}{\sin\varphi_j}, \frac{1}{|\cos\varphi_j|}\right\}.$$

This can be done by the chirp-z algorithm; see section 1.3.6. The Pasciak algorithm runs exactly as the standard Fourier algorithm except that in Step 2 the interpolation is done with the points ξ_k rather than by nearest neighbor. See Schulte (1994) for details.

Both modifications of Algorithm 5.4 greatly improve standard Fourier reconstruction but do not always achieve the accuracy of filtered backprojection. For other improved versions, see Cheung and Lewitt (1991).

5.2.2 The gridding method

The gridding method is presently considered to be the most accurate Fourier reconstruction method. It was introduced in radio astronomy by Brouw (1975) and was transferred to the radiological field by O'Sullivan (1985) and Kaveh and Soumekh (1987). The essential feature of the gridding method is the use of a weight function W which is nonzero in the reconstruction region $|x| < \rho$, $x \in \mathbb{R}^2$, which vanishes outside $|x| \geq a > \rho$, and whose

Fourier transform is concentrated as much as possible around 0. With W such a function, we have

$$
\begin{aligned}
(Wf)^\wedge(\xi) &= \frac{1}{2\pi}(W * f)^\wedge(\xi) \\
&= \frac{1}{2\pi}\int_{\mathbb{R}^2} \hat{W}(\xi - \eta)\hat{f}(\eta)d\eta \\
&= \frac{1}{2\pi}\int_0^\infty \sigma \int_{S^1} \hat{W}(\xi - \sigma\theta)\hat{f}(\sigma\theta)d\theta d\sigma \\
&= (2\pi)^{-3/2}\int_0^\infty \sigma \int_{S^1} \hat{W}(\xi - \sigma\theta)\hat{g}(\theta,\sigma)d\theta d\sigma.
\end{aligned}
\tag{5.41}
$$

The idea is to evaluate $(Wf)^\wedge$ on a Cartesian grid; this is what "gridding" refers to. Then Wf can be obtained by an inverse 2D FFT on this Cartesian grid, and the reconstruction is completed by removing the weight W.

For the success of the method, it is crucial that (5.41) is discretized properly. Using the trapezoidal rule with stepsize $\Delta\varphi = \frac{\pi}{p}$ in the angle and $\Delta\sigma$ for the σ integral, we obtain approximately

$$
(Wf)^\wedge\left(\frac{\pi}{\rho}k\right) = \frac{\frac{\pi}{p}\Delta\sigma}{(2\pi)^{3/2}}\sum_{\ell=0}^\infty \sigma_\ell \sum_{j=0}^{2p-1} \hat{W}\left(\frac{\pi}{\rho}k - \ell\Delta\sigma\theta_j\right)\hat{g}(\theta_j, \ell\Delta\sigma),
\tag{5.42}
$$

where $\sigma_\ell = \ell\Delta\sigma$. In order to find a good value for $\Delta\sigma$, we determine the bandwidth of the integrand in (5.41) as a function of σ. The function $\sigma \to \hat{g}(\theta, \sigma)$ has obviously bandwidth ρ, while the function $\sigma \to \hat{W}(\xi - \sigma\theta)$ has bandwidth a. In fact,

$$
\begin{aligned}
\int_{\mathbb{R}^1} \hat{W}(\xi - \sigma\theta)e^{-is\sigma}d\sigma &= \frac{1}{2\pi}\int_{\mathbb{R}^1}\int_{|x|\leq a} W(x)e^{-ix\cdot(\xi-\sigma\theta)}dx\,e^{-is\sigma}d\sigma \\
&= \frac{1}{2\pi}\int_{|x|\leq a} W(x)e^{-ix\cdot\xi}\int_{\mathbb{R}^1}e^{i(x\cdot\theta - s)\sigma}d\sigma dx \\
&= \int_{|x|\leq a} W(x)e^{-ix\cdot\xi}\delta(x\cdot\theta - s)dx \\
&= 0
\end{aligned}
$$

for $|s| > a$. Hence the function $\sigma \to \sigma\hat{W}(\xi - \sigma\theta)\hat{g}(\theta,\sigma)$ has bandwidth $a + \rho$, suggesting that a stepsize $\Delta\sigma \leq 2\pi/(a + \rho)$ is sufficient for the σ integral in (5.41). In this derivation, we ignored that the integral extends over $[0, \infty)$ rather than $(-\infty, +\infty)$.

In order to study the accuracy of the trapezoidal rule of band-limited functions over $[0, \infty)$, we start out from Poisson's formula (1.11) for $\xi = 0$, which we write as

$$
\int_{\mathbb{R}^1} f(\sigma)d\sigma = \Delta\sigma\sum_\ell f(\ell\Delta\sigma) - (2\pi)^{1/2}\sum_{\ell\neq 0}\tilde{f}\left(\frac{2\pi\ell}{\Delta\sigma}\right).
$$

We use this formula for $f = g\,\mathrm{sgn}$ with $\mathrm{sgn}(\sigma)$ the sign of σ and $g(0) = 0$. From (1.13) we see that $\tilde{f} = iH\tilde{g}$ with H the Hilbert transform, and hence

$$\int_{\mathbb{R}^1} g(\sigma) \, \text{sgn}(\sigma) d\sigma = \Delta\sigma \sum_\ell g(\ell\Delta\sigma) \, \text{sgn}(\ell\Delta\sigma) + r,$$

$$r = -(2\pi)^{1/2} i \sum_{\ell \neq 0} (H\tilde{g}) \left(\frac{2\pi\ell}{\Delta\sigma} \right)$$

$$= -\frac{1}{\pi}(2\pi)^{1/2} i \sum_{\ell \neq 0} \int_{\mathbb{R}^1} \frac{\tilde{g}(s)}{\frac{2\pi\ell}{\Delta\sigma} - s} ds$$

$$= -\frac{2}{\pi}(2\pi)^{1/2} i \sum_{\ell=1}^{\infty} \int_{\mathbb{R}^1} \frac{s\tilde{g}(s)}{(\frac{2\pi\ell}{\Delta\sigma})^2 - s^2} ds$$

$$= \frac{2}{\pi}(2\pi)^{1/2} \sum_{\ell=1}^{\infty} \int_{\mathbb{R}^1} \frac{\widetilde{g'}(s)}{(\frac{2\pi\ell}{\Delta\sigma})^2 - s^2} ds$$

since $s\tilde{g}(s) = i\widetilde{g'}(s)$. If g has bandwidth A and $\Delta\sigma \ll 2\pi/A$, then s^2 can be neglected in the denominator of the integrand, and we have approximately

$$r = \frac{2}{\pi}(2\pi)^{1/2} \sum_{\ell=1}^{\infty} \frac{1}{(\frac{2\pi\ell}{\Delta\sigma})^2} \int_{-A}^{A} \widetilde{g'}(s) ds$$

$$= \frac{1}{6}(\Delta\sigma)^2 g'(0),$$

where we have used that $\sum_{\ell=1}^{\infty} 1/\ell^2 = \pi^2/6$. Hence to good accuracy,

$$\int_{\mathbb{R}^1} g(\sigma) \, \text{sgn}(\sigma) d\sigma = \Delta\sigma \sum_\ell g(\ell\Delta\sigma) \, \text{sgn}(\ell\Delta\sigma) + \frac{1}{6}(\Delta\sigma)^2 g'(0).$$

For $g(\sigma) = \sigma G(\sigma)$, G even, this reads

$$\int_0^\infty \sigma G(\sigma) d\sigma = \Delta\sigma \sum_{\ell=0}^{\infty} \sigma_\ell G(\ell\Delta\sigma),$$

$$\sigma_\ell = \begin{cases} \ell\Delta\sigma, & \ell > 0, \\ \Delta\sigma/12, & \ell = 0. \end{cases}$$

The term $\frac{\Delta\sigma}{12} G(0)$ corrects the trapezoidal rule for the error generated by truncating the range of integration at 0. It was introduced in the context of the gridding method by Schomberg and Timmer (1995) on a purely empirical basis, albeit with a slightly different factor. (In our notation, they suggested $1/4\pi$ instead of $1/12$.)

We use the corrected trapezoidal rule for the σ integral in (5.41). The only change we have to make in (5.42) is to put $\sigma_0 = \Delta\sigma/12$ rather than $\sigma_0 = 0$. The latter choice of σ_0 yields reconstructions whose mean value is slightly off the correct value.

ALGORITHM 5.5 (gridding method for standard parallel geometry)

Data: The numbers $g_{j,\ell} = g(\theta_j, s_\ell)$, $j = 0, \ldots, p - 1$, $\ell = -q, \ldots, q$, from (5.12).

Step 1: For $j = 0, \ldots, p - 1$, carry out the discrete Fourier transform

$$\hat{g}_{j,r} = (2\pi)^{-1/2} \frac{\rho}{q} \sum_{\ell=-q}^{q} e^{-i\rho\Delta\sigma \ell r/q} g_{j,\ell}, \quad r = -Q, \ldots, Q,$$

of length $2Q$, where $Q = \frac{\pi}{\rho\Delta\sigma}q$ and $\Delta\sigma \ll \frac{2\pi}{a+\rho}$.

Extend $\hat{g}_{j,r}$ to $j = 0, \ldots, 2p - 1$ by $\hat{g}_{j+p,r} = \hat{g}_{j,-r}$, $j = 0, \ldots, p - 1$. $\hat{g}_{j,r}$ is an approximation to $\hat{g}(\theta_j, r\Delta\sigma)$.

Step 2: For each $k \in \mathbb{Z}^2$, $|k| \leq q$, compute

$$z_k = \frac{\frac{\pi}{\rho}\Delta\sigma}{(2\pi)^{3/2}} \sum_{\ell=0}^{Q} \sum_{j=0}^{2p-1} \sigma_\ell \hat{W}\left(\frac{\pi}{\rho}k - \ell\Delta\sigma\theta_j\right) \hat{g}_{j,\ell}.$$

Since $\hat{W}$ is decaying fast only a few terms of the sum actually have to be computed: ℓ, j can be restricted to those values for which $|\frac{\pi}{\rho}k - \ell\Delta\sigma\theta_j| \leq K$. z_k is an approximation to $(Wf)^\wedge(\frac{\pi}{\rho}k)$.

Step 3: Compute an approximation f_m to $f(\frac{\rho}{q}m)$, $m \in \mathbb{Z}^2$, $|m| \leq q$, by

$$f_m = \frac{1}{2\pi}\left(\frac{\pi}{\rho}\right)^2 \frac{1}{W(\frac{\rho}{q}m)} \sum_{|k| \leq q} e^{i\pi mk/q} z_k.$$

A good choice for the function W is $W(x) = W_1(x_1)W_1(x_2)$, where for $|x_1| \leq a$

$$W_1(x_1) = I_0\left(K\sqrt{a^2 - x_1^2}\right)$$

with the modified Bessel function I_0 of order zero; see section 1.3.5. Then $\hat{W}(\xi) = \hat{W}_1(\xi_1)\hat{W}_1(\xi_2)$ with

$$\hat{W}_1(\xi_1) = \sqrt{\frac{2}{\pi}} \frac{\sinh\left(a\sqrt{K^2 - \xi_1^2}\right)}{\sqrt{K^2 - \xi_1^2}};$$

see Oberhettinger (1993). Note that W is just the 2D version of the function ϕ from section 4.4. For $|\xi_1| \geq K$, we have

$$\left|\frac{\hat{W}_1(\xi)}{\hat{W}_1(0)}\right| \leq \frac{aK}{\sinh(aK)}.$$

This is negligibly small for modest values of aK.

As an alternative to Algorithm 5.5, one can apply the 2D version of the ned algorithm in section 4.4 directly to a discrete version of (5.36). This leads to an algorithm very similar to the gridding method.

Good values for the parameter in Algorithm 5.5 are $a = 2\rho$, $aK = 9\pi/2$, and $\Delta\sigma = \frac{\pi}{a}$; hence $Q = 2q$.

Of course, the gridding idea extends immediately to inverting the Radon transform in 3D; see Schaller, Flohr, and Steffen (1998).

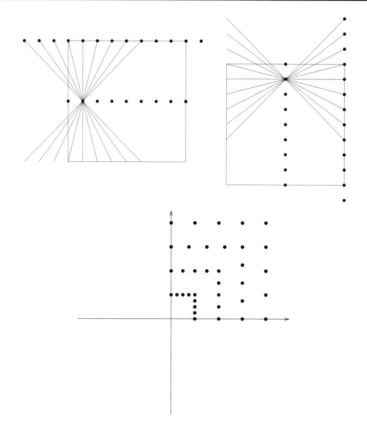

Figure 5.5. *Top: Line pattern used in the linogram algorithm* ($p = q = 4$). *Bottom: Points at which the Fourier transform of f is computed in the linogram algorithm* ($p = 4$).

5.2.3   The linogram algorithm

This algorithm does not need interpolation in Fourier space. It assumes g to be sampled in such a way that the discrete 1D Fourier transforms provide $\hat{f}$ on a grid on which the 2D inverse Fourier transform can be done by the chirp-z algorithm. Again we describe the algorithm for the reconstruction of a function with essential bandwidth Ω in $|x| \leq \rho$.

To begin with we assume $g(\theta, s)$ to be sampled for

$$\theta_j = (\cos\varphi_j, \sin\varphi_j)^T, \quad \varphi_j = \arctan(j/p), \quad j = -p, \ldots, p,$$
$$s_{j,\ell} = \frac{\rho \cos\varphi_j}{q}\ell, \qquad \ell = -q, \ldots, q.$$

For $p = q$ this scanning geometry can be generated by connecting points on the top boundary of a square with sidelength 2ρ with those on the midline, the spacing between adjacent points being ρ/q; see Figure 5.5.

A discrete Fourier transform with respect to s yields approximately

$$\hat{g}(\theta_j, \sigma) = (2\pi)^{-1/2} \frac{\rho \cos \varphi_j}{q} \sum_{\ell=-q}^{q} e^{-i\sigma s_{j,\ell}} g(\theta_j, s_{j,\ell})$$

provided that the Nyquist condition is satisfied. This is the case if $\frac{\rho}{q} \leq \frac{\pi}{\Omega}$. For $\sigma = k\pi/(\rho \cos \varphi_j)$, $k = -p, \ldots, p$, we get

$$\hat{g}\left(\theta_j, \frac{k\pi}{\rho \cos \varphi_j}\right) = (2\pi)^{-1/2} \frac{\rho \cos \varphi_j}{q} \sum_{\ell=-q}^{q} e^{-i\pi k\ell/q} g(\theta_j, s_{j,\ell}).$$

By (5.36) this yields $\hat{f}$ at the points

$$\frac{k\pi}{\rho \cos \varphi_j} \theta_j = \frac{k\pi}{\rho} \begin{pmatrix} 1 \\ \tan \varphi_j \end{pmatrix} = \frac{k\pi}{\rho} \begin{pmatrix} 1 \\ j/p \end{pmatrix}$$

in the Fourier $\xi_1 - \xi_2$ plane. They cover the region $|\xi_1| \geq |\xi_2|$ in an uneven way.

In order to get a similar coverage for $|\xi_2| \geq |\xi_1|$, we make use of $g(\theta, s)$ for

$$\bar{\theta}_j = (\cos \bar{\varphi}_j, \sin \bar{\varphi}_j)^T, \quad \bar{\varphi}_j = \operatorname{arccot}(j/p), \quad j = -p, \ldots, p,$$

$$\bar{s}_{j,\ell} = \frac{\rho \sin \bar{\varphi}_j}{q} \ell, \quad \ell = -q, \ldots, q.$$

These lines are obtained from the previous ones by a rotation through the angle $\pi/2$. From this data we get, exactly as above,

$$\hat{g}\left(\bar{\theta}_j, \frac{k\pi}{\rho \sin \bar{\varphi}_j}\right) = (2\pi)^{-1/2} \frac{\rho \sin \bar{\varphi}_j}{q} \sum_{\ell=-q}^{q} e^{-i\pi k\ell/q} g(\bar{\theta}_j, \bar{s}_{j,\ell})$$

and hence the values of $\hat{f}$ at

$$\frac{k\pi}{\rho \sin \bar{\varphi}_j} \bar{\theta}_j = \frac{k\pi}{\rho} \begin{pmatrix} \cot \bar{\varphi}_j \\ 1 \end{pmatrix} = \frac{k\pi}{\rho} \begin{pmatrix} j/p \\ 1 \end{pmatrix}.$$

Combining the two data sets leads to the values of $\hat{f}$ at the points

$$\frac{k\pi}{\rho} \begin{pmatrix} j/p \\ 1 \end{pmatrix}, \quad \frac{k\pi}{\rho} \begin{pmatrix} 1 \\ j/p \end{pmatrix}, \quad k, j = -p, \ldots, p, \tag{5.43}$$

in the Fourier plane. They cover a square of sidelength $\frac{2\pi}{\rho} p$ around the origin. For $p \geq \rho\Omega/\pi$ this square covers the circle of radius Ω outside of which $\hat{f}$ is essentially zero.

The points (5.43) lie on concentric squares of sidelength $2\pi k/\rho$, the spacing of the points on these squares being $k\pi/(\rho p)$; see Figure 5.5. For $|k| \leq p$ this is not larger than the Nyquist rate π/ρ for correct sampling of $\hat{f}$. Thus by a somewhat loose application of the sampling theorem to irregular sampling, we conclude that it is possible to recover $\hat{f}$, and hence f. Combining this with our findings above, we conclude that $p, q \geq \rho\Omega/\pi$ are the conditions for correct sampling in the linogram algorithm.

Now the key observation is that the inverse Fourier transform on the "grid" (5.43) can be done in $O(p^2 \log p)$ time by the chirp-z algorithm; see section 1.3.6.

Following Edholm, Herman, and Roberts (1988), we decompose f into $f_T + f_C$, where

$$
\hat{f}_T(\xi_1, \xi_2) = \left\{ \begin{array}{ll} \hat{f}(\xi_1, \xi_2), & |\xi_1| \geq |\xi_2|, \\ 0, & |\xi_1| < |\xi_2|, \end{array} \right.
$$

$$
\hat{f}_C(\xi_1, \xi_2) = \left\{ \begin{array}{ll} 0, & |\xi_1| \geq |\xi_2|, \\ \hat{f}(\xi_1, \xi_2), & |\xi_1| < |\xi_2|. \end{array} \right.
$$

In the inversion formula

$$
f_T(x_1, x_2) = \frac{1}{2\pi} \int \int e^{i(\xi_1 x_1 + \xi_2 x_2)} \hat{f}_T(\xi_1, \xi_2) d\xi_1 d\xi_2
$$

we discretize the ξ_1 integral with stepsize π/ρ, obtaining

$$
f_T(\rho m_1/p, x_2) = \frac{1}{2\pi} \frac{\pi}{\rho} \sum_{k=-p}^{p-1} e^{ikm_1\pi/p} \int e^{i\xi_2 x_2} \hat{f}_T\left(k\frac{\pi}{\rho}, \xi_2\right) d\xi_2
$$

to good accuracy because π/ρ is the Nyquist rate for $\hat{f}$. The ξ_2 integral is now discretized with stepsize $|k|\pi/(\rho p)$, which is also correct in the sense of the sampling theorem, to obtain

$$
f_T(\rho m_1/p, \rho m_2/p) = \frac{1}{2\pi} \frac{\pi}{\rho} \sum_{k=-p}^{p} e^{i\pi km_1/p} \frac{|k|\pi}{\rho p} \sum_{j=-p}^{p} e^{i\pi jm_2(\frac{k}{p})/p} \hat{f}\left(k\frac{\pi}{\rho}, k\frac{\pi}{\rho}\frac{j}{p}\right),
$$

$$
\tag{5.44}
$$

where we have written $\hat{f}$ instead of $\hat{f}_T$ since the argument is in $|\xi_1| \geq |\xi_2|$. We remark that evoking the sampling theorem here is not quite rigorous since the support of f_T cannot be expected to be in $|x| \leq \rho$, but apparently the analysis is valid nevertheless.

The evaluation of the j-sum in (5.44) can be done by the chirp-z algorithm with $p \log_2 p$ operations, resulting in $p^2 \log p$ operations for all the j sums. The k sums can be done by a straight FFT. So the overall complexity of (5.44) is $p^2 \log p$. f_C is dealt with correspondingly. Thus the linogram algorithm is a $p^2 \log p$ algorithm.

We remark that the linogram idea is not restricted to inverting the Radon transform. It can be used whenever the data in Fourier space are on concentric squares or cubes. This occurs, e.g., in MRI and PET; see Axel et al. (1990) and Herman, Roberts, and Axel (1992).

Note that the linogram algorithm requires a sampling scheme for the Radon transform that differs from the sampling geometries we considered in section 5.1.

5.2.4   Fourier reconstruction in diffraction tomography and MRI

The gridding idea can also be applied in diffraction tomography (section 3.3) and MRI (section 3.4). In diffraction tomography, we use Theorem 3.1 as a substitute for (5.36). In the 2D case, we have for $|\sigma| \le k$

$$\hat{f}((\pm a(\sigma) - k)\theta + \sigma\theta_\perp) = \frac{i}{k}\sqrt{\frac{2}{\pi}}a(\sigma)e^{ir(k \mp a(\sigma))}\hat{g}_\pm(\theta, \sigma),$$

where $\theta = (\cos\varphi, \sin\varphi)^T$, $\theta_\perp = (-\sin\varphi, \cos\varphi)^T$, $a(\sigma) = \sqrt{k^2 - \sigma^2}$, and

$$g_\pm(\theta, s) = (U_{\pm r}f)(\theta, s\theta_\perp).$$

This formula is used in the gridding process exactly as (5.36). In the convolution integral

$$(Wf)^\wedge(\xi) = \frac{1}{2\pi}\int_{\mathbb{R}^2}\hat{W}(\xi - \zeta)\hat{f}(\zeta)d\zeta$$

we make the change of variable $\zeta_\pm = (\pm a(\sigma) - k)\theta + \sigma\theta_\perp$, expressing $\zeta \in \mathbb{R}^2$ by the new variables $\varphi \in [0, 2\pi)$ and $\sigma \in [-k, k]$. For the $+$ sign, the map $(\varphi, \sigma) \to \zeta_+$ maps $[0, 2\pi) \times [0, k]$ in a one-to-one fashion onto $|\zeta| \le \sqrt{2}k$, and the same applies to $[0, 2\pi) \times [-k, 0]$. Likewise, for the $-$ sign, $(\varphi, \sigma) \to \zeta_-$ maps $[0, 2\pi) \times [0, k]$ in a one-to-one fashion onto the annulus $\sqrt{2}k \le |\zeta| \le 2k$, and the same is true for $[0, 2\pi) \times [-k, 0]$. The Jacobian of this transformation is in all cases

$$\left|\frac{\partial\zeta}{\partial(\varphi, \sigma)}\right| = \left|\det\left((\mp a(\sigma) - k)\theta_\perp - \sigma\theta, \mp\frac{\sigma}{a(\sigma)}\theta + \theta_\perp\right)\right|$$
$$= \frac{k|\sigma|}{a(\sigma)}.$$

Thus

$$\int_{|\zeta|\le 2k}\hat{W}(\xi - \zeta)\hat{f}(\zeta)d\zeta$$
$$= \frac{k}{2}\int_0^{2\pi}\int_{-k}^k\frac{|\sigma|}{a(\sigma)}\left(\hat{W}(\xi - \zeta_+)\hat{f}(\zeta_+) + \hat{W}(\xi - \zeta_-)\hat{f}(\zeta_-)\right)d\sigma\,d\varphi$$
$$= \frac{ie^{irk}}{\sqrt{2\pi}}\int_0^{2\pi}\int_{-k}^k|\sigma|\left(\hat{W}(\xi - \zeta_+)e^{-ira(\sigma)}\hat{g}_+(\theta, \sigma) + \hat{W}(\xi - \zeta_-)e^{ira(\sigma)}\hat{g}_-(\theta, \sigma)\right)d\sigma\,d\varphi.$$

In the discretization of this integral, one has to take into account the singularity of $\hat{g}_\pm(\theta, \sigma)$ at $\sigma = \pm k$. This singularity is of the type $1/a(\sigma)$, as can be seen from Theorem 3.1. It can be removed by the change of variables $\sigma = k\sin t$, $-\pi/2 \le t \le \pi/2$. Evaluating $\hat{g}_\pm(\theta, k\sin t)$ on an equispaced t-grid is another instance of the nonequispaced FFT of type ner; see section 4.4. After having carried out the discretization, the gridding method can be applied exactly as in section 5.2.2.

In magnetic resonance imaging, $\hat{f}$ is often measured on a curve $\xi = \xi(t)$, the so-called k-trajectory (Twieg (1983)); see section 3.4 for the case of a spiral as k-trajectory. For the gridding process, the k-trajectory is imbedded into a transformation $\xi = \xi(t, s)$, which maps $\xi \in \mathbb{R}^2$ in a one-to-one way onto a domain of the space of the parameters t, s such that $\xi(t, 0) = \xi(t)$. After introducing in the convolution integral t and s as new parameters, the gridding process can be carried out as above.

5.3   Iterative Methods

A plethora of iterative methods has been proposed for the numerical solution of discrete models in tomography. However, only the algebraic reconstruction technique (ART) and EM have found widespread use. Thus we concentrate on these two methods and we survey the others in subsection 5.3.3.

5.3.1   ART

ART is simply the well-known Kaczmarz method for solving (over- or underdetermined) linear systems. Let $R_j f = g_j$ be such a system with $R_j : H \to H_j$, $j = 1, \ldots, p$, bounded linear operators from the Hilbert space H onto (surjection) the Hilbert space H_j, $j = 1, \ldots, p$. We write

$$R = \begin{pmatrix} R_1 \\ \vdots \\ R_p \end{pmatrix}, \quad g = \begin{pmatrix} g_1 \\ \vdots \\ g_p \end{pmatrix}, \quad Rf = g.$$

The orthogonal projection P_j in H onto the affine subspace $R_j f = g_j$ is given by

$$P_j f = f + R_j^*(R_j R_j^*)^{-1}(g_j - R_j f). \tag{5.45}$$

We put for $\omega > 0$

$$P_j^\omega = (1 - \omega)I + \omega P_j, \quad P^\omega = P_p^\omega \ldots P_1^\omega.$$

The Kaczmarz procedure with relaxation factor ω for solving $Rf = g$ is then

$$f^{k+1} = P^\omega f^k. \tag{5.46}$$

We describe one step explicitly. Putting $f^{k,0} = f^k$ and computing $f^{k,j}$, $j = 1, \ldots, p$, according to

$$f^{k,j} = P_j^\omega f^{k,j-1} = f^{k,j-1} + \omega R_j^*(R_j R_j^*)^{-1}(g_j - R_j f^{k,j-1}), \quad j = 1, \ldots, p, \tag{5.47}$$

we have $f^{k+1} = f^{k,p}$. For $\omega = 1$ and a linear system $Rf = g$ consisting of p scalar equations in n unknowns, this method was suggested by Kaczmarz (1937). With $a_1, \ldots, a_p$ the rows of R, it reads

$$f^{k,j} = f^{k,j-1} + \omega \frac{g_j - a_j f^{k,j-1}}{\|a_j\|^2} a_j^T, \quad j = 1, \ldots, p.$$

We work out the details of (5.47) for 2D transmission tomography in the standard parallel geometry (5.12). In that case,

$$(R_j f)(s) = (Rf)(\theta_j, s) = g_j(s)$$

with R the 2D Radon transform, considered as an operator from $H = L_2(|x| < \rho)$ into $L_2(S^1 \times (-\rho, \rho))$. Thus R_j is an operator from H into $H_j = L_2(-\rho, \rho)$. From (2.8) we get

$$(R_j^* g)(x) = g(x \cdot \theta_j), \quad |x| < \rho,$$

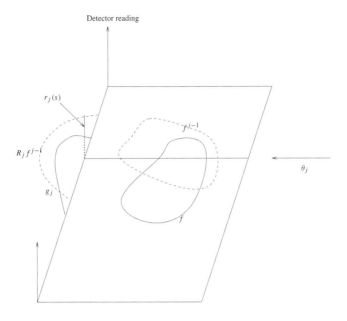

Figure 5.6. *ART for 2D transmission tomography.*

and hence

$$(R_j R_j^* g)(s) = 2\sqrt{\rho^2 - s^2} g(s), \quad |s| < \rho.$$

Thus (5.47) reads

$$f^{k,j}(x) = f^{k,j-1}(x) + \frac{\omega}{2\sqrt{\rho^2 - (x \cdot \theta_j)^2}} r_j(x \cdot \theta_j),$$

$$r_j = g_j - R_j f^{k,j-1}. \tag{5.48}$$

This is easy to visualize; see Figure 5.6. g_j is the projection of the true object f as seen by the detector for direction θ_j. $R_j f^{k,j-1}$ is the projection of the current approximation $f^{k,j-1}$. The discrepancy $r_j(s) = g_j(s) - (R_j f^{k,j-1})(s)$ at detector position s must come from a mismatch of f and $f^{k,j-1}$ along the line $x \cdot \theta_j = s$. There is no information whatsoever concerning where on this line the mismatch occurs. Thus all we can do to correct the mismatch is to spread the discrepancy $r_j(s)$ evenly about the line $x \cdot \theta_j = s$, possibly with a suitable weight. This is exactly what (5.48) is doing.

We carry out the convergence analysis for a method slightly more general than (5.47). We replace the operator $R_j R_j^*$ of that formula by an arbitrary positive definite operator C_j in H_j. This yields

$$f^{k,j} = f^{k,j-1} + \omega R_j^* C_j^{-1}(g_j - R_j f^{k,j-1}), \quad j = 1, \dots, p,$$

$$f^{k,0} = f^k, \quad f^{k+1} = f^{k,p}. \tag{5.49}$$

Special cases are the Landweber iteration ($p = 1$, $C_1 = I$; see Hanke, Neubauer, and Scherzer (1995)) and fixed-block ART (dim H_j finite, C_j diagonal; see Censor and Zenios (1997)). We consider only the consistent case in which $Rf = g$ has a solution.

THEOREM 5.1. *Let C_j be bounded and positive definite, and let $C_j \geq R_j R_j^* > 0$, $j = 1, \ldots, p$. Let $Rf = g$ be consistent. Then the iteration (5.49) is convergent, and*

$$f^k \to P_R f^0 + R^+ g,$$

where P_R is the orthogonal projection on $\ker(R)$ and R^+ is the generalized inverse of R (see section 1.3.3).

Proof. For $C_j = R_j R_j^*$ this is essentially Theorem 3.9 of Natterer (1986). We give a more elementary proof along the lines of Tanabe (1971).

Let f^+ be the minimal norm solution of $Rf = g$, i.e., $Rf^+ = g$ and $f^+ \in \ker(R)^\perp$, and let $e^k = f^k - f^+$. Then

$$e^{k+1} = Q e^k, \quad Q = Q_p \cdots Q_1,$$
$$Q_j = I - \omega R_j^* C_j^{-1} R_j, \quad j = 1, \ldots, p.$$

Q has the invariant subspaces $\ker(R)$ and $\ker(R)^\perp$, and $Q = I$ on $\ker(R)$. We show that $Q^k \to 0$ as $k \to \infty$ strongly on $\ker(R)^\perp$, proving the theorem.

We have

$$\|Q_j f\|^2 = \|f\|^2 - 2\omega(f, R_j^* C_j^{-1} R_j f) + \omega^2 (R_j^* C_j^{-1} R_j f, R_j^* C_j^{-1} R_j f)$$
$$= \|f\|^2 - 2\omega(R_j f, C_j^{-1} R_j f) + \omega^2 (R_j R_j^* C_j^{-1} R_j f, C_j^{-1} R_j f).$$

Since $R_j R_j^* \leq C_j$, we have

$$(R_j R_j^* C_j^{-1} R_j f, C_j^{-1} R_j f) \leq (C_j C_j^{-1} R_j f, C_j^{-1} R_j f)$$
$$= (R_j f, C_j^{-1} R_j f),$$

and hence

$$\|Q_j f\|^2 \leq \|f\|^2 - 2\omega(R_j f, C_j^{-1} R_j f) + \omega^2 (R_j f, C_j^{-1} R_j f)$$
$$= \|f\|^2 - \omega(2 - \omega)(R_j f, C_j^{-1} R_j f). \tag{5.50}$$

Since C_j is positive definite and $0 < \omega < 2$, we see that $\|Q_j f\| \leq \|f\|$, with equality only for $R_j f = 0$. It follows that $\|Qf\| \leq \|f\|$, with equality only for $f \in \ker(R)$. If $0 \neq f \in \ker(R)^\perp$, then $\|Qf\| < \|f\|$, because otherwise $f \in \ker(R)$, and hence $f = 0$. For $\ker(R)^\perp$ finite dimensional, it follows that Q is a contraction on $\ker(R)^\perp$, and hence $Q^k \to 0$ strongly on $\ker(R)^\perp$. In the infinite dimensional case, this follows from the following fact: Let Q be a self-adjoint operator in a Hilbert space with $\|Q\| \leq 1$ and $\|Qf\| < \|f\|$ for $f \neq 0$. Then $Q^k \to 0$ strongly as $k \to \infty$.

For the proof of this fact, we first observe that the sequence $\varepsilon_k = \|Q^k f\|$ is nonincreasing and hence convergent. It suffices to show that its limit ε is zero. We have

$$\|Q^{2k} f - Q^{2k+2m} f\|^2 = \|Q^{2k} f\|^2 + \|Q^{2k+2m} f\|^2 - 2(Q^{2k+m} f, Q^{2k+m} f)$$
$$= \varepsilon_{2k}^2 + \varepsilon_{2k+2m}^2 - 2\varepsilon_{2k+m}^2 \to 0$$

as $k \to \infty$ for each m, and hence $Q^{2k} f \to g$ for some g as $k \to \infty$. It follows that

$$\|g\| = \lim_k \|Q^{2k} f\| = \varepsilon,$$
$$\|Qg\| = \lim_k \|Q^{2k+1} f\| = \varepsilon,$$

and hence $\|Qg\| = \|g\|$. This is possible only for $g = 0$. Hence $\varepsilon = 0$. This establishes $Q^k \to 0$ strongly in $\ker(R)^\perp$.

To finish the proof, we write

$$e^0 = f^0 - f^+ = P_R f^0 + (I - P_R) f^0 - f^+.$$

Since $Q = I$ on $\ker(R)$ and $f^+, (I + P_R) f^0 \in \text{range}(R^*)$, we have

$$f^k - f^+ = e^k = Q^k e^0 = P_R f^0 + Q^k((I - P_R) f^0 - f^+) \to P_R f^0$$

as $k \to \infty$. □

As a by-product the proof provides interesting information about the possible gain in accuracy in one step of the iteration. From (5.50) we get

$$\|f^{k,j} - f\|^2 \le \|f^{k,j-1} - f\|^2$$
$$- \omega(2 - \omega)(R_j f^{k,j-1} - g_j, C_j^{-1}(R f^{k,j-1} - g_j)),$$

(5.51)

where $f = P_R f^0 + R^+ g$ is the limit. Thus the error becomes smaller whenever the residual $R_j f^{k,j-1} - g_j$ does not vanish, and the amount of the improvement can easily be computed.

Theorem 5.1 is clearly reminiscent of the SOR theory for linear systems; see Ortega and Rheinboldt (1970). In fact, there are close connections between the Kaczmarz method for $Rf = g$ and the SOR method for $RR^* u = g$. More precisely, we have the next theorem.

THEOREM 5.2. *Let u^k be the SOR iterates for $RR^* u = g$, i.e.,*

$$u^{k+1} = C_\omega u^k + c_\omega,$$
$$C_\omega = I - \omega(D + \omega L)^{-1} RR^*, \quad c_\omega = \omega(D + \omega L)^{-1} g.$$

Then $f^k = R^* u^k$ are the Kaczmarz iterates (5.46) for $Rf = g$.

So far we have considered the pure linear algebra point of view. In order to learn more about the speed of convergence and the qualitative behavior of the iterates, we exploit the analytic structure of the problems in tomography. We consider the case of reconstruction from complete projections. Let $H = L_2(B)$, let B be the unit ball in $\mathbb{R}^n$, and let $H_j = L_2(-1, +1; w^{1-n})$ with $w(s) = (1 - s^2)^{1/2}$. The maps $R_j : H \to H_j$ are defined by

$$(R_j f)(s) = (Rf)(\theta_j, s), \quad j = 1, \dots, p,$$

with R the Radon transform (2.1), are bounded and surjective. The adjoint $R_j^* : H_j \to H$ is given by

$$(R_j^* g)(x) = (w^{1-n} g)(x \cdot \theta_j);$$

compare (2.7). A straightforward computation shows that

$$R_j R_j^* = \frac{1}{n-1} |S^{n-2}| I.$$

Hence (5.45) reads

$$P_j f(x) = f(x) + \frac{n-1}{|S^{n-2}|} (w^{1-n}(g_j - R_j f))(x \cdot \theta_j), \qquad (5.52)$$

and the ART iteration (5.47) assumes the form

$$f^{k,j}(x) = f^{k,j-1}(x) + \omega'(w(g_j - R_j f^{k,j-1}))(x \cdot \theta_j), \qquad \omega' = \frac{(n-1)\omega}{|S^{n-2}|}.$$

From Theorem 5.1 we know that, in the consistent case, $f^k \to f^+$, where f^+ is the solution of minimal norm. The errors $e^k = f^+ - f^k$ satisfy

$$e^k = Q^\omega e^{k-1}, \qquad Q^\omega = Q_p^\omega \cdots Q_1^\omega, \qquad Q_j^\omega = (1-\omega)I + \omega Q_j,$$

where Q_j is the orthogonal projection onto the subspace $R_j f = 0$. We obtain Q_j from (5.52) with $g_j = 0$, i.e.,

$$Q_j f(x) = f(x) - \frac{n-1}{|S^{n-2}|} (w^{1-n} R_j f)(x \cdot \theta_j).$$

Let C_m^λ, $\lambda > -1/2$, be the Gegenbauer polynomial of degree m, i.e., the orthogonal polynomials on $[-1, +1]$ with weight $(1 - s^2)^{\lambda - 1/2}$; see section 1.3.5. We put

$$C_{m,j}(x) = C_m^{n/2}(x \cdot \theta_j), \qquad C_m = \langle C_{m,1}, \ldots, C_{m,p} \rangle.$$

THEOREM 5.3. *Let* $\alpha_m(t) = \frac{\pi^{(n-1)/2}}{\Gamma(\frac{n+1}{2})} \frac{C_m^{n/2}(t)}{C_m^{n/2}(1)}$. *Then*

$$Q_j C_{m,i} = C_{m,i} - \frac{n-1}{|S^{n-2}|} \alpha_m(\theta_i \cdot \theta_j) C_{m,j}.$$

The theorem was obtained by Hamaker and Solmon (1978). It implies that C_m is an invariant subspace of Q_j and hence of Q_j^ω and of Q^ω. We compute a matrix representation of Q^ω in C_m. One can show that

$$\dim C_m = \min\{p, M\}, \qquad M = \binom{m+n-1}{n-1}, \qquad (5.53)$$

provided that

$$\theta_j \neq \pm \theta_k, \qquad k \neq j, \qquad k, j = 1, \ldots, p. \qquad (5.54)$$

For $M > p$, convergence on $\mathcal{C}_m$ is of no interest since for these m the functions in $\mathcal{C}_m$ represent details that, by our resolution analysis in section 4.2, cannot be resolved anyway. Therefore, we assume in the following that $M \leq p$.

As a direct consequence of Theorem 5.3, Q_j^ω in $\mathcal{C}_m$ is represented by the $p \times p$ matrix

$$A_{m,j}(\omega) = \begin{pmatrix} 1 & & & & \\ & 1 & & & \\ -\omega\alpha_{m,j,1} & \cdots & 1-\omega & \cdots & -\omega\alpha_{m,j,p} \\ & & 1 & & \\ & & & & 1 \end{pmatrix}, \quad \alpha_{m,k,j} = \frac{n-1}{|S^{n-2}|}\alpha_m(\theta_k \cdot \theta_j),$$

which differs from the unit matrix only in row j. For $n = 2$ and $\theta_j = (\cos\varphi_j, \sin\varphi_j)^T$ we have $M = m + 1$ and

$$\alpha_{m,k,j} = \begin{cases} \dfrac{\sin((m+1)(\varphi_k-\varphi_j))}{(m+1)\sin(\varphi_k-\varphi_j)}, & \varphi_k \neq \varphi_j, \\ 1, & \varphi_k = \varphi_j. \end{cases}$$

The matrix representation of Q^ω in $\mathcal{C}_m$ is

$$A_m(\omega) = A_{m,p}(\omega) \cdots A_{m,1}(\omega). \tag{5.55}$$

One can also show that

$$\text{range}(R^*) = \bigoplus_{m=0}^{\infty} \mathcal{C}_m.$$

For $f^0 \in \text{range}(R^*)$, all e^k are in range(R^*). Thus we can study the speed of convergence for each $\mathcal{C}_m$ separately simply by computing the spectral radius $\rho_m(\omega)$ of Q^ω on $\mathcal{C}_m$ for all m with $M \leq p$. This is facilitated by the fact that the inner products of the $\mathcal{C}_{m,i}$ are known: With some constant $c(n, m)$ we have

$$\int_{|x|<1} C_{m,k}(x)C_{m,j}(x)dx = c(n, m)C_m^{n/2}(\theta_k \cdot \theta_j).$$

Numerical results for $\rho_m(\omega)$ are presented in Figure 5.7 for $n = 2$ and $p = 30$ directions θ_j.

The crucial point is that the $\rho_m(\omega)$ depend decisively on the way in which the directions θ_j are ordered. First, we consider the sequential order, i.e., $\varphi_j = \frac{j-1}{p}\pi$, $j = 1, \ldots, p$. In Figure 5.7(a) we see that for $\omega = 1$, convergence is fast on the $\mathcal{C}_m$ with m large, i.e., on the high-frequency components, while convergence is slow on the $\mathcal{C}_m$ with m small, i.e., on the low-frequency components. The situation is just the other way around for $\omega = 0.1$. Thus for $\omega = 1$, the high-frequency components (such as noise) show up early in the iteration, while overall features are determined later. It is clear that this is not a desirable behavior. For $\omega = 0.1$ the iterations first determine the smooth parts of f and the small details only later. This is clearly more desirable. Thus surprisingly small values of ω (e.g., $\omega = 0.05$) are quite common in ART.

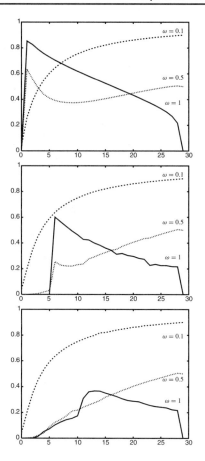

Figure 5.7. *Spectral radius $\rho_m(\omega)$ of Q^ω in $\mathcal{C}_m$ for $n = 2$, $p = 30$ as a function of m.* (a) *Sequential order of directions.* (b) *Nonsequential order.* (c) *Random order.*

The situation changes drastically if the linear order of directions is given up in favor of a nonsequential order; see Figure 5.7(b). For $\omega = 1$ we now have fast convergence on all subspaces $\mathcal{C}_m$, i.e., for all spatial frequencies. The practical consequence is that it is advisable to use an order different from the sequential one. This was discovered by Hamaker and Solmon (1978) and was rediscovered in Herman and Meyer (1993). A good strategy for choosing an order is to make directions as orthogonal as possible to the previous ones. For example, for 18 parallel projections in the plane, the directions 0, 90, 140, 50, 110, 30, 160, 70, 130, 20, 100, 170, 40, 80, 150, 10, 60, 120 degrees seem to be favorable. In fact, Hamaker and Solmon (1978) showed that they are the best possible for $p = 18$. However, a random choice of directions is almost as good; see Figure 5.7(c).

It is interesting to compare ART with other iterative methods, such as the Landweber iteration, which came to be known as SIRT (simultaneous iterative reconstruction technique) in tomography. The difference from (5.52) is that the update is done only after a complete sweep through all the directions. This leads to

$$f^{k+1} = f^k + \omega \sum_{j=1}^{p} R_j^* C_j^{-1}(g_j - R_j f^k).$$

Introducing $e^k = f^k - f^+$, we get

$$e^{k+1} = \overline{Q}^\omega e^k,$$

where now, for $C_j = R_j R_j^*$,

$$\overline{Q}^\omega = I - \omega \sum_{j=1}^{p} R_j^* C_j^{-1} R_j$$

$$= I + \omega \sum_{j=1}^{p} (Q_j - I)$$

with Q_j as above. Thus by Theorem 5.3, $\mathcal{C}_m$ is again an invariant subspace of $\overline{Q}^\omega$, and the matrix representation of $\overline{Q}^\omega$ is

$$\overline{A}_m(\omega) = I - \omega \alpha_m,$$

where α_m is the (p, p)-matrix with elements $\alpha_{m,i,j}$, $i, j = 1, \ldots, p$. For evenly spaced directions θ_j, i.e., $\varphi_j = (j - 1)\pi/p$, $j = 1, \ldots, p$, the eigenvalues of α_m are easy to compute. Using the identity

$$(m + 1)\alpha_{m,k,j} = e^{im\psi} + e^{i(m-2)\psi} + \cdots + e^{-im\psi},$$

where $\psi = \pi(k - j)/p$, the eigenvalue equation $\alpha_m x = \lambda x$, $x = (x_0, \ldots, x_{p-1})^T$, reads

$$(m + 1) \sum_{j=0}^{p-1} \sideset{}{'}\sum_{\ell=-m}^{m} e^{i\pi\ell(k-j)/p} x_j = \lambda x_k, \quad k = 0, \ldots, p - 1,$$

where the prime at the ℓ-sum indicates that $\ell + m$ is even. Putting $\ell + m = 2\nu$, rearranging yields

$$(m + 1) \sum_{\nu=0}^{m} e^{2\pi i \nu k/p} \sum_{j=0}^{p-1} e^{-2\pi i \nu j/p} y_j = \lambda y_k, \quad k = 0, \ldots, p - 1,$$

where $y_j = e^{i\pi m j/p} x_j$, $j = 0, \ldots, p - 1$. With the matrix $F = (e^{-2\pi i jk/p})_{j,k=0,\ldots,p-1}$ and $y = (y_0, \ldots, y_{p-1})^T$, this reads

$$\frac{m+1}{p} F^{-1} P F y = \lambda y,$$

where P is the diagonal matrix with $m + 1$ 1's and $p - m - 1$ 0's on the diagonal. It follows that α_m has the eigenvalue $\frac{p}{m+1}$ with multiplicity $m + 1$ and 0 with multiplicity $p - m - 1$. Thus the spectral radius $\overline{\rho_m}(\omega)$ of $\overline{Q}^\omega$ on $\mathcal{C}_m$ is

$$\overline{\rho_m}(\omega) = \left| 1 - \frac{\omega p}{m + 1} \right|.$$

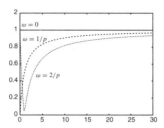

Figure 5.8. *Spectral radius $\overline{\rho_m}(\omega)$ of $\overline{Q}^\omega$ in $\mathcal{C}_m$ for $n = 2$, $p = 30$.*

Hence the condition for convergence of SIRT is $0 < \omega < \frac{2}{p}$.

Comparing the graph of $\overline{\rho_m}(\omega)$ in Figure 5.8 with $\rho_m(\omega)$ in Figure 5.7 makes clear why ART (with a good arrangement of directions or a favorable choice of ω) is so much better than SIRT.

In practice, ART is applied to a discretized version of the linear integral equation governing a certain imaging system, e.g., the Radon integral equation. One represents the unknown function f by an expansion of the form

$$f = \sum_{k=1}^{N} f_k B_k$$

with certain basis functions B_k. These basis functions can be chosen, for example, as the characteristic functions of pixels or voxels. It has been suggested to use radially symmetric functions, the so-called "blobs"; see Lewitt (1992) and Marabini et al. (1999). With g_i the ith measurements, we then obtain

$$g_i = \sum_{k=1}^{N} a_{ik} f_k,$$

where a_{ik} is the ith measurement of B_k. In imaging, this approach is sometimes called a series expansion method, while in numerical analysis, one would call it a projection method, or more specifically a collocation method.

5.3.2 The EM algorithm

This is an iterative algorithm for maximizing the likelihood function L from (3.9). Taking the logarithm of L and omitting an additive constant, we can as well maximize the log likelihood function

$$\ell(f) = \sum_{i=1}^{n} (g_i \log(Af)_i - (Af)_i). \qquad (5.56)$$

In order to avoid purely technical difficulties, we assume $A, g > 0$ elementwise. One can easily verify that the Hessian of ℓ is negative semidefinite, i.e., ℓ is concave. Thus local maxima of ℓ in $f \geq 0$ are also global ones, and f is a global maximum if and only if the Kuhn–Tucker conditions

$$\frac{\partial \ell}{\partial f_\ell}(f) = 0 \quad \text{for } f_\ell > 0,$$

$$\frac{\partial \ell}{\partial f_\ell}(f) \geq 0 \quad \text{for } f_\ell = 0$$

are satisfied. We have

$$\nabla \ell(f) = A^T \left(\frac{g}{Af} - 1 \right),$$

where 1 is a vector with only 1's as components and all arithmetic operations between vectors are componentwise. It follows that each global maximum f of ℓ in $f \geq 0$ satisfies

$$f A^T \left(\frac{g}{Af} - 1 \right) = 0.$$

Normalizing A such that each column sum is 1, i.e., $A^T 1 = 1$, this reads

$$f = f A^T \frac{g}{Af}. \tag{5.57}$$

The EM algorithm is the most simple iterative method for solving (5.57):

$$f^{k+1} = f^k A^T \frac{g}{Af^k}, \quad k = 0, 1, \dots. \tag{5.58}$$

It was shown by Shepp and Vardi (1982) that this is an instance of the EM algorithm of Dempster, Laird, and Rubin (1977). The convergence was proved by Vardi, Shepp, and Kaufman (1985).

THEOREM 5.4. *Let $f^0 > 0$. Then (5.58) converges to a maximizer of (5.56).*

Proof. We follow Mülthei and Schorr (1987) and Iusem (1991). The proof makes use of Jensen's inequality

$$\log \sum_{i=1}^n \alpha_i \beta_i \geq \sum_{i=1}^n \alpha_i \log \beta_i,$$

which holds whenever $\alpha_i, \beta_i \geq 0$ and $\sum_{i=1}^n \alpha_i = 1$. It is just another way of stating that log is a concave function. We also need some elementary properties of the Kullback–Leiber distance

$$L(x, y) = \sum_{i=1}^n \left(x_i \log \frac{x_i}{y_i} + y_i - x_i \right),$$

which is defined for $x, y \in \mathbb{R}^n$, $x \geq 0$, where $t \log t = 0$ for $t = 0$. Putting $\varphi_u(t) = t - u \log t$, we have

$$L(x, y) = \sum_{i=1}^n \left(\varphi_{x_i}(y_i) - \varphi_{x_i}(x_i) \right).$$

For each $u \geq 0$, we have $\varphi_u \geq 0$ for $t \geq 0$, and φ_u assumes its unique minimum at $t = u$. Also, $\varphi_u(t) \to \varphi_u(u)$ for u fixed implies $t \to u$. Hence $L(x, y) \geq 0$, $L(x, \cdot)$ assumes its unique minimum 0 at $y = x$, and $y \to x$ if $L(x, y) \to L(x, x)$.

In the first step of the proof, we show that

$$\ell(f^{k+1}) \geq \ell(f^k), \quad k = 1, 2, \ldots. \tag{5.59}$$

We start out from the identity

$$\sum_{i=1}^{n} g_i \log(Af)_i = \sum_{i=1}^{n} g_i \sum_{\ell=1}^{m} \frac{a_{i\ell} h_\ell}{(Ah)_i} \left[\log(a_{i\ell} f_\ell) - \log\left(\frac{a_{i\ell} f_\ell}{(Af)_i}\right) \right],$$

which holds for $h, f \in \mathbb{R}^m$, $h, f > 0$. Since for $k > 0$

$$\sum_{i=1}^{n} (Af^k)_i = \sum_{\ell=1}^{m} f_\ell^k = \sum_{i=1}^{n} g_i, \tag{5.60}$$

we have for $k > 0$

$$\ell(f^{k+1}) - \ell(f^k) = \sum_{i=1}^{n} g_i \log(Af^{k+1})_i - \sum_{i=1}^{n} g_i \log(Af^k)_i.$$

Applying the identity with $h = f^k$ and $f = f^k, f^{k+1}$, respectively, we obtain

$$\ell(f^{k+1}) - \ell(f^k) = \sum_{i=1}^{n} g_i \sum_{\ell=1}^{m} \frac{a_{i\ell} f_\ell^k}{(Af^k)_i} \left[\log(a_{i\ell} f_\ell^{k+1}) - \log\left(\frac{a_{i\ell} f_\ell^{k+1}}{(Af^{k+1})_i}\right) \right]$$

$$- \sum_{i=1}^{n} g_i \sum_{\ell=1}^{m} \frac{a_{i\ell} f_\ell^k}{(Af^k)_i} \left[\log(a_{i\ell} f_\ell^k) - \log\left(\frac{a_{i\ell} f_\ell^k}{(Af^k)_i}\right) \right]$$

$$= \sum_{i=1}^{n} g_i \sum_{\ell=1}^{m} \frac{a_{i\ell} f_\ell^k}{(Af^k)_i} \left[\log\left(\frac{f_\ell^{k+1}}{f_\ell^k}\right) - \log\left(\frac{f_\ell^{k+1}(Af^k)_i}{f_\ell^k(Af^{k+1})_i}\right) \right]$$

$$= \sum_{\ell=1}^{m} f_\ell^{k+1} \log\left(\frac{f_\ell^{k+1}}{f_\ell^k}\right) - \sum_{i=1}^{n} g_i \sum_{\ell=1}^{m} \frac{a_{i\ell} f_\ell^k}{(Af^k)_i} \log\left(\frac{f_\ell^{k+1}(Af^k)_i}{f_\ell^k(Af^{k+1})_i}\right).$$

Applying Jensen's inequality to the ℓ sum in the double sum, we obtain

$$\ell(f^{k+1}) - \ell(f^k) \geq \sum_{\ell=1}^{m} f_\ell^{k+1} \log\left(\frac{f_\ell^{k+1}}{f_\ell^k}\right) - \sum_{i=1}^{n} g_i \log \sum_{\ell=1}^{m} \frac{a_{i\ell} f_\ell^{k+1}}{(Af^{k+1})_i}$$

$$= L(f^{k+1}, f^k) - \sum_{i=1}^{n} g_i \log 1 \geq 0.$$

In the second step, we show that for each limit point f^* of the sequence (f^k), we have

$$L(f^*, f^{k+1}) \leq L(f^*, f^k), \quad k = 1, 2, \ldots. \tag{5.61}$$

With x^ℓ, y^ℓ the vectors whose components are

$$x_i^\ell = \frac{a_{i\ell}g_i/(Af^*)_i}{(A^T(g/Af^*))_\ell}, \quad y_i^\ell = \frac{a_{i\ell}g_i/(Af^k)_i}{(A^T(g/Af^k))_\ell}, \quad i = 1, \ldots, n,$$

we have $\sum_{i=1}^n x_i^\ell = \sum_{i=1}^n y_i^\ell = 1$ and

$$0 \le \sum_{\ell=1}^m {}' f_\ell^* L(x^\ell, y^\ell)$$

$$= \sum_{\ell=1}^m f_\ell^{*'} \sum_{i=1}^n x_i^\ell \log \frac{x_i^\ell}{y_i^\ell}$$

$$= \sum_{\ell=1}^m {}' f_\ell^* \sum_{i=1}^n \frac{a_{i\ell}g_i/(Af^*)_i}{(A^T(g/Af^*))_\ell} \log \frac{(Af^k)_i(A^T(g/Af^k))_\ell}{(Af^*)_i(A^T(g/Af^*))_\ell}$$

$$= \sum_{\ell=1}^m {}' f_\ell^* \sum_{i=1}^n \frac{a_{i\ell}g_i/(Af^*)_i}{A^T(g/Af^*)_\ell} \log \frac{(Af)_i^k f_\ell^{k+1} f_\ell^*}{(Af^*)_i f_\ell^* f_\ell^k},$$

where the prime indicates that the sum extends only over ℓ with $f_\ell^* > 0$. Since

$$f^* = f^* A^T(g/Af^*),$$

we have

$$\left(A^T\left(\frac{g}{Af^*}\right)\right)_\ell = 1 \quad \text{if } f_\ell^* > 0.$$

It follows that

$$0 \le \sum_{\ell=1}^m f_\ell^* \sum_{i=1}^n a_{i\ell} \frac{g_i}{(Af^*)_i} \log \frac{(Af^k)_i f_\ell^{k+1}}{(Af^*)_i f_\ell^k}$$

$$= \sum_{\ell=1}^m f_\ell^* \sum_{i=1}^n a_{i\ell} \frac{g_i}{(Af^*)_i} \left(\log \frac{(Af^k)_i}{(Af^*)_i} + \log \frac{f_\ell^{k+1}}{f_\ell^k}\right)$$

$$= \sum_{i=1}^n g_i \log \frac{(Af^k)_i}{(Af^*)_i} + \sum_{\ell=1}^m f_\ell^* \log \frac{f_\ell^{k+1}}{f_\ell^k}$$

$$= \ell(f^k) - \ell(f^*) + L(f^*, f^k) - L(f^*, f^{k+1}).$$

Now (5.61) follows from (5.59).

In the final step, we take f^* as the limit of a subsequence (f^{k_s}). Then $L(f^*, f^{k_s}) \to 0$ as $s \to \infty$. Since $L(f^*, f^k)$ is nonincreasing, we have $L(f^*, f^k) \to 0$ as $k \to \infty$. From the properties of L, it follows that $f^k \to f^*$. In order to show that f^* is a maximizer of ℓ, we check the Kuhn–Tucker conditions. They are obviously satisfied for $f_\ell^* > 0$. For $f_\ell^* = 0$, we have

$$f_\ell^{k+1} = f_\ell^0 \left(A^T \frac{g}{Af^0}\right)_\ell \cdot \ldots \cdot \left(A^T \frac{g}{Af^k}\right)_\ell \to 0$$

as $k \to \infty$. Since $(A^T g/Af^k)_\ell \to (A^T g/Af^*)_\ell$ this is only possible if $(A^T g/Af^*)_\ell \le 1$, i.e., the Kuhn–Tucker conditions are satisfied for $f_\ell^* = 0$, too. $\Box$

The problems with EM are the notoriously slow convergence and the lacking smoothness of the iterates ("checkerboard effect," i.e., the pixels show up conspicuously in the iterates). So, in its original form (5.58), EM is not very useful.

The convergence of EM can be accelerated considerably by splitting A and g into submatrices A_j and subvectors g_j, $j = 1, \ldots, p$, such that

$$A = \begin{pmatrix} A_1 \\ \vdots \\ A_p \end{pmatrix}, \quad g = \begin{pmatrix} g_1 \\ \vdots \\ g_p \end{pmatrix},$$

$$A_j : \mathbb{R}^n \to \mathbb{R}^{m_j}, \quad g_j \in \mathbb{R}^{m_j},$$

and doing (5.58) for each submatrix individually. We assume the A_j to be balanced, i.e., $a = A_j^T 1$ is independent of j. In this way, we obtain

$$\begin{aligned} f^{k,0} &= f^k, \\ f^{k,j} &= f^{k,j-1} \frac{1}{a} A_j^T \frac{g_j}{A_j f^{k,j-1}}, \quad j = 1, \ldots, p, \\ f^{k+1} &= f^{k,p}. \end{aligned} \qquad (5.62)$$

This is the ordered subset EM (OSEM) algorithm of Hudson and Larkin (1994). Note that (5.62) is just a multiplicative version of the Kaczmarz method (5.47) for the solution of $Af = g$.

The convergence properties of OSEM are difficult to assess. If all the sequences $(f^{k,j})$ converged to a common limit f^* as $k \to \infty$, then f^* would be a common maximizer of the log likelihood functions for each of the systems $A_j f = g_j$, $j = 1, \ldots, p$. Since these systems are not likely to be consistent in concrete applications, such a common maximizer cannot reasonably be expected to exist. Thus OSEM is not likely to converge, except in the consistent case. In fact, convergence can be proved in the consistent case by a straightforward extension of the proof of Theorem 5.4, if the A_j are balanced.

Now we investigate the speed of convergence of EM and OSEM (in the consistent case). As suggested by Tanaka (1987) we introduce a relaxation parameter ω. Putting

$$G_j(f) = f \left(\frac{1}{a} A_j^T \frac{g}{Af} \right)^\omega, \quad j = 1, \ldots, p,$$

the relaxed OSEM algorithm reads

$$f^{k+1} = G(f^k), \quad G^\omega = G_p^\omega o \cdots o G_1^\omega, \qquad (5.63)$$

where o means composition. For $\omega = 1$ we regain standard OSEM, and for $p = 1$ we regain standard EM with relaxation.

Anticipating convergence, we have that the speed of convergence is governed by the Jacobian $G'(f)$ for a fixed point f of (5.63). Assuming $Af = g$, we readily obtain

$$G'(f) = \prod_{j=1}^{p} \left(I - \omega \frac{f}{a} A_j^T \frac{1}{g_j} A_j \right). \qquad (5.64)$$

It is interesting to compare this with the corresponding operator

$$Q = \prod_{j=1}^{p} (I - \omega A_j^* C_j A_j) \tag{5.65}$$

for the Kaczmarz method (5.49) applied to the system $A_j f = g_j$, $j = 1, \ldots, p$. Viewing A_j as a linear map from $\mathbb{R}^n$ into $\mathbb{R}^{m_j}$ endowed with the inner products

$$(x, y)_f = \left(\frac{a}{f} x, y \right), \quad (x, y)_{g_j} = \left(\frac{1}{g_j} x, y \right),$$

where $(\cdot, \cdot)$ is the natural inner product in $\mathbb{R}^n$, $\mathbb{R}^{m_j}$, respectively, we have

$$A_j^* = \frac{f}{a} A_j^T \frac{1}{g_j},$$

and hence

$$Q = \prod_{j=1}^{p} \left(I - \omega \frac{f}{a} A_j^T C_j \frac{1}{g_j} A_j \right).$$

Thus for $C_j = I$, (5.64) and (5.65) are the same. We conclude that the speed of convergence of OSEM and ART are the same, and that, by and large, our convergence analysis of ART in the previous section applies to OSEM as well. In particular, OSEM is faster than EM in the same sense that ART is faster than Landweber, and for relaxed OSEM very small relaxation factors are favorable. Also, the speed of convergence of OSEM depends on the ordering of the equations, exactly in the same way as in ART.

Now we address the second problem of EM, namely, the lack of smoothness. We consider only EM, the extension to OSEM being obvious. The most simple advice to prevent the iterates from becoming too rough is to stop the iteration early. Another possibility is to carry out a smoothing step after each iteration (EMS algorithm of Silverman, Jones, and Nychka (1990)). Finally, one can add a penalty term $-B(f)$ to (5.56), i.e., one maximizes $\ell(f) - B(f)$ rather than $\ell(f)$. $B(f)$ may be interpreted in a Bayesian framework or simply as a penalty discouraging roughness. Typically,

$$B(f) = (f - \overline{f})^T B(f - \overline{f}),$$

where $\overline{f}$ is a reference picture and B is a positive definite matrix. Maximizing $\ell(f) - B(f)$ leads to

$$f = f A^T \frac{g}{Af} - f \nabla B(f). \tag{5.66}$$

Several iterative methods for solving (5.66) were suggested. In the OSL algorithm of Green (1990) one iterates according to

$$f^{k+1} = f^k A^T \frac{g}{Af^k} - f^{k+1} \nabla B(f^k)$$

or

$$f^{k+1} = \frac{f^k}{1 + \nabla B(f^k)} A^T \frac{g}{Af^k}.$$

This algorithm preserves positivity, as does the original EM algorithm. Setzepfandt (1992) suggested solving

$$f^{k+1} = f^k A^T \frac{g}{A f^k} - f^{k+1} \nabla B(f^{k+1})$$

for f^{k+1} by the SOR Newton method; see Ortega and Rheinboldt (1970). If B is a diagonal matrix, then this equation is of second order in f^{k+1} and can be solved explicitly; see Levitan and Herman (1987).

5.3.3 Other iterative algorithms

We give only a short description of some of the other algorithms, together with their main properties. For a survey, see Censor (1981).

First, there are several versions of ART, all of them dealing with fully discretized problems; see Gordon, Bender, and Herman (1970). We mention only Hildreth's algorithm, which is designed to compute a solution of minimal norm to the system

$$Af \le g, \tag{5.67}$$

where A is an (m, n)-matrix, $m \le n$. The idea behind this reformulation is to account for measurement and modeling errors. Introducing Lagrangian multipliers $\lambda_i \in \mathbb{R}^m$, the minimum norm solution f to (5.67) is easily seen to be characterized by

$$f = A^T \lambda, \quad \lambda^T (g - Af) = 0, \qquad \lambda \ge 0, \quad Af \le g.$$

It can be computed iteratively in the following way. Let $f^0 = 0$, $\lambda^0 = 0$. If f^{k-1}, λ^{k-1} is computed, determine f^k, λ^k by

$$
\begin{aligned}
f^{k,0} &= f^{k-1}, \quad \lambda^{k,0} = \lambda^{k-1}, \\
f^{k,i} &= f^{k,i-1} + c_i a_i, \quad \lambda^{k,i} = \lambda^{k,i-1} - c_i e_i, \\
c_i &= \min\left(\lambda^{k,i-1}, \ \omega \frac{g_i - a_i \cdot f^{k-1,i}}{\|a_i\|^2} \right), \quad i = 1, \dots, m,
\end{aligned}
$$

where $a_i \in \mathbb{R}^n$ is the ith row of A and e_i is the ith unit vector in $\mathbb{R}^m$, and put $f^k = f^{k,m}$, $\lambda^k = \lambda^{k,m}$.

The projection on convex subsets (POCS) algorithm goes one step farther and replaces the half-spaces $(Af)_i \le g_i$, $i = 1, \dots, m$, by arbitrary convex sets C_i. The problem is to find an f in the intersection $C_1 \cap \cdots \cap C_m$ of these convex sets; see Sezan and Stark (1987) and Bauschke and Borwein (1996) for a more recent exposition. Let P_i be the orthogonal projection onto C_i. Then POCS iterates according to

$$f^{k+1} = P_m \cdots P_1 f^k.$$

The purpose behind the multiplicative algebraic reconstruction technique (MART) is to replace the cost function $\|f\|$ by the entropy

$$E(f) = -\sum_{i=1}^n f_i \log f_i. \tag{5.68}$$

In accordance with the probabilistic interpretation of the entropy, we assume $f \geq 0$. The MART update is

$$f_j^{k,i} = f_j^{k,i-1} \left(\frac{g_i}{a_i \cdot f^{k,i-1}} \right)^{a_{ij}}, \quad j = 1, \ldots, n. \tag{5.69}$$

If $Af = g$ has a solution at all, MART converges to the one with minimal entropy $E(f)$. If (5.69) is replaced by

$$f_j^{k,i} = f_j^{k,i-1} \frac{1}{1 - a_{ij} c_i f_j^{k,i-1}}, \quad j = 1, \ldots, n,$$

$$c_i = \omega \left(1 - \frac{a_i \cdot f^{k-1,i}}{g_i} \right) t_i, \tag{5.70}$$

$$t_i = \min_j \left\{ \frac{1}{a_{ij} f_j^{k-1,i-1}} : a_{ij} \neq 0 \right\},$$

then f^k converges for $f^0 > 0$ to the solution of $Af = g$ for which the so called log-entropy

$$-\sum_i \log f_i$$

is minimal. (5.69) and (5.70) are examples of multiplicative algorithms; see Pierro (1991). Another example for a multiplicative algorithm is the EM algorithm (5.58).

5.4   Direct Algebraic Algorithms

In direct algebraic algorithms (DART), one considers the measurements g_j as bounded linear functionals $g_j = R_j f$ on $L_2(G)$, where G is the reconstruction region. One then determines a "solution" to the underdetermined system $g_j = R_j f$, $j = 1, \ldots, m$, for example, the Moore–Penrose generalized solution, a Tikhonov–Phillips regularized solution, or a Bayesian estimate. In all cases one has to invert a huge matrix, which factors if the scanning geometry has enough symmetries, such as rotational symmetry. The matrix can then be inverted efficiently by FFT methods, resulting in algorithms that are comparable in efficiency with filtered backprojection. The advantage of DART is that the ray geometry can be modeled easily and there are no discretization errors at all. The disadvantage is that the implementation is not quite straightforward, and very big matrices, depending only on the scanning geometry, have to be precomputed and stored.

Assume that the functionals R_j can be represented as

$$R_j f = (\chi_j, f), \quad j = 1, \ldots, m,$$

with the inner product $(,)$ in $L_2(C)$. χ_j are typically characteristic functions of the rays, which we assume to be of finite width. These rays are called "natural pixels" in Buonocore, Brody, and Macovski (1981). The χ_j may also be more general functions supported by the rays, modeling nonuniform detector sensitivity and the like. The Moore–Penrose generalized solution is

$$f_{MP} = R^* r, \quad Sr = g. \tag{5.71}$$

Here $R : L_2(G) \rightarrow \mathbb{R}^m$ is the operator

$$R = \begin{pmatrix} R_1 \\ \vdots \\ R_p \end{pmatrix},$$

and its adjoint $R^* : \mathbb{R}^m \rightarrow L_2(G)$ is

$$R^* r = \sum_{j=1}^{m} \chi_j r_j. \tag{5.72}$$

$S = RR^*$ is the Gram matrix of the χ_i, i.e.,

$$S_{ij} = (\chi_i, \chi_j), \quad i, j = 1, \ldots, m. \tag{5.73}$$

Of course, $Sr = g$ need not have a unique solution. In the case of nonuniqueness it does not matter which solution we take.

Instead of the Moore–Penrose solution we may take the Tikhonov–Phillips regularized solution, i.e., the minimizer of

$$\|Rf - g\|^2 + \gamma \|f\|^2$$

with the regularization parameter $\gamma > 0$. The solution is

$$f_{TP} = R^* r, \quad (S + \gamma I)r = g. \tag{5.74}$$

Still another possibility is Bayesian estimation. Here we think of $f(x)$ as a random variable with mean value $\overline{f}(x)$ and covariance

$$F(x, x') = E((f(x) - \overline{f}(x))(f(x') - \overline{f}(x'))),$$

where E is the mathematical expectation. The Bayes estimate for f is (see, e.g., Papoulis (1965))

$$f_B = \overline{f} + FR^* r, \quad (S^F + \Sigma)r = g - R\overline{f}, \tag{5.75}$$

where Σ is the covariance matrix of the noise in g and

$$S_{ij}^F = (\chi_i, F\chi_j), \quad i, j = 1, \ldots, m.$$

Here F is the integral operator

$$(Fu)(x) = \int_G F(x, y)u(y)dy,$$

and FR^* is the generalized backprojection operator

$$FR^* r = \sum_{i=1}^{m} \eta_i r_i, \quad \eta_i(x) = \int_G F(x, y)\chi_i(y)dy.$$

Note that the support of η_i is no longer the ray supporting χ_i but a bit larger, in general.

In all cases, the computation procedure consists of two steps. First, one has to solve the linear system $Sr = g$ or one of its variants. The dimension of this system corresponds to the number of measurements and is typically very large. So direct solution of this system is not feasible. Now assume that the measurements come in p groups with q items each. By abuse of notation, we write

$$R_{j\ell} f = g_{j\ell}, \quad R_{j\ell} f = (f, \chi_{j\ell}).$$

Assume further that group j is obtained from group $j - 1$ by an isometry U, i.e.,

$$\chi_{j,\ell} = \chi_{j-1,\ell} \circ U^{-1}, \tag{5.76}$$

and that $U^p = I$. Then

$$(\chi_{j\ell}, \chi_{ik}) = (\chi_{0\ell} \circ U^{-j}, \chi_{0k} \circ U^{-i})$$
$$= (\chi_{0\ell}, \chi_{0k} \circ U^{j-i})$$

depends only on $j - i$, i.e.,

$$S = \begin{pmatrix} S_0 & S_1 & \cdots & S_{p-1} \\ S_{-1} & S_0 & \cdots & S_{p-2} \\ S_{1-p} & \cdots & \cdots & S_0 \end{pmatrix}, \quad (S_j)_{k\ell} = (\chi_{j\ell}, \chi_{0k}), \quad \ell, k = 1, \ldots, q,$$

with $q \times q$ matrices S_j, and $S_j = S_{j+p}$. Thus S is a block cyclic convolution with blocks of size $q \times q$. Using FFT, the system $Sr = g$ can be solved with O $(q^2 p + pq \log p)$ operations provided the inverses (or generalized inverses) of

$$\hat{S}_k = \frac{1}{p} \sum_{j=0}^{p} e^{-2\pi i k j / p} S_j, \quad k = 0, \ldots, p - 1,$$

are precomputed and stored. This requires O $(q^3 p + q^2 p \log p)$ operations.

Once r is computed, the reconstruction is finished by computing

$$(R^* r)(x) = \sum_{j,\ell} r_{j\ell} \chi_{j\ell}(x)$$
$$= \sum_{\substack{j,\ell \\ x \in L_{j\ell}}} r_{j\ell} \chi_{j\ell}(x), \tag{5.77}$$

where $L_{j\ell} = \text{supp}(\chi_{j\ell})$ is the ray. Equation (5.77) is just a discrete version of the familiar backprojection operator.

5.5 3D Algorithms

Due to the greater geometric flexibility, the variety of reconstruction algorithms is much larger in 3D than in 2D. Therefore, we restrict ourselves to the derivation of the underlying inversion formulas. Their computer implementation parallels the 2D case.

5.5.1 The FDK approximate formula

The FDK approximate formula is presently the most widely used formula for cone beam scanning with a circle as source curve. None of the exact inversion formulas from section 2.3 applies to this situation. Thus we do not aim at exact inversion. We rather describe the ingenious approximate formula, which was given by Feldkamp, Davis, and Kress (1984).

To fix ideas, we assume the source to be on the circle of radius r in the horizontal $x_1 - x_2$ plane. For the source $r\theta$, $\theta \in S^1$, we denote by $g(\theta, y)$ the line integral of f along the line joining $r\theta$ with the detector $y \in \theta^\perp$, i.e.,

$$g(\theta, y) = (Df) \left(r\theta, \frac{y - r\theta}{|y - r\theta|} \right);$$

see Figure 3.3. As usual we assume f to be zero outside $|x| \leq \rho < r$. The idea of FDK is as follows. Consider the plane $\pi(x, \theta)$ through $r\theta$ and x that intersects $\theta^\perp$ in a horizontal line. Compute in this plane the contribution of the linear fan beam inversion formula (5.35) to $(V_\Omega * f)(x)$ which belongs to θ. Finally, integrate all those contributions over θ, disregarding the fact that they come from different planes. These planes form a sheaf with vertex x. The result is the FDK reconstruction at x.

First, we introduce a coordinate system in $\theta^\perp$. For $\theta = (\cos\varphi, \sin\varphi, 0)^T$, we put $\theta_\perp = (\sin\varphi, -\cos\varphi, 0)^T$. Then $\theta_\perp, e_3$ is an orthonormal basis in $\theta^\perp$. The line through $r\theta$ and x hits $\theta^\perp$ at $y = y_2\theta_\perp + y_3e_3$, where

$$y_2 = \frac{r}{r - x \cdot \theta} x \cdot \theta_\perp, \quad y_3 = \frac{r}{r - x \cdot \theta} x_3. \tag{5.78}$$

The line $\mathbb{R}\theta_\perp + y_3e_3$, where $\theta^\perp$ and $\pi(x, \theta)$ intersect, plays the role of the detector line in (5.35). We distinguish the point y_3e_3 of the detector line as origin in $\pi(x, \theta)$. Then the coordinates x' of x in $\pi(x, \theta)$ are $x' = x - y_3e_3$, and the direction vector lying above (or beneath) θ in $\pi(x, \theta)$ is

$$\theta' = (r\theta - y_3e_3)/r', \quad r' = (r^2 + y_3^2)^{1/2}.$$

Note that r' is the distance of $r\theta$ to the origin in $\pi(x, \theta)$. The contribution of the integral in (5.35) to $(V_\Omega * f)(x)$ which belongs to θ' is

$$I(x, \theta) = \frac{r'^2}{(r' - x' \cdot \theta')^2} \int_{-\rho}^{\rho} v_\Omega \left(\frac{r'x' \cdot \theta_\perp}{r' - x' \cdot \theta'} - y_2' \right) g(\theta, y_2'\theta_\perp + y_3e_3) \frac{r'dy_2'}{(r'^2 + y_2'^2)^{1/2}}.$$

A straightforward but unpleasant computation shows that

$$x' \cdot \theta' = \frac{r'}{r} x \cdot \theta.$$

Using this and $x' \cdot \theta_\perp = x \cdot \theta_\perp$, we obtain

$$I(x, \theta) = \frac{r^2}{(r - x \cdot \theta)^2} \int_{-\rho}^{\rho} v_\Omega(y_2 - y_2') g(\theta, y_2'\theta_\perp + y_3e_3) \frac{\sqrt{r^2 + y_3^2} dy_2'}{\sqrt{r^2 + y_2'^2 + y_3^2}}.$$

This is the contribution from the direction θ' in $\pi(x, \theta)$ to the filtered backprojection approximation to $f(x)$ as given by (5.35). In order to compute this approximation exactly, we would have to integrate over the corresponding contributions for all directions in $\pi(x, \theta)$. This is impossible, since we do not have the necessary sources in $\pi(x, \theta)$. The idea of FDK is to integrate instead over all the sources we actually have, i.e., to take

$$f(x) \sim \int I(x, \theta) d\theta'$$

as an approximation to $f(x)$. Viewing θ' as a function of θ, we thus arrive at

$$f(x) \sim \int_{S^1} I(x, \theta) \frac{r}{r'} d\theta$$

$$= \int_{S^1} \frac{r^2}{(r - x \cdot \theta)^2} \int_{-\rho}^{\rho} v_\Omega(y_2 - y_2') g(\theta, y_2'\theta_\perp + y_3 e_3) \frac{r \, dy_2'}{\sqrt{r^2 + y_2'^2 + y_3^2}} d\theta$$

(5.79)

with y_2, y_3 from (5.78). This is the FDK approximate formula. It can be implemented in very much the same way as (5.35), leading to a reconstruction algorithm of the filtered backprojection type. The data are first weighted with the factor $r/\sqrt{r^2 + y_2'^2 + y_3^2}$, then filtered along horizontal lines with one of the filters v_Ω from section 5.1, and finally backprojected with weight $r^2/(r - x \cdot \theta)^2$.

The idea of the FDK algorithm can easily be extended to a helical scanning helical source curve; see Wang et al. (1993).

5.5.2 Grangeat's method

This method requires a source curve with the following property: Each plane hitting $\text{supp}(f)$ contains at least one source; i.e., for each $x \in \text{supp}(f)$ and each $\theta \in S^2$, there is a source (a point on the curve) $a(x, \theta)$ such that $x \cdot \theta = a(x, \theta) \cdot \theta$. Note that this condition is a little weaker than Tuy's condition in section 2.3.

We start out from Radon's inversion formula

$$f(x) = -\frac{1}{8\pi^2} \int_{S^2} \frac{\partial^2}{\partial s^2} (Rf)(\theta, x \cdot \theta) d\theta;$$

(5.80)

see (2.14) for $n = 3$. In view of the property of our curve, we have

$$(Rf)(\theta, x \cdot \theta) = (Rf)(\theta, a(x, \theta) \cdot \theta).$$

Now we make use of Theorem 2.19, obtaining

$$\frac{\partial}{\partial s}(Rf)(\theta, x \cdot \theta) = \int_{\omega \in \theta^\perp \cap S^2} \frac{\partial}{\partial \theta}(Df)(a(x, \theta), \omega) d\omega.$$

From this formula, $\frac{\partial^2}{\partial s^2}(Rf)(\theta, s)$ can be computed for $s = x \cdot \theta$ for each x with $f(x) \neq 0$. Using this in (5.80), we obtain $f(x)$.

Grangeat's method permits exact reconstruction. For the reconstruction of f at some point x it uses only those values of $(Df)(a(x,\theta),\omega)$ for which ω is almost perpendicular to θ, i.e., it requires only those rays that run in a small cone whose axis joins x with an arbitrary source.

An algorithm based on Grangeat's formula consists of three steps. First, we have to compute for $g = Df$ the function

$$G(a,\theta) = \int_{\omega\in\theta^\perp\cap S^2} \frac{\partial}{\partial\theta} g(a,\omega)d\omega$$

$$= -\int_{S^2} \delta'(\theta\cdot\omega)g(a,\omega)d\omega.$$

The first formula requires awkward numerical differentiation, while the second one is conveniently implemented by approximating δ' by a smooth function w_Ω with

$$\hat{w}_\Omega(\sigma) = (2\pi)^{-1/2}i\sigma\hat\phi\left(\frac{\sigma}{\Omega}\right),$$

where $\hat\phi$ is a filter as in section 5.1, i.e.,

$$w_\Omega(s) = \frac{1}{2\pi}\int_{-\Omega}^{\Omega} i\sigma\hat\phi\left(\frac{\sigma}{\Omega}\right)e^{is\sigma}d\sigma = \Omega^2 w(s\Omega),$$

$$w(s) = -\frac{1}{2\pi}\int_{-1}^{+1} \sigma\hat\phi(\sigma)\sin(s\sigma)d\sigma.$$

In a second step, we have to compute $\frac{\partial}{\partial s}(Rf)(\theta,s)$ from Grangeat's formula

$$\frac{\partial}{\partial s}(Rf)(\theta,a\cdot\theta) = G(a,\theta).$$

The assumption underlying Grangeat's method is that each plane $x\cdot\theta = s$ hitting the support of f contains a source a, i.e., $s = a\cdot\theta$. Thus $\frac{\partial}{\partial s}Rf$ is completely determined by G.

For some s there may be several sources a such that $s = a\cdot\theta$. In principle, it would suffice to use just one of them, ignoring all the other measurements. From the point of view of noise propagation, it is desirable to use all the measurements, if possible with identical weights. This can be achieved in the following way. Let B be a function positive in $[-\varepsilon,\varepsilon]$ and zero elsewhere. Let $a_1,\ldots,a_p$ be the available sources. Then

$$\frac{\partial}{\partial s}(Rf)(\theta,s) \sim \frac{\sum_{j=1}^p G(a_j,\theta)B(s-a_j\cdot\theta)}{\sum_{j=1}^p B(s-a_j\cdot\theta)}.$$

In the third step, we have to backproject $\frac{\partial^2}{\partial s^2}(Rf)(\theta,s)$. This can be done by the two-stage algorithm in section 5.5.5.

Grangeat's method can also be obtained by Tuy's inversion formula (Theorem 2.20), as was observed by Zeng, Clack, and Gullberg (1994). Since $(Df)(x,\cdot)$ is homogeneous of order -1, we have

$$(Df)^\wedge(x, \theta) = (2\pi)^{-3/2} \int_{\mathbb{R}^3} (Df)(x, y)e^{-i\theta \cdot y} dy$$

$$= (2\pi)^{-3/2} \int_{S^2} \int_0^\infty (Df)(x, r\omega)e^{-ir\theta \cdot \omega} r^2 dr d\omega$$

$$= (2\pi)^{-3/2} \int_{S^2} \int_0^\infty (Df)(x, \omega)e^{-ir\theta \cdot \omega} r dr d\omega$$

$$= (2\pi)^{-3/2} \int_{S^2} (Df)(x, \omega) \int_{-\infty}^{+\infty} \frac{r + |r|}{2} e^{-ir\theta \cdot \omega} dr d\omega$$

$$= i\pi (2\pi)^{-3/2} \int_{S^2} (Df)(x, \omega)\delta'(\theta \cdot \omega) d\omega + \cdots,$$

where the dots stand for an even function of θ. Since an even function averages out in Tuy's formula, we obtain from Theorem 2.20

$$f(x) = \pi (2\pi)^{-3} \int_{S^2} (a'(\lambda) \cdot \theta)^{-1} \frac{d}{d\lambda} \int_{S^2} (Df)(a(\lambda), \omega)\delta'(\theta \cdot \omega) d\omega d\theta.$$

The ω-integral can be further simplified by the formula

$$\int_{S^2} g(\omega)\delta'(\theta \cdot \omega) d\omega = -\int_{S^2 \cap \theta^\perp} \frac{\partial}{\partial \theta} g(\omega) d\omega,$$

where $\frac{\partial}{\partial \theta}$ denotes the directional derivative in direction θ. Hence

$$f(x) = -\frac{1}{8\pi^2} \int_{S^2} (a'(\lambda) \cdot \theta)^{-1} \frac{d}{d\lambda} \int_{\theta^\perp \cap S^2} \frac{\partial}{\partial \theta} (Df)(a(\lambda), \omega) d\omega d\theta.$$

Here $\frac{\partial}{\partial \theta}$ acts on the second argument of Df. In this form, Tuy's formula is equivalent to Grangeat's method since, with $s = a \cdot \theta$,

$$\frac{ds}{d\lambda} = a'(\lambda) \cdot \theta.$$

5.5.3 Filtered backprojection for the cone beam transform

One can also use Grangeat's formula to derive the 3D analogue of the filtered backprojection algorithm. We start out from the case $n = 3$ of (5.1), i.e.,

$$(V * f)(x) = \int_{S^2} \int_{\mathbb{R}^1} v(x \cdot \theta - s)(Rf)(\theta, s) ds d\theta.$$

Here R is the 3D Radon transform and $V = R^*v$. Following Dietz (1999), we perform an integration by parts, obtaining

$$(V * f)(x) = \int_{S^2} \int_{\mathbb{R}^1} w(x \cdot \theta - s) \frac{\partial}{\partial s} (Rf)(\theta, s) ds d\theta,$$

where $w' = v$. Let $a = a(\lambda)$, $\lambda \in \Lambda \subseteq \mathbb{R}^1$, be a parametric representation of the source curve A. We want to substitute λ for s in the inner integral by putting $s = a(\lambda) \cdot \theta$. If the condition underlying Grangeat's method is met, then each s in the support of $(Rf)(\theta, \cdot)$ can be reached in this way. However, there may be more than one λ for which $s = a(\lambda) \cdot \theta$, i.e., there may be more than one source in the plane $x \cdot \theta = s$. Therefore, we choose a function $M(\theta, \lambda)$ such that

$$\sum_{\substack{\lambda \\ s = a(\lambda) \cdot \theta}} M(\theta, \lambda) = 1$$

for each s. The simplest choice is $M(\theta, \lambda) = 1/n(\theta, a(\lambda) \cdot \theta)$, where $n(\theta, s)$ is the number of λ's for which $s = a(\lambda) \cdot \theta$. Unfortunately, this choice does not lead to a smooth function M. Therefore, other choices of M are to be preferred; see the references below.

The result of the substitution $s = a(\lambda) \cdot \theta$ is

$$(V * f)(x) = \int_{S^2} \int_\Lambda w((x - a) \cdot \theta) \frac{\partial}{\partial s}(Rf)(\theta, a \cdot \theta) M(\theta, \lambda) |a' \cdot \theta| d\lambda d\theta,$$

where $a = a(\lambda)$. We use Grangeat's formula

$$\frac{\partial}{\partial s}(Rf)(\theta, a \cdot \theta) = G(a, \theta)$$

to obtain

$$(V * f)(x) = \int_{S^2} \int_\Lambda w((x - a) \cdot \theta) G(a, \theta) |a' \cdot \theta| M(\theta, \lambda) d\lambda d\theta$$

$$= \int_\Lambda G^w(a, x - a) d\lambda,$$

$$G^w(a, x) = \int_{S^2} w(x \cdot \theta) G(a, \theta) |a' \cdot \theta| M(\theta, \lambda) d\lambda d\theta.$$

This formula can be used as the starting point of a reconstruction algorithm of the filtered backprojection type. Further simplifications are possible. For the choice $V = \delta$, we have from Theorem 2.4

$$v = -\frac{1}{8\pi^2} \delta'', \quad w = -\frac{1}{8\pi^2} \delta'.$$

This makes G^w a function homogeneous of degree -2 in the second argument. Hence we have

$$f(x) = \int_\Lambda |x - a|^{-2} G^w \left(a, \frac{x - a}{|x - a|}\right) d\lambda,$$

$$G^w(a, \omega) = -\frac{1}{8\pi^2} \int_{S^2} \delta'(\omega \cdot \theta) G(a, \theta) |a' \cdot \theta| M(\theta, \lambda) d\theta, \quad \omega \in S^2.$$

This formula was obtained by Defrise and Clack (1994) and Kudo and Saito (1994).

5.5.4 Filtered backprojection for the ray transform

Orlov's inversion formula (Theorem 2.16) can be implemented exactly as Radon's inversion formula in 2D, leading to the filtered backprojection algorithm for the inversion of P, provided $g(\theta, x) = (Pf)(\theta, x)$ is given for $\theta \in S_0^2$, $x \perp \theta$, S_0^2 satisfying Orlov's condition; see Defrise, Townsend, and Clack (1989). Filtered backprojection algorithms based on Orlov's formula integrate over all of $\theta^\perp$. In practice $g(\theta, x)$ often is not available for all $x \in \theta^\perp$. This problem is dealt with in section 6.2.3.

5.5.5 The Radon transform in 3D

We start out from (5.1) for $n = 3$. Representing $\theta \in S^2$ by

$$\theta = \theta(\varphi, \psi) = \begin{pmatrix} \sin\psi\,\cos\varphi \\ \sin\psi\,\sin\varphi \\ \cos\psi \end{pmatrix}, \quad 0 \leq \varphi < 2\pi, \quad 0 \leq \psi \leq \pi,$$

(5.1) reads

$$(V * f)(x) = \int_0^{2\pi} \int_0^\pi (g(\theta(\varphi, \psi), \cdot) * v)(x \cdot \theta(\varphi, \psi)) \sin\psi\,d\psi\,d\varphi. \tag{5.81}$$

Assuming the convolution $g * v$ to be done, this amounts to computing for each reconstruction point x a 2D integral. The complexity of such an algorithm for resolution Ω is as follows. From section 4.3 we know that the number of directions is at least $\rho^2 \Omega^2 / 2$. Doing the reconstruction on a $q \times q \times q$ grid with $q = \rho\Omega/\pi$ leads to an operation count of order Ω^5.

It is possible to reduce this to Ω^4 by exploiting the structure of (5.81). Putting

$$h_\varphi(s, t) = \int_0^\pi (g(\theta(\varphi, \psi), \cdot) * v)(s\cos\psi + t\sin\psi) \sin\psi\,d\psi, \tag{5.82}$$

we have

$$(V * f)(x) = \int_0^{2\pi} h_\varphi(x_3, x_1\cos\varphi + x_2\sin\varphi)\,d\varphi. \tag{5.83}$$

The last two formulas are essentially 2D backprojections. In accordance with our analysis in section 5.1, they have to be discretized with stepsizes $\Delta\varphi$, $\Delta\psi \leq \pi/(\Omega\rho)$; see (5.18). (5.82) has to be evaluated for $\frac{2\pi}{\Delta\varphi} = 2\Omega\rho$ values of φ, (5.83) for $2\Omega\rho/\pi$ values of x_3, yielding $O(\Omega^4)$ operations if the 2D backprojections are done in the straightforward way. We remark that this can be further reduced to $\Omega^3 \log\Omega$ if the fast backprojection from section 5.1.5 is used.

An appropriate filter v in (5.82) is v_Ω from (5.10) and (5.11). We also can take v as $-c\delta''$, mimicking (2.19). With a suitable choice of c we then have

$$f(x) = \frac{1}{4\pi} \int_0^{2\pi} h_\varphi(x_3, x_1\cos\varphi + x_2\sin\varphi)\,d\varphi,$$

$$h_\varphi(s, t) = -\frac{1}{2\pi} \int_0^\pi g''(\theta(\varphi, \psi), s\cos\psi + t\sin\psi) \sin\psi\,d\psi.$$

In this form (5.82)–(5.83) is reminiscent of the two-stage algorithm of Marr, Chen, and Lauterbur (1981), except that the Hilbert transforms of that algorithm are no longer present.

5.6   Circular Harmonic Algorithms

By circular harmonic algorithms, we mean methods that exploit the radial symmetry of the reconstruction problem. They start with a Fourier transform in the angular variable and provide the angular Fourier coefficients of the sought-for density function. In principle, such algorithms can be obtained from Cormack's inversion formula (2.24); see Hansen (1981), Hawkins and Barrett (1986), and Chapman and Cary (1986). However, we find it more convenient to start out from the discrete versions of (5.1) already derived in section 5.1. We simply introduce polar coordinates for x in (5.19) for the parallel case and (5.26) for the fan beam case.

First, we study the sampling requirements in polar coordinates. Assume f to be Ω-band-limited. On putting $x = t\theta(\varphi)$, $f(x)$ becomes a function of φ, t, which we denote by $F(\varphi, t)$. It is clear that the proper sampling interval for F as a function of t is $\Delta t \leq \pi/\Omega$. In order to find the correct sampling condition in φ, we compute the partial Fourier transform of F with respect to φ, i.e.,

$$
\begin{aligned}
\hat{F}(k, t) &= \frac{1}{2\pi} \int_0^{2\pi} e^{-ik\varphi} F(\varphi, t) d\varphi \\
&= \frac{1}{2\pi} \int_0^{2\pi} e^{-ik\varphi} f(t\theta(\varphi)) d\varphi \\
&= \frac{1}{(2\pi)^2} \int_0^{2\pi} e^{-ik\varphi} \int_{|\xi|<\Omega} e^{it\theta(\varphi)\cdot\xi} \hat{f}(\xi) d\xi d\varphi \\
&= \frac{1}{2\pi} \int_{|\xi|<\Omega} \frac{1}{2\pi} \int_0^{2\pi} e^{it\theta(\varphi)\xi - ik\varphi} d\varphi \, \hat{f}(\xi) d\xi \\
&= \frac{1}{2\pi} \int_{|\xi|<\Omega} J_k(|\xi|t) e^{-ik\psi} \hat{f}(\xi) d\xi,
\end{aligned}
$$

where ψ is the argument of ξ; see the derivation of (4.17). By Debye's asymptotic relation, we conclude that $\hat{F}(k, t) \sim 0$ for $\Omega t < k$. Thus if f is supported in $|x| < \rho$ and is essentially Ω-band-limited, then F is properly sampled if

$$
\Delta\varphi \leq \frac{\pi}{\Omega\rho}, \quad \Delta t \leq \frac{\pi}{\Omega}.
$$

As in section 5.1, we deal with the parallel and fan beam cases separately.

5.6.1   Standard parallel scanning

Putting $x = x_{ik} = s_i\theta(\varphi_k)$ in (5.19) yields

$$
(V_\Omega * f)(x_{ik}) = \frac{2\pi}{p} \Delta s \sum_{\ell=-q}^{q} \sum_{j=0}^{p-1} v_\Omega(s_i \cos(\varphi_{j-k}) - s_\ell) g(\theta_j, s_\ell).
$$

Note that the sampling of $V_\Omega * f$ under the conditions (5.13) and (5.18) is correct. In order to make the convolution cyclic, we extend $g(\theta_j, s_\ell)$ by putting $g(\theta_{j+p}, s_\ell) = g(\theta_j, -s_\ell)$. Then

$$(V_\Omega * f)(x_{ik}) = \frac{\pi}{p} \Delta s \sum_{\ell=-q}^{q} \sum_{j=0}^{2p-1} v_\Omega(s_i \cos(\varphi_{j-k}) - s_\ell) g(\theta_j, s_\ell).$$

Defining

$$h_{\ell ik} = \frac{\pi}{p} \sum_{j=0}^{2p-1} v_\Omega(s_i \cos(\varphi_{j-k}) - s_\ell) g(\theta_j, s_\ell), \tag{5.84}$$

$$\ell = -q, \ldots, q, \quad i = 0, \ldots, q, \quad k = 0, \ldots, 2p - 1,$$

we have

$$(V_\Omega * f)(x_{ik}) = \Delta s \sum_{\ell=-q}^{q} h_{\ell ik}. \tag{5.85}$$

These relations define Algorithm 5.6.

ALGORITHM 5.6 (circular harmonic algorithm for standard parallel scanning)

Data: The values $g_{j,\ell} = g(\theta_j, s_\ell)$, $j = 0, \ldots, p-1$, $\ell = -q, \ldots, q$, from (5.12), extended by $g_{j+p,\ell} = g_{j,-\ell}$ to $j = 0, \ldots, 2p - 1$.

Step 1: Precompute the numbers

$$v_{\ell,i,j} = v_\Omega(s_i \cos \varphi_j - s_\ell),$$

$$\ell = -q, \ldots, q, \quad i = 0, \ldots, q, \quad j = 0, \ldots, 2p - 1.$$

Step 2: For $i = 0, \ldots, q$, $\ell = -q, \ldots, q$, carry out the discrete convolution

$$h_{\ell ik} = \frac{\pi}{p} \sum_{j=0}^{2p-1} v_{\ell,i,j-k} g_{j,\ell}, \quad k = 0, \ldots, 2p - 1.$$

Step 3: For $i = 0, \ldots, q$, $k = 0, \ldots, 2p - 1$, compute the sums

$$f_{CH}(x_{ik}) = \frac{\rho}{q} \sum_{\ell=-q}^{q} h_{\ell ik}.$$

The third step needs $4pq^2$ additions, while the second step can be done in $O(q^2 p \log p)$ operations using FFT.

Result: $f_{CH}(x_{ik})$ is an approximation to $f(x_{ik})$.

5.6.2   Standard fan beam scanning

Putting $x_{ik} = t_i \theta(\beta_k)$ in (5.26), $t_i = \Delta t \cdot i$, $\Delta t = \rho/q$, $\beta_k = k\Delta\beta$, we get

$$(V_\Omega * f)(x_{ik}) \qquad\qquad\qquad\qquad\qquad\qquad\qquad\qquad\qquad\qquad (5.86)$$

$$= r\Delta\alpha\,\Delta\beta \sum_{\ell=-q}^{q} \sum_{j=0}^{p-1} v_\Omega \left(t_i \cos\left(\beta_{k-j} - \alpha_\ell + \frac{\pi}{2}\right) - r\sin\alpha_\ell \right) \cdot g(\beta_j, \alpha_\ell)\cos\alpha_\ell.$$

Note that the choice (4.27) for $\Delta\beta$ is not quite sufficient for sampling $V_\Omega * f$, which would require $\Delta\beta \leq \pi/(\Omega\rho)$. We ignore this subtle inconsistency.

Defining

$$v_{\ell,i,j} = v_\Omega \left(t_i \cos\left(\beta_j - \alpha_\ell + \frac{\pi}{2}\right) - r\sin\alpha_\ell \right)\cos\alpha_\ell, \qquad\qquad (5.87)$$

we arrive at the following algorithm.

ALGORITHM 5.7 (circular harmonic reconstruction for standard fan beam scanning)

Data: The values $g_{j,\ell} = g(\beta_j, \alpha_\ell)$, $j = 0, \ldots, p-1$, $\ell = -q, \ldots, q$, from (5.23).

Step 1: Precompute the numbers $v_{\ell,i,j}$, $\ell = -q, \ldots, q$, $i = 0, \ldots, q$, $j = 0, \ldots, p-1$, from (5.87).

Step 2: For $\ell = -q, \ldots, q$, $i = 0, \ldots, q$, carry out the convolutions

$$h_{\ell i k} = \Delta\beta \sum_{j=0}^{p-1} v_{\ell,i,k-j} g_{j,\ell}, k = 0, \ldots, p-1.$$

Step 3: For $i = 0, \ldots, q$, $k = 0, \ldots, p-1$ compute the sums

$$f_{CH}(x_{ik}) = r\Delta\alpha \sum_{\ell=-q}^{q} h_{\ell i k}.$$

Result: $f_{CH}(x_{ik})$ is an approximation to $f(x_{ik})$.

Again the overall complexity of the algorithm is $O(q^2 p \log p)$. This is slightly more (by a factor of $\log p$) than for the filtered backprojection algorithm. However, circular harmonic algorithms are even simpler than the filtered backprojection algorithm: one only has to do real convolutions (Step 2) and additions (Step 3). Circular harmonic algorithms do the reconstruction on a grid in polar coordinates. Interpolation to a Cartesian grid (for instance, for display) is not critical and can be done by linear interpolation.

The advantage of circular harmonic algorithms over the filtered backprojection is that they can be justified by a rigorous application of sampling theorems. No additional approximations, such as the interpolation in the backprojection step or the homogeneity approximation in the fan beam case (see (5.29)–(5.30)) are needed. Thus circular harmonic algorithms outperform the filtered backprojection algorithm if one of those additional approximations becomes critical. Such a case occurs in the fan beam geometry if the sources are close to the reconstruction region, i.e., $\rho \sim r$. In that case, the circular harmonic algorithm is the algorithm of choice.

The disadvantage of the circular harmonic algorithm is not so much its slightly increased complexity, which is easily compensated for by its simplicity. Its main drawback is that it starts with a Fourier transform in the angular variable. This is considered impractical in medical applications because one wants to process each projection separately.

5.7   ART for Nonlinear Problems

In section 5.3.1, we dealt with the Kaczmarz method for linear problems. It is easy to extend the method to nonlinear systems:

$$R_j(f) = g_j, \quad j = 1, \ldots, p, \tag{5.88}$$

where R_j is a differentiable operator from a Hilbert space H into a Hilbert space H_j. We write $R(f) = g$ for (5.88). An obvious extension of (5.49) to (5.88) is

$$f^{k,j} = f^{k,j-1} + \omega R_j'(f_{j-1})^* C_j^{-1}(g_j - R_j(f_{j-1})),$$

$$f^{k,0} = f^k, \quad f^{k+1} = f^{k,p}, \tag{5.89}$$

where $R_j'(f)$ is the derivative of R_j at f.

In the applications to nonlinear tomography in section 7, the evaluation of $R_j(f)$ calls for the solution of a linear boundary value problem of a partial differential equation, while the computation of $R_j'(f)^* g_j$ for $g_j \in H_j$ requires the solution of the adjoint linearized problem. Methods using the latter feature are often called "dual field methods" or "adjoint differentiation."

Based on the analysis in the linear case, we expect convergence for $C_j \geq R_j'(f_{j-1}) R_j'(f_{j-1})^*$ and $0 < \omega < 2$. In fact, Meyn (1983) and Martinez and De Sampaio (1986) proved local convergence for $C_j = R_j'(f_{j-1}) R_j'(f_{j-1})^*$ and H, H_j finite dimensional subject to the following assumptions:

(i) There exists a (nonlinear) projection $U : H \to R^{-1}(g)$ such that

$$\|f - U(f)\| = \min_{R(u)=g} \|f - u\|,$$

and U is continuous.

(ii) There exists a solution $\tilde{f}$ of $R(f) = g$ such that

$$f - \tilde{f} \perp \ker(R'(\tilde{f}))$$

for all f with $U(f) = \tilde{f}$.

These conditions are certainly quite natural and generically satisfied in concrete cases. On the other hand, they are very difficult to verify in the problems we are going to deal with. Therefore, we do not extend the convergence proof in the above references to (5.88), even though, based on our analysis of the linear case, this would be very easy. Rather, we leave the question of convergence open and remind the reader of some of the favorable properties of (5.89), which we already encountered in the linear case, in particular (5.51).

Chapter 6

Problems That Have Peculiarities

6.1 Unknown Orientations

In section 3.5, we were lead to the problem of reconstructing a function f from its projections at unknown orientations. Assuming the projection direction to be e_3 and observing that the barycenter of the rotated object can easily be found from the barycenter of the projections, we arrive at the following problem.

Let $U_1, \ldots, U_p \in SO(3)$ be rotations, and let $f_j(x) = f(U_j^{-1}x)$. Determine f from

$$g_j(x') = (Pf_j)(e_3, x), \qquad x = \begin{pmatrix} x' \\ 0 \end{pmatrix}, \quad x' \in \mathbb{R}^2. \tag{6.1}$$

The crux of the matter is that U_j are unknown. Of course, U_j are determined only up to a common rotation. We describe three methods for the determination of U_j from the projections g_j.

6.1.1 The geometric method

This method goes back to the original paper of Crowther, DeRosier, and Klug (1970) and has been further developed by Goncharov (1987) and Van Heel (1987); see also Goncharov (1988a, 1988b, 1990) and Gel'fand and Goncharov (1990). It exploits consistencies between the 2D Radon transforms of the g_j, meaning that these Radon transforms coincide along certain lines. Let R_2, R_3 be the 2D and 3D Radon transform, respectively. Then for each $\theta' \in S^1$,

$$R_2 g_j(\theta', \cdot) = R_3 f(U_j^{-1}\theta, \cdot), \quad \theta = \begin{pmatrix} \theta' \\ 0 \end{pmatrix}.$$

Thus if $\theta'_{jk} \in S^1$ are such that

$$U_j^{-1}\theta_{jk} = U_k^{-1}\theta_{kj}, \qquad \theta_{jk} = \begin{pmatrix} \theta'_{jk} \\ 0 \end{pmatrix}, \quad j \neq k, \quad j, k = 1, \ldots, p, \tag{6.2}$$

then

139

$$R_2 g_j(\theta'_{jk}, \cdot) = R_2 g_k(\theta'_{kj}, \cdot). \tag{6.3}$$

This means that the values of $R_2 g_j$ along the line $\theta' = \theta'_{jk}$ are the same as the values of $R_2 g_k$ along the line $\theta' = \theta'_{kj}$. We assume that the directions θ'_{jk} are uniquely determined by (6.3). They can be found by searching for common lines in $R_2 g_j$, $R_2 g_k$. One possibility for doing this is to compute the cross correlation of $R_2 g_j$, $R_2 g_k$ and to determine its maximum; see Wuschke (1990).

Once θ_{jk} have been found, we compute U_j from (6.2). It is clear that U_j are determined only up to a common unitary factor, i.e., one U_j is arbitrary. We express U_j by its Euler angles $\alpha_j, \beta_j, \gamma_j, 0 \le \alpha_j, \gamma_j < 2\pi, 0 \le \beta_j \le \pi$; i.e.,

$$U_j = u_1(\gamma_j) u_2(\beta_j) u_1(\alpha_j),$$

where $u_1(\alpha)$ and $u_2(\alpha)$ are counterclockwise rotations by an angle α in the x_1, x_2 and the x_2, x_3 plane, respectively. Since one U_j is arbitrary, the nonlinear system (6.2) contains $3(p-1)$ unknowns $\alpha_j, \beta_j, \gamma_j, j = 2, \ldots, p$. The number of equations in (6.2) is $p^2 - p$. For $p = 3$, we have six equations for six unknowns, and we can hope that (6.2) is uniquely solvable. Henceforth, we assume $p = 3$.

In order to solve (6.2) for $\alpha_j, \beta_j, \gamma_j$, we introduce the directions

$$\begin{aligned}
\theta_1 &= U_2^{-1}\theta_{23} = U_3^{-1}\theta_{32}, \\
\theta_2 &= U_3^{-1}\theta_{31} = U_1^{-1}\theta_{13}, \\
\theta_3 &= U_1^{-1}\theta_{12} = U_2^{-1}\theta_{21}.
\end{aligned} \tag{6.4}$$

Since

$$\begin{aligned}
\theta_1 \cdot U_2^{-1}e_3 &= U_2\theta_1 \cdot e_3 = \theta_{23} \cdot e_3 = 0, \\
\theta_3 \cdot U_2^{-1}e_3 &= U_2\theta_3 \cdot e_3 = \theta_{21} \cdot e_3 = 0,
\end{aligned}$$

$U_2^{-1}e_3$ is orthogonal to θ_1, θ_3, hence a multiple of $\theta_1 \times \theta_3$, and correspondingly for the other directions. Hence

$$\begin{aligned}
U_1^{-1}e_3 &= \delta_1 \theta_2 \times \theta_3, \\
U_2^{-1}e_3 &= \delta_2 \theta_3 \times \theta_1, \\
U_3^{-1}e_3 &= \delta_3 \theta_1 \times \theta_2
\end{aligned} \tag{6.5}$$

with some $\delta_j \in \mathbb{R}$, which is determined uniquely up to the sign. Expressing U_1 by its Euler angles, the first equation of (6.5) reads

$$\begin{pmatrix} \sin \alpha_1 \, \sin \beta_1 \\ \cos \alpha_1 \, \sin \beta_1 \\ \cos \beta_1 \end{pmatrix} = \delta_1 \theta_2 \times \theta_3. \tag{6.6}$$

Since the sign of δ_1 is unknown, this equation admits two solutions, (α_1, β_1) and (α'_1, β'_1), which, viewed as spherical coordinates, correspond to antipodal points on the unit sphere.

For the determination of γ_1, we use the third equation of (6.4) in the form $U_1\theta_3 = \theta_{12}$. Expressed in the Euler angles, it reads

$$u_1(-\gamma_1)\theta_{12} = u_2(\beta_1)u_1(\alpha_1)\theta_3. \tag{6.7}$$

It is readily verified that $u_2(\beta_1')u_1(\alpha_1') = Du_2(\beta_1)u_1(\alpha_1)$ with D the diagonal matrix with diagonal entries $-1, 1, -1$. The last element on the left-hand side of (6.7) is independent of γ_1. Thus in the generic case, the last equation of (6.7) tells us whether (α_1, β_1) or its antipodal point (α_1', β_1') is the right solution of (6.6). Once this decision is made, (6.7) is readily solved for γ_1. Summing up, we see that (6.5) can be solved uniquely for the Euler angles $\alpha_j, \beta_j, \gamma_j$ if only $\theta_1, \theta_2, \theta_3$ are known, irrespective of the indeterminacy of the sign of δ_j.

So everything boils down to computing the directions $\theta_1, \theta_2, \theta_3$ introduced in (6.4). Since

$$\theta_1 \cdot \theta_2 = U_3^{-1}\theta_{32} \cdot U_3^{-1}\theta_{31} = \theta_{32} \cdot \theta_{31} = \theta_{32}' \cdot \theta_{31}' \tag{6.8}$$

and similarly

$$\theta_2 \cdot \theta_3 = \theta_{13}' \cdot \theta_{12}', \qquad \theta_3 \cdot \theta_1 = \theta_{21}' \cdot \theta_{23}', \tag{6.9}$$

the angles between θ_j are known. From these angles we can compute θ_j up to a common rotation, which reflects the inherent nonuniqueness of the rotations U_j mentioned above. We choose this common rotation in such a way that

$$\theta_3 = \begin{pmatrix} 0 \\ 0 \\ 1 \end{pmatrix}, \qquad \theta_2 = \begin{pmatrix} 0 \\ \sin \vartheta \\ \cos \vartheta \end{pmatrix}, \qquad \theta_1 = \begin{pmatrix} \cos \varphi \, \sin \psi \\ \sin \varphi \, \sin \psi \\ \cos \psi \end{pmatrix},$$

where $0 \le \vartheta \le \pi, 0 \le \psi \le \pi, 0 \le \varphi < 2\pi$. Then (6.8)–(6.9) can be rewritten as

$$\cos \psi = \theta_{21}' \cdot \theta_{23}', \quad \cos \vartheta = \theta_{13}' \cdot \theta_{12}', \quad \sin \vartheta \sin \varphi \sin \psi + \cos \vartheta \cos \psi = \theta_{32}' \cdot \theta_{31}'.$$

These equations determine ψ, φ, and $\sin \varphi$. Thus $\theta_1, \theta_2, \theta_3$ are uniquely determined up to a reflection of θ_1 with respect to the plane spanned by θ_2, θ_3.

6.1.2   The moment method

This method was introduced by Goncharov (1987); see also Goncharov (1988a) and Goncharov and Gel'fand (1988). The method relies on consistency conditions between the moments

$$M_{k_1,\ldots,k_m}^j = \int_{\mathbb{R}^3} x_{k_1} \cdots x_{k_m} f(U_j^{-1}x)dx$$

of the rotated object. Here $1 \le k_i \le 3$. If $k_i \le 2$, we have

$$M_{k_1,\ldots,k_m}^j = \int_{\mathbb{R}^2} x_{k_1}' \cdots x_{k_m}' \int_{\mathbb{R}} f(U_j^{-1}x)dx_3dx',$$

where $x = \binom{x'}{x_3}$. The $\mathbb{R}$ integral is just the ray transform of f_j in direction e_3, and hence

$$M_{k_1\ldots,k_m}^j = \int_{\mathbb{R}^2} x_{k_1}' \cdots x_{k_m}' g_j(x')dx'.$$

Thus all the moments with $k_i \leq 2$ can be computed from the data.

Now let $U_j = (u^j_{k\ell})_{k,\ell=1,\ldots,3}$ and $U_1 = I$. Then

$$M^j_{k_1,\ldots,k_m} = \sum_{1 \leq \ell_1,\ldots,\ell_m \leq 3} u^j_{k_1\ell_1} \cdots u^j_{k_m\ell_m} M^1_{\ell_1,\ldots,\ell_m}.$$

For $m = 2$, this reads

$$M^j_{k_1,k_2} = \sum_{1 \leq \ell_1,\ell_2 \leq 3} u^j_{k_1\ell_1} u^j_{k_2\ell_2} M^1_{\ell_1,\ell_2}, \qquad j = 2,\ldots,p. \tag{6.10}$$

The moments are symmetrical functions of their subscripts. Thus (6.10) consists of $6(p-1)$ equations. The unknowns in (6.10) are the $3(p-1)$ Euler angles hidden in the $u^j_{k\ell}$ and the $3p$ moments that contain the subscript 3. This makes $6p - 6$ equations for $6p - 3$ unknowns. In order to get an overdetermined system, we consider also the moments with $m = 3$, i.e.,

$$M^j_{k_1,k_2,k_3} = \sum_{1 \leq \ell_1,\ell_2,\ell_3 \leq 3} u^j_{k_1\ell_1} u^j_{k_2\ell_2} u^j_{k_3\ell_3} M^1_{\ell_1,\ell_2,\ell_3}, \qquad j = 2,\ldots,p. \tag{6.11}$$

Taking into account symmetry, these are $10(p-1)$ equations. Besides the $3(p-1)$ Euler angles, they contain as unknowns the $6p$ moments containing 3 as subscript, the other ones being determined from the data. Combining (6.10) and (6.11), we thus have $16(p-1)$ equations for $12p - 3$ unknowns. We can hope that, in the generic case, these equations determine the Euler angles for $p \geq 4$.

6.1.3   The method of Provencher and Vogel

In this method, we start from the expansion

$$f = \sum_{m=0}^{\infty} \sum_{\ell=0}^{\infty} \sum_{|k| \leq \ell} f_{m\ell k} \psi_{m\ell k} \tag{6.12}$$

of f with respect to an orthonormal system $\psi_{m\ell k}$ with the following properties:

$$\hat{\psi}_{m\ell k} = \lambda_m \psi_{m\ell k},$$
$$\psi_{m\ell k}(U^j x) = \sum_{|k'| \leq \ell} R^{j,\ell}_{k,k'} \psi_{m\ell k'}(x). \tag{6.13}$$

Here λ_m are known complex numbers, and $R^{j,\ell}_{k,k'}$ are known functions of the Euler angles $\alpha_j, \beta_j, \gamma_j$ of U^j.

Let $f_j(x) = f(U_j^{-1}x)$ as above. Then from Theorem 2.11,

$$\hat{f}_j(\xi) = (2\pi)^{-1/2}(Pf_j)^\wedge(e_3, \xi), \quad \xi = \begin{pmatrix} \xi' \\ 0 \end{pmatrix},$$
$$= (2\pi)^{-1/2} \hat{g}_j(\xi')$$

with the data function g_j from (6.1). Thus

$$\hat{g}_j(\xi') = (2\pi)^{1/2}\hat{f}_j(\xi) = (2\pi)^{1/2}\hat{f}(U_j\xi)$$

$$= (2\pi)^{1/2}\sum_{m=0}^{\infty}\sum_{\ell=0}^{\infty}\sum_{|k|\le\ell} f_{m\ell k}\hat{\psi}_{m\ell k}(U_j\xi)$$

$$= (2\pi)^{1/2}\sum_{m=0}^{\infty}\sum_{\ell=0}^{\infty}\sum_{|k|\le\ell} f_{m\ell k}\lambda_m\psi_{m\ell k}(U_j\xi)$$

$$= (2\pi)^{1/2}\sum_{m=0}^{\infty}\sum_{\ell=0}^{\infty}\sum_{|k|,|k'|\le\ell} f_{m\ell k}\lambda_m R_{k,k'}^{j,\ell}\psi_{m\ell k'}(\xi). \tag{6.14}$$

The idea is to solve (6.14) simultaneously for the $f_{m\ell k}$ (providing the function f by (6.12)) and the Euler angles. If the sum in (6.12) is truncated at $m = \ell = N$, then the number of unknowns in (6.14) is $\frac{1}{2}N(N+1)(N+2) + 3(p-1)$ for p projections. Due to this large number of unknowns, the method has not been used much. For details see Provencher and Vogel (1983).

6.1.4 The 2D case

If the objects rotate only around a fixed axis perpendicular to the direction of the projections, the problem can be considered separately in each plane perpendicular to the axis of rotation. We end up with a 2D problem in each plane. This 2D problem is conveniently modeled by the 2D Radon transform. With

$$U_j = \begin{pmatrix} \cos\alpha_j & -\sin\alpha_j \\ \sin\alpha_j & \cos\alpha_j \end{pmatrix},$$

the unknown rotations around the fixed axis, the data are

$$g_j = (Rf_j)(e_2,\cdot) = (Rf)(U_j^{-1}e_2,\cdot), \quad j = 1,\ldots,p, \tag{6.15}$$

where e_2 is the direction of the projection.

The moment method assumes the following form in 2D; see Gel'fand and Goncharov (1989). From Theorem 2.8 we know that

$$q_m(\varphi) = \int s^m (Rf)(\theta, s)ds, \qquad \theta = \begin{pmatrix} \cos\varphi \\ \sin\varphi \end{pmatrix},$$

is a homogeneous polynomial of degree m in θ with the parity of m. Hence

$$q_m(\varphi) = a_{m,m}\cos m\varphi + a_{m,m-2}\cos(m-2)\varphi + \cdots$$
$$+ a_{m,-m}\sin m\varphi + a_{m,-m+2}\sin(m-2)\varphi + \cdots$$

with real coefficients $a_{m,m},\ldots,a_{m,-m}$. In terms of the polynomial q_m, (6.15) reads

$$q_m(\alpha_j) = \int s^m g_j(s)ds, \qquad j = 1,\ldots,p. \tag{6.16}$$

For each $m = 0, 1, \ldots$, this constitutes a system of p equations for $p - 1$ angles $\alpha_2, \ldots, \alpha_p$ (α_1 being arbitrary, e.g., $\alpha_1 = 0$) and $m + 1$ coefficients $a_{m,m}, a_{m,m-2}, \ldots, a_{m,-m}$. Combining the cases $m = 2$ and $m = 3$, we thus get $2p$ equations for $p + 6$ unknowns. It may be expected that these equations determine the angles uniquely if $p \geq 6$.

6.2   Incomplete Data

We speak—somewhat vaguely—of incomplete data if an integral geometric transform such as Rf, Pf, Df is partially unknown, or, equivalently, if not all the lines or planes meeting the object can be measured. We give a few examples for R:

  (a) Limited angle problems. Here $(Rf)(\theta, \cdot)$ is known only for θ in a subset of a half-sphere.
  (b) Exterior problems. Here $(Rf)(\cdot, s)$ is known only for $|s| > a$, and $f(x)$ is sought only for $|x| > a$.
  (c) Truncated problems. Here $(Rf)(\cdot, s)$ is known only for $|s| < a$.

Similar situations occur with the other transforms. The incompleteness of data may cause several difficulties. The most typical one is instability. This is because stability results such as Theorems 2.10 and 2.18 do not apply to incomplete data problems, and the favorable decay rates for the singular values in (2.27) and (2.39) no longer hold. Thus the stability analysis of section 4.1 is not valid for incomplete data. Other difficulties are nonuniqueness or simply the lack of reconstruction algorithms.

6.2.1   Uniqueness and stability

As for uniqueness, we have the following facts; see Smith et al. (1977) and Natterer (1986), Chapter II.3.

THEOREM 6.1. *Let $f \in \mathcal{S}(\mathbb{R}^n)$ and K be a convex compact set in $\mathbb{R}^n$. If $(Rf)(\theta, s) = 0$ for each plane $x \cdot \theta = s$ not meeting K, then $f = 0$ outside K. If $(Pf)(\theta, x) = 0$ for each line $x + \mathbb{R}\theta$, then $f = 0$ outside K.*

THEOREM 6.2. *Let $S_0 \subseteq S^{n-1}$ be a set of directions such that no nontrivial homogeneous polynomial vanishes on S_0. Let $f \in \mathcal{S}(\mathbb{R}^n)$ have compact support. If $(Rf)(\theta, \cdot) = 0$ for $\theta \in S_0$, then $f = 0$. If $(Pf)(\theta, \cdot) = 0$ for all $\theta \in S_0$, then $f = 0$.*

THEOREM 6.3. *Let K be a ball in $\mathbb{R}^n$, let A be an infinite set outside K, and let $f \in \mathcal{S}(\mathbb{R}^n)$ have support in K. If $(Df)(a, \cdot) = 0$ for $a \in A$, then $f = 0$.*

It follows from Theorem 6.1 that exterior problems are uniquely solvable if f has compact support. However, this is not of much use in practice because exterior problems are severely ill-posed; see below. The assumption of compact support is essential, as can be seen from the singular value decomposition of the exterior Radon transform; see Quinto (1983a), (1982).

Theorem 6.2 implies that limited angle problems are uniquely solvable. Again, this is not of much help in practice since limited angle problems are severely ill-posed. Truncated problems for R in odd dimension are uniquely solvable. This follows from the local character of Radon's inversion formula (Theorem 2.6). For $n = 2$, this is not the case, nor is it true for P, D in any dimension. Let us consider the 2D Radon transform. We construct a function f with support in the unit circle whose Radon transform $(Rf)(\cdot, s)$ vanishes for $|s| < a$. We only have to take an even function $g \in \mathcal{S}(\mathbb{R}^1)$ that vanishes in $[-a, a]$ and put

$$f(x) = -\frac{1}{\pi} \int_{|x|}^{\infty} (s^2 - |x|^2)^{-1/2} g'(s) ds.$$

By Cormack's inversion formula 2.24, f is a solution to $Rf = g$, and for suitable choices of g outside $[-a, a]$, f does not vanish identically.

Similarly, Theorem 6.3 tells us that the reconstruction of a compactly supported function from sources on an arbitrarily small curve is in principle possible. But the reconstruction process has reasonable stability properties only if the source curve satisfies a rather restrictive condition; see section 5.5.

So much for uniqueness. As for stability, we used two tools in section 4.1: the SVD and stability estimates. We want to look at incomplete data problems from these points of view. We start with the SVD for the limited angle problem. We consider only the case $n = 2$ and assume $(Rf)(\theta, \cdot)$ to be given only on $S_\phi = \{\theta : \theta = (\cos \varphi, \sin \varphi)^T, |\varphi| \le \phi\}$, where $\phi \le \pi/2$.

THEOREM 6.4. *The singular values of the operator*

$$R : L_2(|x| < 1) \to L_2(S_\phi \times [-1, +1]; (1 - s^2)^{-1/2}) \tag{6.17}$$

are given by

$$\sigma_{m\ell} = \left(\frac{2\pi}{m+1} \lambda_\ell \left(m+1, \frac{\phi}{\pi} \right) \right)^{1/2},$$

$$m = 0, 1, \ldots, \quad \ell = 0, 1, \ldots, m,$$

where $\lambda_\ell(m + 1, \frac{\phi}{\pi})$ are the eigenvalues of the $(m + 1, m + 1)$ matrix

$$A_m(\phi) = \begin{pmatrix} a_0 & a_1 & \cdots & a_m \\ a_1 & a_0 & \cdots & a_{m-1} \\ \vdots & & & \\ a_m & a_{m-1} & \cdots & a_0 \end{pmatrix}, \quad a_\ell = \frac{1}{\pi} \begin{cases} 2\phi, & \ell = 0, \\ \frac{\sin 2\ell\phi}{\ell}, & \ell \ne 0. \end{cases}$$

For the proof, see Davison (1983) and Louis (1980). The eigenvalues $\lambda_\ell(m+1, \phi/\pi)$ have been studied in Slepian (1978). A fraction $2\phi/\pi$ of these eigenvalues is close to 1, and the rest are close to 0. Thus the number of small singular values of R is proportional to the size of the missing angular range. If the missing range is small, i.e., ϕ close to $\pi/2$, then

$$\frac{\sigma_{00}}{\sigma_{mm}} = \sqrt{m+1} \left(1 + m \frac{\phi - \pi/2}{\pi} + O(\phi - \pi/2)^2 \right);$$

see Louis (1986). Thus if the missing range is small, the decay of the singular values is essentially still polynomial, indicating modest ill-posedness. On the other hand, if the missing range is large, i.e., ϕ close to 0, then

$$\frac{\sigma_{00}}{\sigma_{mm}} = 2^{1/2}\pi^{-3/4}m^{1/4}\left(\frac{2}{\phi}\right)^m (1+\mathrm{O}(\phi)).$$

Now the decay is truly exponential, and hence the problem is severely ill-posed. Practical experience shows that it is quite difficult to get decent reconstructions for $\phi < \pi/3$, i.e., from an angular range of less than 120°. In Louis (1986), some of the singular functions that belong to the small singular values are depicted. They are characterized by steep gradients perpendicular to the directions of lines that are not measured, indicating that such features are difficult to reconstruct.

The SVD of truncated transforms was studied by Maass (1992), as follows.

THEOREM 6.5. *The singular values of the operator*

$$R : L_2(\mathbb{R}^2) \to L_2(S^1 \times [-1, +1]) \tag{6.18}$$

are a two-parameter family $\sigma_{m\ell}$, $m = 0, 1, \ldots, \ell = 0, \pm 1, \pm 2, \ldots$, with

$$\sigma_{m\ell} = \begin{cases} \mathrm{O}(m^{-1/2}), & \ell \text{ fixed}, \quad m \to \infty, \\ \mathrm{O}(m^{-1/4}), & m = \ell \to \infty, \\ \mathrm{O}(\ell^{-1/2}), & m \text{ fixed}, \quad \ell \to \infty. \end{cases}$$

This modest decay of the singular values indicates that the generalized inverse of R (remember that R is not invertible) can be computed in a fairly stable way. One can show (see Maass (1992), Louis and Rieder (1989), Natterer (1986), and Leahy, Smith, and Solmon (1979)) that the functions in the null space of R are almost constant. That means that one can reconstruct up to an additive almost constant function in a fairly stable way. We shall take this up again in section 6.5, on local tomography.

The SVD for the exterior problem was given by Quinto (1983a). This analysis reveals that the operator

$$R : L_2(|x| > 1) \to L_2(S^{n-1} \times [1, \infty)) \tag{6.19}$$

has a large null space that is spanned by the functions

$$|x|^{-n-k}Y_\ell(x/|x|), \qquad 0 \le k < \ell, \quad k - \ell \text{ even},$$

with the spherical harmonics Y_ℓ of degree ℓ; see section 1.3.5. This does not contradict Theorem 6.1, because these functions are not in $S(\mathbb{R}^n)$. However, these functions suggest that the operator R restricted to functions of compact support does have very small singular values, leading to severe instability of the inversion problem. This is corroborated by Cormack's inversion formula (2.24), namely,

$$f_\ell(r) = \frac{1}{\pi}\int_r^\infty (s^2 - r^2)^{-1/2}T_{|\ell|}\left(\frac{s}{r}\right) g_\ell'(s)ds.$$

Here $s/r \geq 1$. Since the Chebyshev polynomials $T_{|\ell|}(x)$ increase exponentially in ℓ for $|x| \geq 1$ (see section 1.3.5), the exponential instability becomes apparent.

The second method to judge stability in section 4.1 was by stability estimates. In the following, we use and extend a method of Finch (1985) to show that such stability estimates cannot exist for incomplete data problems, indicating severe ill-posedness. The idea is very simple. Suppose we have a linear operator $A : L_2(\Omega_1) \rightarrow L_2(\Omega_2)$, where Ω_1, Ω_2 are domains in $\mathbb{R}^n$. Suppose we want to show that an estimate of the form

$$\|f\|_{H^s(\Omega_1)} \leq C \|Af\|_{H^{s+t}(\Omega_2)} \quad \text{for all } f \in H^s(\Omega_1) \tag{6.20}$$

cannot possibly exist, not even for arbitrary large values of t. For this purpose it suffices to produce a function $f \notin H^s(\Omega_1)$ for which $Af \in C^\infty(\Omega_2)$. In other words, if nonsmoothness of f cannot be seen in the data $g = Af$, then a stability estimate does not exist, and the problem of inverting A is seriously ill-posed.

We apply this principle first to the limited angle problem. Let $f \in \mathcal{S}(\mathbb{R}^2)$ have support in $|x| \leq 1$ and assume $f(0) \neq 0$. Put $f_+(x) = f(x)$ if x is in the upper half-plane and $f_+(x) = 0$ otherwise. Let $g = Rf_+$ in $S_\phi \times R$. If $\phi < \frac{\pi}{2}$, g is smooth in $S_\phi \times \mathbb{R}$: the discontinuity of f_+ along the horizontal axis affects only the values of g outside $S_\phi \times \mathbb{R}$. Thus an estimate such as (6.20) cannot exist, and we arrive again at the conclusion that the limited angle problem (6.17) is seriously ill-posed. For the exterior problem (6.19), a similar construction is possible. The discontinuity of f_+ along the horizontal axis does not show up in $g = R_+f$ on $S^1 \times [1, \infty)$. For the truncated problem, such a construction is not possible—every discontinuity of f along curves is picked up by the truncated Radon transform (6.18). Thus an estimate (6.20) may well exist in the orthogonal complement of the kernel of (6.18). This is in fact the case. We will take up this again in section 6.5 on local tomography. For the time being, we only formulate a rule of thumb for an incomplete data problem to be only modestly ill-posed. All lines (or planes, circles, etc.) that are tangent to curves of discontinuity of f should be measured. It should be clear from the previous examples that this condition guarantees an estimate (6.20) and hence a certain degree of stability.

6.2.2 Reconstruction methods

Due to the reasons explained in the previous section the quality of reconstruction suffers seriously from the incompleteness of data, irrespective of the reconstruction algorithm. Some favorable cases are described in the following sections.

In some cases, explicit inversion formulas are available, such as Cormack's formula (2.24) for the exterior problem (6.19) or the formulas of Denisjuk and Palamodov (1988) and Ramm (1992) for the limited angle problem. These formulas necessarily contain seriously unstable operations, such as multiplication with exponentially growing factors (as in Cormack's formula), extrapolations (as in the Denisjuk–Palamodov formula), or analytic continuation, as in Ramm (1992).

A general approach to incomplete data problems is data completion. One simply estimates the data in the missing range, either from information about the object (such as its boundary) or by mathematical extrapolation into the missing range. Often this extrapolation is done with respect to consistency conditions in the range of the relevant integral transforms, such as Theorem 2.8 for R and Theorem 2.15 for P; see Lewitt et al. (1978), Natterer (1986), and Louis and Rieder (1989). Again these extrapolations suffer from instabilities. The results are mixed. Projection completion removes the most conspicuous artifacts but tends to introduce new ones that are quite disturbing.

Iterative methods can be applied to incomplete data without any preprocessing of the data. This does not mean that the results are always satisfactory. An important feature of iterative methods is the possibility to incorporate a priori knowledge about the object to be reconstructed.

6.2.3   Truncated projections in PET

The filtered backprojection algorithm in section 5.5.4 for the ray transform P cannot be used directly for 3D PET (see section 3.2) since it requires $(Pf)(\theta, \cdot)$ to be known in all of $\theta^\perp$. Unfortunately, due to the finite height of the cylindrical detector, only truncated projections are available.

The usual way out is the reprojection algorithm of Kinahan and Rogers (1990). One computes a preliminary reconstruction using only directions θ that are orthogonal to the axis of the cylinder. This amounts to a 2D reconstruction in each slice perpendicular to the axis. From this preliminary reconstruction, the missing line integrals are computed, completing the measured truncated data set. To this completed data set the filtered backprojection algorithm can be applied.

A more elegant method for completing the projections makes use of John's differential equation, which we have already used in section 2.3 for the cone beam transform. For the ray transform, it assumes a particularly simple form if we replace the cylindrical detector by a pair of parallel plane detectors of finite height. Assuming the detector planes to be parallel to the $x - z$ plane and positioned at $y = y_1, y_2$, respectively, the data function is

$$g(x_1, z_1, x_2, z_2) = \int_0^1 f((1-t)x_1 + tx_2, (1-t)y_1 + ty_2, (1-t)z_1 + tz_2)dt,$$

$$x_1, x_2 \in \mathbb{R}^1, \quad -L/2 \le z_1, \quad z_2 \le L/2.$$

L is the height of the plane detectors. Our aim is to express $g_z(x_1, x_2) = g(x_1, z, x_2, z)$ in terms of all the measured data, if possible with equal weights to minimize noise. g_z is a reparametrized version of the Radon transform of $f(\cdot, \cdot, z)$ (in fact, the linogram transform; see section 5.2.3). Once g_z is known we can reconstruct $f(\cdot, \cdot, z)$ by any of the 2D algorithms in section 5.

It is readily verified that g satisfies John's differential equation

$$\frac{\partial^2 g}{\partial x_1 \partial z_2} - \frac{\partial^2 g}{\partial x_2 \partial z_1} = 0.$$

Let $\hat{g}$ be the Fourier transform of g with respect to x_1, x_2, i.e.,

$$\hat{g}(\xi_1, z_1, \xi_2, z_2) = \frac{1}{2\pi} \int_{\mathbb{R}^1} \int_{\mathbb{R}^1} e^{-i(\xi_1 x_1 + \xi_2 x_2)} g(x_1, z_1, x_2, z_2) dx_1 dx_2.$$

Then

$$\xi_1 \frac{\partial \hat{g}}{\partial z_2} - \xi_2 \frac{\partial \hat{g}}{\partial z_1} = 0.$$

This means that for ξ_1, ξ_2 fixed, $\hat{g}$ is constant along each straight line with direction $\xi = (\xi_1, \xi_2)^T$. Thus

$$\hat{g}_z(\xi_1, \xi_2) = \hat{g}(\xi_1, z, \xi_2, z) = \frac{1}{\ell_+ - \ell_-} \int_{\ell_-}^{\ell_+} \hat{g}(\xi_1, z + \ell\xi_1, \xi_2, z + \ell\xi_2) d\ell, \qquad (6.21)$$

where $\ell_+ = \ell_+(z, \xi)$, $\ell_- = \ell_-(z, \xi)$ are such that $z + \ell\xi_1$, $z + \ell\xi_2$ are in the measured region for $\ell_- \leq \ell \leq \ell_+$, i.e., $-L/2 \leq z + \ell\xi_i \leq L/2$, $i = 1, 2$, $\ell_- \leq \ell \leq \ell_+$. This solves our problem of expressing g_z in such a way that all of the available data are used.

The implementation of (6.21) is tricky since $\hat{g}$ does not exist as a function but only as a distribution and since it requires awkward interpolation between the cylindrical detector of a real PET scanner and the plane detectors we assumed above. Defrise and Liu (1999) found an elegant, more direct treatment of the cylindrical detector. We return to the cylindrical geometry, representing the line integrals by

$$g(\varphi, s, z, t) = \int f(s\theta + \ell\theta_\perp, z + \ell t) d\ell,$$

where $\theta = (\cos \varphi, \sin \varphi)^T$, $\theta_\perp = (-\sin \varphi, \cos \varphi)^T$. Assuming the detector to have radius r and height L, the function g is available at least for

$$|s| \leq r, \quad 0 \leq \varphi \leq 2\pi, \quad 0 \leq t \leq t_0, \quad rt_0 \leq z \leq L + rt_0$$

for some $t_0 > 0$. The problem is to express the function $g_z(\varphi, s) = g(\varphi, s, z, 0)$, which is simply the Radon transform of $f(\cdot, \cdot, z)$, using all the measured data. The reconstruction can then be done again by applying a 2D reconstruction algorithm for each z.

John's equation now reads

$$\frac{\partial^2 g}{\partial \varphi dz} + \frac{\partial^2 g}{\partial s dt} + st \frac{\partial^2 g}{\partial^2 z^2} = 0.$$

For the proof, we interchange differentiation with integration, obtaining

$$\left(\frac{\partial^2}{\partial \varphi \partial z} + \frac{\partial^2}{\partial s \partial t} + st \frac{\partial^2}{\partial z^2} \right) \int f(s\cos\varphi - \ell\sin\varphi, s\sin\varphi + \ell\cos\varphi, z + \ell t) d\ell$$

$$= \int \left((-s\sin\varphi - \ell\cos\varphi) \frac{\partial^2 f}{\partial x \partial z} + (s\cos\varphi - \ell\sin\varphi) \frac{\partial^2 f}{\partial y \partial z} \right.$$

$$\left. + \ell\cos\varphi \frac{\partial^2 f}{\partial x \partial z} + \ell\sin\varphi \frac{\partial^2 f}{\partial y \partial z} + st \frac{\partial^2 f}{\partial z^2} \right) d\ell$$

$$= \int \left(-s\sin\varphi \frac{\partial^2 f}{\partial x \partial z} + s\cos\varphi \frac{\partial^2 f}{\partial y \partial z} + st \frac{\partial^2 f}{\partial z^2} \right) d\ell$$

$$= s \int \frac{d}{d\ell} \frac{\partial f}{\partial z} d\ell$$

$$= 0,$$

the arguments of f being the same at each occurrence.

Now let $\hat{g}$ be the Fourier transform of g with respect to φ, s, i.e.,

$$\hat{g}(k, \sigma, z, t) = (2\pi)^{-3/2} \int_0^{2\pi} \int_{\mathbb{R}^1} e^{-i(k\varphi + s\sigma)} g(\varphi, s, z, t) d\varphi ds$$

for $k \in \mathbb{Z}$ and $\sigma \in \mathbb{R}^1$. Then

$$k \frac{\partial \hat{g}}{\partial z} + \sigma \frac{\partial \hat{g}}{\partial t} = -t \frac{\partial^3 \hat{g}}{\partial z^2 \partial \sigma}.$$

This can be written as

$$\frac{d}{dt} \hat{g}(k, \sigma, z + kt, \sigma t) = -t \frac{\partial^3 \hat{g}}{\partial z^2 \partial \sigma}(k, \sigma, z + kt, \sigma t),$$

and hence

$$\hat{g}_z(k, \sigma) = \hat{g}(k, \sigma, z, 0) = \hat{g}(k, \sigma, z + kt_1, \sigma t_1)$$

$$+ \int_0^{t_1} t \frac{\partial^3 \hat{g}}{\partial z^2 \partial \sigma}(k, \sigma, z + kt, \sigma t) dt$$

for each $t_1 = t_1(z, k, \sigma)$ such that $z + kt, \sigma t$ are in the measured region for $0 \le t \le t_1$. This formula permits exact determination of g_z using the whole data set. Previously published approximate and exact methods can be derived from it.

Another possibility for reconstruction from truncated projections is as follows. Assume that for each point x in the reconstruction region (which may well be a subset of the object) all the lines in the planes through x perpendicular to a set $S_1^2 \subseteq S^2$ of directions are measured. In PET, S_1^2 would be a cone around the axis of the scanner. Then $f(x)$ can be reconstructed by any 2D reconstruction procedure applied to any of those planes. The final value of $f(x)$ is obtained by averaging over all these planes. Following the procedure in Defrise et al. (1989), one can show that this leads to a filtered backprojection algorithm with the TTR kernel of Ra et al. (1982) as filter.

6.2.4   Conical tilt problem in electron tomography

In section 3.5, we mentioned the problem of reconstructing f from $(Pf)(\theta, \cdot)$ if θ is restricted to the set

$$S_0^2 = \{\theta(\varphi, \psi) : \psi = \psi_0\},$$

where

$$\theta(\varphi, \psi) = \begin{pmatrix} \sin \psi \, \cos \varphi \\ \sin \psi \, \sin \varphi \\ \cos \psi \end{pmatrix}.$$

Here we use Theorem 2.17 in the form

$$(P^*h)^\wedge(\xi) = (2\pi)^{1/2} \int_{S_0^2} \hat{h}(\theta, E_\theta \theta) \delta(\theta \cdot \xi) d\theta.$$

For $h = \delta_\theta$ the δ function in $\theta^\perp$, we have $\hat{h} = (2\pi)^{-1}$, hence

$$(P^*\delta_\theta)^\wedge(\xi) = (2\pi)^{-1/2} \int_{S_0^2} \delta(\theta \cdot \xi)d\theta$$

$$= (2\pi)^{-1/2} \int_0^{2\pi} \delta(|\xi'|\cos\varphi\sin\psi_0 + \xi_3\cos\psi_0)\sin\psi_0 d\varphi,$$

where $\xi = (\xi', \xi_3)^T$. This vanishes for $|\xi_3| > |\xi'|\tan\psi_0$, while in the opposite case,

$$(P^*\delta_\theta)^\wedge(\xi) = (2\pi)^{-1/2} \frac{2}{\sqrt{|\xi'|^2 - \frac{\xi_3^2}{\tan^2\psi_0}}}.$$

Thus we obtain from (2.34)

$$\hat{H}\hat{f} = (P^*Pf)^\wedge,$$

where

$$\hat{H}(\xi) = \begin{cases} 4\pi(|\xi'|^2 - \xi_3^2/\tan^2\psi)^{-1/2}, & |\xi_3| < |\xi'|\tan\psi, \\ 0 & \text{otherwise.} \end{cases}$$

This leads to the weighted backprojection algorithm for conical tilt geometry in electron tomography; see Frank (1992).

6.3 Discrete Tomography

We speak of discrete tomography if the function to be reconstructed assumes only discrete values. A typical example is the reconstruction of the characteristic function of a set that is 1 in the interior and 0 outside the set. The methods and algorithms of discrete tomography are quite different from the continuous case. They belong to fields such as combinatorics, convex analysis, linear and integer programming, and measure theory; see Gardner (1995).

   We start with the problem of reconstructing the characteristic function of convex sets in $\mathbb{R}^2$ from line integrals. We have the following uniqueness results.

THEOREM 6.6. *Let* K_1, $K_2 \subseteq \mathbb{R}^2$ *be compact and convex with nonempty interior, and let* f_1, f_2 *be the characteristic functions of* K_1, K_2, *respectively. If* $(Df_1)(a_i, \cdot) = (Df_2)(a_i, \cdot)$ *for three points* a_1, a_2, a_3 *outside* K *that are not collinear, then* $f_1 = f_2$.

   Comparing this with the uniqueness theorems in section 6.2, we see that reconstructing characteristic functions of convex sets requires much less data than reconstructing general functions. Algorithms have been developed specifically for convex sets (see Falconer (1983) and Dartmann (1991)) for the reconstruction from two exterior point sources.

   A numerical procedure that can be used for sets K that are star-like with respect to the origin is as follows. Represent K in polar coordinates by

$$x = F(\omega), \quad \omega \in S^1,$$

where $F(\omega) > 0$. Assume that $g = Rf$, where f is the characteristic function of K, is measured for a few directions θ. From Theorem 2.1 we easily obtain

$$\hat{g}(\theta, s) = \int_{S^1} F^2(\omega) G(\sigma \theta \cdot \omega F(\omega)) d\omega,$$

where

$$G(u) = \begin{cases} u^{-2}((1 + iu)e^{-iu} - 1), & u \neq 0, \\ \frac{1}{2}, & u = 0; \end{cases}$$

see Natterer (1986). For each measured θ, this is a nonlinear integral equation for F. Since G is smooth, it is severely ill-posed. The numerical solution must include some regularization; see section 4.1. By solving for F, it is possible to reconstruct fairly complex sets K with very few (say two to four) directions θ; see Lohmann (1983).

In a further step away from continuous tomography, the domain of the functions to be reconstructed is often assumed to be discrete, too. Problems like this occur in computer vision (Horn (1986)), electron microscopy (Schwander et al. (1993)), and medicine (Slump and Gerbrandes (1982)). In a typical case, an (m, n) matrix $A = (a_{ij})$ whose entries are either 0 or 1 has to be reconstructed from its row sums $h_1, \ldots, h_m$ and its column sums $v_1, \ldots, v_n$, representing two orthogonal projections of the discrete function given by A.

It is clear that the problem is not uniquely solvable. The matrices

$$\begin{pmatrix} 1 & 0 \\ 0 & 1 \end{pmatrix}, \quad \begin{pmatrix} 0 & 1 \\ 1 & 0 \end{pmatrix}$$

have the same row and column sums, but they are not the same. Submatrices of this structure (i.e., if for some (i_1, j_1), (i_2, j_2) we have $a_{i_1, j_1} = a_{i_2, j_2} = \vartheta$, $a_{i_1, j_2} = a_{i_2, j_1} = 1 - \vartheta$ with ϑ either 0 or 1) are called switching components. If a matrix A has such a switching component, then the reconstruction problem is obviously not uniquely solvable. Changing all the elements in a switching component is called a switching operation. A switching operation does not change column and row sums. In fact, this is the only possible nonuniqueness in the reconstruction of a binary pattern from its row and column sums.

THEOREM 6.7. *Let A, B be (m, n) matrices with only 1 and 0 as entries. If the column sums and the row sums of A, B are the same, then A can be transformed into B by a finite number of switching operations.*

For a proof, see Ryser (1957). An algorithm based on Theorem 6.7 was described by Chang (1971). Algorithms based on minimum cost capacitated network flow were given in Slump and Gerbrandes (1982). For a state-of-the-art review, see Gritzmann et al. (1998).

6.4   Simultaneous Reconstruction of Attenuation and Activity

This is a problem that comes up, e.g., in emission tomography; see section 3.2. We restrict ourselves to the 2D case. We have to solve the equation

$$g = R_\mu f \tag{6.22}$$

with R_μ the attenuated Radon transform (see section 2.4) in SPECT and

$$g = e^{-R\mu} Rf \qquad (6.23)$$

for PET. Both equations have to be solved for f. If μ is known, then (6.22) and (6.23) are linear integral equations for f which can be solved by one of the methods of section 5. Thus the usual procedure is to determine μ by separate transmission scans prior to or simultaneously with the emission scan; see Bailey, Hutton, and Walker (1987). Often a separate transmission scan is considered as too demanding, and simple techniques for correcting for attenuation are used; see Chang (1978) and Bellini, Piacentini, and Rocca (1979).

We study here the case in which μ is unknown. In an early attempt to deal with the problem, Censor et al. (1979) simply considered (6.22) as an underdetermined nonlinear system for μ, f and solved it by an iterative procedure.

Another possibility is based on consistency conditions in the range of R_μ, R, respectively; see Theorems 2.22 and 2.8. Beginning with the former, assume that the SPECT data $g = R_\mu f$ from (6.22) is known. Then according to Theorem 2.22,

$$\int_{R^1} \int_{S^1} s^m e^{ik\varphi + \frac{1}{2}(I+iH)R\mu(\theta,s)} g(\theta, s) d\theta ds = 0 \qquad (6.24)$$

for $0 \le m < k$. We consider (6.24) as a nonlinear system for the unknown attenuation μ, which can be set up as soon as the SPECT data g is known. The idea is to solve (6.24) for μ. Once μ is known, (6.22) can be solved for f. Similarly, for the PET case (6.23), we use Theorem 2.8 to obtain

$$\int_{\mathbb{R}^1} \int_{S^1} s^m e^{ik\varphi} e^{R\mu(\theta,s)} g(\theta, s) d\theta ds = 0 \qquad (6.25)$$

for $|k| > m \ge 0$. Again, (6.25) is a nonlinear system for μ.

Neither (6.24) nor (6.25) is, in general, uniquely (not to speak of stably) solvable for μ. For instance, if f is a radial function, then (6.24) and (6.25) are satisfied for any radial function μ. However, in the absence of radial symmetry, uniqueness is not altogether impossible. We have the following uniqueness theorem (see Natterer (1983) and Boman (1990) for an extension).

THEOREM 6.8. *Suppose f is a finite linear combination of Dirac measures, i.e.,*

$$f = \sum_{k=1}^{N} f_k \delta(x - x_k), \qquad f_k \ne 0.$$

Let $g = R_{\mu_0} f$ for some $\mu_0 \in C_0^\infty(\mathbb{R}^2)$. If $\mu \in C_0^\infty(\mathbb{R}^2)$ satisfies (6.24), and if there exists a half-line starting at some x_k and missing the supports of μ and μ_0, then

$$D\mu(\theta, x_k) = D\mu_0(\theta, x_k) \qquad (6.26)$$

for all $\theta \in S^1$ and $k = 1, \ldots, N$.

The theorem reduces the question of uniqueness to the uniqueness problem for the cone beam transform D for finitely many sources. Strictly speaking, there is no uniqueness in (6.26), but it is clear from Chapter 5 that μ can be computed from (6.26) with good accuracy for sufficiently many suitably placed sources x_k. Unfortunately, (6.26) is not of much practical use since $D\mu(\theta, x_k)$ is determined only in an extremely unstable way by the data g in (6.22).

The situation becomes much more favorable if μ is suitably restricted. Consider, e.g., the case in which μ is a radial function with support in $|x| < 1$. Put

$$h = e^{\frac{1}{2}(I+iH)R\mu}, \qquad g_k(s) = \int_{S^1} e^{ik\varphi} g(\theta, s) d\theta.$$

Note that h is a function of s alone with $\operatorname{Re} h(s) = 1$. Then (6.24) for $m = 0$ reads

$$\int h(s) g_k(s) ds = 0, \quad k = 1, 2, \ldots. \tag{6.27}$$

This system is not uniquely solvable for h. It becomes trivial for f, a radial function. However, if we put

$$f(x) = f_0 \delta(x - x_0) + f_c(x) \tag{6.28}$$

with a sufficiently smooth function f_c and $|x_0| = 1$, then we have the next theorem (see Natterer (1990)).

THEOREM 6.9. *Assume f to be of the form (6.28). Then h is uniquely determined by (6.27) and $\operatorname{Re} h(s) = 1$, provided f_0 does not belong to an exceptional set which accumulates only at zero. In that case, h can be recovered stably from g in the following sense: the linear operator $g \to h$ is bounded as an operator from $L_2(S^1 \times [-1, +1])$ into $L_2([-1, +1]; (1 - s^2)^{-1/2})$.*

Thus for a sufficiently strong external source f_0, the function h, hence $R\mu$, is determined by the data g in a perfectly stable manner. Of course, this result is of only limited practical value in emission tomography since human beings are not radially symmetric. However, the result shows the way to situations in which μ can be determined from emission scans. For instance, if μ is constant in a domain, then only the boundary of this domain has to be determined. How this can be done is shown in Natterer and Herzog (1992). If μ can be obtained by an affine distortion of a known attenuation distribution μ_0, then only this affine transformation has to be computed. This is the subject of Welch et al. (1997) and Natterer (1993).

A completely different approach to determining μ from emission data $g = R_\mu f$ has been suggested by Bronnikov (1995). It does not require μ to be of special structure, but μ has to be small and f has to be close to a constant. More precisely, assume that $f = e^{-\varphi}$ in the reconstruction region $|x| < \rho$, and let f, μ vanish outside $|x| < \rho$. Then

$$f(x) e^{-\int_0^\infty \mu(x+t\theta^\perp) dt} = e^{\varphi(x) - \int_0^\infty \mu(x+t\theta^\perp) dt}$$

$$= 1 + \varphi(x) - \int_0^\infty \mu(x + t\theta^\perp) dt + O(\varphi^2 + \mu^2).$$

Neglecting the second order terms, we obtain approximately

$$g(\theta, s) - g(-\theta, s) = \int \left\{ \int_t^\infty \mu(s\theta + \tau\theta^\perp) d\tau - \int_{-\infty}^{-t} \mu(s\theta + \tau\theta^\perp) d\tau \right\} dt.$$

This is a linear integral equation for μ. Of course, it is not uniquely solvable. But computing the generalized solution is always possible and does lead to an attenuation map.

Finally, for the exponential Radon transform T_μ (see section 2.4), Hertle (1988) found a very simple and satisfactory solution to the problem of recovering μ from $g = T_\mu f$. A slight extension of his result applies to the case where μ depends on θ. It reads as follows.

THEOREM 6.10. *Let $f \in \mathcal{S}(\mathbb{R}^2)$ and $g = T_\mu f$. Then*

$$\frac{d\mu}{d\varphi} a_0 - \mu a_1 = \frac{da_0}{d\varphi},$$

$$a_k(\varphi) = \int s^k g(\theta, s) ds, \quad \theta = (\cos\varphi, \sin\varphi)^T.$$

The proof is by verification.

6.5   Local Tomography

We call a reconstruction procedure local if the computation of f at the point x requires only values of line or plane integrals which meet an arbitrarily small neighborhood of x. An example for a local formula is Radon's inversion formula (2.19) for $n = 3$. We write it as

$$f(x) = -\frac{1}{8\pi^2} \int_{S^2} g''(\theta, x \cdot \theta) d\theta, \quad g = Rf, \tag{6.29}$$

where g'' is the second derivative of g with respect to the second argument. For $n = 2$, the corresponding formula (2.18),

$$f(x) = \frac{1}{4\pi} \int_{S^1} (Hg')(\theta, x \cdot \theta) d\theta, \quad g = Rf, \tag{6.30}$$

is not local due to the presence of the Hilbert transform H. None of the inversion formulas for P, D from sections 2.2 and 2.3 is local.

In order to get a local inversion formula in $\mathbb{R}^2$, we drop H in (6.30) and raise the order of differentiation by 1; i.e., we compute

$$(\Lambda f)(x) = \frac{-1}{4\pi} \int_{S^1} g''(\theta, x \cdot \theta) d\theta. \tag{6.31}$$

From Theorem 2.4, we obtain

$$(\Lambda f)^\wedge(\xi) = -(2\pi)^{-1/2} \frac{1}{|\xi|} (g'')^\wedge \left(\frac{\xi}{|\xi|}, |\xi| \right)$$

$$= (2\pi)^{-1/2} |\xi| \hat{g} \left(\frac{\xi}{|\xi|}, |\xi| \right) \tag{6.32}$$

$$= |\xi| \hat{f}(\xi),$$

where we have used Theorem 2.1 again.

Now we consider $f \in L_1(\mathbb{R}^2)$. The singular support of f is the complement of the largest set on which f is C^∞:

$$x \notin \text{sing supp}(f) \Leftrightarrow x \in \cup\{U : f \in C^\infty(U)\}.$$

In short, we consider $\text{sing supp}(f)$ as the locus of the singularities of f. Λ is an elliptic pseudodifferential operator; see Taylor (1996). Such operators preserve the singular support.

THEOREM 6.11. *Let $f \in L_1(\mathbb{R}^n)$. Then*

$$\text{sing supp}(f) = \text{sing supp}(\Lambda f).$$

This means that the local formula (6.31) produces a function Λf with the same singularities as f. Since the high-frequency components become magnified by the application of Λ, the singularities of f are even more pronounced in Λf. Thus, even though the values of Λf may be completely different from those of f, jumps in f occur at the same places in Λf as in f, and they are even more visible in Λf. This fits nicely into what we found in section 6.2 about the interior problem: If we restrict the scanning to a region of interest, we no longer have uniqueness, but rapid changes in the density can still be recovered.

Moreover, Λf not only contains information about the locus of jump discontinuities of f but also about the size of the jumps. To see this, we express Λf without Fourier transforms. The Fourier transformation of $|\xi|$, viewed as a tempered distribution, is $c|x|^{-3}$, where $c > 0$; see Schwartz (1973). Thus

$$(\Lambda f)(x) = -\frac{c}{2\pi} \int |x - y|^{-3} f(y) dy.$$

This integral is a finite part integral; see Schwartz (1973). If $x \notin \text{supp}(f)$, then the integral exists in the usual sense. Thus if $Y \subseteq \mathbb{R}^2$ is compact and χ_Y is the characteristic function of Y, then for $x \notin Y$,

$$(\Lambda \chi_Y)(x) = -\frac{c}{2\pi} \int_Y |x - y|^{-3} dy. \tag{6.33}$$

Now we consider the following simple situation. Let Y_1, Y_2 be open sets whose smooth boundaries have a common part Γ but whose interiors do not intersect. Let

$$f = c_1 \chi_{Y_1} + c_2 \chi_{Y_2}.$$

We want to find $c_1 - c_2$ from Λf.

THEOREM 6.12. *Let x_0 be an interior point of Γ. Then*

$$\lim_{Y_2 \ni x \to x_0} \frac{\Lambda f(x)}{\Lambda f_{Y_1}(x)} = c_1 - c_2.$$

Proof. We have

$$f = (c_1 - c_2)\chi_{Y_1} + c_2 \chi_{Y_1 \cup Y_2},$$

and hence

$$\frac{\Lambda f}{\Lambda \chi_{Y_1}} - (c_1 - c_2) = c_2 \frac{\Lambda \chi_{Y_1 \cup Y_2}}{\Lambda \chi_{Y_1}}.$$

Since $\chi_{Y_1 \cup Y_2}$ is equivalent to a C^∞ function in a neighborhood of x_0, $\Lambda \chi_{Y_1 \cup Y_2}(x)$ is bounded as $x \to x_0$. Hence it suffices to show that $|\Lambda \chi_{Y_1}(x)| \to \infty$ as $x \to x_0$. This is obvious from (6.33).   □

It is clear that Theorem 6.12 extends to much more general situations and how it can be used for local reconstructions of jump discontinuities; see Faridani et al. (1992, 1990) and Spyra et al. (1990). In Faridani et al. (1997), the operator Λ is replaced by $\Lambda + \mu \Lambda^{-1}$, which is also local and produces reconstructions that are even more similar to f than Λf. Kuchment, Lancaster, and Mogilevskaya (1995) extend local tomography to more general Radon transforms and to incomplete data problems. A penetrating analysis of local tomography based on microlocal analysis was given by Quinto (1993).

A purely geometric view of local tomography was developed by Ramm and Zaslavsky (1993). It is based on the following simple observation. Suppose f is a piecewise smooth function with jumps only along smooth manifolds. Then Rf is smooth everywhere except at points (θ, s) which parametrize tangent hyperplanes to manifolds along which f has a jump discontinuity. Thus if f has a jump discontinuity along a manifold $x_n = g(x')$, $x' = (x_1, \ldots, x_{n-1})^T$, then Rf has a jump discontinuity along the manifold in (θ, s) space, which is made up by the tangent planes along $x_n = g(x')$. The tangent plane in $x = (x', x_n)^T$, $x_n = g(x')$ is given by

$$\begin{aligned} y_n &= \xi' \cdot y' - \xi_n, \qquad\qquad\qquad\qquad (6.34) \\ \xi' &= \nabla g(x'), \quad \xi_n = \xi' \cdot x' - g(x'). \end{aligned}$$

The transformation $x \to \xi = (\xi', \xi_n)$ is well known as the Legendre transform. It maps the manifold $x_n = g(x')$ onto the manifold $\xi_n = h(\xi')$, where

$$h(\xi') = \xi' \cdot x' - g(x').$$

Here x', ξ' are related by $\xi' = \nabla g(x')$. Thus the Legendre transform maps surfaces of discontinuity of f into surfaces of discontinuity of Rf. Note that we have expressed Rf in the coordinate ξ introduced in (6.34), the relation of ξ to the usual coordinates θ, s being obvious.

In the application to local tomography, we first find the singularities of Rf. This is a local operation. In a second step, we find the singularities of f from those of Rf. This is greatly facilitated by the fact that the Legendre transform is involutory. Let $\xi_n = h(\xi')$ be the Legendre transform of $x_n = g(x')$, i.e.,

$$h(\xi') = \xi' \cdot x' - g(x'), \quad \xi' = \nabla g(x').$$

Then for $i = 1, \ldots, n-1$,

$$\begin{aligned} \frac{\partial}{\partial \xi_i} h(\xi') &= x_i + \sum_{j=1}^{n-1} \xi_j \frac{\partial x_j}{\partial \xi_i} - \sum_{j=1}^{n-1} \frac{\partial g}{\partial x_j} \frac{\partial x_j}{\partial \xi_i} \\ &= x_i. \end{aligned}$$

Hence

$$x' = \nabla h(\xi'), \quad g(x') = x' \cdot \xi' - h(\xi'),$$

i.e., the Legendre transform applied to $\xi_n = h(\xi')$ yields $x_n = g(x')$. Thus in order to find the discontinuities of f, we simply have to apply the Legendre transform to the manifold $\xi_n = h(\xi')$ of discontinuities of Rf.

As an example, take f to be the characteristic function of the unit ball. The top half of the unit sphere is $x_n = g(x')$, $g(x') = \sqrt{1 - |x'|^2}$, $|x'| < 1$. Putting $\xi' = \nabla g(x') = -x'/\sqrt{1 - |x'|^2}$, we obtain $x' = -\xi'/\sqrt{1 + |\xi'|^2}$. Thus the Legendre transform of $x_n = g(x')$ is $\xi_n = h(\xi')$, where

$$h(\xi') = \xi' \cdot x' - g(x') = -\sqrt{1 + |\xi'|^2}.$$

We compare with the Radon transform of f, i.e.,

$$(Rf)(\theta, s) = \frac{|s^{n-2}|}{n-1} \left\{ \begin{array}{ll} \sqrt{1 - s^2}^{n-1}, & |s| \leq 1, \\ 0, & |s| > 1 \end{array} \right\}.$$

The coordinates ξ and (θ, s) are interrelated by $s = \xi_n/\sqrt{1 + |\xi'|^2}$. Hence the singularities of Rf in the ξ plane are at $\xi_n = \pm\sqrt{1 + |\xi'|^2}$, the lower branch of which is $\xi_n = h(\xi')$. The Legendre transform of the lower branch takes us back to the top half of the unit sphere.

The use of the Legendre transform in local tomography has been studied in numerous papers; see Ramm and Katsevich (1996). For an extension to the ray transform, see Ramm and Zaslavsky (1994).

Local inversion formulas have also been derived for the fan beam transform D in $\mathbb{R}^3$ by Louis and Maass (1993). Assume that $g(a, \theta) = (Df)(a, \theta)$ is available for $a \in A$ and $\theta \in S^2$, where A is some curve outside supp(f). We define as the adjoint of D the operator

$$(D^*g)(x) = \int_A g\left(a, \frac{x - a}{|x - a|}\right) da,$$

where da is some measure on A. Then we define the local reconstruction of f by

$$\Lambda_A f = \Delta D^* g$$

with Δ as the Laplacian. By a straightforward calculation, we obtain

$$(\Lambda_A f)^\wedge(\xi) = |\xi| \int \hat{f}(t|\xi|)|t| C_A(\xi, t) dt,$$

$$C_A(\xi, t) = -|\xi| \int_A e^{-i(1-t)a \cdot \xi} da.$$

If $|\xi|$ is sufficiently large, then the integrand is oscillating except for $t = 1$. Thus $C_A(\xi, t)$ is negligible except for t close to 1. This means that

$$(\Lambda_A f)^\sim(\xi) \sim |\xi| \hat{f}(\xi).$$

Hence Λ_A behaves essentially as Λ. This becomes more obvious if we compute $C_A(\xi, t)$ for A, the circle in the $x_1 - x_2$ plane with radius ρ around the origin. In that case,

$$C_A(\xi, t) = 2\pi\rho|\xi|J_0(\rho(1-s)|\xi'|),$$

where $\xi = (\xi', \xi_3)^T$ and J_0 is the Bessel function of the first kind of order 0. For $\rho \to \infty$, one obtains

$$(\Lambda_A f)^\wedge(\xi) \longrightarrow \frac{|\xi|}{|\xi'|}(\Lambda f)^\wedge(\xi).$$

This again shows the similarity between Λ_A and Λ. This correspondence was fully explored in the framework of microlocal analysis by Katsevich (1999).

6.6 Few Data

In many applications the number of line integrals that can be measured is quite small. We mention plasma physics (Howard (1996)), acoustic pyrometry (Sielschott and Derichs (1995)), and the various instances of process tomography (Beck et al. (1995)).

It is clear from section 4.3 that the spatial resolution is limited if only a few projections are available. For instance, for p equally distributed complete views, the resolution in a ball of radius ρ is $\frac{2\pi}{\Omega}$ with

$$\rho\Omega = \begin{cases} p & \text{for the ray transform,} \\ ((n-1)!p)^{1/(n-1)} & \text{for the Radon transform;} \end{cases} \tag{6.35}$$

see section 4.3. Strictly speaking these relations hold only for p large. However, they are sufficiently accurate for p quite small. The same applies to the other asymptotic results in section 4.3. They are valid for very small numbers of data points, as was demonstrated by Bertero and Caponnetto (1997). In particular, the results on efficient sampling (see Figure 4.7) remain valid for small data sets. Thus if the amount of data is restricted but the geometry can be chosen freely, it is a good idea to resort to the efficient sampling schemes (4.22) and (4.29). See Desbat (1993, 1996) for applications.

As for algorithms, the filtered backprojection algorithm also performs well on small data sets, provided the data is regular (i.e., the projection directions are equally spaced) and the resolution Ω is adjusted to the small number of data. However, since the number of degrees of freedom is small, very simple algorithms become competitive. For instance, one can always represent the unknown function f by

$$f(x) = \sum_{k=1}^{m} f_k \phi(x - x_k),$$

where x_k are points in the reconstruction region and ϕ is a radial symmetric function that peaks at 0, e.g.,

$$\phi(x) = e^{-\lambda|x|}$$

with some $\lambda > 0$. The expansion coefficients f_k are determined by collocation: if the measurements are $g_j = R_j f$, $j = 1, \dots, p$ with linear functionals R_j, then

$$g_j = \sum_{k=1}^{m} a_{jk} f_k, \quad a_{jk} = R_j(\phi(x - x_k)). \tag{6.36}$$

The linear system (6.36) can be under- or overdetermined. It can be solved by any of the methods from section 4.1, preferably by the truncated SVD (4.2); see Sielschott (1997).

Chapter 7

Nonlinear Tomography

In this section, we present tomographic techniques that require the solution of intrinsically nonlinear problems. These techniques are not yet established as standard imaging tools in radiology or science, and they are still the subject of mainly academic research.

Nonlinear tomographic problems can be modeled as inverse problems for partial differential equations. Linearized versions lead to problems very similar to integral geometry, except that the straight lines are replaced by more complex shapes, such as weight functions in strip-like (sometimes rather banana-shaped) domains. The bulk of the practically oriented work exploits this fact and deals with nonlinear tomography simply with the algorithms of linear tomography. If the background (against which the linearization is done) is constant, then Fourier transform–based methods can be used, too. For the fully nonlinear problems, we give only a description of the nonlinear ART algorithm. A comprehensive treatment of the many methods that are being developed is altogether impossible.

7.1 Tomography with Scatter

In our treatment of transmission and emission tomography in sections 3.1 and 3.2, we ignored scatter. In practice, scatter is taken care of by simple correction procedures; see Welch and Gullberg (1997).

Tomography with scatter can be modeled by the transport equation. Let $\Omega \subseteq \mathbb{R}^n$ be a convex domain that contains the object to be imaged. Let $u(x, \theta)$ be the particle flux in direction $\theta \in S^{n-1}$ at $x \in \Omega$. u satisfies the stationary one-speed transport equation

$$\theta \cdot \nabla u(x, \theta) + \mu(x)u(x, \theta) = \mu_s(x) \int_{S^{n-1}} \eta(x, \theta, \theta')u(x, \theta')d\theta' + q(x, \theta). \qquad (7.1)$$

Here $\mu = \mu_s + \mu_a$, where μ_a the absorption coefficient is the attenuation coefficient, μ_s is the scattering coefficient, and η is the scattering kernel, which we assume to be normalized, i.e.,

$$\int_{S^{n-1}} \eta(x, \theta, \theta')d\theta' = 1.$$

q is the source term. See Barrett et al. (1999) for the derivation of (7.1) in the context of emission tomography. As a boundary condition for (7.1), we have

$$u(x, \theta) = g^-(x, \theta) \quad \text{for } x \in \partial\Omega, \quad \nu(x) \cdot \theta \le 0, \tag{7.2}$$

with ν as the exterior normal on $\partial\Omega$. (7.2) specifies the incoming particle flux. The boundary value problem (7.1)–(7.2) admits under natural assumptions on μ, μ_s, η, q, g^- a unique solution u; see, e.g., Case and Zweifel (1967) and Dautray and Lions (1993).

In tomography, one wants to determine μ (and, if possible, μ_s and η) from measurements of the outgoing radiation

$$g^+(x, \theta) = u(x, \theta), \quad x \in \partial\Omega, \quad \nu(x) \cdot \theta > 0, \tag{7.3}$$

for all (or sufficiently many) incoming radiation patterns g^-. This is an inverse problem for the transport equation. The linear operator $\Lambda(\mu, \mu_s)$ which maps g^- onto g^+ is called the albedo operator.

If $\mu_s = 0$, i.e., no scatter is present, this inverse problem can be readily reduced to the integral geometric problems of sections 3.1 and 3.2. In this case, (7.1)–(7.2) can be solved as an initial value problem along the ray $\{y = x + t\theta : t \ge 0\}$ with initial values $g^-(x, \theta)$ for $x \in \partial\Omega$, $\nu(x) \cdot \theta \le 0$ (method of characteristics). We obtain for y on the ray

$$u(y, \theta) = g^-(x, \theta)\rho(x, y) + \int_x^y q(x', \theta)\rho(x', y)dx', \quad \rho(x, y) = e^{\int_x^y \mu(x')dx'}, \tag{7.4}$$

where integration is along the straight line connecting x, y.

For $y \in \Omega$, $\theta \in S^{n-1}$, we only have to find $x \in \partial\Omega$ such that $\theta = (y - x)/|y - x|$ to obtain $u(y, \theta)$ from (7.4).

Now let $y, x \in \partial\Omega$. Putting $\theta = (y - x)/|y - x|$, we have $\nu(y) \cdot \theta > 0$ and $\nu(x) \cdot \theta \le 0$. Hence

$$g^+(y, \theta) = g^-(x, \theta)\rho(x, y) + \int_x^y q(x', \theta)\rho(x', y)dx'. \tag{7.5}$$

If, as assumed, g^+ and g^- are known, then (7.5) is an integral equation for q and μ. In transmission tomography, we have no internal sources, i.e., $q = 0$; hence

$$\rho(x, y) = \frac{g^+(y, \theta)}{g^-(x, \theta)}, \tag{7.6}$$

which is (3.1), except for notation. In emission tomography (SPECT; see section 3.2), we have no incoming radiation, i.e., $g^- = 0$, and the source is isotropic, i.e., $q(x, \theta) = q(x)$. Hence

$$g^+(y, \theta) = \int_x^y q(x')\rho(x', y)dx'. \tag{7.7}$$

This is (3.5), again except for notation. So much for the case $\mu_s = 0$.

For $\mu_s > 0$, we still can extract ρ from g^+, g^- (assuming $q = 0$ and μ, μ_s, η to be continuous) provided g^- is properly chosen. Let

$$g^-(x, \theta) = \begin{cases} 1, & |\theta - \theta_0| < \varepsilon, \\ 0 & \text{otherwise} \end{cases} \tag{7.8}$$

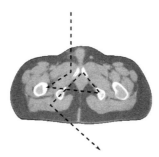

Figure 7.1. *Optical tomography. The detector responses are measured for many positions of the laser source. In practice, far more scattering events occur.*

with $\theta_0 \in S^{n-1}$ and ε small. Considering the scattering integral in (7.1) as the source term, (7.5) reads

$$g^+(y, \theta) = g^-(x, \theta)\rho(x, y) + \int_x^y \mu_s(x') \int_{S^{n-1}} \eta(x', \theta, \theta')u(x', \theta')d\theta'dx'$$
$$= g^-(x, \theta)\rho(x, y) + H(x, y),$$

where $\theta = (y - x)/|y - x|$ and H is continuous. Now let $y \in \partial\Omega$ be fixed. Choose $x_0 \in \partial\Omega$ such that $\theta = \theta_0$ and $x_\varepsilon \in \partial\Omega$ such that $|\theta - \theta_0| = \varepsilon$. Then

$$g^+(y, \theta_0) = \rho(x_0, y) + H(x_0, y),$$

$$g^+(y, \theta) = H(x_\varepsilon, y). \tag{7.9}$$

As $\varepsilon \to 0$, $x_\varepsilon \to x_0$, and we can find $\rho(x_0, y)$ from g^+. Varying θ_0, we can find ρ for all x, $y \in \partial\Omega$, hence μ. Similarly, one can find $\mu_s \eta$. This program has been carried out in Choulli and Stefanov (1996), Antyufeev and Bondarenko (1996), and Anikonov, Kovtanyuk, and Prokhorov (1999). Practically, this is difficult to do since highly collimated sources such as (7.8) are difficult to make and (7.9) is subject to cancellation.

7.2 Optical Tomography

In optical tomography, one illuminates the object to be imaged with light in the near infrared (NIR; 700–1000 nm) region; see Figure 7.1. Human tissue is relatively transparent to NIR light, which penetrates small objects such as the female breast and heads of preterm infants. See Singer et al. (1990) and Navarro and Profio (1988) for early attempts and Arridge (1999) for a state-of-the-art review.

7.2.1 The transport model

The most comprehensive model for optical tomography is the transport equation for the particle flux u in a convex region $\Omega \subseteq \mathbb{R}^3$ containing the object. It reads

$$\frac{1}{c}\frac{\partial u}{\partial t}(x,\theta,t) + \theta \cdot \nabla u(x,\theta,t) + \mu(x)u(x,\theta,t)$$

$$= \mu_s(x)\int_{S^2} \eta(\theta \cdot \theta')u(x,\theta',t)d\theta', \qquad (7.10)$$

where $\mu = \mu_a + \mu_s$ with μ_a, μ_s as the absorption and the scattering coefficients, respectively. The particle speed c is assumed to be constant and known. The scattering kernel η is normalized such that

$$\int_{S^2} \eta(\theta \cdot \theta')d\theta' = 1.$$

We consider only Henyey–Greenstein scattering, in which case

$$\eta(s) = \frac{1}{4\pi}\frac{1-g^2}{(1+g^2-2gs)^{3/2}}.$$

The parameter $g \in (-1,1)$ is a measure for anisotropy, with $g = 0$ corresponding to isotropic scattering.

For $t = 0$, we assume

$$u(x,\theta,0) = 0, \quad x \in \Omega, \quad \theta \in S^2. \qquad (7.11)$$

We model the incoming flux by the boundary condition

$$u(x,\theta,t) = g^-(x,\theta,t), \quad x \in \partial\Omega, \quad \nu(x)\cdot\theta \le 0, \quad t \ge 0, \qquad (7.12)$$

where ν is the exterior normal on $\partial\Omega$. Alternatively, we could model the incoming flux by a source distribution q on the right-hand side of (7.10). By looking at the distributional form of (7.10), we readily see that (7.12) corresponds to the source distribution $\nu(x)\cdot\theta g^-(x,\theta,t)$, concentrated on $\partial\Omega$.

As in the preceding section, the problem (7.10)–(7.12) admits a unique solution under natural assumptions on μ, μ_s, η. Again the problem is to recover these parameters (or some of them) from measurements of the outgoing flux. The measured quantity in optical tomography is

$$g(x,t) = \frac{1}{4\pi}\int_{S^2} \nu(x)\cdot\theta u(x,\theta,t)d\theta, \quad x \in \partial\Omega, \quad t \ge 0. \qquad (7.13)$$

We assume g to be known for many incoming fluxes g^-. See Kaltenbach and Kaschke (1993) and Arridge and Hebden (1997) for a thorough discussion of the physical aspects.

Typical values of μ_a, μ_s in optical tomography are $\mu_a = 0.1 - 1.0$ mm^{-1}, $\mu_s = 100 - 200$ mm^{-1}. This means that the mean free path of the particles is between 0.005 and 0.01 mm, which is very small compared to a typical object. Thus the predominant phenomenon in optical tomography is scatter rather than transport. Therefore, one can replace the transport equation (7.10) by a much simpler parabolic equation, the diffusion approximation.

7.2.2   The diffusion model

Due to the prevalence of scatter, the flux is essentially isotropic a small distance away from the sources; i.e., it depends only linearly on θ. Thus we may describe the process adequately by the first few moments,

$$u_0(x, t) = \frac{1}{4\pi} \int_{S^2} u(x, \theta, t) d\theta,$$

$$u_1(x, t) = \frac{1}{4\pi} \int_{S^2} \theta u(x, \theta, t) d\theta,$$

$$u_2(x, t) = \frac{1}{4\pi} \int_{S^2} \theta \theta^T u(x, \theta, t) d\theta,$$

of u. Integrating (7.10) over S^2 and using the normalization of η, we obtain

$$\frac{1}{c} \frac{\partial u_0}{\partial t}(x, t) + \nabla \cdot u_1(x, t) + \mu_a(x) u_0(x, t) = 0.$$

Similarly, multiplying (7.10) with θ and integrating over S^2 yields

$$\frac{1}{c} \frac{\partial u_1}{\partial t}(x, t) + \nabla \cdot u_2(x, t) + \mu(x) u_1(x, t) = \bar{\eta} \mu_s(x) u_1(x, t),$$

where $\nabla \cdot u_2$ means that ∇ is applied to the rows of u_2. $\bar{\eta}$ is the mean scattering cosine

$$\bar{\eta} = \frac{1}{4\pi} \int_{S^2} \theta' \cdot \theta \eta(\theta \cdot \theta') d\theta', \tag{7.14}$$

which does not depend on θ. This formula is obtained in the following way. It is clear that

$$\int_{S^2} \theta \eta(\theta \cdot \theta') d\theta = \bar{\eta} \theta'$$

with some constant $\bar{\eta}$. We obtain (7.14) by multiplying this equation with θ' and integrating over S^2. Introducing the reduced scattering coefficient

$$\mu_s' = (1 - \bar{\eta}) \mu_s, \tag{7.15}$$

we can write the equations for u_0, u_1 in the more concise form

$$\frac{1}{c} \frac{\partial u_0}{\partial t} + \nabla \cdot u_1 + \mu_a u_0 = 0,$$

$$\frac{1}{c} \frac{\partial u_1}{\partial t} + \nabla \cdot u_2 + (\mu_a + \mu_s') u_1 = 0. \tag{7.16}$$

Now we make the decisive approximation. We assume that u depends only linearly on θ, i.e.,

$$u(x, \theta, t) = \alpha u_0(x, t) + \beta \theta \cdot u_1(x, t). \tag{7.17}$$

For the constants α, β we easily obtain $\alpha = 1, \beta = 3$ by computing the moments of order
0 and 1 of (7.17). Expressing u_2 by (7.17) in terms of u_0, u_1 it follows that

$$\nabla \cdot u_2 = \frac{1}{3}\nabla u_0.$$

Eliminating $\nabla \cdot u_2$ from (7.16), we obtain a closed system for u_0, u_1:

$$\frac{1}{c}\frac{\partial u_0}{\partial t} + \nabla \cdot u_1 + \mu_a u_0 = 0,$$

$$\frac{1}{c}\frac{\partial u_1}{\partial t} + \frac{1}{3}\nabla u_0 + (\mu_a + \mu_s')u_1 = 0.$$

(7.18)

This is called the P_1-approximation; see Case and Zweifel (1967). To obtain the diffusion
approximation, we go one step farther, assuming that u is almost stationary in the sense that
$\partial u_1/\partial t$ is negligible in the second equation of (7.18). In that case, we have approximately

$$u_1 = -D\nabla u_0, \qquad D = \frac{1}{3(\mu_a + \mu_s')}.$$

(7.19)

This is called Fick's law, and D is the diffusion coefficient. Inserting (7.19) into the first
equation of (7.18), we finally arrive at the diffusion approximation

$$\frac{1}{c}\frac{\partial u_0}{\partial t} - \nabla \cdot (D\nabla u_0) + \mu_a u_0 = 0$$

(7.20)

of (7.10). This is the most commonly used model for photon migration in tissue. It is used
almost exclusively in optical tomography.

We still have to derive the initial and boundary conditions for (7.20). From (7.11),
we immediately obtain

$$u_0(x, 0) = 0.$$

(7.21)

From the boundary condition (7.12), we obtain

$$v(x) \cdot \int_{v(x)\cdot\theta \leq 0} \theta u(x, \theta, t)d\theta = v(x) \cdot \int_{v(x)\cdot\theta \leq 0} \theta g^-(x, \theta, t)d\theta, \quad x \in \partial\Omega, \quad t \geq 0.$$

From (7.17) and (7.19), we get

$$u(x, \theta, t) = \frac{1}{4\pi}u_0(x, t) - \frac{3}{4\pi}\theta \cdot D(x)\nabla u_0(x, t).$$

Observing that

$$v \cdot \int_{v\cdot\theta \leq 0} \theta d\theta = -\pi, \qquad v \cdot \int_{v\cdot\theta \leq 0} \theta_i \theta_j d\theta = \begin{cases} 0, & i \neq j, \\ \frac{2\pi}{3}v_i, & i = j, \end{cases}$$

we obtain for an isotropic distribution $g^-(x, \theta, t) = g^-(x, t)$

$$-\pi u_0(x, t) - 3\frac{2\pi}{3}Dv(x) \cdot \nabla u_0(x, t) = -\pi g^-(x, t)$$

or

$$u_0 + 2D\frac{\partial u_0}{\partial v} = g^- \tag{7.22}$$

on $\partial\Omega$. This translates the boundary condition (7.12) into the diffusion model. The equation (7.13) for the measurements reads

$$g(x,t) = v(x) \cdot u_1(x,t) = -Dv(x) \cdot \nabla u_0(x,t)$$

by (7.19), and hence

$$g = -D\frac{\partial u_0}{\partial v} \tag{7.23}$$

on $\partial\Omega$.

The initial boundary value problem (7.20)–(7.22) admits a unique solution u_0 under natural assumptions. The inverse problem of optical tomography in the diffusion approximation calls for the determination of D, μ_a from the values of g for all incoming isotropic light distributions g^-. Putting $f = g^- - 2g^+$, this means that from knowing g^+ for each choice of the boundary values $u_0 = g$ for (7.20), we have to determine D, μ_a. This can be expressed conveniently by the Dirichlet-to-Neuman map $\Lambda(D, \mu_a)$, which is defined as the linear operator associating with each function f on $\partial\Omega \times \mathbb{R}_+$ the function $\Lambda(D, \mu_a)g = -D\partial u_0/\partial v$ on $\partial\Omega \times \mathbb{R}_+$, where u_0 is the solution of (7.20) with boundary values $u_0 = f$ on $\partial\Omega \times \mathbb{R}_+$.

Optical tomography can be done in the time domain and the frequency domain. In the time domain, g^- is a light flash emanating from sources on $\partial\Omega$. This is modeled as

$$g^-(x,t) = g^-(x)\delta(t), \tag{7.24}$$

where g^- is the source distribution on $\partial\Omega$. Typically, g^- is a δ-like function concentrated at a source $s \in \partial\Omega$. The response $g^+(x,t)$ at detector $x \in \partial\Omega$ is a function of t that is nonzero for $t \geq t_0$, peaks shortly afterward, and levels off as $t \to \infty$; see Figure 7.2.

In frequency domain optical tomography, g^- is a time-harmonic function

$$g^-(x,t) = g^-(x)e^{i\omega t}. \tag{7.25}$$

For t large, u_0 is time harmonic, too, and we have

$$u_0(x,t) = v(x)e^{i\omega t}, \tag{7.26}$$

where v satisfies

$$-\nabla \cdot (D\nabla v) + \left(\mu_a + i\frac{\omega}{c}\right)v = 0 \quad \text{in } \Omega,$$

$$v + 2D\frac{\partial v}{\partial v} = g^- \quad \text{on } \partial\Omega, \tag{7.27}$$

the detector response being

$$g = -D\frac{\partial v}{\partial v} \quad \text{on } \partial\Omega. \tag{7.28}$$

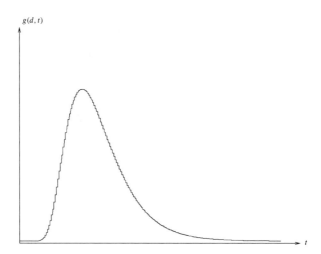

$g(d,t)$

t

Figure 7.2. *Typical detector response in time domain optical tomography.*

The problem is to recover D, μ_a from knowing g for all source distributions g^- and for one (or some few) frequencies ω. This is tantamount to saying that for each function g on $\partial\Omega$, we know $\Lambda(D, \mu_a)g$, where $\Lambda(D, \mu_a)$ is the Dirichlet-to-Neuman map for (7.27). A special case arises for $\omega = 0$ (continuous wave (CW) or steady state (DC)), which is identical to the stationary or time-independent case of (7.20) and (7.22)–(7.23).

Problem (7.27)–(7.28) can be further simplified by the Liouville transformation. Putting

$$v = D^{-1/2}u,$$

(7.27) becomes

$$-\Delta u + qu = 0, \qquad q = \frac{\mu_a + i\omega/c}{D} + \frac{\Delta D^{1/2}}{D^{1/2}}.$$

If q is real (i.e., $\omega = 0$), we have the uniqueness theorem of Sylvester and Uhlmann (1986): Suppose that $\partial u/\partial v$ is known on $\partial\Omega$ for each u on $\partial\Omega$; then q is uniquely determined. This result was extended to $\omega \neq 0$ by Grinberg (1998), provided q is close to a constant. From this latter result, we get an important uniqueness result for optical tomography, as follows.

If $\omega \neq 0$ and μ_a, D are sufficiently close to constants, then μ_a and D can be determined simultaneously.

For $\omega = 0$, simultaneous determination of μ_a, D is not possible. The degree of nonuniqueness has been explored by Arridge and Lionheart (1998).

7.2.3 The linearized problem

Most of the work in optical tomography is based on linearization. As an example, we consider the frequency domain case (7.27)–(7.28). We assume that approximations D_0, μ_0 for D, μ_a are available such that $D = D_0 + H$, $\mu_a = \mu_0 + h$ with H, h small and, for simplicity, $D = D_0$ near $\partial\Omega$. Let v_0 be the solution of (7.27) for $D = D_0$, $\mu_a = \mu_0$, i.e.,

$$-\nabla \cdot (D_0 \nabla v_0) + \left(\mu_0 + i\frac{\omega}{c}\right) v_0 = 0 \quad \text{in } \Omega,$$

$$v_0 + 2D_0 \frac{\partial v_0}{\partial \nu} = g^- \quad \text{on } \partial\Omega. \tag{7.29}$$

Putting $v = v_0 + w$ and subtracting (7.29) from (7.28), we obtain, ignoring second order terms in H, h, w,

$$-\nabla \cdot (D_0 \nabla w) + \left(\mu_0 + i\frac{\omega}{c}\right) w = \nabla \cdot (H \nabla v_0) - h v_0 \quad \text{in } \Omega,$$

$$w + 2D_0 \frac{\partial w}{\partial \nu} = 0 \quad \text{on } \partial\Omega. \tag{7.30}$$

The linearized problem consists of determining H, h from knowing

$$-D_0 \frac{\partial w}{\partial \nu} = g^+ + D_0 \frac{\partial v_0}{\partial \nu} \tag{7.31}$$

for all choices of g^- in (7.29).

With G_0 as the Green's function of (7.30), we can write the solution w to (7.30) as

$$w(x) = \int_\Omega G_0(x, y)(\nabla \cdot (H \nabla v_0)(y) - h(y)v_0(y))dy$$

$$= -\int_\Omega \nabla_y G_0(x, y) \cdot \nabla v_0(y)H(y)dy - \int_\Omega G_0(x, y)v_0(y)h(y)dy.$$

From (7.28) we obtain for each detector $x \in \partial\Omega$

$$g(x) = -D_0 \frac{\partial v_0}{\partial \nu}(x) + D_0(x) \int_\Omega \frac{\partial}{\partial \nu_x} \nabla_y G_0(x, y) \cdot \nabla v_0(y)H(y)dy$$

$$+ D_0(x) \int_\Omega \frac{\partial}{\partial \nu_x} G_0(x, y)v_0(y)h(y)dy.$$

Since $D = D_0$ is known on $\partial\Omega$, we obtain the integral equation

$$g(x) = -D_0 \frac{\partial v_0}{\partial \nu}(x) + \int_\Omega J(x, y)H(y)dy + \int_\Omega K(x, y)h(y)dy, \quad x \in \partial\Omega,$$

where the kernel

$$J(x, y) = D_0 \frac{\partial}{\partial \nu_x} \nabla_y G_0(x, y) \cdot \nabla v_0(y), \qquad K(x, y) = D_0 \frac{\partial}{\partial \nu_x} G_0(x, y)v_0(y)$$

is known. Typically, the source distribution g^- is concentrated at some source $s \in \partial\Omega$. Assuming that g^- is the δ function on $\partial\Omega$ concentrated at s, K is large in a banana-shaped region joining x and s; see Figure 7.3. Thus the linearized problem is similar to transmission tomography, with the straight lines replaced by banana-shaped regions.

Many researchers, e.g., Hoogenraad et al. (1997), use algorithms for transmission tomography such as ART or filtered backprojection (see sections 5.1 and 5.3) for reconstruction in optical tomography.

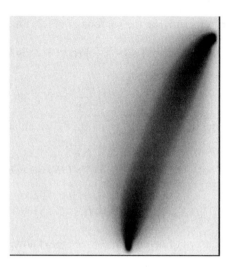

Figure 7.3. *Weight function K of the linearized problem.*

7.2.4   Calderon's method

If the known approximations D_0, μ_0 to D, μ in the previous sections are constant, then an explicit solution of the linearized problem (7.30)–(7.31) in terms of Fourier transforms is possible by a procedure due to Calderon (1980). We extend Calderon's method to complex potentials, using a technique of Grinberg (1998).

Let L be the differential operator defined by

$$Lz = -\nabla \cdot (D_0 \nabla z) + \left(\mu_0 + i\frac{\omega}{c}\right) z$$

with D_0, μ_0 constant. By Green's formula,

$$\int_\Omega (Lwz - wLz)dx = -D_0 \int_{\partial\Omega} \left(\frac{\partial w}{\partial \nu}z - w\frac{\partial z}{\partial \nu}\right) d\sigma$$

with ν as the exterior normal and σ as the surface measure on $\partial\Omega$. Now let z be any solution to $Lz = 0$, and let w be the solution to (7.30). Then

$$\int_\Omega (\nabla \cdot (H\nabla v_0) - hv_0)z\,dx = -D_0 \int_{\partial\Omega} \left(\frac{\partial w}{\partial \nu}z - w\frac{\partial z}{\partial \nu}\right) d\sigma. \qquad (7.32)$$

Since D_0, μ_0 are constant, the function z defined by

$$z(x) = e^{\varsigma \cdot x}$$

with $\varsigma \subset \mathbb{C}^3$ satisfying

$$-D_0\varsigma \cdot \varsigma + \mu_0 + i\frac{\omega}{c} = 0 \qquad (7.33)$$

is a solution to $Lz = 0$. For each $\xi \in \mathbb{R}^3$, (7.33) has the solutions

$$\varsigma^\pm = \pm(\alpha + i\beta)\eta - \frac{i}{2}\xi,$$

where $\eta \in \xi^\perp$, $|\eta| = 1$, and

$$\alpha = \sqrt{\frac{\omega}{2cD_0}}\left(\delta + \sqrt{1+\delta^2}\right)^{1/2}, \qquad \beta = \sqrt{\frac{\omega}{2cD_0}}(\delta + \sqrt{1+\delta^2})^{-1/2},$$

$$\delta = \frac{cD_0}{\omega}\left(\frac{\mu_0}{D_0} + \frac{1}{4}|\xi|^2\right).$$

Thus $z_\xi = e^{\varsigma^+ \cdot x}$ solves $Lz_\xi = 0$ for each $\xi \in \mathbb{R}^3$. Likewise, $v_{0\xi} = e^{\varsigma^- \cdot x}$ is a solution to (7.29) for

$$g^- = g_\xi^- = v_{0\xi} + 2D_0\frac{\partial v_{0\xi}}{\partial \nu} = (1 + 2D_0\nu \cdot \varsigma^-)e^{\varsigma^- \cdot x}.$$

For this choice of g^-,

$$g = g_\xi = -D_0\frac{\partial v}{\partial \nu} = -D_0\frac{\partial v_{0\xi}}{\partial \nu} - D_0\frac{\partial w}{\partial \nu}$$

is known. Hence $\frac{\partial w}{\partial \nu}$ and, because of $w + 2D_0\frac{\partial w}{\partial \nu} = 0$, w are known on $\partial\Omega$. This means that the right-hand side of (7.32),

$$-t(\xi) = -D_0\int_{\partial\Omega}\left(\frac{\partial w}{\partial \nu}z_\xi - w\frac{\partial z_\xi}{\partial \nu}\right)d\sigma,$$

is known for each $\xi \in \mathbb{R}^3$. Using $v = v_0 + w$, (7.31), and the boundary condition of v in (7.27), and observing that $Lv_{0\xi} = 0$, we have

$$t(\xi) = \int_{\partial\Omega}\left(g_\xi^+ z_\xi - (g_\xi^- - 2g_\xi^+)\frac{\partial z_\xi}{\partial \nu}\right)d\sigma$$

$$= \int_{\partial\Omega} g_\xi^+(x)(1 + 2v(x) \cdot \varsigma^+(x))e^{\varsigma^+ \cdot x}d\sigma(x) + t_0(\xi), \qquad (7.34)$$

$$t_0(\xi) = -\int_{\partial\Omega}(1 + 2D_0\nu(x) \cdot \varsigma^-)(v(x) \cdot \varsigma^+)e^{-i\xi \cdot x}d\sigma(x).$$

After an integration by parts, (7.32) reads

$$\int_\Omega (H\nabla v_{0\xi} \cdot \nabla z_\xi + hv_{0\xi}z_\xi)dx = t(\xi).$$

Inserting $v_{0\xi}$, z_ξ, we obtain

$$\int_\Omega (\varsigma^+ \cdot \varsigma^- H(x) + h(x))e^{-i\xi x}dx = t(\xi).$$

Now,

$$\varsigma^+ \cdot \varsigma^- = -\frac{1}{2}|\xi|^2 - \frac{\mu_0}{D_0} - i\frac{\omega}{cD_0},$$

and hence

$$\left(\frac{1}{2}\Delta - \frac{\mu_0}{D_0} - \frac{i\omega}{cD_0}\right)H + h = (2\pi)^{-3/2}\tilde{t}(x) \tag{7.35}$$

with $\tilde{t}$ as the inverse Fourier transform of t. For $\omega > 0$ we first recover H from the imaginary part of this equation and then h from the real part.

Calderon's solution of the linearized problem provides valuable insight into the nature of the problem in frequency domain. First, it corroborates that uniqueness of the simultaneous determination of H, h can be expected for $\omega \neq 0$. Second, it tells us that the problem is severely ill-posed. This follows from the exponential growth of $e^{\varsigma^+ \cdot x}$ in (7.34) as $|\xi| \to \infty$: We have

$$\varsigma^+ = O(|\xi|) \quad \text{as } |\xi| \to \infty.$$

Thus the inverse Fourier transform $\tilde{t}$ in (7.35) does not exist as a function, and strong filtering has to be used.

A practical reconstruction method has not yet been derived from Calderon's method; however, see Schotland (1997).

7.2.5 The transport-backtransport algorithm

The transport-backtransport algorithm is the nonlinear Kaczmarz method of section 5.7 for the transport model of section 7.2.1. We assume that we have p incoming fluxes g_j^- in $[0, T]$, $j = 1, \ldots, p$. The operator R_j is defined as follows: Let $u = u_j$ be the solution of (7.10)–(7.12), and define $R_j\binom{\mu_a}{\mu_s}$ to be the detector output (7.13), i.e.,

$$R_j\begin{pmatrix} \mu_a \\ \mu_s \end{pmatrix} = \frac{1}{4\pi}\int_{S^2} \nu(x) \cdot \theta u_j(x, \theta, t)d\theta, \qquad x \in \partial\Omega, \quad 0 \leq t \leq T. \tag{7.36}$$

The problem is to recover μ_a, μ_s from

$$R_j\begin{pmatrix} \mu_a \\ \mu_s \end{pmatrix} = g_j \quad \text{in } \partial\Omega \times [0, T], \quad j = 1, \ldots, p, \tag{7.37}$$

g_j being the detector output for incoming radiation g_j^-. We use the unknowns μ_a, μ_s rather than $\mu = \mu_a + \mu_s$, μ_s to separate scattering from absorption phenomena in the algorithm.

We consider R_j as an operator from $L_2(\Omega) \times L_2(\Omega)$ into $L_2(\partial\Omega \times [0, T])$. This is questionable, since the natural spaces are $L_\infty(\Omega) \times L_\infty(\Omega)$ and $L_1(\partial\Omega \times [0, T])$, respectively; see Dorn (1997). We ignore this subtle inconsistency.

We compute the derivative of R_j by formally linearizing around μ_a, μ_s, obtaining

$$R_j'\begin{pmatrix} \mu_a \\ \mu_s \end{pmatrix}\begin{pmatrix} h \\ k \end{pmatrix} = \frac{1}{4\pi}\int_{S^2} \nu(x) \cdot \theta w(x, \theta, t)d\theta, \tag{7.38}$$

where w is the solution of

$$\frac{1}{c}\frac{\partial w}{\partial t}(x,\theta,t) + \theta \cdot \nabla w(x,\theta,t) + \mu_a(x)w(x,\theta,t) \tag{7.39}$$

$$- \mu_s(x)\left(\int_{S^2} \eta(\theta \cdot \theta')w(x,\theta',t)d\theta' - w(x,\theta,t)\right) \tag{7.40}$$

$$= k(x)\left(\int_{S^2} \eta(\theta \cdot \theta')u_j(x,\theta',t)d\theta' - u_j(x,\theta,t)\right) - h(x)u_j(x,\theta,t)$$

in $\Omega \times S^2 \times [0,T]$,

$$w(x,\theta,0) = 0 \quad \text{in } \Omega \times S^2, \tag{7.41}$$

$$w(x,\theta,t) = 0 \quad \text{for } x \in \partial\Omega, \qquad v(x) \cdot \theta \le 0, \quad 0 \le t \le T. \tag{7.42}$$

The adjoint of $R'_j\left(\begin{smallmatrix}\mu_a\\\mu_s\end{smallmatrix}\right)$ is formally given by

$$\left(\left(R'_j\left(\begin{matrix}\mu_a\\\mu_s\end{matrix}\right)\right)^* r\right)(x)$$

$$= \int_0^T \int_{S^2} \left(\begin{matrix}-u_j(x,\theta,t)\\ \int_{S^2} \eta(\theta \cdot \theta')u_j(x,\theta',t)d\theta' - u_j(x,\theta,t)\end{matrix}\right) z(x,\theta,t)d\theta dt, \tag{7.43}$$

where z is the solution of the adjoint problem

$$-\frac{\partial z}{\partial t}(x,\theta,t) - \theta \cdot \nabla z(x,\theta,t) + \mu_a(x)z(x,\theta,t)$$

$$- \mu_s(x)\left(\int_{S^2} \eta(\theta \cdot \theta')z(x,\theta',t)d\theta' - z(x,\theta,t)\right) = 0 \tag{7.44}$$

in $\Omega \times S^2 \times [0,T]$,

$$z(x,\theta,T) = 0 \quad \text{on } \Omega \times S^2, \tag{7.45}$$

$$z(x,\theta,t) = r(x,\theta,t), \qquad x \in \partial\Omega, \quad v(x)\theta \ge 0, \quad t \in [0,T]. \tag{7.46}$$

This can be shown by verifying the identity

$$\left(R'_j\left(\begin{matrix}\mu_a\\\mu_s\end{matrix}\right)\left(\begin{matrix}h\\k\end{matrix}\right), r\right)_{L_2(\partial\Omega\times[0,T])} = \left(\left(\begin{matrix}h\\k\end{matrix}\right), \left(R'_j\left(\begin{matrix}\mu_a\\\mu_s\end{matrix}\right)\right)^* r\right)_{L_2(\Omega)\times L_2(\Omega)}$$

for smooth functions h, k on Ω and r on $\partial\Omega \times [0,T]$. This is an exercise in integration by parts; see Dorn (1997) and Natterer (1996).

For the operator C_j in (5.89), we simply take a multiple of the identity. The factor can be absorbed into the parameter ω. Then the restriction $0 < \omega < 2$ loses significance and we have to determine a suitable value of ω by trial and error.

Now one sweep of the Kaczmarz procedure (5.89) goes as follows. Let μ_a^0, μ_s^0 be an initial approximation. We describe the step $\mu_a^k, \mu_s^k \to \mu_a^{k+1}, \mu_s^{k+1}$.

Let $\mu_a^{k,0} = \mu_a^k$, $\mu_s^{k,0} = \mu_s^k$.

For $j = 1, \ldots, p$,

1. *the transportation step:*

   Solve (7.10)–(7.12) for $\mu_a = \mu_a^{k,j-1}$, $\mu_s = \mu_s^{k,j-1}$, and $g^- = g_j^-$. Denote the solution by u_j.

2. *computation of the residual:*

$$r_j(x,t) = \frac{1}{4\pi} \int_{S^2} \nu(x) \cdot \theta u_j(x,\theta,t) d\theta - g_j(x,t), \qquad x \in \partial\Omega, \quad 0 \le t \le T.$$

3. *the backtransportation step:*

   Solve the adjoint problem (7.44)–(7.46) by $\mu_a = \mu_a^{k,j-1}$, $\mu_s = \mu_s^{k,j-1}$, $r = r_j$. Denote the solution by z_j and put

$$\mu_a^{k,j} = \mu_a^{k,j-1} + \omega \int_0^T \int_{S^2} u_j(x,\theta,t) z_j(x,\theta,t) d\theta dt,$$

$$\mu_s^{k,j} = \mu_s^{k,j-1} - \omega \int_0^T \int_{S^2} \left(\int_{S^2} \eta(\theta \cdot \theta') u_j(x,\theta',t) d\theta' - u_j(x,\theta,t) \right) z_j(x,\theta,t) d\theta dt.$$

Put $\mu_a^{k+1} = \mu_a^{k,p}$, $\mu_s^{k+1} = \mu_s^{k,p}$.

The algorithm is stopped when $r_1, \dots, r_p$ are sufficiently small.

The algorithm is easily interpreted from a physical point of view. For the current guess $\mu_a^{(j-1)}$, $\mu_s^{(j-1)}$ and for the given incoming flux g_j^-, the detector output is computed and compared to the measured detector output g_j, yielding the residual flux r_j. This residual flux is used as incoming flux with direction and time reversed, yielding the flux z_j in Ω. For each $x \in \Omega$ we compute the update for μ_a, μ_s as a weighted average of z_j, the weight being determined by u_j. z_j is sometimes called the importance. Note that the update for μ_s is zero if u_j is isotropic. This means that μ_s can be recovered only if u_j is sufficiently direction dependent. For numerical results, see Dorn (1998).

7.2.6 The diffusion-backdiffusion algorithm

Now we apply the nonlinear Kaczmarz method to the diffusion approximation of section 7.2.2 in frequency domain. We assume that we have p incoming fluxes g_j^-, $j = 1, \dots, p$. The operator R_j associates with D, μ_a the detector response

$$R_j \begin{pmatrix} D \\ \mu_a \end{pmatrix} = -D \frac{\partial v_j}{\partial \nu} \quad \text{on } \partial\Omega, \tag{7.47}$$

where $v = v_j$ is the solution to (7.27) with $g^- = g_j^-$. The problem is to determine D, μ_a from

$$R_j \begin{pmatrix} D \\ \mu_a \end{pmatrix} = g_j, \qquad j = 1, \dots, p, \tag{7.48}$$

where g_j is the measured detector output. For simplicity, we assume D to be known on $\partial\Omega$. We consider R_j as an operator from $L_2(\Omega) \times L_2(\Omega)$ into $L_2(\partial\Omega)$, although Sobolev spaces would be more natural. Linearizing formally around D, μ_a, we obtain

$$R'_j \begin{pmatrix} D \\ \mu_a \end{pmatrix} \begin{pmatrix} H \\ h \end{pmatrix} = -D \frac{\partial w}{\partial \nu} \quad \text{on } \partial\Omega, \tag{7.49}$$

where w is the solution to

$$-\nabla \cdot (D\nabla w) + \left(\mu_a + i\frac{\omega}{c}\right) w = \nabla \cdot (H\nabla v_j) - hv_j \quad \text{in } \Omega,$$
$$w = 0 \quad \text{on } \partial\Omega. \tag{7.50}$$

The adjoint of $R'_j(\begin{smallmatrix} D \\ \mu_a \end{smallmatrix})$ is considered as an operator from $L_2(\partial\Omega)$ into $L_2(\Omega) \times L_2(\Omega)$. Formally, we obtain

$$\left(R'_j \begin{pmatrix} D \\ \mu_a \end{pmatrix}\right)^* r = \begin{pmatrix} -\nabla \overline{v}_j \cdot \nabla z \\ -\overline{v}_j z \end{pmatrix}, \tag{7.51}$$

where z is the solution of the adjoint equation

$$-\nabla \cdot (D\nabla z) + \left(\mu_a - i\frac{\omega}{c}\right) z = 0 \quad \text{in } \Omega,$$
$$z = r \quad \text{on } \partial\Omega. \tag{7.52}$$

This can be verified by Green's formula

$$\int_\Omega \left(\left(-\nabla \cdot (D\nabla w) + \left(\mu_a + i\frac{\omega}{c}\right) w\right) \overline{z} - w \overline{\left(-\nabla \cdot (D\nabla z) + \left(\mu_a - i\frac{\omega}{c}\right) z\right)} \right) dx$$
$$= -\int_{\partial\Omega} D \left(\frac{\partial w}{\partial \nu} \overline{z} - w \frac{\overline{\partial z}}{\partial \nu} \right) d\sigma$$

applied to w from (7.50) and z from (7.52).

With C_j a rough approximation to $R'_j(\begin{smallmatrix} D \\ \mu_0 \end{smallmatrix})(R'_j(\begin{smallmatrix} D \\ \mu_0 \end{smallmatrix}))^*$, the Kaczmarz method (5.89) goes as follows. Let D^0, μ_a^0 be initial approximations to D, μ_a. We describe the step D^k, $\mu_a^k \to D^{k+1}, \mu_a^{k+1}$.

Let $D^{k,0} = D^k$, $\mu_a^{k,0} = \mu_a^k$.

For $j = 1, \ldots, p$,

1. *the diffusion step:*

    Solve (7.27) for $D = D^{k,j-1}$, $\mu_a = \mu_a^{k,j-1}$, and $g^- = g_j^-$. Denote the solution by v_j.

2. *compute the weighted residual:*

$$r_j = C_j^{-1} \left(-D^{k,j-1} \frac{\partial v_j}{\partial \nu} - g_j \right) \quad \text{on } \partial\Omega.$$

3. *the backdiffusion step:*

    Solve the adjoint problem (7.52) with $D = D^{k,j-1}$, $\mu_a = \mu_a^{k,j-1}$, $r = r_j$. Denote the solution by z_j and put

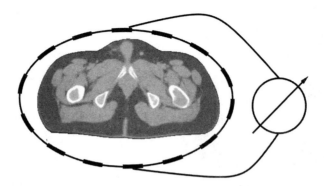

Figure 7.4. *Impedance tomography. Many current patterns are applied and the resulting voltages are measured.*

$$D^{k,j} = D^{k,j-1} + \omega \nabla \bar{v}_j \cdot \nabla z_j,$$
$$\mu_a^{k,j} = \mu_a^{k,j-1} + \omega \bar{v}_j z_j.$$

Put $D^{k+1} = D^{k,p}$, $\mu_a^{k+1} = \mu_a^{k,p}$. In general this update is complex valued. There are several ways to obtain a real update; see Dierkes (2000).

The physical interpretation of the algorithm is similar to the transport-backtransport algorithm, except that now diffusion plays the role of transportation. For numerical results see Arridge and Schweiger (1997) and Dierkes (2000). Many of the algorithms published in the literature are similar to the algorithm suggested here; see Arridge and Schweiger (1999) for a survey on iterative algorithms. For alternatives, see Klibanov, Lucas, and Frank (1999).

7.3   Impedance Tomography

In impedance tomography, one determines the conductivity f inside an object $\Omega \subseteq \mathbb{R}^n$ by applying currents to electrodes at the surface of the object and measuring the resulting voltages; see Figure 7.4.

A simple mathematical model is as follows; see Cheney, Isaacson, and Newell (1999). With u the voltage inside Ω, we have

$$\nabla \cdot (f \nabla u) = 0 \quad \text{in } \Omega. \tag{7.53}$$

Let $E_\ell \subseteq \partial \Omega$, $\ell = 1, \ldots, q$, be the electrodes on $\partial \Omega$. The voltages measured at the electrodes are

$$u + Z_\ell f \frac{\partial u}{\partial \nu} = V^\ell \quad \text{on } E_\ell, \quad \ell = 1, \ldots, q, \tag{7.54}$$

where Z_ℓ is the contact impedance assumed to be known. Between electrodes the current is zero, i.e.,

$$f \frac{\partial u}{\partial \nu} = 0 \quad \text{on } \partial \Omega \backslash (E_1 \cup \cdots \cup E_q). \tag{7.55}$$

Finally, the currents applied to the electrodes are

$$g^\ell = \int_{E_\ell} f \frac{\partial u}{\partial \nu} d\sigma, \quad \ell = 1, \ldots, q. \tag{7.56}$$

The boundary value problem (7.53)–(7.55) has a unique solution under natural conditions. The problem is to recover f from the values in (7.56) for many current patterns.

The inverse problem (7.53)–(7.56) is essentially the same as the inverse problem (7.27)–(7.28) of optical tomography for $\mu_a = 0$, $\omega = 0$, except that the role of the electrodes has been made more explicit. Therefore, the treatment of the linearized problem, including Calderon's method, is the same. We only work out the details of the Kaczmarz method.

Let

$$g_j = \begin{pmatrix} g_j^1 \\ \vdots \\ g_j^q \end{pmatrix}, \quad V_j = \begin{pmatrix} V_j^1 \\ \vdots \\ V_j^q \end{pmatrix}, \quad j = 1, \ldots, p,$$

be the applied current patterns and the measured voltages, respectively. With $u = u_j$ the solution of (7.53)–(7.55) with $V^\ell = V_j^\ell$, we define the operator $R_j : L_2(\Omega) \to \mathbb{R}^q$ by

$$(R_j(f))_\ell = \int_{E_\ell} f \frac{\partial u_j}{\partial \nu} d\sigma, \quad \ell = 1, \ldots, q.$$

The problem is to determine f from

$$R_j(f) = g_j, \quad j = 1, \ldots, p. \tag{7.57}$$

The derivative of R_j and its adjoint are obtained exactly as in (7.49)–(7.52). For R'_j we get

$$(R'_j(f)h)_\ell = \int_{E_\ell} f \frac{\partial w}{\partial \nu} d\sigma$$

with w the solution of

$$\nabla \cdot (f \nabla w) = -\nabla \cdot (h \nabla u_j) \quad \text{in } \Omega,$$

$$w + Z_\ell f \frac{\partial w}{\partial \nu} = 0 \quad \text{on } E_1 \cup \cdots \cup E_q, \tag{7.58}$$

$$f \frac{\partial w}{\partial \nu} = 0 \quad \text{on } \partial\Omega \backslash (E_1 \cup \cdots \cup E_q).$$

The operator $(R'_j(f))^* : \mathbb{R}^q \to L_2(\Omega)$ turns out to be

$$R'_j(f)^* r = \nabla u_j \cdot \nabla z,$$

where z is the solution of

$$\nabla \cdot (f \nabla z) = 0 \quad \text{in } \Omega,$$

$$z + Z_\ell f \frac{\partial z}{\partial \nu} = r_\ell \quad \text{on } E_\ell, \quad \ell = 1, \ldots, q, \tag{7.59}$$

$$f \frac{\partial z}{\partial \nu} = 0 \quad \text{on } \partial\Omega - (E_1 \cup \cdots \cup E_q).$$

All we need for the Kaczmarz method (5.89) is an approximation C_j to $R'_j(f)(R'_j(f))^*$. An easy way to compute such an approximation—which is just a $q \times q$ matrix—is to solve (7.58)–(7.59) for a background conductivity f. Then the algorithm reads as follows. Again we describe the step $f^k \rightarrow f^{k+1}$.

Let $f^{k,0} = f^k$.
For $j = 1, \ldots, p$,

1. Solve (7.53)–(7.55) for $f = f^{k,j-1}$ and $V^\ell = V^\ell_j, \ell = 1, \ldots, q$. Denote the solution by u_j.

2. Compute the residuals d_j with components

$$d^\ell_j = \int_{E_\ell} f \frac{\partial u_j}{\partial \nu} d\sigma - g^\ell_j, \quad \ell = 1, \ldots, q,$$

and the weighted residual $r_j = C^{-1}_j d_j$.

3. Solve the adjoint problem (7.59) with $f = f^{k,j-1}, r^\ell = r^\ell_j$. Denote the solution by z_j and put

$$f^{k,j} = f^{k,j-1} + \omega \nabla u_j \cdot \nabla z_j.$$

Put $f^{k+1} = f^{k,p}$.

Numerical results with this algorithm were obtained by Biedenstein (1996). By and large, they correspond to the results of other algorithms for the fully nonlinear problem. Most of the practical algorithms (e.g., the NOSER algorithm of Cheney et al. (1990)) are linear approximations.

7.4 Ultrasound Tomography

Ultrasound is a venerable imaging technique in medicine, science, and nondestructive testing. In most applications, the images are produced from the backscatter, as in the familiar B-scan images; see Morneburg (1995). The mathematics behind these techniques is fairly simple. They essentially translate the travel time between scatterer and transducer into an image.

Ultrasound tomography is a much more demanding venture. It makes use not only of the reflected wave but also of the transmitted wave, very much in the same way X-rays are used in transmission tomography. The aim is to produce images of a quality comparable to X-ray transmission tomography. Unfortunately, the low penetration of ultrasound in human tissue restricts ultrasound tomography to small objects, most notably the female breast.

A prototype ultrasonic scanner was developed by Waag (1998); see Figure 7.5.

It consists of a cylindrical water tank with a ring of 2048 transducers. Any 128 contiguous transducers can be fired simultaneously to produce a plane wave, which interacts with the object. The resulting scattered wave is measured by the transducers. The prototype is designed to image cylindrical objects.

Wave propagation in biological tissue is described by linear wave equations. Several versions have been derived in the literature; see Nachman, Smith, and Waag (1990), Charlier

Figure 7.5. *Ultrasound tomography scanner.*

and Crowet (1985), and Johnson et al. (1982). Fortunately, these equations largely coincide; only the physical interpretation varies.

Ultrasound tomography can be done in the time domain and the frequency domain.

7.4.1 Frequency domain ultrasound tomography

In frequency domain ultrasound, the relevant differential equation is the Helmholtz equation

$$\Delta u + k^2(1 + f)u = 0, \tag{7.60}$$

where $k = \frac{2\pi}{\lambda}$, λ the wavelength, is the wave number of the irradiating wave and f is a complex valued function of $x \in \mathbb{R}^n$. In Johnson et al. (1982),

$$f = \frac{c_0^2}{c^2} - 1 + \frac{i}{k}\frac{\alpha c_0}{c^2},$$

where c is the speed of sound and α the attenuation. We assume $f = 0$ outside $|x| \leq \rho$, i.e., $\alpha = 0$ and $c = c_0$ in $|x| > \rho$. We seek solutions of (7.60) of the form

$$u = e^{ikx\cdot\theta} + v,$$

where $\theta \in S^{n-1}$ is the direction of the incoming wave and v is the scattered wave, which satisfies the Sommerfeld radiation condition

$$\lim_{r\to\infty} \max_{|x|=r} |x|^{\frac{n-1}{2}} \left(\frac{\partial v}{\partial \nu} - ikv\right) = 0, \tag{7.61}$$

where ν is the exterior normal on $|x| = r$. (7.60)–(7.61) is uniquely solvable. The problem is to recover f from the values of u on $|x| = \rho$ for finitely many directions $\theta_1, \ldots, \theta_p$, i.e.,

$$g_j = u \quad \text{on } |x| = \rho, \quad j = 1, \ldots, p, \tag{7.62}$$

where u is the solution of (7.60)–(7.61) for $\theta = \theta_j$.

In section 3.3, we dealt with this problem by linearization. Unfortunately, the Born and Rytov approximations are far from being valid in applications such as breast screening. Thus we have to solve the fully nonlinear problem.

In principle, the Kaczmarz method (5.89) could be applied to (7.60)–(7.62) almost immediately. One could define $R_j(f) = u$ on $|x| = \rho$, where u is the solution to (7.60)–(7.61), and apply (5.89) directly. However, this would entail the solution of the Helmholtz problem (7.60)–(7.61) at each step. Solving (7.60)–(7.61) numerically for the high values of k, which are used in medical applications (typically the size of the object is 100 wavelengths, i.e., $k\rho = \frac{2\pi}{\lambda}\rho \sim 300$), is very difficult.

Fortunately, there is a way out. We do not need to solve the boundary value problem (7.60)–(7.61). We can replace it by an initial value problem that is much easier to solve numerically. First, knowing u on $|x| = \rho$ means that we can compute u in $|x| \geq \rho$. Indeed, u satisfies in $|x| \geq \rho$ the Helmholtz equation with $f = 0$; hence the boundary value problem can easily be solved by series expansion. To fix ideas, let $n = 2$. Then

$$u(r\theta) = \sum_\ell c_\ell e^{i\ell\varphi} H_\ell(kr), \quad \theta = \begin{pmatrix} \cos\varphi \\ \sin\varphi \end{pmatrix}, \tag{7.63}$$

where H_ℓ is the first-kind Hankel function of order ℓ. The coefficients c_ℓ are readily obtained from the data g_j by

$$c_\ell = \frac{1}{2\pi H_\ell(k\rho)} \int_0^{2\pi} g_j(\rho\theta)e^{-i\ell\varphi} d\varphi.$$

Thus for each θ_j, we know u and its normal derivative on the planes $\Gamma_j^\pm = \pm\rho\theta_j + \theta_j^\perp$; see Figure 7.6. This permits us to replace the boundary value problem (7.60)–(7.61) by the initial value problem

$$\Delta u + k^2(1 + f)u = 0,$$

$$u = g_j^-, \quad \frac{\partial u}{\partial\nu} = \frac{\partial g_j^-}{\partial\nu} \quad \text{on } \Gamma_j^-. \tag{7.64}$$

Here g_j^- is the extended data function computed from (7.63), restricted to Γ_j^-.

Initial value problems such as (7.64) are notoriously unstable. However, this instability is a pure high-frequency phenomenon. Consider first the case $f = 0$. Denote by $^\wedge$ the $(n-1)$-dimensional Fourier transform in $\theta_j^\perp$. Then from (7.64), for $\xi \in \theta_j^\perp$,

$$\hat{u}(s\theta_j, \xi) = \hat{g}(\xi)\cos(sa) + \frac{1}{a}\left(\frac{\partial g}{\partial\nu}\right)^\wedge(\xi)\sin(sa),$$

where $a = \sqrt{k^2 - |\xi|^2}$. We see that for $|\xi| < k$, u depends stably on the initial values. Thus if we define the low-pass filtered version $P_\kappa u$ of u by

$$(P_\kappa u)^\wedge(s\theta_j, \xi) = \begin{cases} \hat{u}(s\theta_j, \xi), & |\xi| < \kappa, \\ 0 & \text{otherwise,} \end{cases}$$

$P_\kappa u$ is stably determined by the initial values on Γ_j^- for $\kappa = k$. It can be shown that this is the case also for $f \neq 0$ if κ is chosen slightly smaller than k; see Natterer (1997a). In

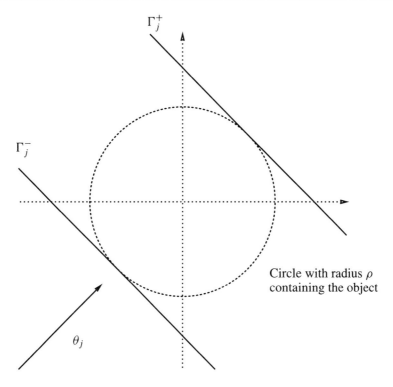

Figure 7.6. *Geometry of the PBP algorithm.*

practice, a value of κ between $0.9k$ and $0.99k$ is sufficient. Initial value techniques are also an essential feature of the algorithm of Borup et al. (1992).

Now we can define the nonlinear operator $R_j : L_2(|x| < \rho) \to L_2(\Gamma_j^+)$ by

$$R_j(f) = P_\kappa u_j|_{\Gamma_j^+},$$

where u_j is the solution to the initial value problem (7.64). Our problem is to solve

$$R_j(f) = g_j^+, \quad j = 1, \dots, p, \tag{7.65}$$

where g_j^+ is the extended data function restricted to Γ_j^+. The reconstruction problem now calls for the determination of f from (7.65).

We proceed exactly as in the previous sections. The derivative $R_j'(f)$ is given by

$$R_j'(f)h = P_\kappa w|_{\Gamma_j^+}, \tag{7.66}$$

where w is the solution of the initial value problem

$$\Delta w + k^2(1 + f)w = -k^2 h u_j,$$

$$w = 0, \quad \frac{\partial w}{\partial \nu} = 0 \quad \text{on } \Gamma_j^-. \tag{7.67}$$

The adjoint $(R'_j(f))^* : L_2(\Gamma^+_j) \to L_2(|x| < \rho)$ is (see Natterer (1996))

$$(R'_j(f))^* r = k^2 \overline{u}_j z,$$

where z is the solution of

$$\Delta z + k^2(1 + \overline{f})z = 0,$$

$$z = 0, \quad \frac{\partial z}{\partial \nu} = P_\kappa r \quad \text{on } \Gamma^+_j. \tag{7.68}$$

Note that z is exactly identical to what is called a backpropagated (Langenberg (1989)) or time-reversed (Fink (1992)) wave.

As operator C_j in (5.89), we take $C_j = R'_j(0)(R'_j(0))^*$. According to (7.67)–(7.68), this operator can be computed by solving

$$\Delta z + k^2 z = 0,$$

$$z = 0, \quad \frac{\partial z}{\partial \nu} = P_\kappa r \quad \text{on } \Gamma^+_j,$$

$$\Delta w + k^2 w = -k^4 z,$$

$$w = 0, \quad \frac{\partial w}{\partial \nu} = 0 \quad \text{on } \Gamma^-_j,$$

and putting

$$C_j r = P_\kappa w$$

on Γ^+_j. By taking the $(n - 1)$-dimensional Fourier transforms in $\theta^\perp_j$, we readily get for $\xi \in \theta^\perp_j, |\xi| < k$

$$\hat{z}(s\theta_j, \xi) = \frac{\hat{r}(\xi)}{a} \sin(s - \rho)a,$$

$$\hat{w}(s\theta_j, \xi) = -\frac{k^4}{a} \int_{-\rho}^{s} \hat{z}(s'\Theta_j, \xi) \sin(s - s')a \, ds',$$

and hence

$$(C_j r)^\wedge(\xi) = k^4 \int_{-\rho}^{\rho} \left(\frac{\sin(s - \rho)a}{a} \right)^2 ds \, \hat{r}(\xi)$$

$$= \frac{k^4}{2a^3}(2\rho a - \cos(2\rho a)\sin(2\rho a))\hat{r}(\xi)$$

$$= \gamma(\xi, k, \rho)\hat{r}(\xi)$$

as long as $|\xi| < k$; see Figure 7.7. Thus the operator C_j^{-1} can be applied by taking Fourier transforms.

The Kaczmarz method (5.89) is now easily described. We call it the propagation-backpropagation (PBP) algorithm. As usual we give the step $f^k \to f^{k+1}$.

Put $f^{k,0} = f^k$.

For $j = 1, \ldots, p$, do

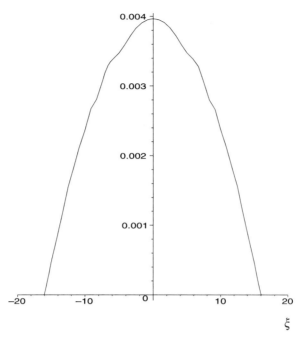

Figure 7.7. *Plot of $\gamma(\xi, k, \rho)^{-1}$ for $\rho = 1$, $k = 16$, $\xi \in [-20, 20]$. Note that C_j^{-1} is a low-pass filter with cutoff frequency k.*

1. *the propagation step:*
   Solve the initial value problem (7.64) with $f = f^{k,j-1}$. Denote the solution by u_j.

2. *compute the residual*

$$d_j = g_j - P_\kappa u_j|_{\Gamma_j^+}$$

   and the weighted residual $r_j = C_j^{-1}d_j$.

3. *the backpropagation step:*
   Solve the initial value problem (7.68) with $f = f^{k,j-1}$ and $r = r_j$. Denote the solution by z_j and put

$$f^{k,j} = f^{k,j-1} + \omega k^2 \overline{u}_j z_j.$$

Put $f^{k+1} = f^{k,P}$.

We visualize the PBP algorithm for the reconstruction of a dot; see Figure 7.8. The data from 16 incoming plane waves are reminiscent of the sinogram in X-ray tomography. The backpropagated residual converges toward the dot. It is easy to imagine that superimposing the backpropagated residuals from different directions reproduces the dot.

A few remarks concerning the numerical solution of (7.64) and (7.68) are in order. First, we do the computations on the function

$$v_j = e^{ikx \cdot \theta_j} u_j$$

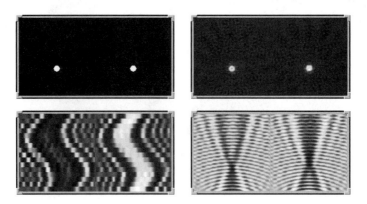

Figure 7.8. *Visualization of the PBP algorithm. In all panels, the left half shows the real part, and the right half shows the imaginary part. Top left: Original. Bottom left: Data. Each of the 16 rows corresponds to the scaled scattered wave at the detector array. Bottom right: Backpropagated first row of data set. Top right: Superimposed backpropagated fields from all 16 directions.*

rather than on u. The reason is that for k large and f small,

$$v_j(x) \sim -\frac{k}{2i}(Rf)(\theta_{j\perp}, x \cdot \theta_{j\perp})$$

for $|x| > \rho$ with R as the Radon transform (2.1) and $\theta_{j\perp}$ as a unit vector perpendicular to θ_j. This follows from neglecting Δv_j and v_j in (7.69) below. Thus we can expect v_j to contain no violent oscillations. v_j satisfies

$$\Delta v_j + 2ik\theta_j \cdot \nabla v_j + k^2(1 + v_j)f = 0. \tag{7.69}$$

It can be solved by a finite difference marching scheme. To fix ideas, we consider the 2D case. We introduce the grid

$$\{x_j^{\ell,m} = \theta_j h\ell + \theta_{j\perp} hm : \ell, m = -q, \ldots, q\}$$

with the stepsize $h = \rho/q$ and approximate (7.69) on this grid by the finite difference equations

$$
\begin{aligned}
4v_j^{\ell,m} - v_j^{\ell+1,m} - v_j^{\ell-1,m} - v_j^{\ell,m+1} - v_j^{\ell,m-1} \\
+ ikh(v_j^{\ell+1,m} - v_j^{\ell-1,m}) + k^2h^2(1 + v_j^{\ell,m})f(x_j^{\ell,m}) = 0,
\end{aligned}
\tag{7.70}
$$

where $v_j^{\ell,m}$ stands for an approximation to $v_j(x_j^{\ell,m})$. Incorporating the initial conditions of (7.64) on Γ_j^- and the boundary condition $u = g_j$ for $m = \pm q$, we can solve (7.70) for $v_j^{\ell,m}$ recursively in ℓ. In order to preserve stability, we have to keep out frequencies beyond κ. This can be done either by restricting the stepsize to $h \geq \pi/\kappa$ or by applying a low pass filter of bandwidth κ to each discrete function $(v_j^{\ell,-q}, \ldots, v_j^{\ell,q})$, $\ell = -q, \ldots, q$, as soon as it is computed. Since a stepsize $h \geq \pi/\kappa$ is usually not sufficient, the latter method is to be preferred. This way of solving (7.70) is clearly reminiscent of the stable marching scheme of Knightly and Mary (1993). By using the fast Fourier transform, v_j can be computed with $O(q^2 \log q)$ operations. Thus a complete sweep of the algorithm is of complexity $pq^2 \log q$. Up to the logarithm, this is the complexity of one sweep of ART in X-ray tomography.

Note that in the three-dimensional case we need only directions θ_j on a great circle of S^2 rather than on all of S^2. This is in agreement with Orlov's completeness condition in section 2.2. For details, see Natterer (1997b).

For the choice of the initial approximation f^0, we empirically found the condition

$$|R(f - f^0)| < \frac{\pi}{k} \tag{7.71}$$

with the Radon transform R. Whenever (7.71) was fulfilled, we observed convergence. For numerical results, see Natterer and Wübbeling (1995). For algorithms based on different principles, see van den Berg and Kleinman (1997), Colton and Monk (1999), and Gutman and Klibanov (1994).

7.4.2 Time domain ultrasound tomography

Since measurements are usually done in the time domain, this is the more natural way to look at the problem. However, the time domain approach suffers from high computation time and its inability to handle problems with dispersion, i.e., if f, as in (7.60), depends on k.

As a model problem, we consider the wave equation

$$\frac{\partial^2 u}{\partial t^2} = c^2(x)\Delta u + q(x, s)\delta(t) \quad \text{in } \Omega \times [0, T] \tag{7.72}$$

with boundary and initial conditions

$$\frac{\partial u}{\partial \nu} = 0 \quad \text{on } \partial\Omega \times [0, T], \quad u = 0, \quad \frac{\partial u}{\partial t} = 0 \quad \text{in } \Omega \times \{0\}. \tag{7.73}$$

Here c is the speed of sound and q is the source term which peaks at the source $s \in \partial\Omega$. For c, q known, (7.72)–(7.73) has a unique solution under natural assumptions. The problem is to find c from knowing

$$g_j = u \quad \text{on } \partial\Omega \times [0, T], \quad j = 1, \ldots, p, \tag{7.74}$$

for the sources $s_1, \ldots, s_p \in \partial\Omega$. We assume that $c^2 = c_0^2(1 + f)$, where f is compactly supported in Ω and c_0 is the speed of sound of the surrounding medium.

The Kaczmarz method for (7.72)–(7.74) is derived exactly in the same way as previously. We introduce the nonlinear map $R_j : L_2(\Omega) \to L_2(\partial\Omega \times [0, T])$ by

$$R_j(f) = u_j|_{\partial\Omega \times [0,T]},$$

where u_j is the solution to (7.72)–(7.73) for $s = s_j$. Again we have to solve

$$R_j(f) = g_j, \quad j = 1, \ldots, p.$$

The derivative of R_j is (at least formally) given by

$$R'_j(f)h = w_j|_{\partial\Omega \times [0,T]},$$

where w_j is the solution of

$$\frac{\partial^2 w_j}{\partial t^2} = (1+f)\Delta w_j + h\Delta u_j \quad \text{in } \Omega \times [0,T],$$

$$\frac{\partial w_j}{\partial v} = 0 \quad \text{on } \partial\Omega \times [0,T], \quad w_j = 0, \quad \frac{\partial w_j}{\partial t} = 0 \quad \text{on } \Omega \times \{0\}.$$

The adjoint $(R'_j(f))^* : L_2(\partial\Omega \times [0,T]) \to L_2(\Omega)$ is

$$(R'_j(f))^* r = \int_0^T z\Delta u_j \, dt,$$

where z is the solution of

$$\frac{\partial^2 z}{\partial t^2} = \Delta((1+f)z) \quad \text{in } \Omega \times [0,T], \tag{7.75}$$

$$\frac{\partial z}{\partial v} = r \quad \text{on } \partial\Omega \times [0,T], \quad z = 0, \quad \frac{\partial z}{\partial t} = 0 \quad \text{on } \Omega \times \{T\}. \tag{7.76}$$

Note that z is nothing but the time-reversed wave generated by the residual r on $\partial\Omega$; see Fink (1992).

As operator C_j in (5.91), we simply take the identity. The step $f^k \to f^{k+1}$ of the Kaczmarz method now reads as follows.

Put $f^{k,0} = f^k$.

For $j = 1, \ldots, p$, do

1. *the propagation step:*
   Solve the initial boundary value problem (7.72)–(7.73) with $f = f^{k,j-1}$ and $s = s_j$.
   Denote the solution by u_j.

2. *compute the residual:*

$$r_j = g_j - u_j|_{\partial\Omega \times [0,T]}.$$

3. *the backpropagation step:*
   Solve the final boundary value problem (7.75)–(7.76) with $f = f^{k,j-1}$ and $r = r_j$.
   Denote the solution by z_j and put

$$f^{k,j} = f^{k,j-1} + \omega \int_0^T z_j \Delta u_j \, dt.$$

Put $f^{k+1} = f^{k,p}$.

Due to our choice $C_j = I$, the inequality $0 < \omega < 2$ is meaningless. The parameter ω has to be determined by trial and error. The propagation and backpropagation step can be done conveniently by (almost identical) finite difference methods.

The algorithm is very similar to the one suggested in Gauthier, Virienz, and Tarantola (1986), Nolet (1987), and Tarantola (1987), except that the update in our algorithm is done for each source s_j separately. In view of our convergence analysis for the Kaczmarz method in section 5.3.1, this difference is essential for the convergence behavior. The algorithm has been tested extensively by Sielschott (2000). For related work see Zhou et al. (1997), Plessix de Roeck, and Chavent (1999), and Minkoff and Symes (1997).

Bibliography

H. Aben and A. Puro (1997), Photoelastic tomography for three-dimensional birefringence studies, *Inverse Problems* **13**, 215–221.

M. Abramowitz and I.A. Stegun (1970), *Handbook of Mathematical Functions*. Dover, New York.

R.A. Adams (1975), *Sobolev Spaces*. Academic Press, New York.

V. Aguilar and P. Kuchment (1995), Range conditions for the multidimensional exponential x-ray transform, *Inverse Problems* **11**, 977–982.

C.B. Ahn, J.H. Kim, and Z.H. Cho (1986), High speed spiral-scan echo planar NMR imaging—I, *IEEE Trans. Med. Imag.* **5**, 2–7.

L.E. Andersson (1988), On the determination of a function from spherical averages, *SIAM J. Math. Anal.* **19**, 214–232.

D.S. Anikonov, A.E. Kovtanyuk, and I.V. Prokhorov (1999), Tomography through the transport equation, in C. Börgers and F. Natterer (eds.): *Computational Radiology and Imaging: Theory and Diagnostics*, IMA Vol. Math. Appl. **110**, 33–44. Springer, New York.

V. Antyufeev and A. Bondarenko (1996), X-ray tomography in scattering media, *SIAM J. Appl. Math.* **56**, 573–587.

S.R. Arridge (1999), Optical tomography in medical imaging, *Inverse Problems* **15**, R41–R93.

S.R. Arridge and J.C. Hebden (1997), Optical imaging in medicine II: Modelling and reconstruction, *Phys. Med. Biol.* **42**, 841–853.

S.R. Arridge and W.R.B. Lionheart (1998), Non-uniqueness in optical tomography, *Optics Lett.* **23**, 882–884.

S.R. Arridge and M. Schweiger (1997), A gradient-based optimisation scheme for optical tomography, *Optics Express* **2**, 213–226.

S.R. Arridge and M. Schweiger (1999), A general framework for iterative reconstruction algorithms in optical tomography, using a finite element method, in C. Börgers and F. Natterer (eds.): *Computational Radiology and Imaging: Theory and Diagnostics*, IMA Vol. Math. Appl. **110**, 45–70. Springer, New York.

L. Axel, G.T. Herman, D.A. Roberts, and L. Dougherty (1990), Linogram reconstruction for magnetic resonance imaging (MRI), *IEEE Trans. Med. Imag.* **9**, 447–449.

D.L. Bailey, B.F. Hutton, and P.J. Walker (1987), Improved SPECT using simultaneous emission and transmission tomography, *J. Nuclear Med.* **28**, 844–851.

H.H. Barrett, B. Gallas, E. Clarkson, and A. Clough (1999), Scattered radiation in nuclear medicine: A case study of the Boltzman transport equation, in C. Börgers and F. Natterer (eds.): *Computational Radiology and Imaging: Theory and Diagnostics*, IMA Vol. Math. Appl. **110**, 71–100. Springer, New York.

H.H. Bauschke and J.M. Borwein (1996), On projection algorithms for solving convex feasibility problems, *SIAM Rev.* **38**, 367–426.

M.S. Beck, E. Campogrande, E.A. Hammer, M. Morris, R.A. Williams, and R.C. Waterfall (1995), Process Tomography—A Strategy for Industrial Exploitation, *Proceedings of ECAPT'94, Porto, Portugal*.

S. Bellini, M. Piacentini, and F. Rocca (1979), Compensation of tissue absorption in emission tomography, *IEEE Trans. Acoust. Speech Signal Process.* **27**, 213–218.

C.A. Berenstein and E. Casadio Tarabusi (1991), Inversion formulas for the k-dimensional Radon transform in real hyperbolic spaces, *Duke Math. J.* **62**, 613–632.

M. Bertero and A. Caponnetto (1997), Tomography with a finite set of projections: Singular value decomposition and resolution, *Inverse Problems* **13**, 1191–1206.

M. Bertero and P. Boccacci (1998), *Introduction to Inverse Problems in Imaging*. Institute of Physics Publishing, Bristol, Philadelphia.

G. Besson (1996), CT fan-beam parametrizations leading to shift-invariant filtering, *Inverse Problems* **12**, 815–833.

G. Beylkin (1984), The inversion problem and applications of the generalized Radon transform, *Comm. Pure Appl. Math.* **37**, 579–599.

G. Beylkin (1995), On the fast Fourier transform of functions with singularities, *Appl. Comp. Harm. Anal.* **2**, 363–381.

S. Biedenstein (1996), *Numerische Verfahren zur Impedanz-Tomographie*, Diplomarbeit, Fachbereich Mathematik und Informatik, Universität Münster, Münster, Germany.

J. Boman (1990), On generalized Radon transforms with unknown measures, *Contemp. Math.* **113**, 5–16.

D.T. Borup, S.A. Johnson, W.W. Kim, and M.J. Berggren (1992), Nonperturbative diffraction tomography via Gauss–Newton iteration applied to the scattering integral equation, *Ultrasonic Imaging* **14**, 69–85.

R.N. Bracewell (1956), Strip integration in radio astronomy, *Aus. J. Phys.* **9**, 198–217.

R.N. Bracewell and A.C. Riddle (1967), Inversion of fan-beam scans in radio astronomy, *Astrophys. J.* **150**, 427–434.

A. Brandt, J. Mann, M. Brodski, and M. Galun (1998), A fast and accurate multilevel inversion of the Radon transform, *SIAM J. Appl. Math.* **60**, 437–462.

H. Braun and A. Hauck (1991), Tomographic reconstruction of vector fields, *IEEE Trans. Signal Process.* **39**, 464–471.

W.L. Briggs and V.E. Henson (1995), *The DFT: An Owner Manual for the Discrete Fourier Transform.* SIAM, Philadelphia.

A.V. Bronnikov (1995), Approximate reconstruction of attenuation map in SPECT imaging, *IEEE Trans. Nuclear Sci.* **42**, 1483–1488.

W.N. Brouw (1975), Aperture synthesis, *Methods Comput. Phys. B* **14**, 131–175.

T. Budinger (1996), *Mathematics and Physics of Emerging Biomedical Imaging.* National Academy Press, Washington, DC.

M.H. Buonocore, W.R. Brody, and A. Macovski (1981), A natural pixel decomposition for two-dimensional image reconstruction, *IEEE Trans. Biomed. Engrg.* **28**, 69–77.

A.B. Calderon (1980), On an inverse boundary value problem, *Seminar on Numerical Analysis and Its Applications to Continuum Physics*, 65–73. Soc. Brasileira de Matemàtica, Rio de Janeiro.

K.M. Case and P.F. Zweifel (1967), *Linear Transport Theory.* Addison–Wesley, Reading, MA.

Y. Censor, D.E. Gustafson, A. Lent, and H. Tuy (1979), A new approach to the emission computerized tomography problem: Simultaneous calculation of attenuation and activity coefficients, *IEEE Trans. Nuclear Sci.* **26**, 2775–2779.

Y. Censor (1981), Row-action methods for huge and sparse systems and their applications, *SIAM Rev.* **23**, 444–466.

Y. Censor and S.A. Zenios (1997), *Parallel Optimization*. Oxford University Press, Oxford, UK.

L.T. Chang (1978), A method for attenuation correction in radionuclide computed tomography, *IEEE Trans. Nuclear Sci.* **25**, 638–643.

L.T. Chang and G.T. Herman (1980), A scientific study of filter selection for a fan-beam convolution algorithm, *SIAM J. Appl. Math.* **39**, 83–105.

S.-K. Chang (1971), The reconstruction of binary patterns from their projections, *Comm. ACM* **14**, 21–25.

C.H. Chapman and P.W. Cary (1986), The circular harmonic Radon transform, *Inverse Problems* **2**, 23–49.

J.-P. Charlier and F. Crowet (1985), Wave equations in linear viscoelastic materials, *J. Acoust. Soc. Amer.* **79**, 895–900.

M. Cheney, D. Isaacson, and J.C. Newell (1999), Electrical impedance tomography, *SIAM Rev.* **41**, 85–101.

M. Cheney, D. Isaacson, J.C. Newell, S. Simske, and J. Goble (1990), NOSER: An algorithm for solving inverse conductivity problems, *Internat. J. Imag. Systems Tech.* **2**, 66–75.

W.K. Cheung and R.M. Lewitt (1991), Modified Fourier reconstruction method using shifted transform samples, *Phys. Med. Biol.* **36**, 269–277.

M. Choulli and P. Stefanov (1996), Inverse scattering and inverse boundary value problems for the linear Boltzmann equation, *Comm. Partial Differential Equations* **21**, 763–785.

J.G. Colsher (1980), Fully three-dimensional emission tomography, *Phys. Med. Biol.* **25**, 103–115.

D. Colton and P. Monk (1999), Mathematical problems in microwave medical imaging, in C. Börgers and F. Natterer (eds.): *Computational Radiology and Imaging: Theory and Diagnostics*, IMA Vol. Math. Appl. **110**, 137–156. Springer, New York.

A.M. Cormack (1963), Representation of a function by its line integrals, with some radiological applications I, *J. Appl. Phys.* **34**, 2722–2727.

A.M. Cormack (1964), Representation of a function by its line integrals, with some radiological applications II, *J. Appl. Phys.* **35**, 195–207.

A.M. Cormack (1978), Sampling the Radon transform with beams of finite width, *Phys. Med. Biol.* **23**, 1141–1148.

A.M. Cormack (1981), The Radon transform on a family of curves in the plane I, *Proc. Amer. Math. Soc.* **83**, 325–330.

A.M. Cormack (1982), The Radon transform on a family of curves in the plane II, *Proc. Amer. Math. Soc.* **86**, 293–298.

A.M. Cormack and E.T. Quinto (1980), A Radon transform on spheres through the origin in $\mathbb{R}^n$ and applications to the Daboux equation, *Trans. Amer. Math. Soc.* **260**, 575–581.

R. Courant and D. Hilbert (1962), *Methods of Mathematical Physics*, Vol. II. Wiley-Interscience, New York.

R.A. Crowther, D.J. DeRosier, and A. Klug (1970), The reconstruction of a three-dimensional structure from its projections and its application to electron microscopy, *Proc. Roy. Soc. London* **A317**, 319–340.

M. Dartmann (1991), *Rekonstruktion konvexer, homogener Gebiete aus wenigen Punktquellen*, Diplomarbeit, Fachbereich Mathematik und Informatik, Universität Münster, Münster, Germany.

R. Dautray and J.L. Lions (1993), *Mathematical Analysis and Numerical Methods for Science and Technology*, Vol. 6. Springer, New York.

M.E. Davison (1983), The ill-conditioned nature of the limited angle tomography problem, *SIAM J. Appl. Math.* **43**, 428–448.

S.R. Deans (1983), *The Radon Transform and Some of Its Applications*. Wiley-Interscience, New York.

M. Defrise and R. Clack (1994), A cone-beam reconstruction algorithm using shift-variant filtering and cone-beam backprojection, *IEEE Trans. Med. Imag.* **13**, 186–195.

M. Defrise and X. Liu (1999), A fast rebinning algorithm for 3D positron emission tomography using John's equation, *Inverse Problems* **15**, 1047–1066.

M. Defrise, D.W. Townsend, and R. Clack (1989), Three-dimensional image reconstruction from complete projections, *Phys. Med. Biol.* **34**, 573–587.

A.P. Dempster, N.M. Laird, and D.B. Rubin (1977), Maximum likelihood from incomplete data via the EM algorithm, *J. Roy. Statist. Soc. B* **39**, 1–38.

A. Denisjuk and V.P. Palamodov (1988), Inversion de la transformation de Radon d'après des données incomplêtes, *C. R. Acad. Sci. Paris Sér. I* **307**, 181–183.

L. Desbat (1993), Efficient sampling on coarse grids in tomography, *Inverse Problems* **9**, 251–269.

L. Desbat (1996), Efficient sampling in 3D tomography, in P. Grangeat and J.L. Amans (eds.): *Three Dimensional Image Reconstruction in Radiology and Nuclear Medicine*, 87–102. Kluwer Academic Publishers, Norwell, MA.

A.J. Devaney (1982), A filtered backpropagation algorithm for diffraction tomography, *Ultrasonic Imaging* **4**, 336–350.

Th. Dierkes (2000), *Rekonstruktionsverfahren zur optischen Tomographie*, Dissertation, Fachbereich Mathematik und Informatik, Universität Münster, Münster, Germany.

R.L. Dietz (1999), *Die approximative Inverse als Rekonstruktionsmethode in der Röntgen-Computertomographie*, Dissertation, Universität Saarbrücken, Saarbrücken, Germany.

K.A. Dines and R.J. Lytle (1979), Computerized geophysical tomography, *Proc. IEEE* **67**, 1065–1073.

O. Dorn (1997), *Das inverse Transportproblem in der Lasertomographie*, Dissertation, Fachbereich Mathematik und Informatik, Universität Münster, Münster, Germany.

O. Dorn (1998), A transport-backtransport method for optical tomography, *Inverse Problems* **14**, 1107–1130.

A. Dutt and V. Rohklin (1993), Fast Fourier transforms for nonequispaced data, *SIAM J. Sci. Comput.* **14**, 1368–1393.

P. Edholm, G.T. Herman, and D.A. Roberts (1988), Image reconstruction from linograms: Implementation and evaluation, *IEEE Trans. Med. Imag.* **7**, 239–246.

K.J. Falconer (1983), X-ray problems for point sources, *Proc. London Math. Soc.* **46**, 241–262.

A. Faridani (1990), An application of a multidimensional sampling theorem to computed tomography, *Contemp. Math.* **113**, 65–80.

A. Faridani (1998), Sampling in parallel-beam tomography, in A.G. Ramm (ed.): *Inverse Problems and Imaging*. Plenum Press, New York.

A. Faridani, D.V. Finch, E.L. Ritman, and K.T. Smith (1997), Local tomography II, *SIAM J. Appl. Math.* **57**, 1095–1127.

A. Faridani, F. Keinert, E.L. Ritman, and K.T. Smith (1990), Local and global tomography, in Grünbaum et al. (eds.): *Signal Processing, Part* II, 241–256. Springer, New York.

A. Faridani, E.L. Ritman, and K.T. Smith (1992), Local tomography I, *SIAM J. Appl. Math.* **52**, 459–484.

J.A. Fawcett (1985), Inversion of n-dimensional spherical averages, *SIAM J. Appl. Math.* **45**, 336–341.

E. Feig and P. Greenleaf (1986), Inversion of an integral transform associated with tomography in radar detection, *Inverse Problems* **2**, 405–411.

E. Feig and F.A. Grünbaum (1986), Tomographic methods in image range–Doppler radar, *Inverse Problems* **2**, 185–195.

L.A. Feldkamp, L.C. Davis, and J.W. Kress (1984), Practical cone-beam algorithm, *J. Opt. Soc. Amer. A* **6**, 612–619.

D. Finch (1985), Cone beam reconstruction with sources on a curve, *SIAM J. Appl. Math.* **45**, 665–673.

M. Fink (1992), Time-reversal of ultrasonic fields—Part I: Basic principles, *IEEE Trans. Ultrasonic Ferroelectr. Freq. Control* **39**, 555–567.

K. Fourmont (1999), *Schnelle Fourier-Transformation bei nicht-äquidistanten Gittern und tomographische Anwendungen*, Dissertation, Fachbereich Mathematik und Informatik, Universität Münster, Münster, Germany.

G. Frank (1938), *Verfahren zur Herstellung von Körperschnittbildern mittels Röntgenstrahlen*, Patentschrift 693374, Reichspatentamt, Berlin, Germany.

J. Frank (ed.) (1992), *Electron Tomography*. Plenum Press, New York.

P. Funk (1914), Über Flächen mit lauter geschlossenen geodätischen Linien, *Math. Ann.* **74**, 278–300.

R.J. Gardner (1995), *Geometric Tomography*. Cambridge University Press, Cambridge, UK.

O. Gauthier, J. Virienz, and A. Tarantola (1986), Two-dimensional nonlinear inversion of seismic waveforms: Numerical results, *Geophys.* **51**, 1387–1403.

I.M. Gel'fand and A.B. Goncharov (1987), Recovery of a compactly supported function starting from its integrals over lines intersecting a given set of points in space, *Dokl.* **290** (1986); English translation in *Soviet Math. Dokl.* **34**, 373–376.

M.S. Gel'fand and A.B. Goncharov (1989), Spatial rotational alignment of identical particles in the case of (almost) coaxial projections, *Ultramicroscopy* **27**, 301–306.

M.S. Gel'fand and A.B. Goncharov (1990), Spatial rotational alignment of identical particles given their projections: Theory and practice, *Transl. Math. Monographs* **81**, 97–122.

I.M. Gel'fand, M.I. Graev, and N.Y. Vilenkin (1965), *Generalized Functions, Vol. 5: Integral Geometry and Representation Theory*. Academic Press, New York.

S. Gindikin, J. Reeds, and L. Shepp (1993), Spherical tomography and spherical integral geometry, *Lecture Notes in Appl. Math.* **30**, 83–92. AMS, Providence, RI.

W.A. Götz and H.J. Druckmüller (1996), A fast digital Radon transform—an efficient means for evaluating the Hough transform, *Pattern Recognition* **29**, 711–718.

S.V. Goldin (1986), *Seismic Traveltime Inversion*. Society of Exploration Geophysicists, Tulsa, OK.

A.B. Goncharov (1987), Integral geometry and three-dimensional reconstruction of arbitrary oriented identical particles from electron micrographs, *Soviet Phys. Crystallogr.* **32**, 663–666.

A.B. Goncharov (1988a), Integral geometry and three-dimensional reconstruction of randomly oriented identical particles from their electron micrographs, *Acta Appl. Math.* **11**, 199–211.

A.B. Goncharov (1988b), Methods of integral geometry and recovering a function with compact support from its projections in unknown directions, *Acta Appl. Math.* **11**, 213–222.

A.B. Goncharov (1990), Three-dimensional reconstruction of arbitrarily arranged identical particles given their projections, *Transl. Math. Monographs* **81**, 67–96.

A.B. Goncharov and M.S. Gel'fand (1988), Determination of mutual orientation of identical particles from their projections by the moment method, *Ultramicroscopy* **25**, 317–328.

R. Gorenflo and S. Vessella (1991), *Abel Integral Equations*. Springer, New York.

R. Gordon, R. Bender, and G.T. Herman (1970), Algebraic reconstruction techniques (ART) for three-dimensional electron microscopy and X-ray photography, *J. Theoret. Biol.* **29**, 471–481.

I.S. Gradshteyn and I.M. Ryzhik (1965), *Table of Integrals, Series and Products*. Academic Press, New York.

P. Grangeat (1987), Analyse d'un système d'imagerie 3D par reconstruction à partir de radiographies X en geometrie conique, Ph.D. thesis, École Normale Superieure des Télécommunications, Paris, France.

P. Grangeat (1991), Mathematical framework of cone-beam reconstruction via the first derivative of the Radon transform, in G.T. Herman, A.K. Louis, and F. Natterer (eds.): *Lecture Notes in Math.* **1497**, 66–97. Springer, New York.

P.J. Green (1990), On the use of the EM algorithm for penalized likelihood estimation, *J. Roy. Statist. Soc. B* **52**, 443–452.

N.I. Grinberg (1998), *Inverse Boundary Problem for the Diffusion Equation with the Constant Background: Investigation of Uniqueness*, Technical Report 10/98-N, Fachbereich Mathematik und Informatik, Universität Münster, Münster, Germany.

P. Gritzmann, D. Prangenberg, S. de Vries, and M. Wiegelmann (1998), Success and failure of certain reconstruction and uniqueness algorithms in discrete tomography, *Internat. J. Imag. Systems Tech.* **9**, 101–109.

C.W. Groetsch (1977), *Generalized Inverses of Linear Operators: Representation and Approximation*. Marcel Dekker, New York, Basel.

S. Gutman and M. Klibanov (1994), Iterative method for multidimensional scattering problems at fixed frequencies, *Inverse Problems* **10**, 579–599.

C. Hamaker, K.T. Smith, D.C. Solmon, and S.L. Wagner (1980), The divergent beam X-ray transform, *Rocky Mountain J. Math.* **10**, 253–283.

C. Hamaker and D.C. Solmon (1978), The angles between the null spaces of X-rays, *J. Math. Anal. Appl.* **62**, 1–23.

M. Hanke, A. Neubauer, and O. Scherzer (1995), A convergence analysis of Landweber iteration for nonlinear ill-posed problems, *Numer. Math.* **72**, 21–37.

E.W. Hansen (1981), Circular harmonic image reconstruction, *Appl. Optics* **20**, 2266–2274.

W.G. Hawkins and H.H. Barrett (1986), A numerically stable circular harmonic reconstruction algorithm, *SIAM J. Numer. Anal.* **23**, 873–890.

S. Helgason (1984), *Groups and Geometric Analysis: Integral Geometry, Invariant Differential Operators, and Spherical Functions*. Academic Press, New York.

S. Helgason (1999), *The Radon Transform*, second ed. Birkhäuser, Boston.

H. Hellsten and L.E. Andersson (1987), An inverse method for the processing of synthetic aperture radar data, *Inverse Problems* **3**, 111–124.

G.T. Herman (1980), *Image Reconstruction from Projection: The Fundamentals of Computerized Tomography*. Academic Press, New York.

G.T. Herman and L. Meyer (1993), Algebraic reconstruction techniques can be made computationally efficient, *IEEE Trans. Med. Imag.* **12**, 600–609.

G.T. Herman, D. Roberts, and L. Axel (1992), Fully three-dimensional reconstruction from data collected on concentric cubes in Fourier space: Implementation and a sample application to MRI, *Phys. Med. Biol.* **37**, 673–687.

A. Hertle (1988), The identification problem for the constantly attenuated Radon transform, *Math. Z.* **197**, 13–19.

W.E. Higgins and D.C. Munson (1988), A Hankel transform approach to tomographic image reconstruction, *IEEE Trans. Med. Imag.* **7**, 59–72.

W.S. Hinshaw and A.H. Lent (1983), An introduction to NMR imaging: From the Bloch equation to the imaging equation, *Proc. IEEE* **71**, 338–350.

J.H. Hoogenraad, M.B. van der Mark, S.B. Colak, G.W. Hooft, and E.S. van Linden (1997), First results from the Philips Optical Mammoscope, *SPIE Press* **3194**, 184–190.

B.K.P. Horn (1986), *Robot Vision*. MIT Press and McGraw–Hill, New York.

G.N. Hounsfield (1973), Computerized transverse axial scanning tomography: Part I, Description of the system, *British J. Radiology* **46**, 1016–1022.

J. Howard (1996), Vector tomography applications in plasma diagnostics, *Plasma Phys. Contr. Fusion* **38**, 489–503.

H.M. Hudson and R.S. Larkin (1994), Accelerated EM reconstruction using ordered subsets of projection data, *IEEE Trans. Med. Imag.* **13**, 601–609.

A.N. Iusem (1991), Convergence analysis for a multiplicatively relaxed EM algorithm, *Math. Methods Appl. Sci.* **14**, 573–593.

A.J. Jerry (1977), The Shannon sampling theorem—its various extensions and applications: A tutorial review, *Proc. IEEE* **65**, 1565–1596.

F. John (1955), *Plane Waves and Spherical Means Applied to Partial Differential Equations*. Wiley-Interscience, New York.

S.A. Johnson, F. Stenger, C.H. Wilcox, J. Ball, and M. Berggren (1982), Wave equations and inverse solutions for soft tissue, in *Acoustic Imaging* **11**, 409–424. Plenum, New York.

P.M. Joseph and R.A. Schulz (1980), View sampling requirements in fan beam computed tomography, *Med. Phys.* **7**, 692–702.

S. Kaczmarz (1937), Angenäherte Auflösung von Systemen linearer Gleichungen, *Bull. Acad. Polon. Sci. Lett.* **A35**, 355–357.

G. Kaiser and R. Streater (1992), Windowed Radon transforms, analytic signals, and the wave equation, in C.K. Chui (ed.): *Wavelets: A Tutorial in Theory and Applications*. Academic Press, New York.

A.C. Kak and M. Slaney (1987), *Principles of Computerized Tomography Imaging*. IEEE Press, New York.

J.M. Kaltenbach and M. Kaschke (1993), Frequency- and time-domain modelling of light transport in random media, in G.J. Müller et al. (eds.): *Medical Optical Tomography: Functional Imaging and Monitoring*, SPIE Series **IS11**, 65–86.

A. Katsevich (1999), Cone beam local tomography, *J. Appl. Math.* **59**, 2224–2246.

M. Kaveh and M. Soumekh (1987), Computer assisted diffraction tomography, in H. Stark (ed.): *Image Recovery: Theory and Application*. Academic Press, New York.

D. Kershaw (1962), *The Determination of the Density Distribution of a Gas Flowing in a Pipe from Mean Density Measurements*, Report A.R.L./R1/MATHS 4 105, Admirality Research Laboratory, Teddington, Middlesex, UK.

D. Kershaw (1970), The determination of the density distribution of a gas flowing in a pipe from mean density measurements, *J. Inst. Math. Appl.* **6**, 111–114.

P.E. Kinahan and J.G. Rogers (1990), Analytic three-dimensional image reconstruction using all detector events, *IEEE Trans. Nuclear Sci.* **36**, 964–968.

M.V. Klibanov, T.R. Lucas, and R.M. Frank (1999), Image reconstruction from experimental data in diffusion tomography, in C. Börgers and F. Natterer (eds.): *Computational Radiology and Imaging: Theory and Diagnostics*, IMA Vol. Math. Appl. **110**, 157–182. Springer, New York.

G.H. Knightly and D.F. St. Mary (1993), Stable marching schemes based on elliptic models of wave propagation, *J. Acoust. Soc. Amer.* **93**, 1866–1872.

P. Kuchment, K. Lancaster, and L. Mogilevskaya (1995), On local tomography, *Inverse Problems* **11**, 571–589.

H. Kudo and T. Saito (1994), Derivation and implementation of a cone-beam reconstruction algorithm for nonplanar orbits, *IEEE Trans. Med. Imag.* **13**, 196–211.

L. Kunyansky (2000), *A New SPECT Reconstruction Algorithm Based on the Novikov's Explicit Inversion Formula*, preprint, California Institute of Technology, Pasadena, CA.

K.J. Langenberg (1989), Introduction to the special issue on inverse problems, *Wave Motion* **11**, 99–112.

P.C. Lauterbur (1973), Image formation by induced local interactions: Examples employing nuclear magnetic resonance, *Nature* **242**, 190–191.

M.M. Lavrent'ev (ed.) (1995), *Computerized Tomography*. VSP, Utrecht.

J.V. Leahy, K.T. Smith, and D.C. Solmon (1979), Uniqueness, nonuniqueness and inversion in the x-ray and Radon problems, *Proceedings of the International Symposion on Ill-Posed Problems*, Newark, DE.

E. Levitan and G.T. Herman (1987), A maximum a posteriori probability expection maximation algorithm for image reconstruction in emission tomography, *IEEE Trans. Med. Imag.* **6**, 185–192.

R.M. Lewitt (1978), Image reconstruction from projections III: Projection completion methods (theory), *Optik* **50**, 180–205.

R.M. Lewitt (1992), Alternatives to voxels for image representations in iterative reconstruction algorithms, *Phys. Med. Biol.* **37**, 705–716.

G. Lohmann (1983), *Rekonstruktion sternförmiger, homogener Objekte aus Projektionen*, Diplomarbeit, Fachbereich Mathematik und Informatik, Universität Münster, Münster, Germany.

A.K. Louis (1980), Picture reconstruction from projections in restricted range, *Math. Methods Appl. Sci.* **2**, 109–220.

A.K. Louis (1982), Optimal sampling in nuclear magnetic resonance (NMR) tomography, *J. Comput. Assisted Tomography* **6**, 334–340.

A.K. Louis (1984), Orthogonal function series expansion and the null space of the Radon transform, *SIAM J. Math. Anal.* **15**, 621–633.

A.K. Louis (1986), Incomplete data problems in x-ray computerized tomography I: Singular value decomposition of the limited angle transform, *Numer. Math.* **48**, 251–262.

A.K. Louis and A. Rieder (1989), Incomplete data problems in x-ray computerized tomography II: Truncated projections and region-of-interest tomography, *Numer. Math.* **56**, 371–383.

A.K. Louis and P. Maass (1993), Contour reconstruction in 3-D X-ray CT, *IEEE Trans. Med. Imag.* **12**, 764–769.

R. Marabini, G.T. Herman, and J.M. Carazo (1999), Fully three-dimensional reconstruction in electron microscopy, in C. Börgers and F. Natterer (eds.): *Computational Radiology and Imaging: Theory and Diagnostics*, IMA Vol. Math. Appl. **110**, 251–281. Springer, New York.

R.B. Marr, C.N. Chen, and P.C. Lauterbur (1981), On two approaches to 3D reconstruction in NMR zeugmatography, in G.T. Herman and F. Natterer (eds.): *Mathematical Aspects of Computerized Tomography*, Proceedings, Oberwolfach, 1980. Springer, New York.

P. Maass (1987), The X-ray transform: Singular value decomposition and resolution, *Inverse Problems* **3**, 729–741.

P. Maass (1989), Wideband radar: The hyp transform, *Inverse Problems* **5**, 849–957.

P. Maass (1992), The interior Radon transform, *SIAM J. Appl. Math.* **52**, 710–724.

J.M. Martìnez and R.J.B. DeSampaio (1986), Parallel and sequential Kaczmarz methods for solving underdetermined nonlinear equations, *J. Comput. Appl. Math.* **15**, 311–321.

K.-H. Meyn (1983), Solution of underdetermined nonlinear equations by stationary iteration methods, *Numer. Math.* **42**, 161–172.

D. Miller, M. Oristaglio, and G. Beylkin (1987), A new slant on seismic imaging: Migration and integral geometry, *Geophys.* **52**, 943–964.

S.E. Minkoff and W.W. Symes (1997), Full waveform inversion of marine reflection data in the plane-wave domain, *Geophys.* **62**, 540–553.

H. Morneburg (ed.) (1995), *Bildgebende Systeme für die Medizinische Diagnostik*. Publicis MCD Verlag, Erlangen.

P.M. Morse and H. Feshbach (1953), *Methods of Theoretical Physics*. McGraw–Hill, New York.

H.N. Mülthei and B. Schorr (1987), On an iterative method for a class of integral equations of the first kind, *Math. Methods Appl. Sci.* **9**, 137–168.

A.I. Nachman, J.F. Smith, and R.C. Waag (1990), An equation for acoustic propagation in inhomogeneous media with relaxation losses, *J. Acoust. Soc. Amer.* **88**, 1584–1595.

F. Natterer (1979), On the inversion of the attenuated Radon transform, *Numer. Math.* **32**, 431–438.

F. Natterer (1983), Computerized tomography with unknown sources, *SIAM J. Appl. Math.* **43**, 1201–1212.

F. Natterer (1986), *The Mathematics of Computerized Tomography*. John Wiley, B.G. Teubner, New York, Leipzig.

F. Natterer (1990), An inverse problem for a transport equation, *Contemp. Math.* **113**, 221–231.

F. Natterer (1993), Determination of tissue attenuation in emission tomography of optically dense media, *Inverse Problems* **9**, 731–736.

F. Natterer (1993a), Sampling in fan beam tomography, *SIAM J. Appl. Math.* **53**, 358–380.

F. Natterer (1994), Recent developments in X-ray tomography, *Lectures in Appl. Math.* **30**, 177–198. AMS, Providence, RI.

F. Natterer (1995), Sampling and resolution in CT, in M.M. Lavrent'ev (ed.): *Computerized Tomography*, 343–354. VSP, Utrecht.

F. Natterer (1996), *Numerical Solution of Bilinear Inverse Problems*, Technical Report 19/96-N, Fachbereich Mathematik und Informatik, Universität Münster, Münster, Germany.

F. Natterer (1997a), An initial value approach to the inverse Helmholtz problem at fixed frequency, in H. Engl et al. (eds.): *Inverse Problems in Medical Imaging and Nondestructive Testing*, 159–167. Springer, New York.

F. Natterer (1997b), An algorithm for 3D ultrasound tomography, in G. Chavent and P.C. Sabatier (eds.): *Inverse Problems of Wave Propagation and Diffraction*. Springer, New York.

F. Natterer and A. Faridani (1990), Basic algorithms in tomography, in F.A. Grünbaum et al. (eds.): *Signal Processing Part* II: *Control Theory and Applications*, 321–334. Springer, New York.

F. Natterer and H. Herzog (1992), Attenuation correction in positron emission tomography, *Math. Methods Appl. Sci.* **15**, 321–330.

F. Natterer and F. Wübbeling (1995), A propagation-backpropagation method for ultrasound tomography, *Inverse Problems* **11**, 1225–1232.

G.A. Navarro and A.E. Profio (1988), Contrast in diaphanography of the breast, *Med. Phys.* **15**, 181–187.

S. Nilsson (1997), *Application of Fast Backprojection Techniques for Some Inverse Problems of Integral Geometry*, Linköping Studies in Science and Technology, Dissertation 499, Department of Mathematics, Linköping University, Linköping Sweden.

G. Nolet (1987), Wave form tomography, in G. Nolet (ed.): *Seismic Tomography*. D. Reidel, Boston.

R.G. Novikov (2000), *An Inversion Formula for the Attenuated X-Ray Transform*, preprint, Departement de Mathématique, Université de Nantes, Nantes, France.

H.J. Nussbaumer (1982), *Fast Fourier Transform and Convolution Algorithms*. Springer, New York.

F. Oberhettinger (1993), *Tables of Fourier Transforms and Fourier Transforms of Distributions*. Springer, New York.

S.S. Orlov (1976), Theory of three dimensional reconstruction II: The recovery operator, *Soviet Phys. Crystallogr.* **20**, 429–433.

J.M. Ortega and W.C. Rheinboldt (1970), *Iterative Solution of Nonlinear Equations in Several Variables*. Academic Press, New York.

J.D. O'Sullivan (1985), A fast sinc function gridding algorithm for Fourier inversion in computer tomography, *IEEE Trans. Med. Imag.* **4**, 200–207.

V.P. Palamodov (1991), Inversion formulas for the three-dimensional ray transform, in G.T. Herman, A.K. Louis, and F. Natterer (eds.): *Lecture Notes in Math.* **1497**, 53–62. Springer, New York.

V.P. Palamodov (1995), Localization of harmonic decomposition of the Radon transform, *Inverse Problems* **11**, 1025–1030.

V.P. Palamodov (1996), An inversion method for an attenuated X-ray transform, *Inverse Problems* **12**, 717–730.

V.P. Palamodov (1998), Reconstruction from line integrals in spaces of constant curvature, *Math. Nachrichten* **196**, 167–188.

A. Papoulis (1965), *Probability, Random Variables, and Stochastic Processes.* McGraw–Hill, New York.

J.E. Pasciak (1981), *A note on the Fourier Algorithm for Image Reconstruction*, Brookhaven National Laboratory, Upton, NY.

P.P. Petersen and D. Middleton (1962), Sampling and reconstruction of wave-number-limited functions in N-dimensional euclidean space, *Inform. Control* **5**, 279–323.

A.R. Pierro (1991), Multiplicative iterative methods in computed tomography, in G.T. Herman, A.K. Louis, and F. Natterer (eds.): *Lecture Notes in Math.* **1497**, 167–186. Springer, New York.

R.-E. Plessix, Y.-H. de Roeck, and G. Chavent (1999), Waveform inversion of reflection seismic data for kinematic parameters by local optimization, *SIAM J. Sci. Comput.* **20**, 1033–1052.

W.K. Pratt (1978), *Digital Image Processing*. John Wiley, New York.

J.L. Prince (1995), Tomographic reconstruction of 3-D vector fields using inner product probes, *IEEE Trans. Image Process.* **32**, 216–219.

S.W. Provencher and R.H. Vogel (1983), Regularization techniques for inverse problems in molecular biology, in P. Deuflhard and E. Hairer (eds.): *Numerical Treatment of Inverse Problems in Differential and Integral Equations*. Birkhäuser, Boston.

E.T. Quinto (1982), Null spaces and ranges for classical and spherical Radon transforms, *J. Math. Anal. Appl.* **90**, 408–420.

E.T. Quinto (1983), The invertibility of rotation invariant Radon transforms, *J. Math. Anal. Appl.* **91**, 510–522.

E.T. Quinto (1983a), Singular value decomposition and inversion methods for the exterior Radon transform and a spherical transform, *J. Math. Anal. Appl.* **95**, 437–448.

E.T. Quinto (1993), Singularities of the X-ray transform and limited data tomography in $\mathbb{R}^3$, *SIAM J. Math. Anal.* **24**, 1215–1225.

J.B. Ra, C.B. Lim, Z.H. Cho, S.K. Hilal, and J. Corell (1982), A true three-dimensional reconstruction algorithm for the spherical positron emission tomography, *Phys. Med. Biol.* **27**, 37–50.

J. Radon (1917), Über die Bestimmung von Funktionen durch ihre Integralwerte längs gewisser Mannigfaltigkeiten, *Berichte Sächsische Akademie der Wissenschaften, Math.-Phys. Kl.*, **69**, 262–267.

G.N. Ramachandran and A.V. Lakshminarayanan (1971), Three-dimensional reconstruction from radiographs and electron micrographs: Application of convolutions instead of Fourier transforms, *Proc. Nat. Acad. Sci. USA* **68**, 2236–2240.

A. Ramm (1992), Inversion of limited-angle tomographic data, *Comput. Math. Appl.* **22**, 101–111.

A. Ramm and A. Katsevich (1996), *The Radon Transform and Local Tomography*. CRC Press, Boca Raton, FL.

A. Ramm and A.I. Zaslavsky (1993), Singularities of the Radon transform, Bull. AMS **28**, 109–115.

A. Ramm and A.I. Zaslavsky (1994), X-ray transform, the Legendre transform and envelopes, *J. Math. Anal. Appl.* **183**, 528–546.

P.A. Rattey and A.G. Lindgren (1981), Sampling the 2D Radon transform, *IEEE Trans. Acoust. Speech Signal Process.* **ASSP-29**, 994–1002.

V.G. Romanov (1969), *Integral Geometry and Inverse Problems for Hyperbolic Equations*. Springer, New York.

H.J. Ryser (1957), The combinatorial properties of matrices of zeros and ones, *Canad. J. Math.* **9**, 371–379.

S. Schaller, T. Flohr, and P. Steffen (1998), An efficient Fourier method for 3-D Radon inversion in exact cone-beam CT reconstruction, *IEEE Trans. Med. Imag.* **17**, 244–250.

H. Schomberg and J. Timmer (1995), The gridding method for image reconstruction by Fourier transformation, *IEEE Trans. Med. Imag.* **14**, 596–607.

J.G. Schotland (1997), Continuous wave diffusion imaging, *J. Opt. Soc. Amer. A* **14**, 275–279.

J. Schulte (1994), *Fourier-Rekonstruktion in der Computer-Tomographie*, Diplomarbeit, Fachbereich Mathematik und Informatik, Universität Münster, Münster, Germany.

P. Schwander, C. Kisielowski, M. Seibt, F.H. Baumann, Y. Kim, and A. Ourmazd (1993), Mapping projected potential, interfacial roughness, and composition in general crystalline solides by quantitative transmission electron microscopy, *Phys. Rev. Lett.* **71**, 4150–4153.

L. Schwartz (1973), *Théoriè des Distribution*. Hermann, Paris.

R.T. Seeley (1966), Spherical harmonics, *Amer. Math. Monthly* **73**, 115–121.

B. Setzepfandt (1992), *ESNM: Ein rauschunterdrückendes EM-Verfahren für die Emissionstomographie*, Dissertation, Fachbereich Mathematik und Informatik, Universität Münster, Münster, Germany.

M.I. Sezan and H. Stark (1987), Incorporation of a priori moment information into signal recovery and synthesis problems, *J. Math. Anal. Appl.* **122**, 172–186.

V.A. Sharafutdinov (1994), *Integral Geometry of Tensor Fields*. VSP, Utrecht.

L.A. Shepp and B.F. Logan (1974), The Fourier reconstruction of a head section, *IEEE Trans. Nuclear Sci.* **NS-21**, 21–43.

L.A. Shepp and Y. Vardi (1982), Maximum likelihood reconstruction for emission tomography, *IEEE Trans. Med. Imag.* **1**, 113–122.

H. Sielschott (1997), Measurement of horizontal flow in a large scale furnace using acoustic vector tomography, *Flow Meas. Instrum.* **8**, 191–197.

H. Sielschott (2000), *Rückpropagationsverfahren für die Wellengleichung in bewegtem Medium*, Dissertation, Fachbereich Mathematik und Informatik, Universität Münster, Münster, Germany.

H. Sielschott and W. Derichs (1995), Use of collocation methods under inclusion of a priori information in acoustic pyrometry, in M.S. Beck et al. (eds.): *Process Tomography: Implementation for Industrial Purposes*. UMIST, Manchester, UK.

B.W. Silverman, M.C. Jones, and D.W. Nychka (1990), A smoothed EM approach to indirect estimation problems, with particular reference to stereology and emission tomography, *J. Roy. Statist. Soc. B* **52**, 271–324.

J. Singer, F.A. Grünbaum, P. Kohn, and J. Zubelli (1990), Image reconstruction of the interior of bodies that diffuse radiation, *Science* **248**, 990–993.

D. Slepian (1978), Prolate spheroidal wave functions, Fourier analysis, and uncertainty V: The discrete case, *Bell System Tech. J.* **57**, 1371–1430.

C.H. Slump and J.J. Gerbrandes (1982), A network flow approach to reconstruction of the left ventricle from two projections, *Comput. Graph. Imag. Process.* **18**, 18–36.

B.D. Smith (1985), Image reconstruction from cone-beam projections: Necessary and sufficient conditions and reconstruction methods, *IEEE Trans. Med. Imag.* **4**, 14–25.

K.T. Smith, D.C. Solmon, and S.L. Wagner (1977), Practical and mathematical aspects of the problem of reconstructing a function from radiographs, *Bull. AMS* **83**, 1227–1270.

K.T. Smith and F. Keinert (1985), Mathematical foundations of computed tomography, *Appl. Optics* **24**, 3950–3957.

I.H. Sneddon (1972), *The Use of Integral Transforms*. McGraw–Hill, New York.

G. Sparr, K. Stråhlén, K. Lindström, and H.W. Persson (1995), Doppler tomography for vector fields, *Inverse Problems* **11**, 1051–1061.

W.J.T. Spyra, A. Faridani, K.T. Smith, and E.L. Ritman (1990), Computed tomography imaging of the coronary arterial tree: Use of local tomography, *IEEE Trans. Med. Imag.* **9**, 1–4.

G. Steidl (1998), A note on fast Fourier transforms for nonequispaced grids, *Adv. Comput. Math.* **9**, 337–352.

E.M. Stein and G. Weiss (1971), *Introduction to Fourier Analysis on Euclidean Spaces*. Princeton University Press, Princeton, NJ.

J. Sylvester and G. Uhlmann (1986), A uniqueness theorem for an inverse boundary problem in electrical prospection, *Comm. Pure Appl. Math.* **39**, 92–112.

K. Tanabe (1971), Projection method for solving a singular system of linear equations and its applications, *Numer. Math.* **17**, 203–214.

E. Tanaka (1987), A fast reconstruction algorithm for stationary positron emission tomography based on a relaxed EM algorithm, *IEEE Trans. Med. Imag.* **6**, 98–105.

A. Tarantola (1987), Inversion of travel times and seismic waveforms, in G. Nolet (ed.): *Seismic Tomography*. D. Reidel, Boston.

M.E. Taylor (1996), *Partial Differential Equations* II. Springer, New York.

A.N. Tikhonov and V.Y. Arsenin (1977), *Solution of Ill-Posed Problems*. V.H. Winston & Sons, Washington, DC.

O. Tretiak and C. Metz (1980), The exponential Radon transform, *SIAM J. Appl. Math.* **39**, 341–354.

H.K. Tuy (1983), An inversion formula for cone-beam reconstruction, *SIAM J. Appl. Math.* **43**, 546–552.

D.B. Twieg (1983), The *k* trajectory formulation of the NMR imaging process with applications in analysis and synthesis of imaging methods, *Med. Phys.* **10**, 610–621.

B.K. Vainstein (1970), Finding structure of objects from projections, *Kristallografiya* **15**, 984–902.

P.M. van den Berg and R.E. Kleinman (1997), A contrast source inversion method, *Inverse Problems* **13**, 1607–1620.

M. Van Heel (1987), Angular reconstruction: A posteriori assignment of projection direction for 3D reconstruction, *Ultramicroscopy* **21**, 111–124.

Y. Vardi, L.A. Shepp, and L. Kaufman (1985), A statistical model for positron emission tomography, *J. Amer. Stat. Assoc.* **80**, 8–20.

N.D. Vvedenskaya and S.G. Gindikin (1984), Poisson's formula for the Radon transform, and a numerical algorithm for reconstructing the image, *Soviet Math. Dokl.* **30**, 700–703.

R.C. Waag (1998), *University of Rochester Ring Transducer System*, Technical report, Department of Electrical Engineering and Radiology, University of Rochester, Rochester, NY.

G. Wang, T.H. Lin, P.C. Cheng, and D.M. Shinozaki (1993), A general cone beam reconstruction algorithm, *IEEE Trans. Med. Imag.* **12**, 486–496.

A. Ware (1998), Fast approximate Fourier transforms for irregularly spaced data, *SIAM Rev.* **40**, 838–856.

S. Webb (1990), *From the Watching of Shadows*. Adam Hilger, Bristol, UK.

A. Welch and G.T. Gullberg (1997), Implementation of a model-based nonuniform scatter correction scheme for SPECT, *IEEE Trans. Med. Imag.* **16**, 717–726.

A. Welch, R. Clack, F. Natterer, and G.T. Gullberg (1997), Towards accurate attenuation correction in SPECT without transmission scan, *IEEE Trans. Med. Imag.* **16**, 532–541.

J. Wloka (1953), *Tomografia*, Protokolle des Seminars "Anwendungen der Mathematik" (Lukaszewicz, Perkal, Steinhaus), Universität Breslau, Breslau, Poland.

K. Wuschke (1990), *Die Rekonstruktion von Orientierungen aus Projektionen*, Diplomarbeit, Fachbereich Mathematik und Informatik, Universität Münster, Münster, Germany.

K. Yosida (1968), *Functional Analysis*. Springer, New York.

G.T. Zeng, R. Clack, and R. Gullberg (1994), Implementation of Tuy's cone-beam inversion formula, *Phys. Med. Biol.* **39**, 493–508.

C. Zhou, G.T. Schuster, S. Hassanzadeh, and J.M. Harris (1997), Elastic wave equation traveltime and waveform inversion of Crosswell data, *Geophys.* **62**, 853–867.

Index

Abel integral equation, 5, 32
Aben, 58
Abramowitz, 6, 7, 16
absorption coefficient, 161
acoustic pyrometry, 159
adjoint differentiation, 137
adjoint fields, 137
Aguilar, 27
Ahn, 54
albedo operator, 162
algebraic reconstruction technique, *see* ART

aliasing, 70
Andersson, 35, 55
Anikonov, 163
Antyufeev, 163
Arridge, 163, 164, 168, 176
Arsenin, 63
ART, 110, 111, 124, 137
    nonlinear, 161
    optical tomography, 169
    speed of convergence, 115
artifact, 71, 86, 89
attenuated Radon transform, 28, 99
attenuated ray transform, 27
attenuation, 41, 152
attenuation coefficient, 161
Axel, 108

B-scan, 178
backprojection operator, 10, 18, 35, 60,
       84
backpropagation, 183, 186
backscatter, 178
Bailey, 153
band pass, 49
band-limited, 8, 66, 70, 72

bandwidth, 66, 67
Barrett, 134, 162
barycenter, 139
Bayesian estimate, 125
Beck, 41, 159
Bellini, 153
Bender, 124
Bertero, 6, 159
Bessel function, 7, 73, 80, 159
Besson, 93
Beylkin, 36, 60, 62, 80
Biedenstein, 178
blobs, 118
Bloch equation, 51
Boccacci, 6
Boman, 153
Bondarenko, 163
Born approximation, 46, 47, 61, 180
Borup, 181
Bracewell, 62, 82
Brandt, 95
Braun, 36, 58
Briggs, 8
Brody, 125
Bronnikov, 154
Brouw, 102
Budinger, 41
Buonocore, 125

Calderon, 170
Calderon's method, 170, 177
Caponnetto, 159
Cary, 134
Case, 162, 166
Censor, 112, 124, 153
central slice theorem, 10, 48
Chang, 82, 152, 153

Chapman, 134
Charlier, 178
Chavent, 187
Chebyshev polynomials, 6, 14, 147
checkerboard effect, 122
Chen, 83, 133
Cheney, 176, 178
Cheung, 102
chirp-z, 8, 102, 108
Cho, 54
Choulli, 163
circular harmonic algorithms, 134
Clack, 130, 132, 133
Colsher, 21
Colton, 185
computer vision, 152
cone beam, 23, 43, 93, 131, 148, 153
conical tilt problem, 150
consistency conditions, 153
convolution, 3
Cormack, 15, 36, 62, 75
Cormack's first inversion formula, 15
Cormack's inversion formula, 134, 145, 146
Cormack's second inversion formula, 15
cosine filter, 71, 82, 89, 98
Courant, 49, 61
cross-borehole tomography, 59
Crowet, 179
Crowther, 62, 139
curved manifolds, 31
cutoff, 49

DART, 125
Dartmann, 151
data completion, 147
Dautray, 162
Davis, 128
Davison, 17, 145
De Sampaio, 137
de Roeck, 187
Deans, 2
Debye's asymptotic relation, 7, 73, 85, 88, 134
Defrise, 132, 133, 149, 150
degree of ill-posedness, 65

Dempster, 119
Denisjuk, 147
Derichs, 159
DeRosier, 62, 139
Desbat, 78, 159
Devaney, 48, 49
Dierkes, 176
Dietz, 131
diffraction tomography, 46, 108
diffusion approximation, 164, 166
diffusion coefficient, 166
diffusion model, 165
diffusion-backdiffusion, 174
Dines, 59
Dirac δ function, 4, 9, 81, 96
direct algebraic algorithms, 125
Dirichlet-to-Neuman map, 167
discrete backprojection, 96
discrete Fourier transform, 8
discrete tomography, 151
Doppler tomography, 57
Dorn, 172–174
Druckmüller, 95
dual field method, 137
Dutt, 80

Edholm, 108
electron microscopy, 152
electron tomography, 54, 150
EM, 46, 110, 118, 119, 122
    speed of convergence, 122
emission tomography, 44, 45, 152, 162
essentially band-limited, 66
Euler angles, 140
expectation maximization, *see* EM
exponential Radon transform, 27, 99
exterior problem, 144, 146, 147

Falconer, 151
fan beam, 42, 43, 75, 90, 93
    circular harmonic reconstruction, 136
Faridani, 78, 87, 157
fast backprojection, 95
fast Fourier transform, *see* FFT
Fawcett, 35
FDK approximate formula, 93, 128

Feig, 31, 57
Feig–Greenleaf transform, 30
Feldkamp, 128
Feshbach, 37, 49
few data, 159
FFT, 8
    nonequispaced, 78, 80, 101, 109
Fick's law, 166
filtered backprojection, 10, 28, 56, 81, 86,
        93, 129
    complexity, 85
    fan beam, 92
    few data, 159
    point spread function, 96
    ray transform, 133
Finch, 25, 147
Fink, 182, 186
fixed-block ART, 112
Flohr, 105
Fourier analysis, 3
Fourier reconstruction, 54, 100, 101, 108
Fourier transform, 3, 4, 10
Fourmont, 79, 80, 102
Frank, 55, 62, 151, 176
frequency domain ultrasound tomography,
        179
Funk, 33
Funk–Hecke theorem, 7, 14

Götz, 95
Gardner, 151
Gauthier, 187
Gegenbauer polynomial, 6, 14, 16, 114
Gel'fand, 9, 25, 139, 141, 143
general manifolds, 36
generalized backprojection, 126
generalized inverse, 5, 63
geometric method, 139
Gerbrandes, 152
Gindikin, 15, 34
Goldin, 59
Goncharov, 25, 139, 141, 143
Gordon, 124
Gorenflo, 5
Grünbaum, 57
Gradshteyn, 29, 49, 72

Graev, 9
Gram matrix, 126
Grangeat, 23
Grangeat's formula, 23, 24
    filtered backprojection, 131
Grangeat's method, 129, 130
Green, 123
Green's formula, 170
Green's function, 169
Greenleaf, 31
gridding method, 102, 104, 109
Grinberg, 168, 170
Gritzmann, 152
Groetsch, 5
Gullberg, 130, 161
Gutman, 185
gyromagnetic ratio, 51

Haar measure, 38
Hamaker, 23, 114
Hanke, 112
Hankel function, 47, 180
Hankel inversion formula, 14
Hankel transform, 14, 35
Hansen, 134
harmonic polynomial, 71
Hauck, 36, 58
Hawkins, 134
Hebden, 164
Helgason, 9, 31, 36
helical scanning, 43, 129
Hellsten, 55
Helmholtz decomposition, 37
Helmholtz equation, 180
Henson, 8
Henyey–Greenstein, 164
Herman, 2, 43, 82, 108, 116, 124
Hertle, 155
Herzog, 154
Higgins, 14
Hilbert, 49, 61
Hilbert transform, 5, 11, 12, 133, 155
Hildreth's algorithm, 124
Hinshaw, 51
homogeneity relation, 95
homogeneous polynomial, 19

Hoogenraad, 169
Horn, 152
Hounsfield, 62
Howard, 159
Hudson, 122
Hutton, 153

ideal low pass, 82
ill-posed, 2, 63
impedance tomography, 176
incomplete data, 144, 145, 157
initial value technique, 181
integral geometry, 9
interlaced scanning, 74, 75, 87
invariance, 26, 35
irrotational, 37, 39
Isaacson, 176
Iusem, 119

Jacobi polynomials, 16
Jensen's inequality, 119, 120
Jerry, 65
John, 25
John's differential equation, 25, 148
Johnson, 179
Jones, 123
Joseph, 77

Kaczmarz, 110
Kaczmarz method, 110, 122, 137, 172,
          177, 180, 182, 185
Kaiser, 31
Kak, 2, 48, 97
Kaltenbach, 164
κ-operator, 34
Kaschke, 164
Katsevich, 158, 159
Kaufman, 119
Kaveh, 102
Keinert, 82
Kershaw, 15
Kim, 54
Kinahan, 148
Kirchhoff's formula, 61
Kleinman, 185
Klibanov, 176, 185

Klug, 62, 139
Knightly, 185
Kovtanyuk, 163
Kress, 128
Kuchment, 27, 157
Kudo, 132
Kuhn–Tucker conditions, 118, 121
Kullback–Leiber distance, 119
Kunyansky, 100

Lagrangian multipliers, 124
Laird, 119
Lakshminarayanan, 82
Lancaster, 157
Landweber iteration, 112, 116, 123
Langenberg, 182
Larkin, 122
Larmor frequency, 51
lattice, 66, 68, 88, 90
Lauterbur, 51, 83, 133
Lavrent'ev, 41
Leahy, 146
Legendre polynomials, 6
Legendre transform, 157, 158
Lent, 51
Levitan, 124
Lewitt, 102, 118, 148
limited angle, 144, 145, 147
Lindgren, 75, 77
linogram algorithm, 106, 108, 148
Lionheart, 168
Lions, 162
Liouville transformation, 168
Liu, 149
local tomography, 13, 155, 157, 158
log likelihood, 118
Logan, 62, 82, 87
Lohmann, 152
Louis, 17, 71, 145, 146, 148, 158
low pass, 49, 70
Lucas, 176
Lytle, 59

Mülthei, 119
Maass, 22, 56, 146, 158
Macovski, 125

magnetic resonance imaging, *see* MRI
magnetization, 51
Marabini, 118
Marr, 83, 133
Marr filter, 98
MART, 124
Martinez, 137
Mary, 185
maximum likelihood, 46
Mellin transform, 26
Metz, 28
Meyer, 116
Meyn, 137
microlocal analysis, 157, 159
microwaves, 46
Middleton, 66
Miller, 60, 62
Minkoff, 187
modified Bessel function, 105
Mogilevskaya, 157
moment method, 141
Monk, 185
Moore, 5
Moore–Penrose, 5
Morneburg, 41, 97, 178
Morse, 37, 49
MRI, 51, 108
Munson, 14

Nachman, 178
natural pixels, 125
Navarro, 163
ned, 79, 105
ner, 79, 101, 109
Neubauer, 112
Newell, 176
Nilsson, 35, 56, 95, 96
NIR, 163
noise, 97, 98, 115, 126, 148
Nolet, 187
nonequispaced FFT, 80, 101, 109
nonlinear problems, 137, 161
nonlinear tomography, 161
NOSER, 178
Novikov, 29
Nussbaumer, 8

Nychka, 123
Nyquist condition, 67, 107
Nyquist rate, 107

O'Sullivan, 102
Oberhettinger, 80, 105
optical tomography, 163
ordered subset EM, 122
Oristaglio, 60, 62
Orlov, 18, 19
Orlov's condition, 18, 21, 185
Orlov's inversion formula, 19, 22, 133
Ortega, 113, 124
orthogonal polynomials, 6
OSEM, 122
oversampling, 87

Palamodov, 24, 28, 34, 75, 78, 147
Papoulis, 97, 126
parallel interlaced, 75
parallel scanning, 41, 74, 83, 134
        circular harmonic algorithm, 135
Parseval's relation, 4
Pasciak, 102
PBP, 182
Penrose, 5
PET, 44, 45, 148, 149, 153
Petersen, 66
Petersen–Middleton theorem, 67
photoelastic tomography, 58
Piacentini, 153
Pierro, 125
plasma physics, 159
Plessix, 187
POCS, 124
point spread function, 96
Poisson's formula, 4, 15, 66, 68, 103
polarization, 58
Pratt, 65
Prince, 36
process tomography, 159
Profio, 163
projection theorem, 10
Prokhorov, 163
propagation, 186

propagation-backpropagation algorithm, 182
Provencher, 143
Puro, 58

Quinto, 27, 35, 36, 144, 146, 157

Ra, 150
radar, 55, 57
Radon, 1, 12
Radon normal transform, 36
Radon probe transform, 36
Radon transform, 1, 9
    3D, 133
    ill-posedness, 65
    range, 16
    resolution, 71
    singular value decomposition, 16
Radon's inversion formula, 1, 12, 155
Ram–Lak filter, 82, 98, 99
Ramachandran, 82
Ramm, 147, 157, 158
random variable, 45
Range–Doppler radar, 30, 56
Rattey, 75, 77
ray transform, 17, 50, 148
    convolution, 17
    filtered backprojection, 133
    Fourier transform, 17
    singular value decomposition, 22
rebinning, 43, 93
reciprocal lattice, 66, 67, 75
Reeds, 34
reflection tomography, 60, 62
regularization, 63, 64
regularization parameter, 64
relaxation factor, 110, 122, 123
relaxation times, 51
reprojection algorithm, 148
resolution, 63, 71, 72
Rheinboldt, 113, 124
Riddle, 82
Rieder, 146, 148
Riesz potential, 5, 11, 18, 39
ringing artifact, 71
Roberts, 108

Rocca, 153
Rogers, 148
Rohklin, 80
Romanov, 59
Rubin, 119
Ryser, 152
Rytov approximation, 46, 48, 180
Ryzhik, 29, 49, 72

Saito, 132
sampling, 2, 65
sampling condition, 73
sampling scheme, 75
sampling theorem, 66, 68, 88
    irregular spacing, 107
SAR, 96
scanning geometry, 41
scatter, 161, 164
scattering coefficient, 161
scattering kernel, 161
Schaller, 105
Scherzer, 112
Schlieren tomography, 58
Schomberg, 104
Schorr, 119
Schotland, 172
Schulte, 102
Schulz, 77
Schwander, 152
Schwartz, 3, 25, 156
Schwartz space, 3
Schweiger, 176
Seeley, 6
seismic tomography, 59
Setzepfandt, 124
Sezan, 124
shah distribution, 4
Shannon sampling theorem, 67
Sharafutdinov, 36, 39
Shepp, 34, 45, 62, 82, 87, 119
Shepp–Logan, 87
Shepp–Logan filter, 82, 98
Sielschott, 159, 160, 187
Silverman, 123
simultaneous reconstruction, 152
sinc function, 82

sinc series, 70
Singer, 163
singular support, 156
singular value decomposition, *see* SVD
SIRT, 116
Slaney, 2, 48, 97
Slepian, 145
Slump, 152
Smith, 82, 144
Smith, B. D., 24, 25
Smith, J. F., 178
Smith, K. T., 9, 87, 144, 146
Sneddon, 14, 26
Sobolev spaces, 17
solenoidal, 37, 40
Solmon, 9, 116
Solmon, 9, 114, 116, 146
Sommerfeld radiation condition, 47, 179
SOR, 113
SOR Newton, 124
Soumekh, 102
Sparr, 36
SPECT, 44, 45, 153, 162
spherical harmonics, 6, 7, 13, 14, 16, 146
spin, 51
Spyra, 157
stability, 17, 63, 67
        incomplete data, 144
stability estimates, 145
standard parallel, 75
Stark, 124
Stefanov, 163
Steffen, 105
Stegun, 6, 7, 16
Steidl, 80
Stein, 3
stopping, 64
Streater, 31
SVD, 5, 145, 160
Sylvester, 168
Symes, 187
symmetry, 134
synthetic aperture radar, 55

Tanabe, 112
Tanaka, 122

Tarantola, 187
Taylor, 156
tempered distributions, 3
Tikhonov, 63
Tikhonov–Phillips regularization, 64
time domain ultrasound tomography, 185
time reversal, 182
Timmer, 104
tomography, 1–187
tomography with scatter, 161
Townsend, 133
transmission tomography, 41
transport equation, 161, 163
transport-backtransport algorithm, 172
trapezoidal rule, 8, 67, 85, 103, 104
travel time tomography, 59, 60
Tretiak, 28
truncated projections, 144, 146, 148, 150
truncated singular value decomposition,
        64, 160
TTR kernel, 150
Tuy, 25
Tuy's condition, 25, 129
Tuy's inversion formula, 130
Twieg, 109

Uhlmann, 168
ultrasound, 46
ultrasound tomography, 178
uniqueness
        incomplete data, 144
unknown orientations, 139

Vainstein, 62
van den Berg, 185
Van Heel, 139
Vardi, 45, 119
vector fields, 36
vector tomography, 57
vectorial ray transform, 36
Vessella, 5
Vilenkin, 9
Virienz, 187
Vogel, 143
Vvedenskaya, 15

Waag, 178

Wagner, 9
Walker, 153
Wang, 129
Ware, 79
wave equation, 47, 185
waveform tomography, 60
Webb, 62
weighted transforms, 27
Weiss, 3
Welch, 154, 161
well-posed, 63
windowed ray transform, 31
Wloka, 62
Wuschke, 140

Yosida, 3

Zaslavsky, 157, 158
Zeng, 130
Zenios, 112
Zhou, 187
Zweifel, 162, 166